The Alchemist Who Survived Now Dreams of a Quiet City Life

01

Artist: Guru Mizoguchi
Author: Usata Nonohara
Character Design: ox

STELLATVS-ANNVS VENTORVM-ANN
Mercurius Philosophorum
Sulphur
Fixum
Sal Centrale
Ignes
Quatuor
Terrenum
Vulgaris

The Alchemist Who Survived
Now Dreams of a Quiet City Life ✳✲✳

01 Contents

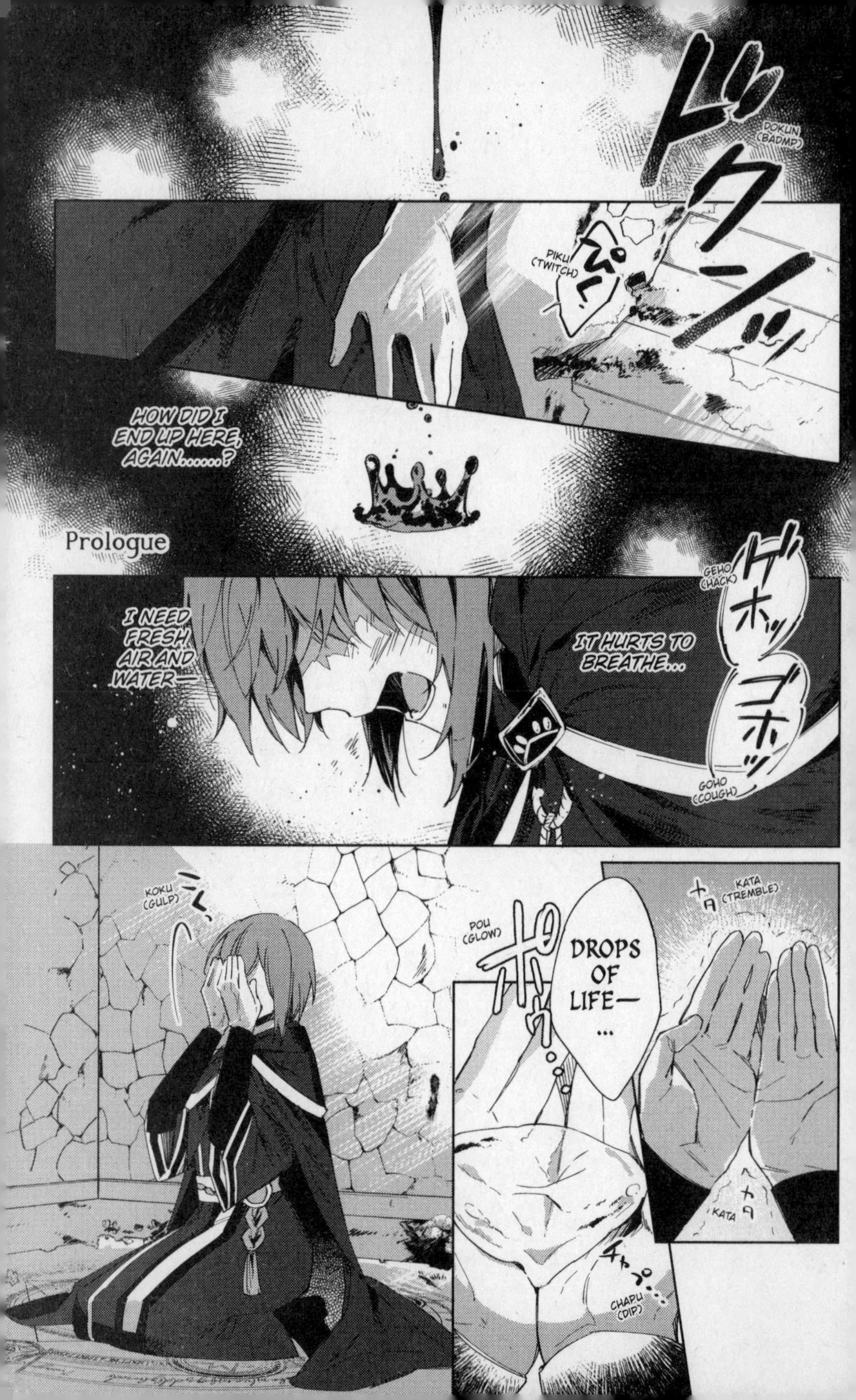
DOKUN (BADMP)
PIKU (TWITCH)
HOW DID I END UP HERE, AGAIN......?
Prologue
GEHO (HACK)
IT HURTS TO BREATHE...
GOHO (COUGH)
I NEED FRESH AIR AND WATER—
KATA (TREMBLE)
DROPS OF LIFE—...
POU (GLOW)
KATA
CHAPU (DIP)
KOKU (GULP)

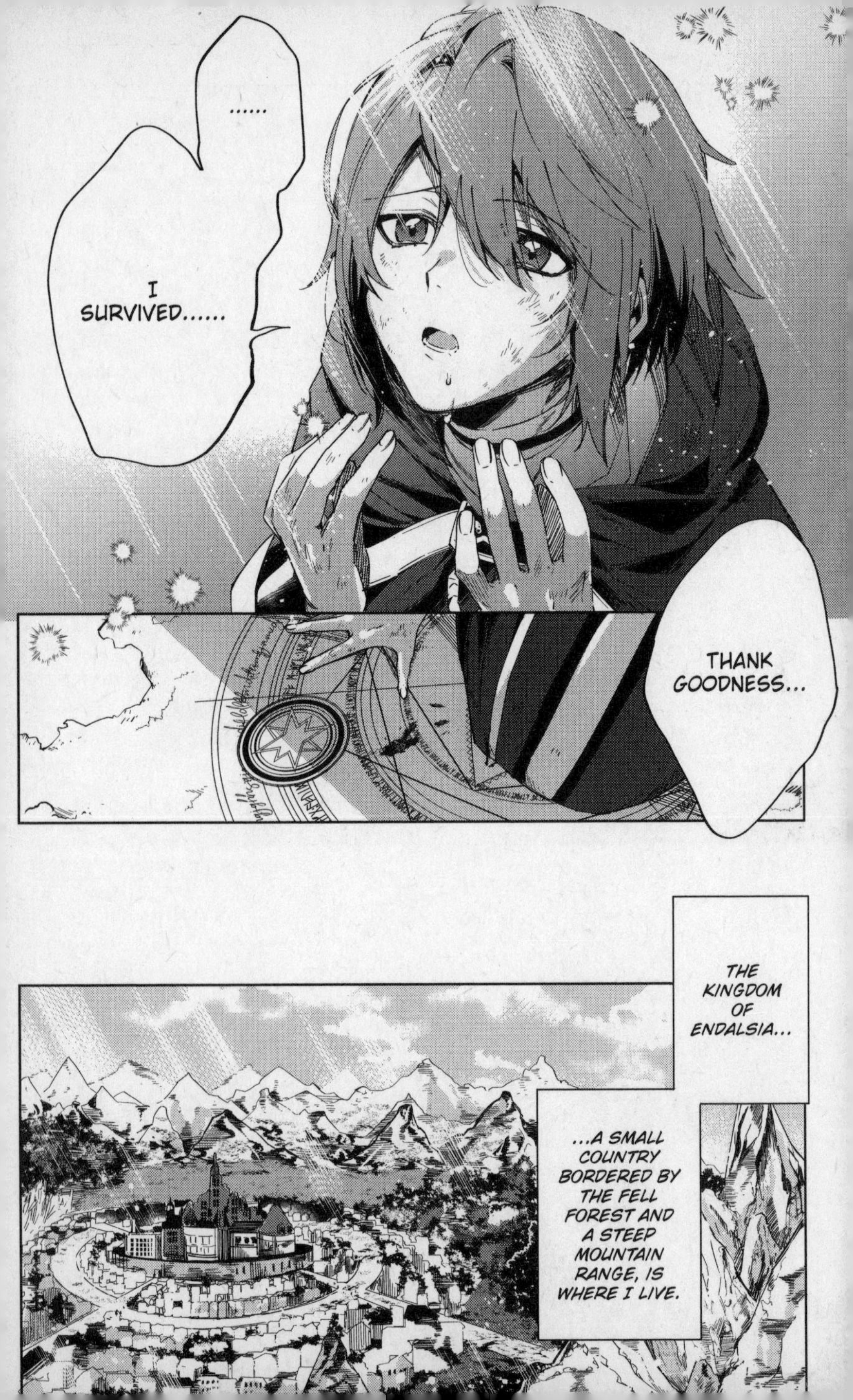
......
I SURVIVED......
THANK GOODNESS...
THE KINGDOM OF ENDALSIA...
...A SMALL COUNTRY BORDERED BY THE FELL FOREST AND A STEEP MOUNTAIN RANGE, IS WHERE I LIVE.

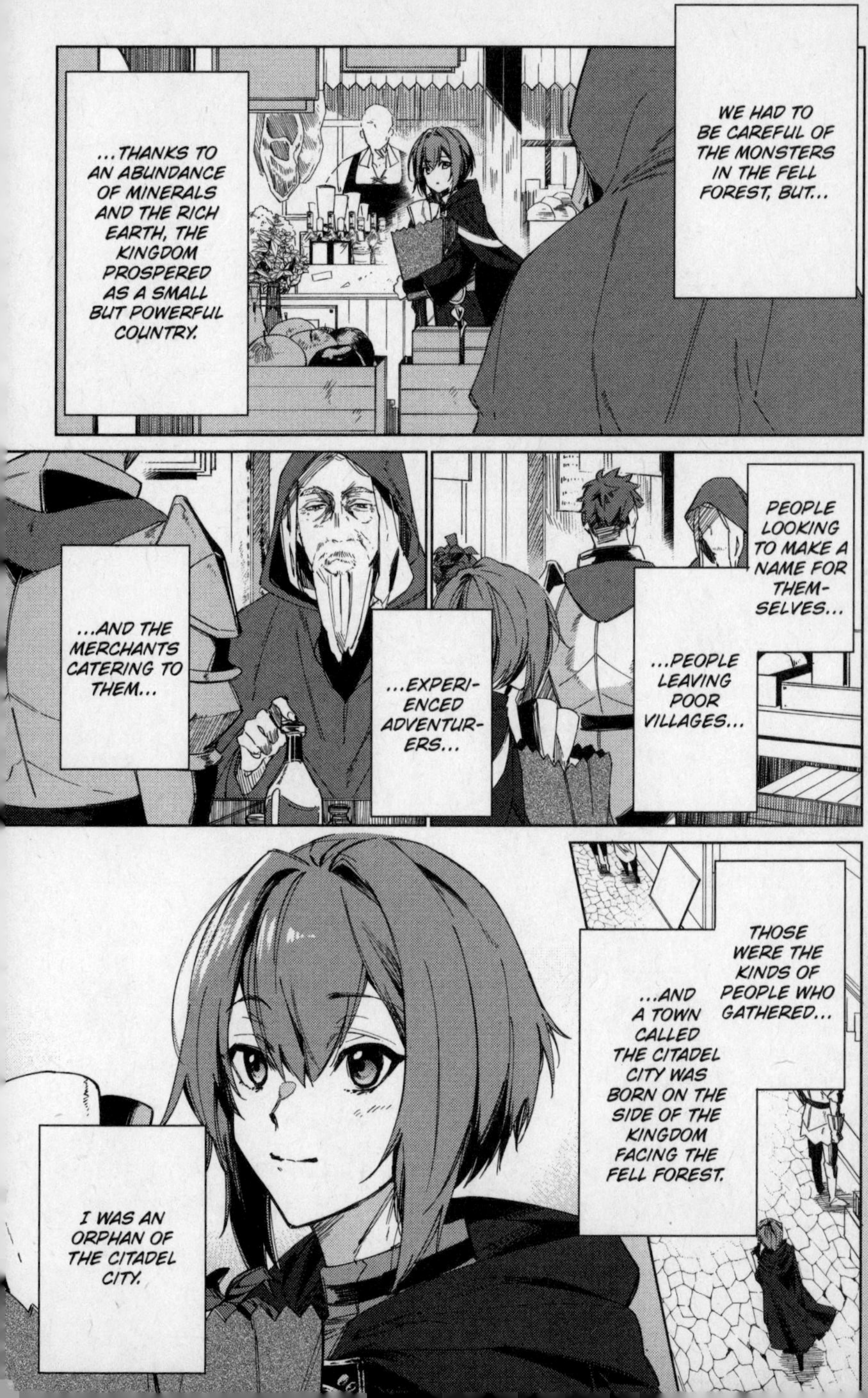
WE HAD TO BE CAREFUL OF THE MONSTERS IN THE FELL FOREST, BUT...
...THANKS TO AN ABUNDANCE OF MINERALS AND THE RICH EARTH, THE KINGDOM PROSPERED AS A SMALL BUT POWERFUL COUNTRY.
PEOPLE LOOKING TO MAKE A NAME FOR THEM-SELVES...
...PEOPLE LEAVING POOR VILLAGES...
...EXPERI-ENCED ADVENTUR-ERS...
...AND THE MERCHANTS CATERING TO THEM...
THOSE WERE THE KINDS OF PEOPLE WHO GATHERED...
...AND A TOWN CALLED THE CITADEL CITY WAS BORN ON THE SIDE OF THE KINGDOM FACING THE FELL FOREST.
I WAS AN ORPHAN OF THE CITADEL CITY.

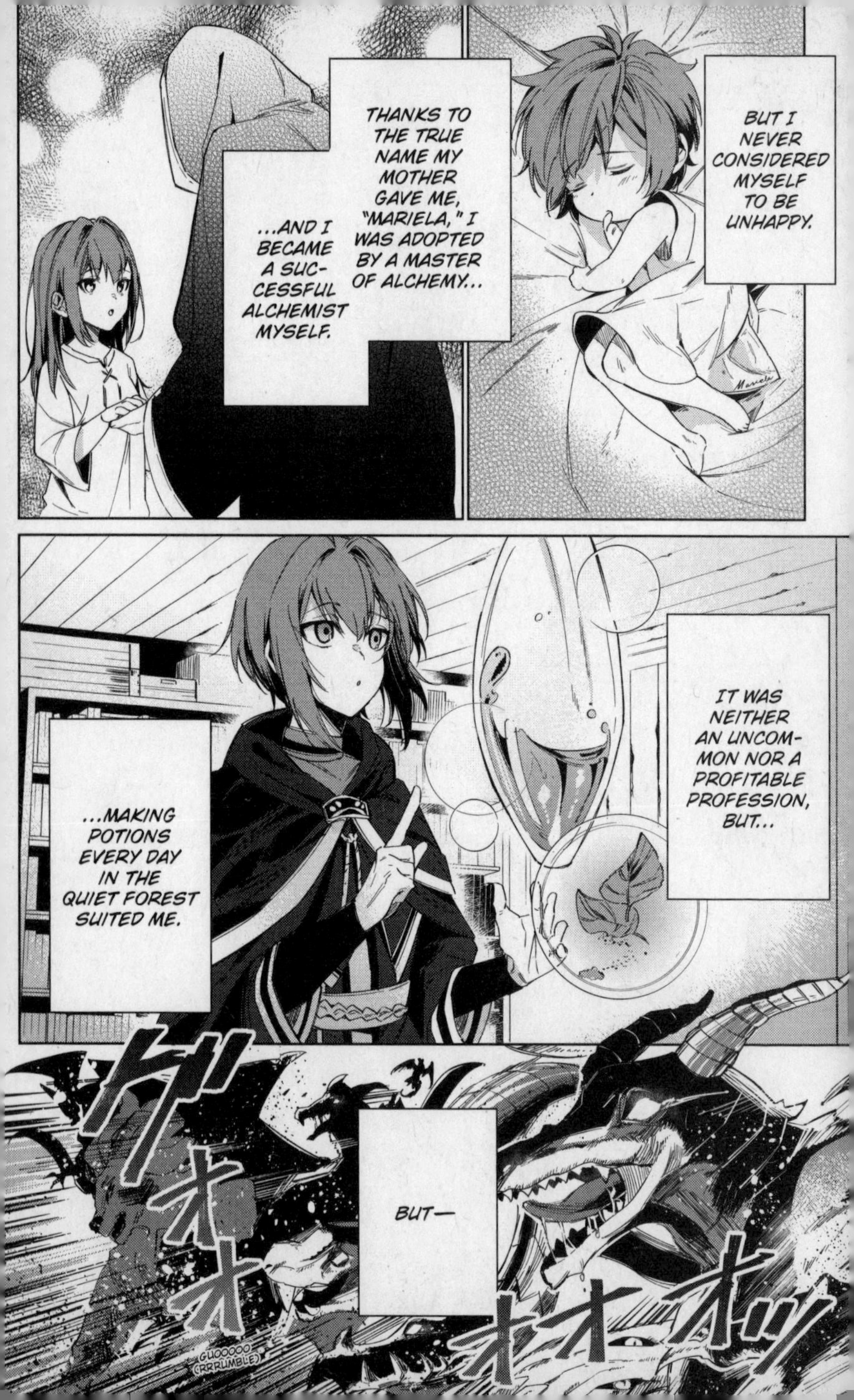
BUT I NEVER CONSIDERED MYSELF TO BE UNHAPPY.
THANKS TO THE TRUE NAME MY MOTHER GAVE ME, "MARIELA," I WAS ADOPTED BY A MASTER OF ALCHEMY...
...AND I BECAME A SUC-CESSFUL ALCHEMIST MYSELF.
IT WAS NEITHER AN UNCOM-MON NOR A PROFITABLE PROFESSION, BUT...
...MAKING POTIONS EVERY DAY IN THE QUIET FOREST SUITED ME.
BUT—
GUOOOOO (RRRUMBLE)

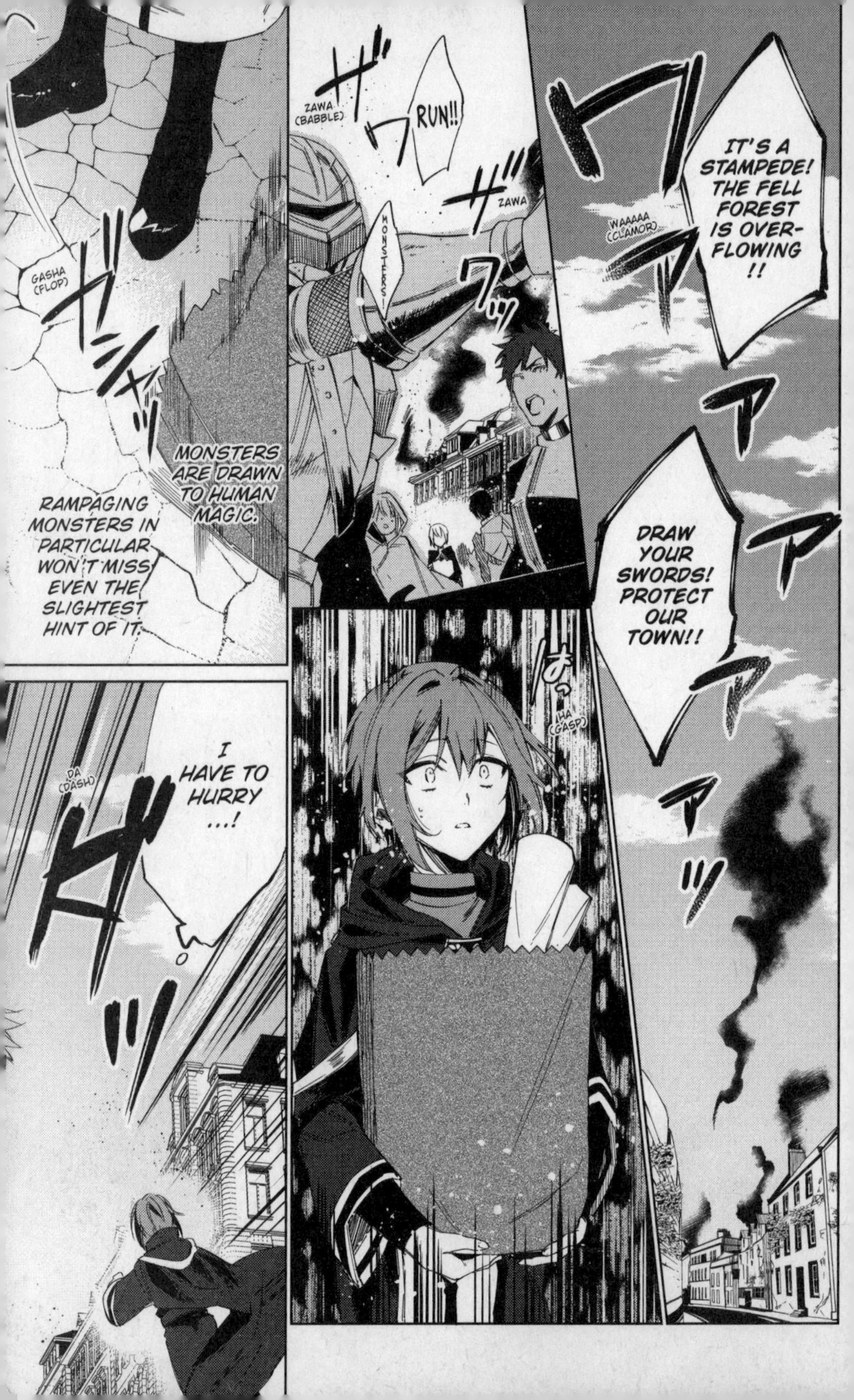
IT'S A STAMPEDE! THE FELL FOREST IS OVER-FLOWING!!
WAAAAA (CLAMOR)
DRAW YOUR SWORDS! PROTECT OUR TOWN!!
RUN!!
ZAWA (BABBLE)
ZAWA
MONSTERS!
GASHA (FLOP)
MONSTERS ARE DRAWN TO HUMAN MAGIC.
RAMPAGING MONSTERS IN PARTICULAR WON'T MISS EVEN THE SLIGHTEST HINT OF IT.
HA (GASP)
DA (DASH)
I HAVE TO HURRY ...!

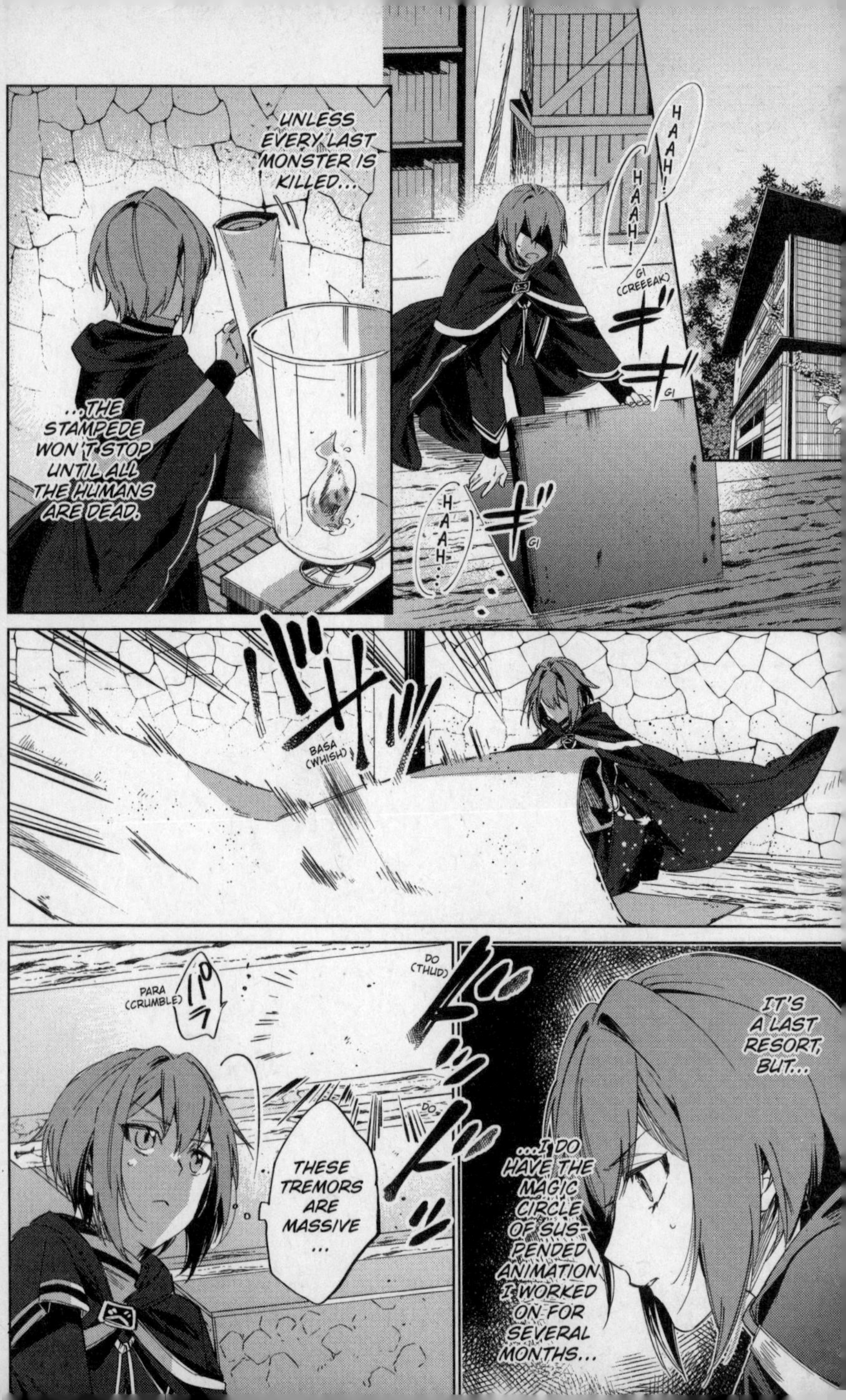
HAAAH! HAAAH!
GI (CREEEAK)
GI
HAAAH...
GI
UNLESS EVERY LAST MONSTER IS KILLED...
...THE STAMPEDE WON'T STOP UNTIL ALL THE HUMANS ARE DEAD.
BASA (WHISH)
IT'S A LAST RESORT, BUT...
...I DO HAVE THE MAGIC CIRCLE OF SUS-PENDED ANIMATION I WORKED ON FOR SEVERAL MONTHS...
DO (THUD)
DO
PARA (CRUMBLE)
THESE TREMORS ARE MASSIVE...

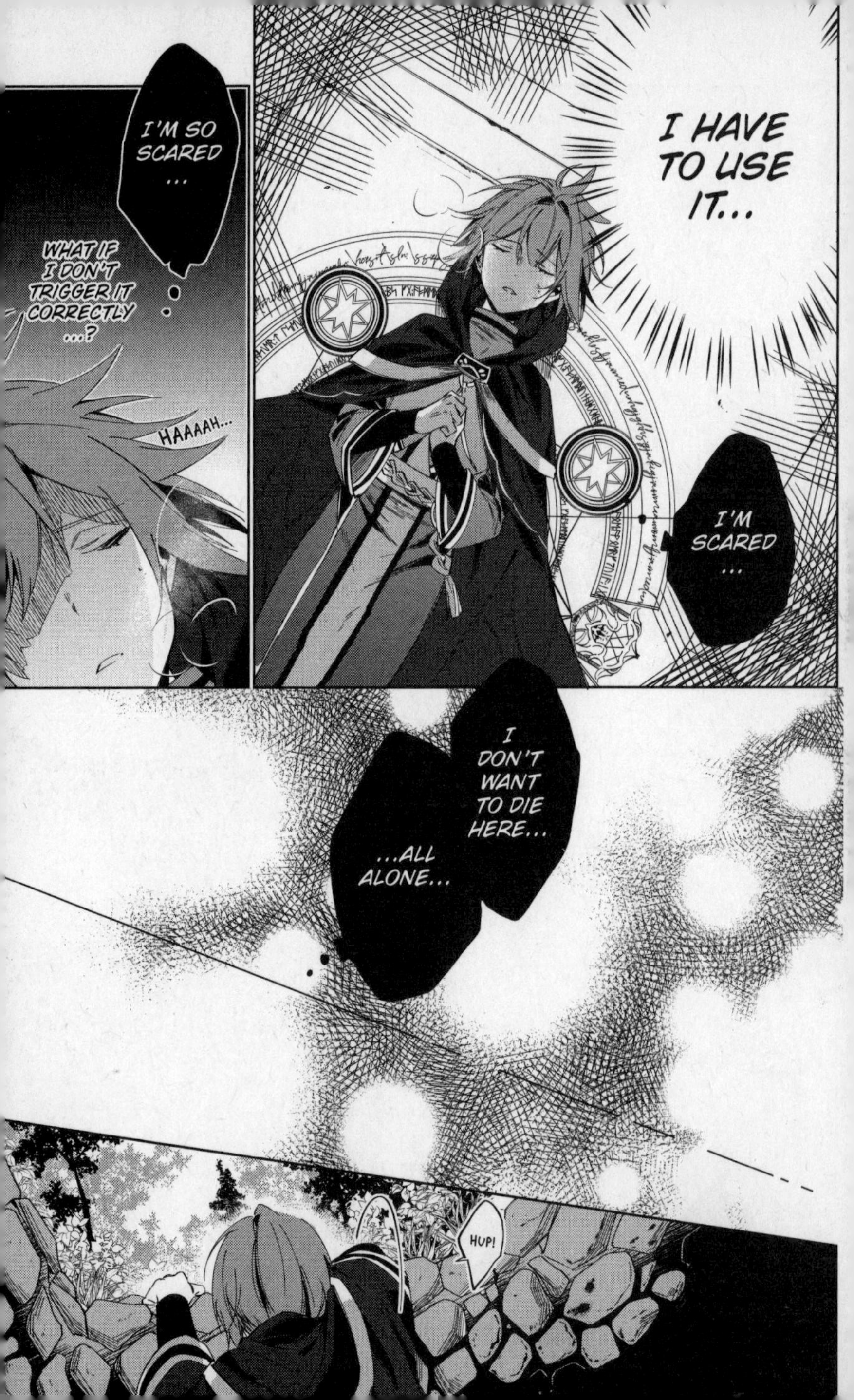
I HAVE TO USE IT...
I'M SCARED...
I'M SO SCARED...
WHAT IF I DON'T TRIGGER IT CORRECTLY...?
HAAAAH...
I DON'T WANT TO DIE HERE...
...ALL ALONE...
HUP!

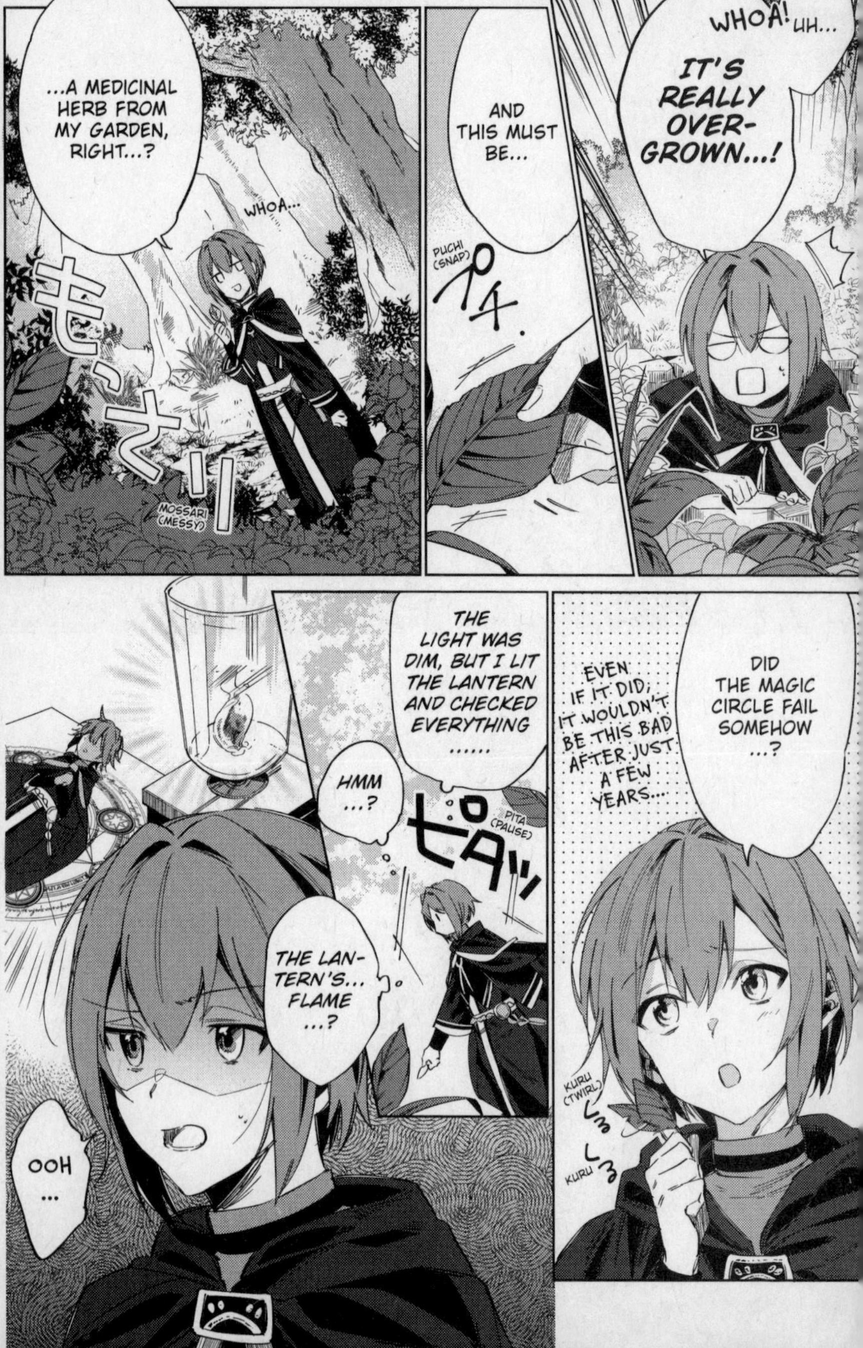
WHOA! UH...
IT'S REALLY OVER-GROWN...!
AND THIS MUST BE...
PUCHI (SNAP)
...A MEDICINAL HERB FROM MY GARDEN, RIGHT...?
WHOA...
MOSSARI (MESSY)
DID THE MAGIC CIRCLE FAIL SOMEHOW ...?
EVEN IF IT DID, IT WOULDN'T BE THIS BAD AFTER JUST A FEW YEARS...
KURU (TWIRL)
KURU
THE LIGHT WAS DIM, BUT I LIT THE LANTERN AND CHECKED EVERYTHING ......
HMM ...?
PITA (PAUSE)
THE LAN-TERN'S... FLAME ...?
OOH ...

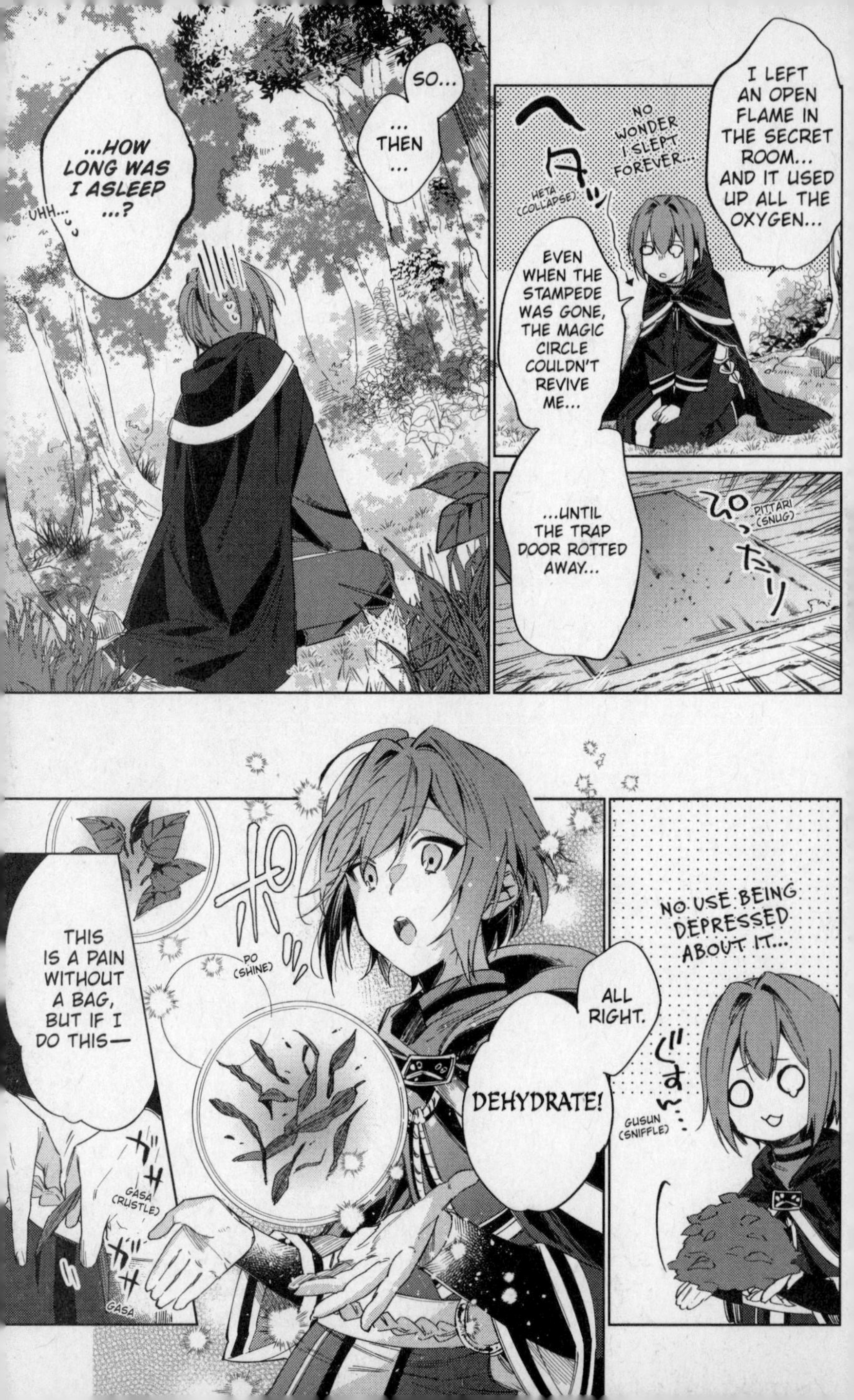
I LEFT AN OPEN FLAME IN THE SECRET ROOM... AND IT USED UP ALL THE OXYGEN...
NO WONDER I SLEPT FOREVER...
HETA (COLLAPSE)
EVEN WHEN THE STAMPEDE WAS GONE, THE MAGIC CIRCLE COULDN'T REVIVE ME...
...UNTIL THE TRAP DOOR ROTTED AWAY...
PITTARI (SNUG)
SO...
... THEN ...
...HOW LONG WAS I ASLEEP ...?
UHH...
NO USE BEING DEPRESSED ABOUT IT...
GUSUN (SNIFFLE)
ALL RIGHT.
THIS IS A PAIN WITHOUT A BAG, BUT IF I DO THIS—
GASA (RUSTLE)
GASA
PO (SHINE)
DEHYDRATE!

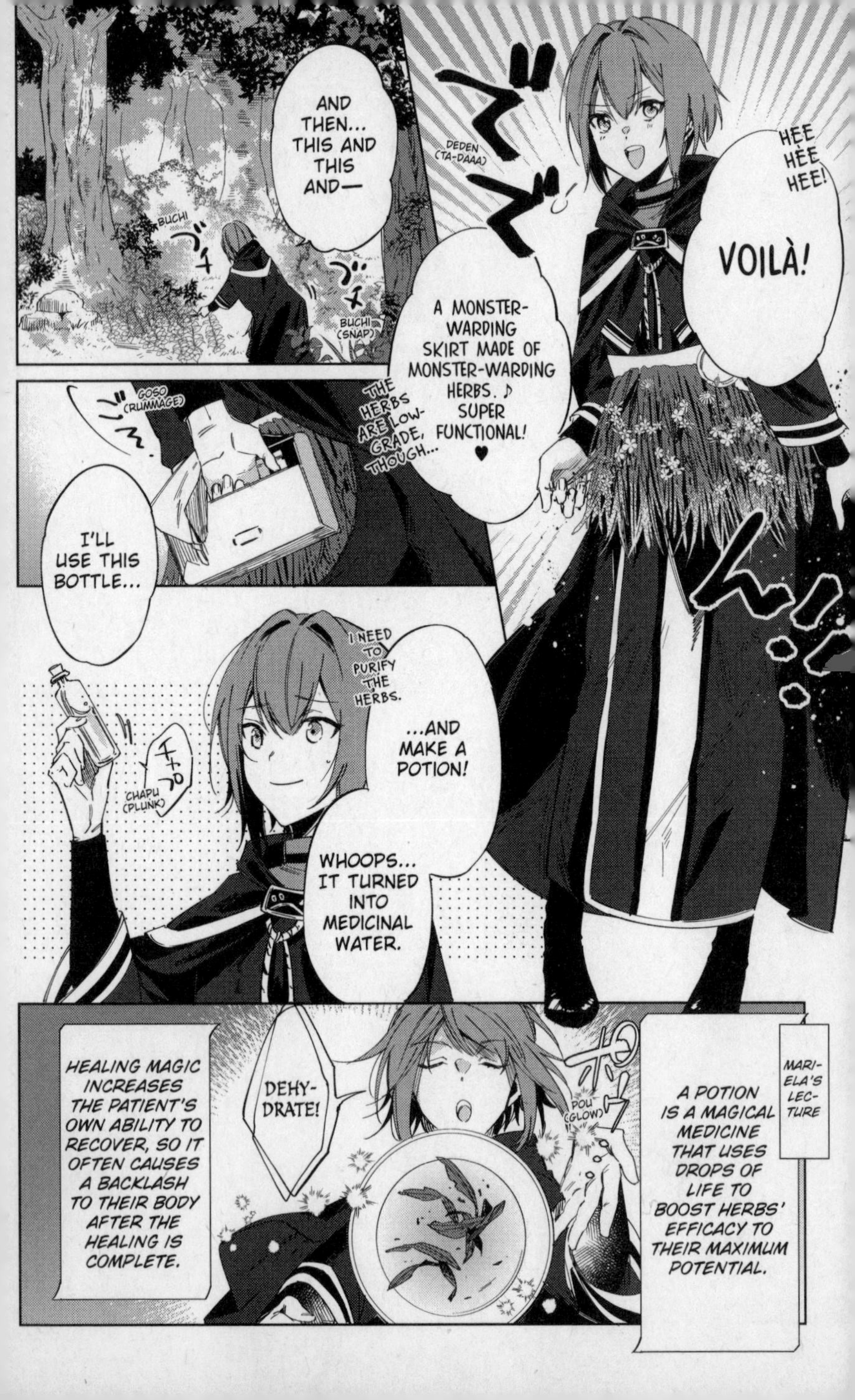
DEDEN (TA-DAAA)
HEE HEE HEE!
VOILÀ!
A MONSTER-WARDING SKIRT MADE OF MONSTER-WARDING HERBS. ♪ SUPER FUNCTIONAL! ♥
THE HERBS ARE LOW-GRADE, THOUGH...
AND THEN... THIS AND THIS AND—
BUCHI
BUCHI (SNAP)
GOSO (RUMMAGE)
I'LL USE THIS BOTTLE...
I NEED TO PURIFY THE HERBS.
...AND MAKE A POTION!
CHAPU (PLUNK)
WHOOPS... IT TURNED INTO MEDICINAL WATER.
MARI-ELA'S LEC-TURE
A POTION IS A MAGICAL MEDICINE THAT USES DROPS OF LIFE TO BOOST HERBS' EFFICACY TO THEIR MAXIMUM POTENTIAL.
POU (GLOW)
DEHY-DRATE!
HEALING MAGIC INCREASES THE PATIENT'S OWN ABILITY TO RECOVER, SO IT OFTEN CAUSES A BACKLASH TO THEIR BODY AFTER THE HEALING IS COMPLETE.

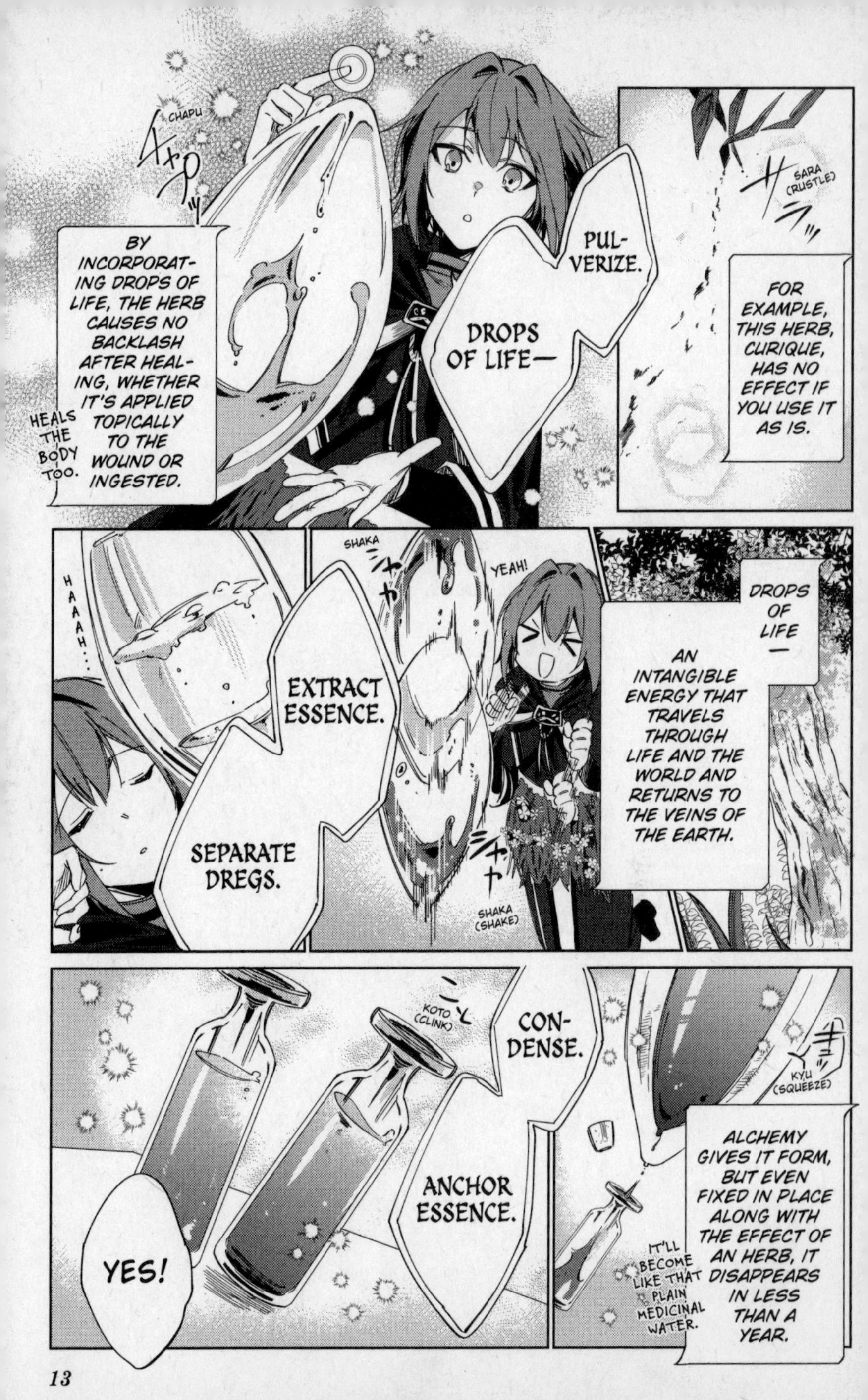
SARA (RUSTLE)
FOR EXAMPLE, THIS HERB, CURIQUE, HAS NO EFFECT IF YOU USE IT AS IS.
CHAPU
PUL-VERIZE.
DROPS OF LIFE—
BY INCORPORATING DROPS OF LIFE, THE HERB CAUSES NO BACKLASH AFTER HEALING, WHETHER IT'S APPLIED TOPICALLY TO THE WOUND OR INGESTED.
HEALS THE BODY TOO.
DROPS OF LIFE —
AN INTANGIBLE ENERGY THAT TRAVELS THROUGH LIFE AND THE WORLD AND RETURNS TO THE VEINS OF THE EARTH.
SHAKA
YEAH!
EXTRACT ESSENCE.
SHAKA (SHAKE)
HAAAAH...
SEPARATE DREGS.
KYU (SQUEEZE)
ALCHEMY GIVES IT FORM, BUT EVEN FIXED IN PLACE ALONG WITH THE EFFECT OF AN HERB, IT DISAPPEARS IN LESS THAN A YEAR.
IT'LL BECOME LIKE THAT PLAIN MEDICINAL WATER.
CON-DENSE.
KOTO (CLINK)
ANCHOR ESSENCE.
YES!

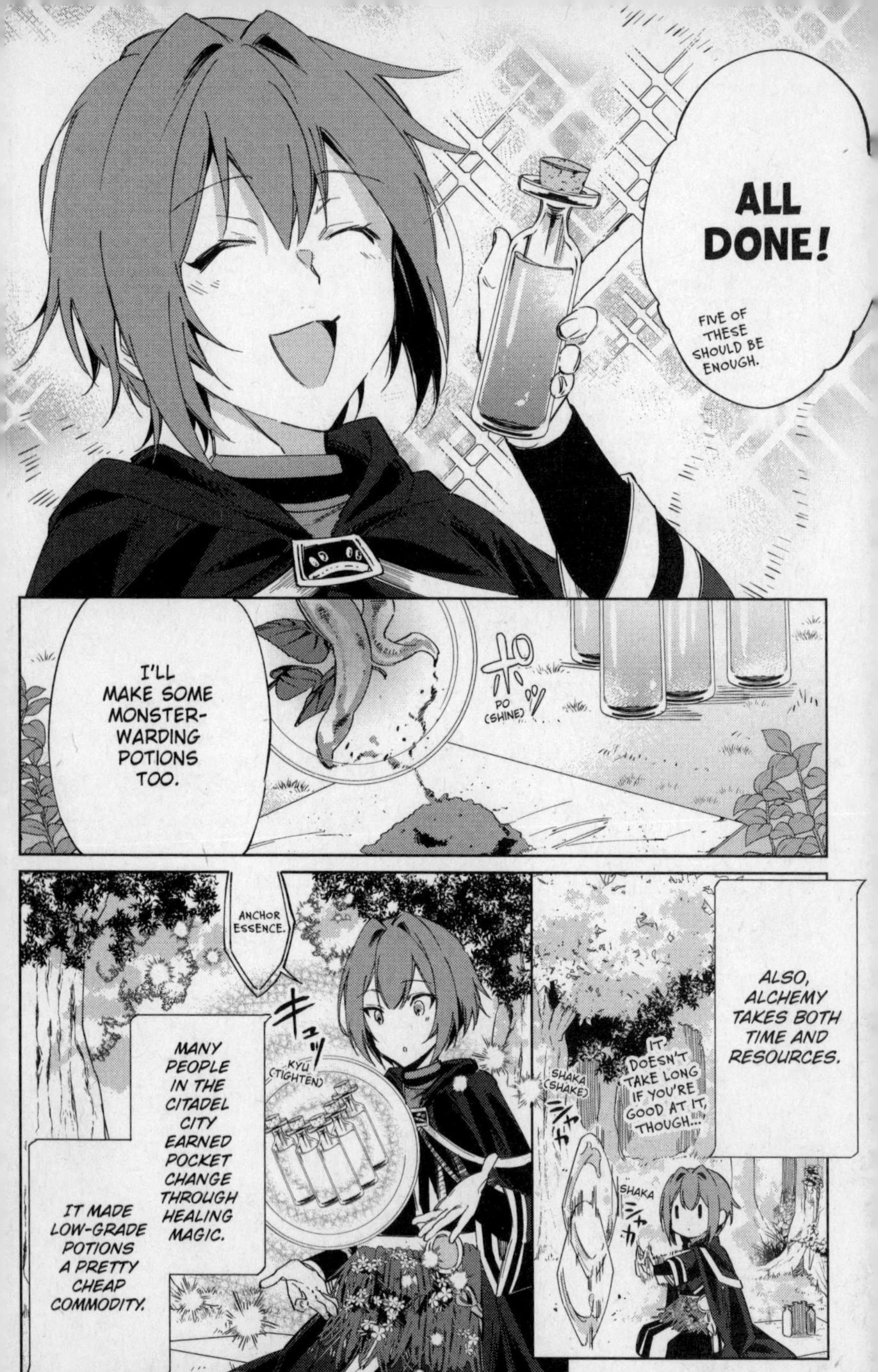
ALL DONE!
FIVE OF THESE SHOULD BE ENOUGH.
PO (SHINE)
I'LL MAKE SOME MONSTER-WARDING POTIONS TOO.
ALSO, ALCHEMY TAKES BOTH TIME AND RESOURCES.
IT DOESN'T TAKE LONG IF YOU'RE GOOD AT IT, THOUGH...
SHAKA (SHAKE)
SHAKA
ANCHOR ESSENCE.
KYU (TIGHTEN)
MANY PEOPLE IN THE CITADEL CITY EARNED POCKET CHANGE THROUGH HEALING MAGIC.
IT MADE LOW-GRADE POTIONS A PRETTY CHEAP COMMODITY.

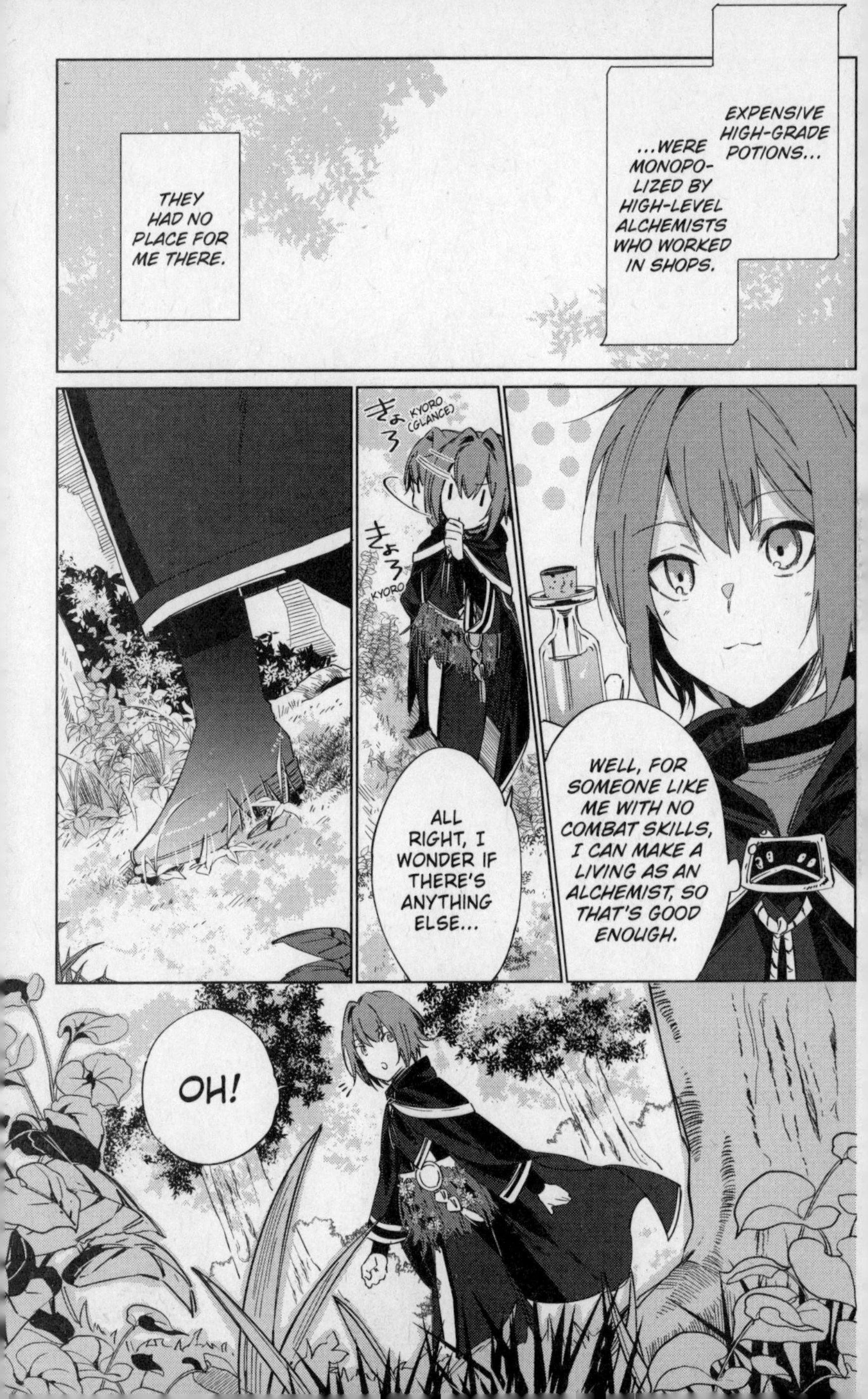
EXPENSIVE HIGH-GRADE POTIONS...
...WERE MONOPOLIZED BY HIGH-LEVEL ALCHEMISTS WHO WORKED IN SHOPS.
THEY HAD NO PLACE FOR ME THERE.
WELL, FOR SOMEONE LIKE ME WITH NO COMBAT SKILLS, I CAN MAKE A LIVING AS AN ALCHEMIST, SO THAT'S GOOD ENOUGH.
きょろ
KYORO (GLANCE)
きょろ
KYORO
ALL RIGHT, I WONDER IF THERE'S ANYTHING ELSE...
OH!

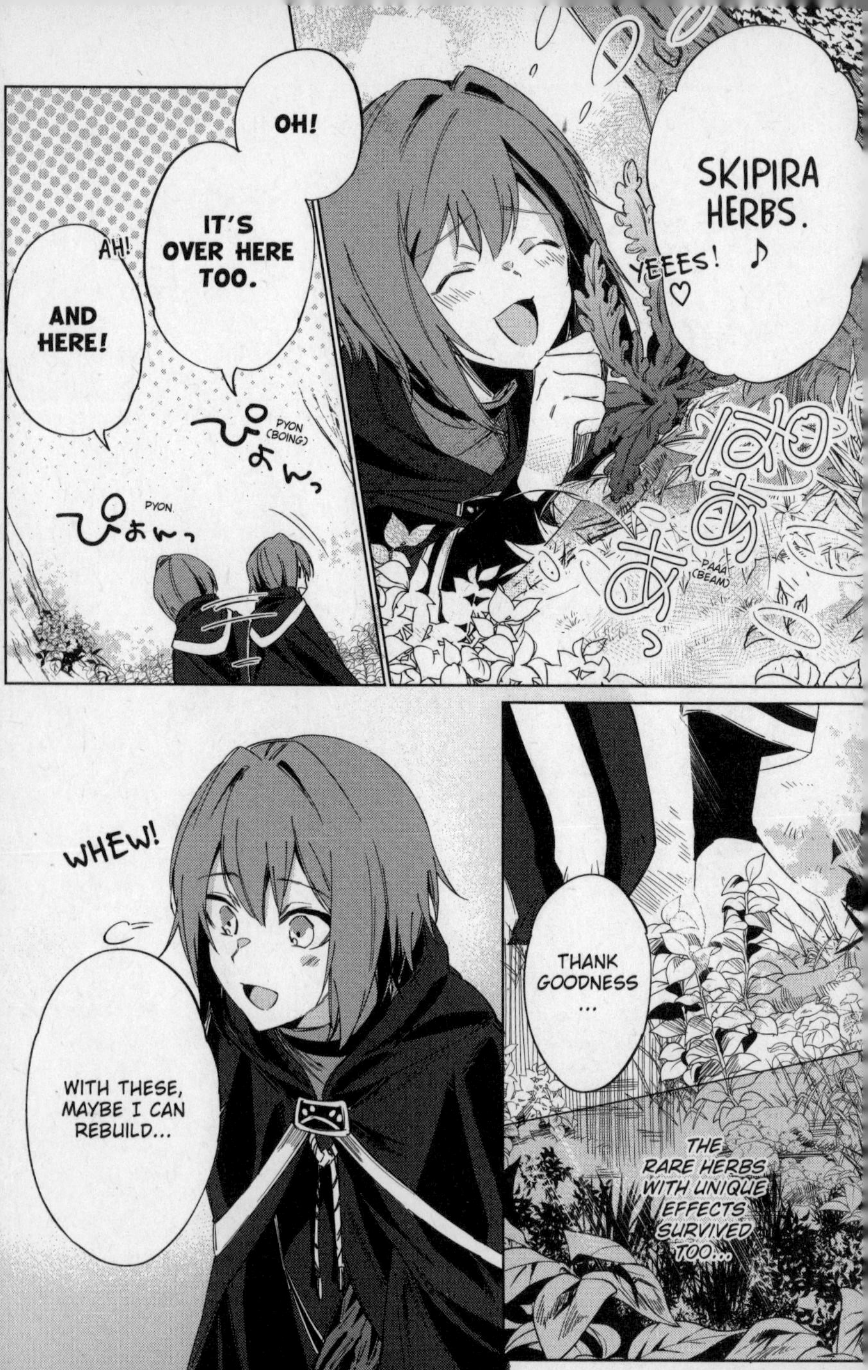
SKIPIRA HERBS.
YEEES! ♪ ♡
ぱあぁっ
PAAA (BEAM)
OH!
IT'S OVER HERE TOO.
AH!
AND HERE!
ぴょんっ
PYON (BOING)
ぴょんっ
PYON.
THANK GOODNESS...
THE RARE HERBS WITH UNIQUE EFFECTS SURVIVED TOO...
WHEW!
WITH THESE, MAYBE I CAN REBUILD...

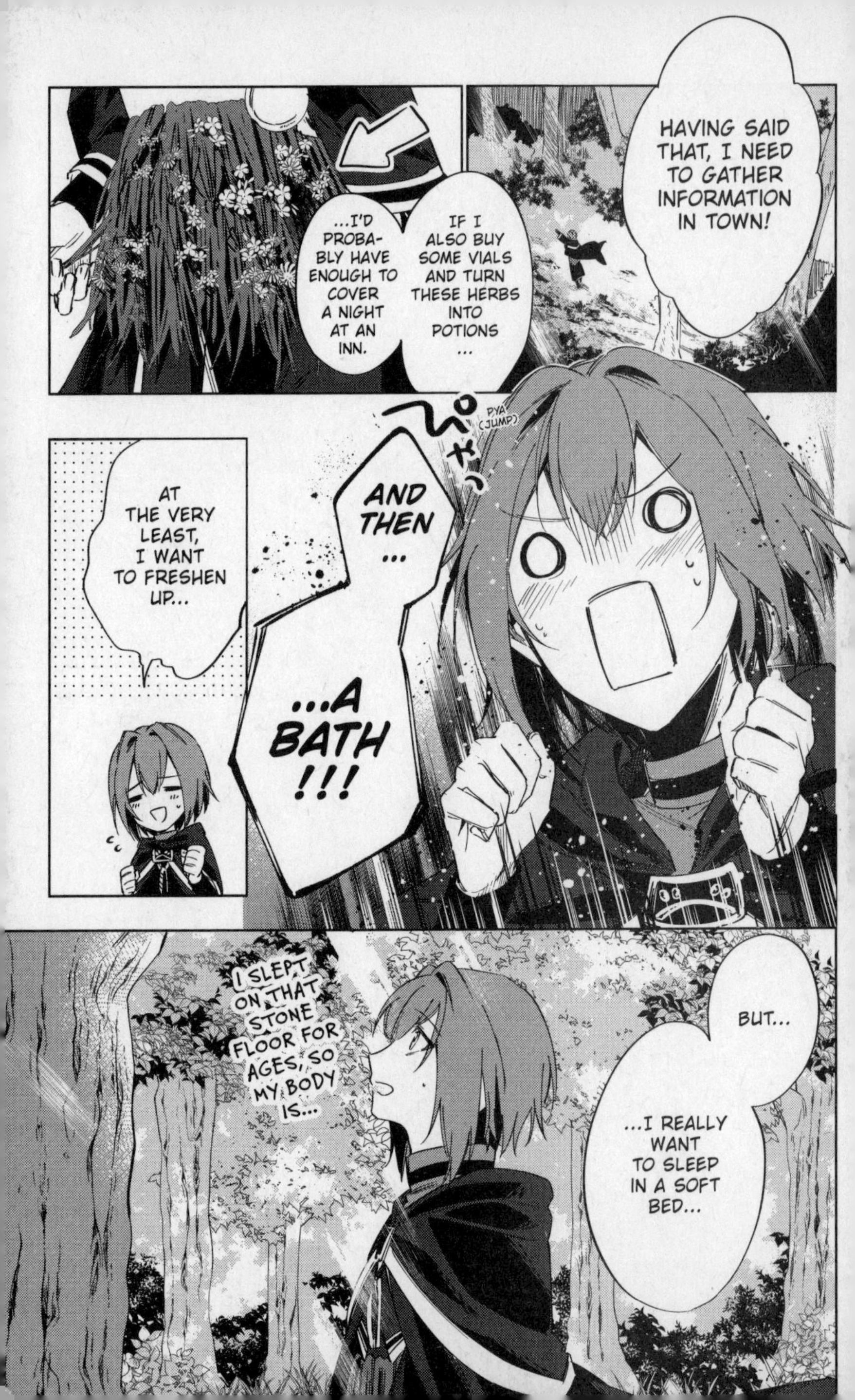
HAVING SAID THAT, I NEED TO GATHER INFORMATION IN TOWN!
IF I ALSO BUY SOME VIALS AND TURN THESE HERBS INTO POTIONS...
...I'D PROBABLY HAVE ENOUGH TO COVER A NIGHT AT AN INN.
PYA (JUMP)
AND THEN...
...A BATH!!!
AT THE VERY LEAST, I WANT TO FRESHEN UP...
BUT...
...I REALLY WANT TO SLEEP IN A SOFT BED...
I SLEPT ON THAT STONE FLOOR FOR AGES, SO MY BODY IS...

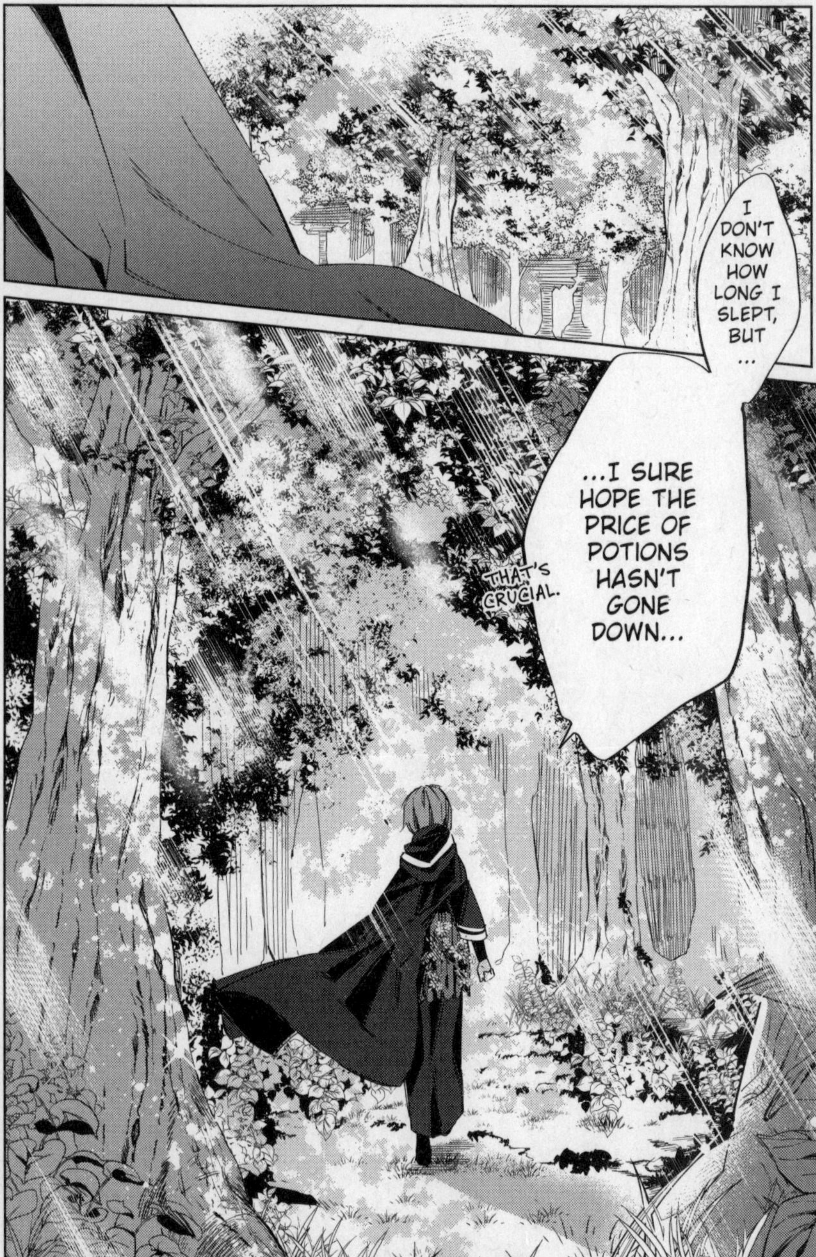
I DON'T KNOW HOW LONG I SLEPT, BUT ...
...I SURE HOPE THE PRICE OF POTIONS HASN'T GONE DOWN...
THAT'S CRUCIAL.

Episode 1

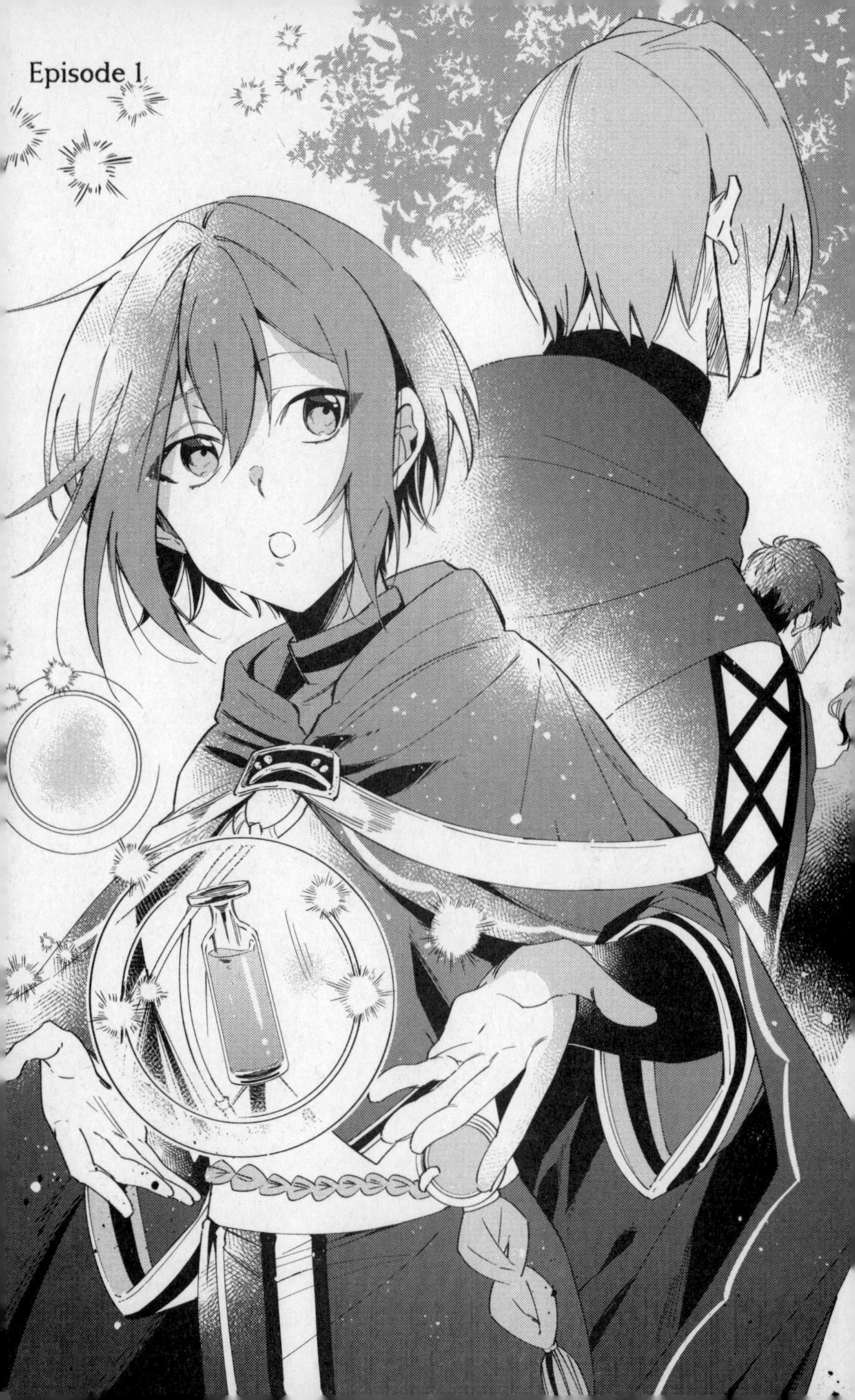

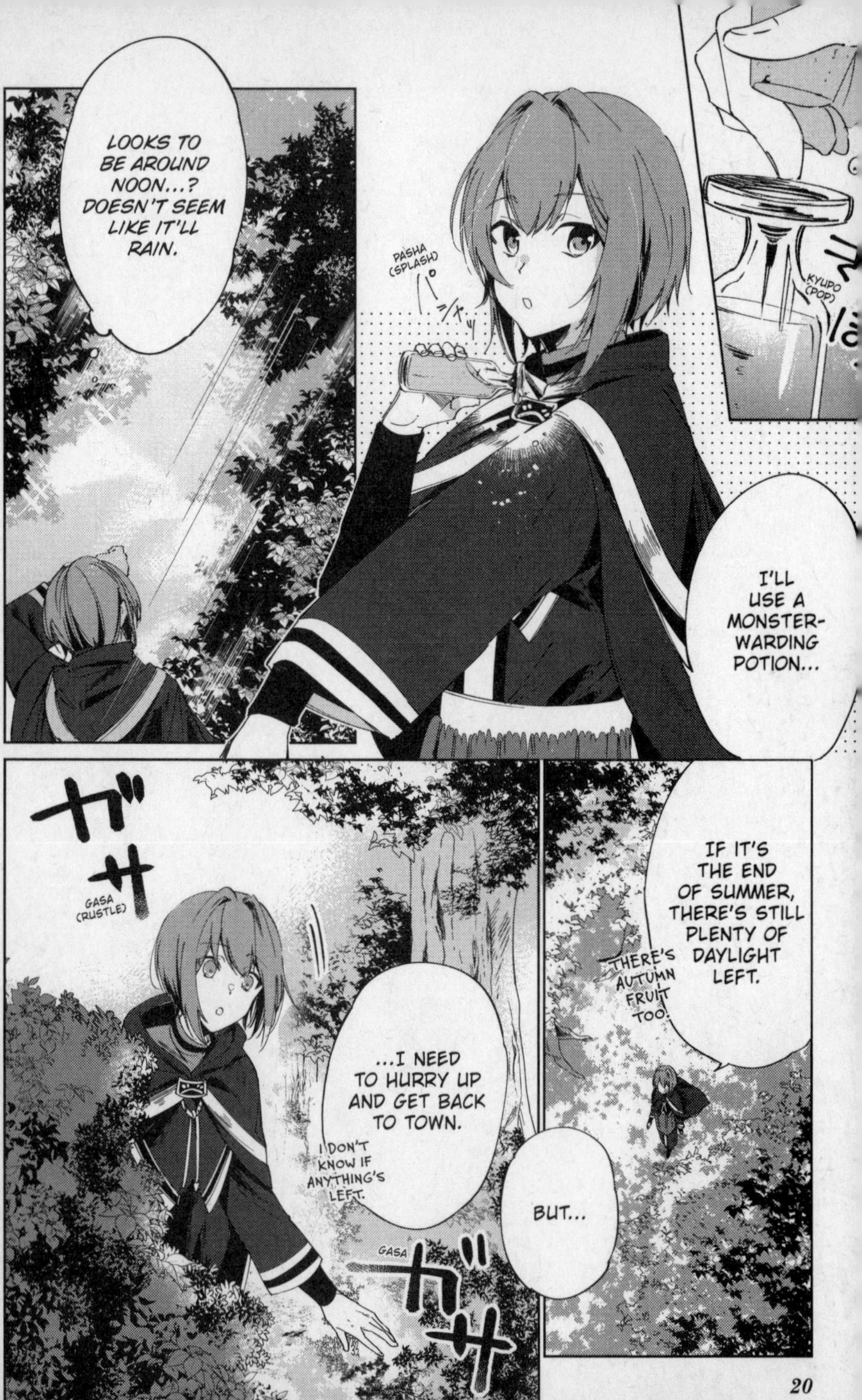

KYUPO (POP)
I'LL USE A MONSTER-WARDING POTION...
PASHA (SPLASH)
LOOKS TO BE AROUND NOON...? DOESN'T SEEM LIKE IT'LL RAIN.
IF IT'S THE END OF SUMMER, THERE'S STILL PLENTY OF DAYLIGHT LEFT.
THERE'S AUTUMN FRUIT TOO.
BUT...
...I NEED TO HURRY UP AND GET BACK TO TOWN.
I DON'T KNOW IF ANYTHING'S LEFT.
GASA
GASA (RUSTLE)

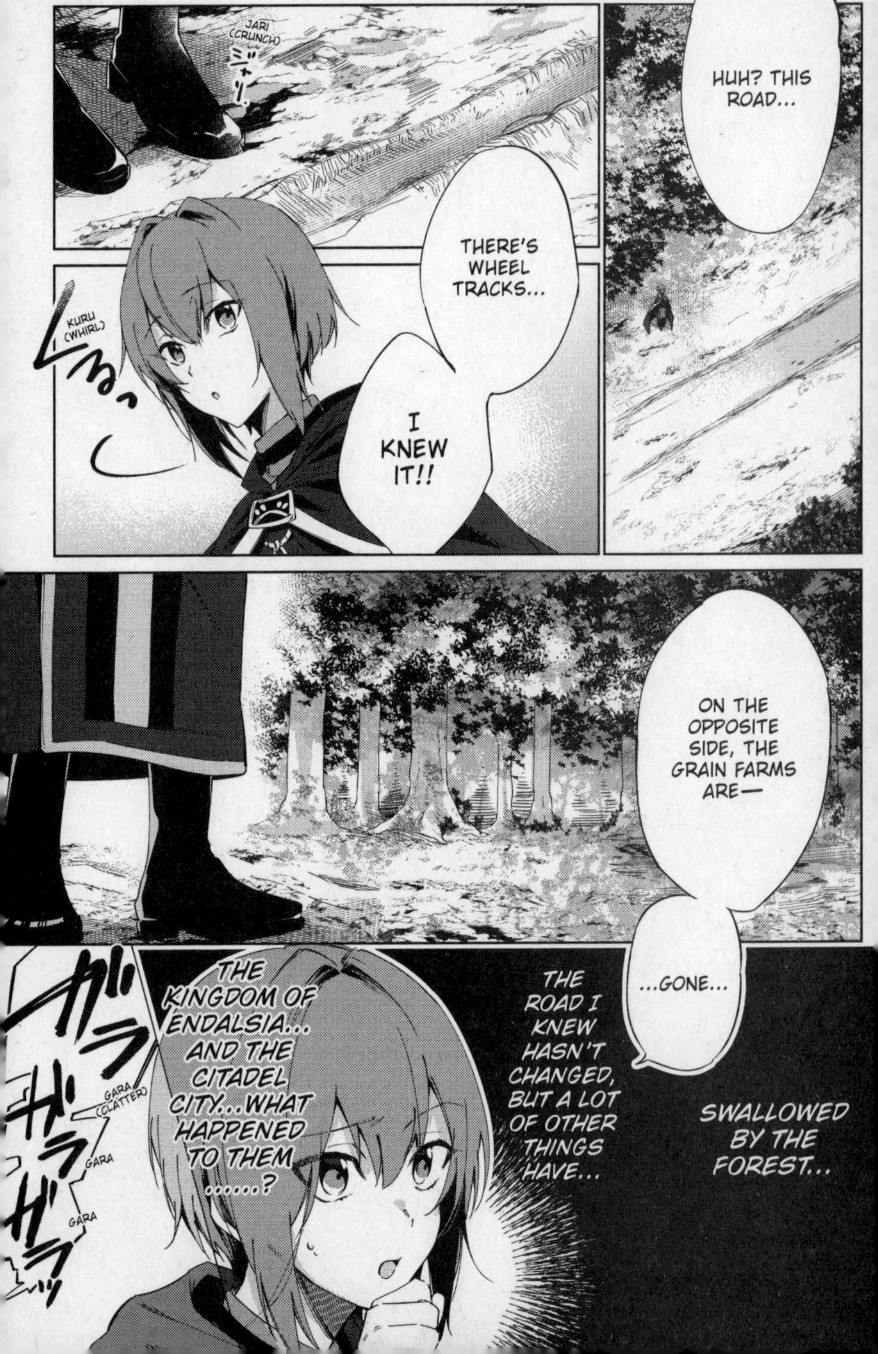
HUH? THIS ROAD...
JARI (CRUNCH)
THERE'S WHEEL TRACKS...
I KNEW IT!!
KURU (WHIRL)
ON THE OPPOSITE SIDE, THE GRAIN FARMS ARE—
...GONE...
SWALLOWED BY THE FOREST...
THE ROAD I KNEW HASN'T CHANGED, BUT A LOT OF OTHER THINGS HAVE...
THE KINGDOM OF ENDALSIA... AND THE CITADEL CITY...WHAT HAPPENED TO THEM ......?
GARA (CLATTER)
GARA
GARA

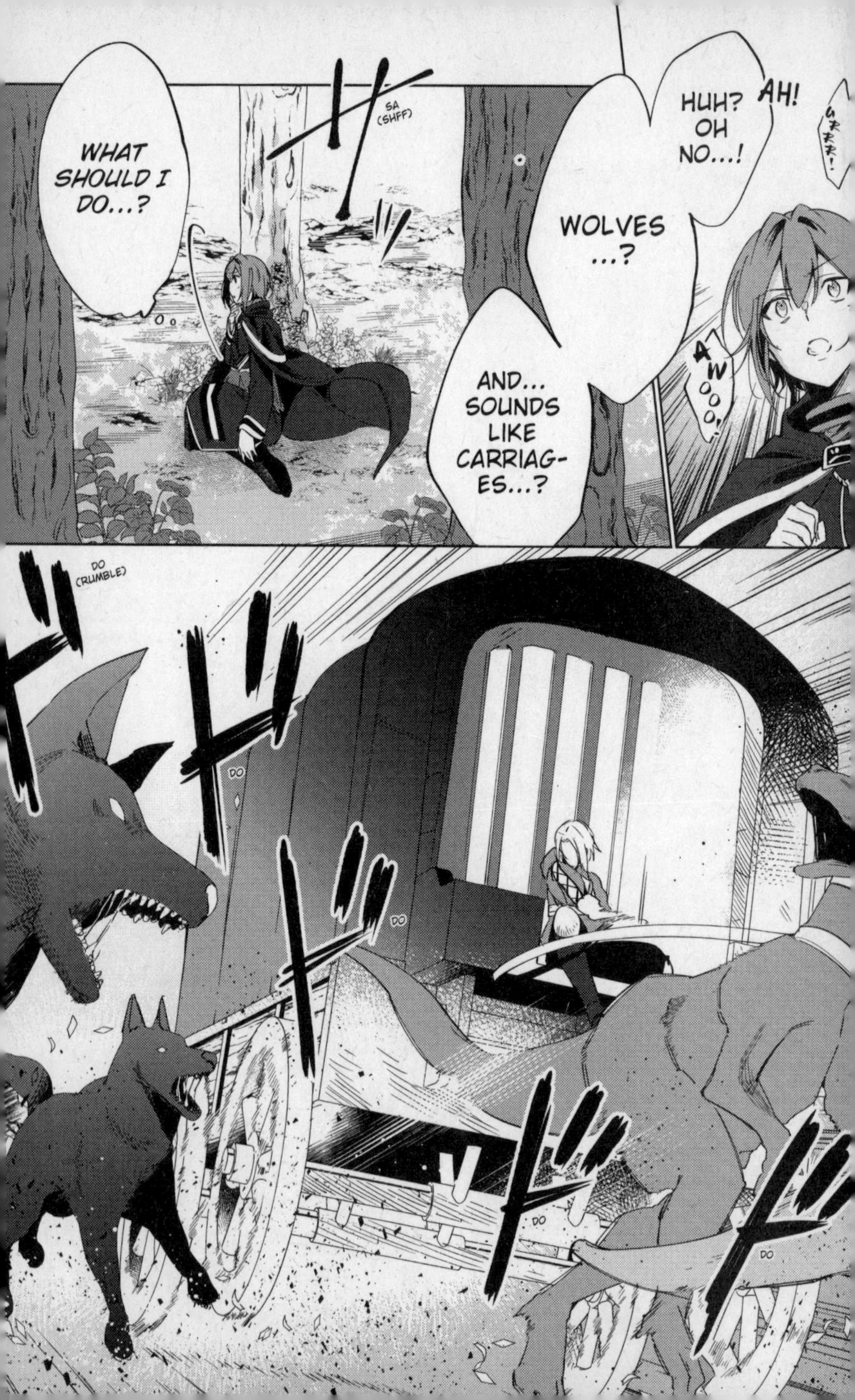
AH!
URRR!
HUH? OH NO...!
WOLVES ...?
AWOOO!
AND... SOUNDS LIKE CARRIAG-ES...?
SA (SHFF)
WHAT SHOULD I DO...?
DO (RUMBLE)
DO
DO
DO
DO

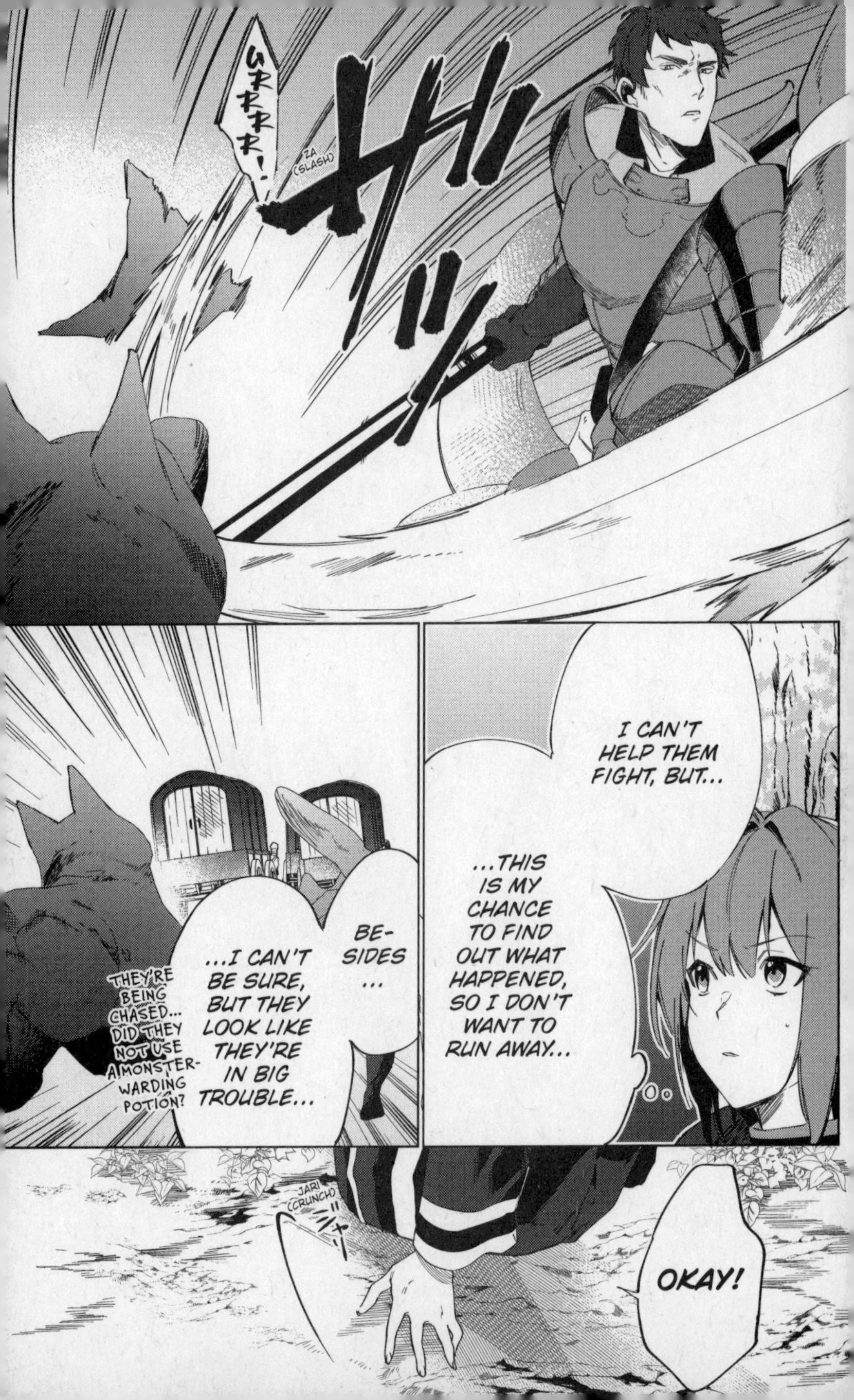
URRRRR!
ZA (SLASH)
I CAN'T HELP THEM FIGHT, BUT...
...THIS IS MY CHANCE TO FIND OUT WHAT HAPPENED, SO I DON'T WANT TO RUN AWAY...
BESIDES...
...I CAN'T BE SURE, BUT THEY LOOK LIKE THEY'RE IN BIG TROUBLE...
THEY'RE BEING CHASED... DID THEY NOT USE A MONSTER-WARDING POTION?
JARI (CRUNCH)
OKAY!

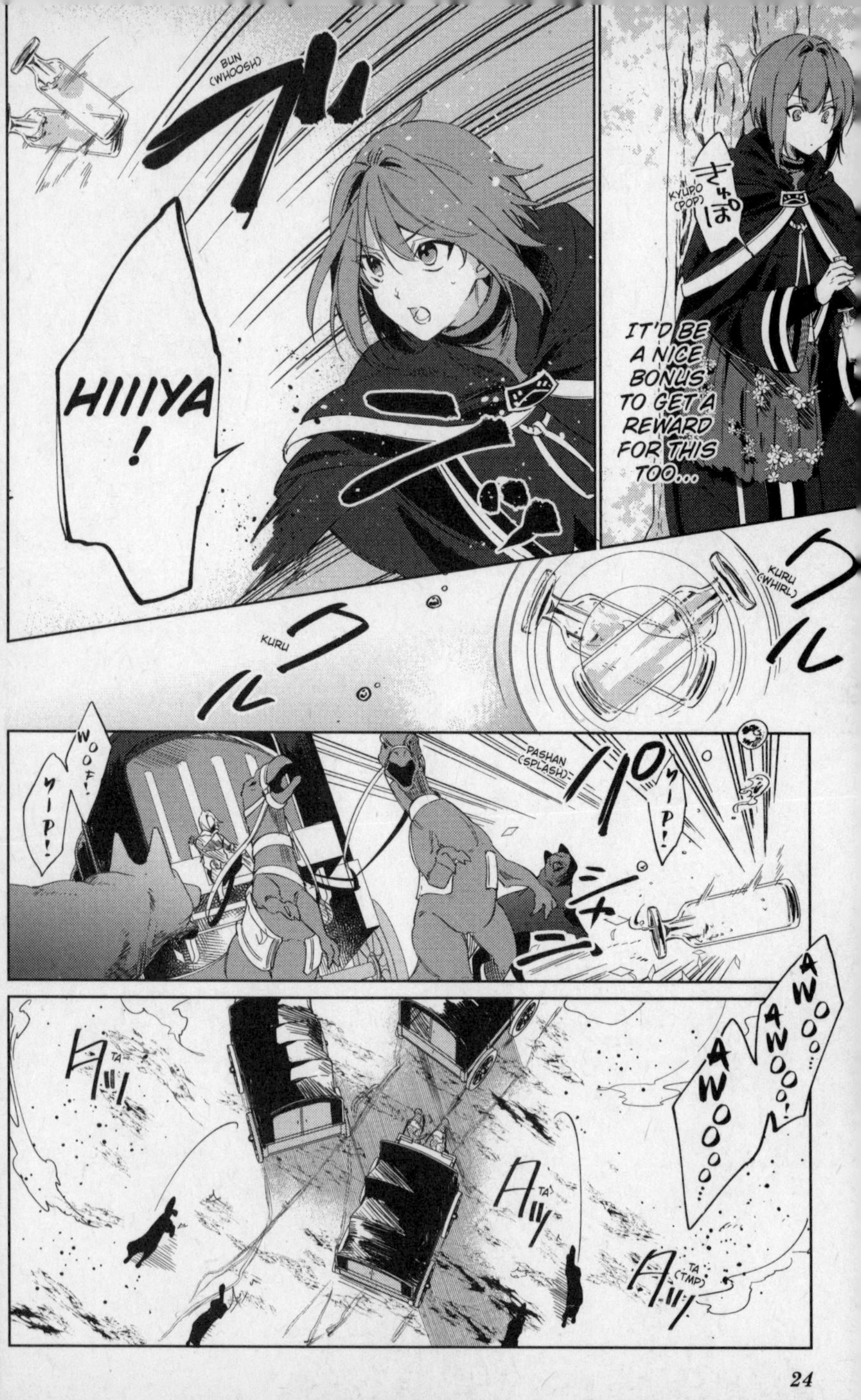
KYUPO (POP)
きゅぽ
IT'D BE A NICE BONUS TO GET A REWARD FOR THIS TOO...
BUN (WHOOSH)
HIIIYA!
KURU (WHIRL)
KURU
PASHAN (SPLASH)
WOOF!
AWOOO...
AWOOO!
AWOOOO...
TA
TA
TA (TMP)

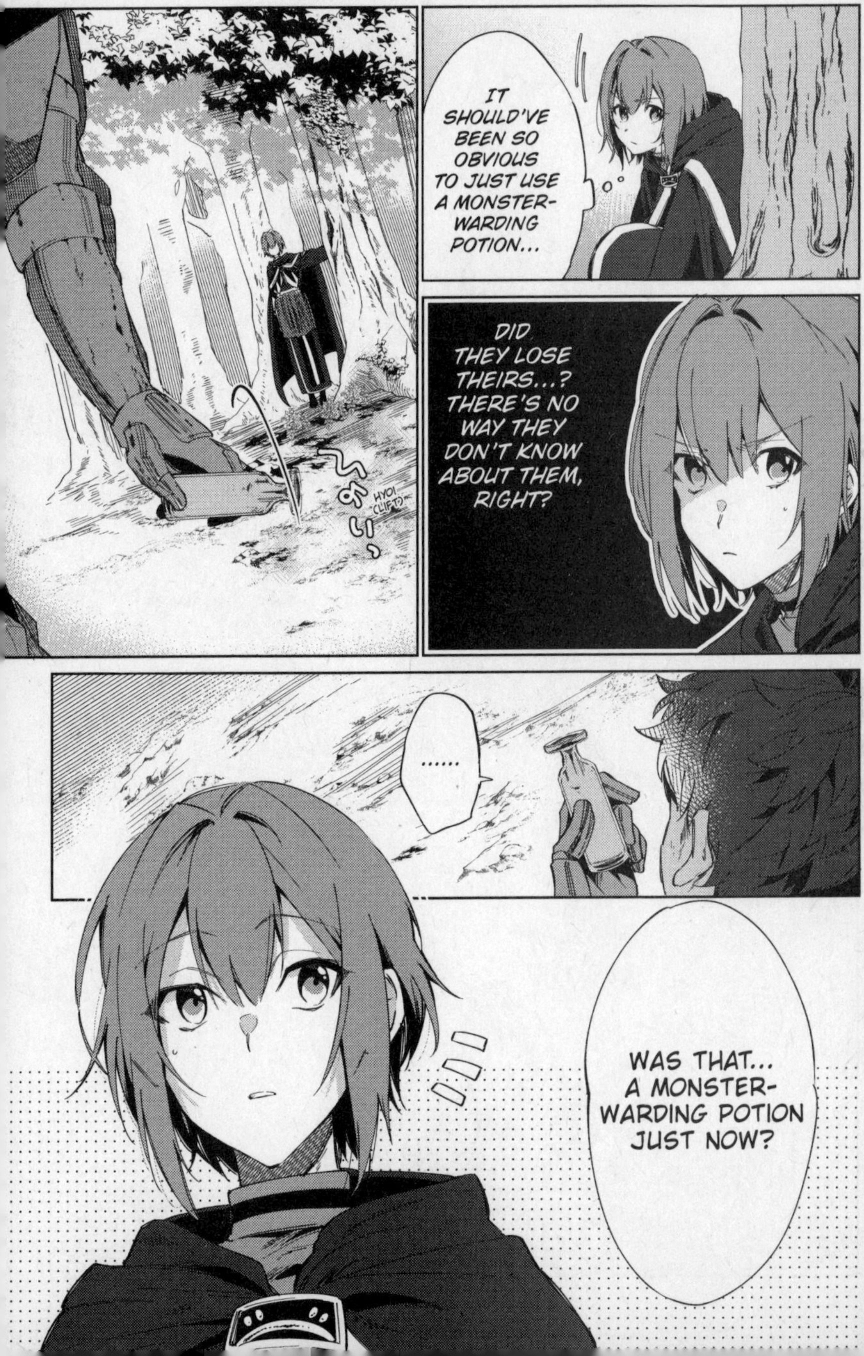
IT SHOULD'VE BEEN SO OBVIOUS TO JUST USE A MONSTER-WARDING POTION...
DID THEY LOSE THEIRS...? THERE'S NO WAY THEY DON'T KNOW ABOUT THEM, RIGHT?
ひょい
HYOI (LIFT)
......
WAS THAT... A MONSTER-WARDING POTION JUST NOW?

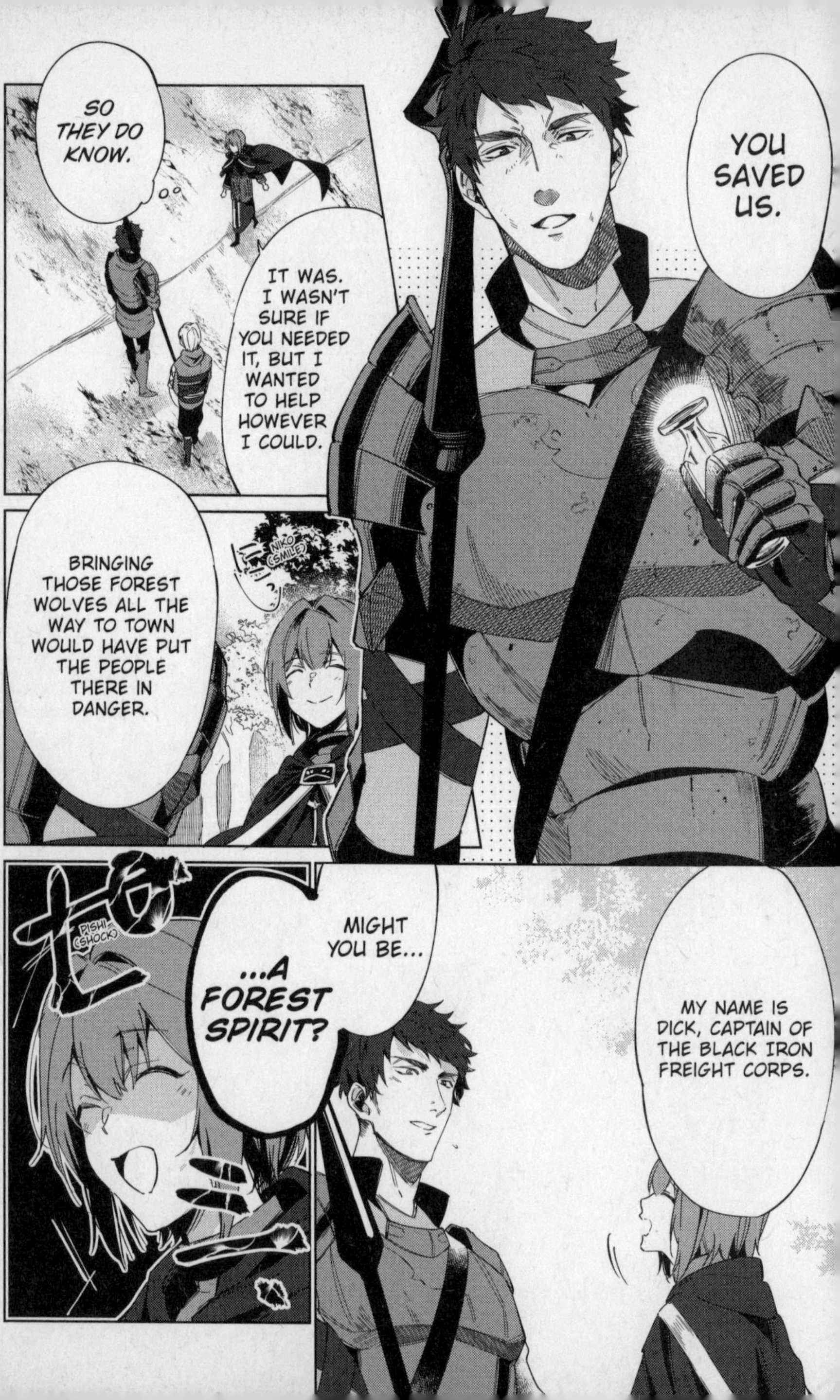
YOU SAVED US.
SO THEY DO KNOW.
IT WAS. I WASN'T SURE IF YOU NEEDED IT, BUT I WANTED TO HELP HOWEVER I COULD.
NIKO (SMILE)
BRINGING THOSE FOREST WOLVES ALL THE WAY TO TOWN WOULD HAVE PUT THE PEOPLE THERE IN DANGER.
MY NAME IS DICK, CAPTAIN OF THE BLACK IRON FREIGHT CORPS.
MIGHT YOU BE...
...A FOREST SPIRIT?
PISHI (SHOCK)

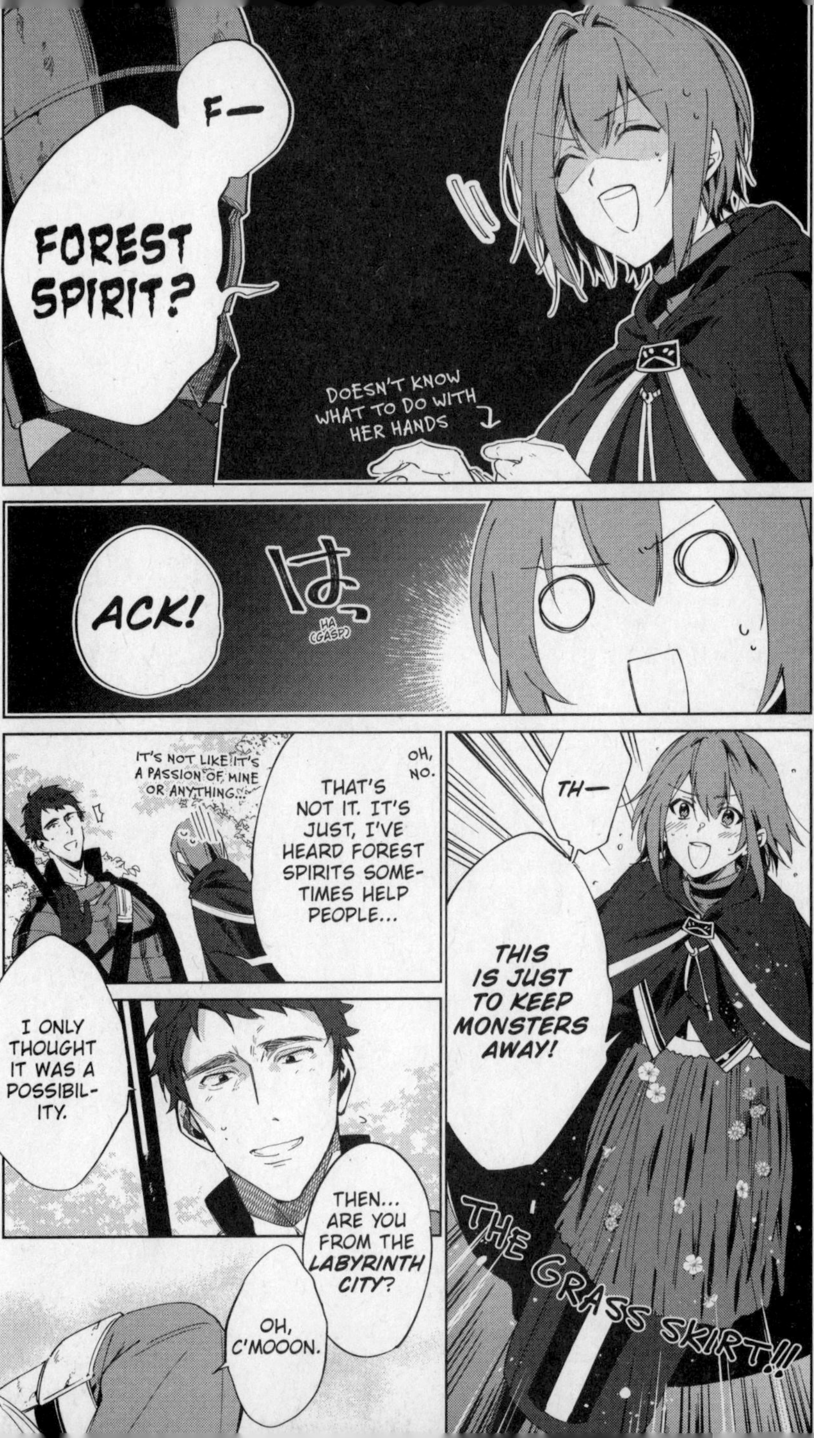
F—
FOREST SPIRIT?
DOESN'T KNOW WHAT TO DO WITH HER HANDS
は
HA (GASP)
ACK!
TH—
THIS IS JUST TO KEEP MONSTERS AWAY!
THE GRASS SKIRT!!
OH, NO.
THAT'S NOT IT. IT'S JUST, I'VE HEARD FOREST SPIRITS SOMETIMES HELP PEOPLE...
IT'S NOT LIKE IT'S A PASSION OF MINE OR ANYTHING...
I ONLY THOUGHT IT WAS A POSSIBILITY.
THEN... ARE YOU FROM THE LABYRINTH CITY?
OH, C'MOOON.

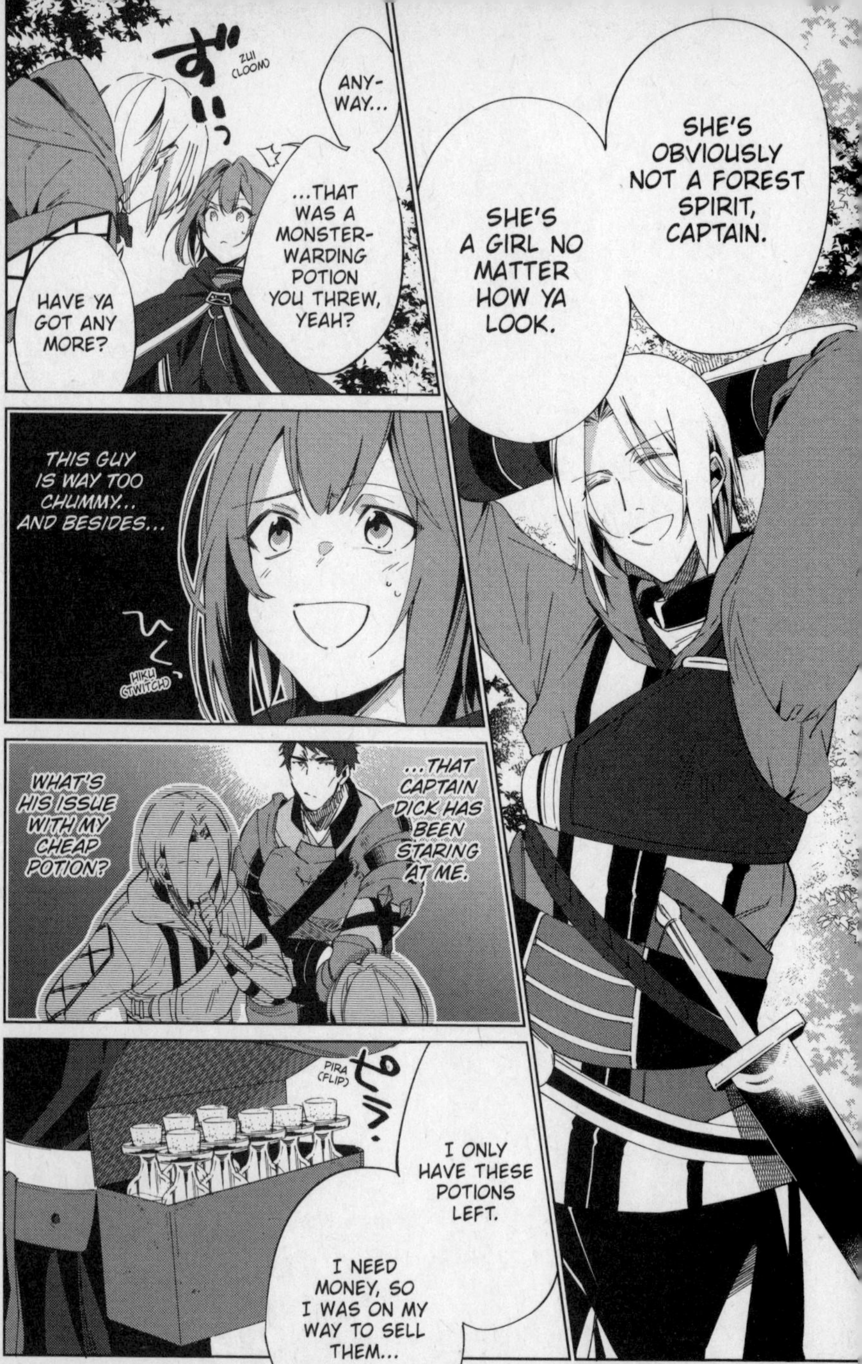
SHE'S OBVIOUSLY NOT A FOREST SPIRIT, CAPTAIN.
SHE'S A GIRL NO MATTER HOW YA LOOK.
ずいっ
ZUI (LOOM)
ANY-WAY...
...THAT WAS A MONSTER-WARDING POTION YOU THREW, YEAH?
HAVE YA GOT ANY MORE?
THIS GUY IS WAY TOO CHUMMY... AND BESIDES...
ひくっ
HIKU (TWITCH)
...THAT CAPTAIN DICK HAS BEEN STARING AT ME.
WHAT'S HIS ISSUE WITH MY CHEAP POTION?
ぴら
PIRA (FLIP)
I ONLY HAVE THESE POTIONS LEFT.
I NEED MONEY, SO I WAS ON MY WAY TO SELL THEM...

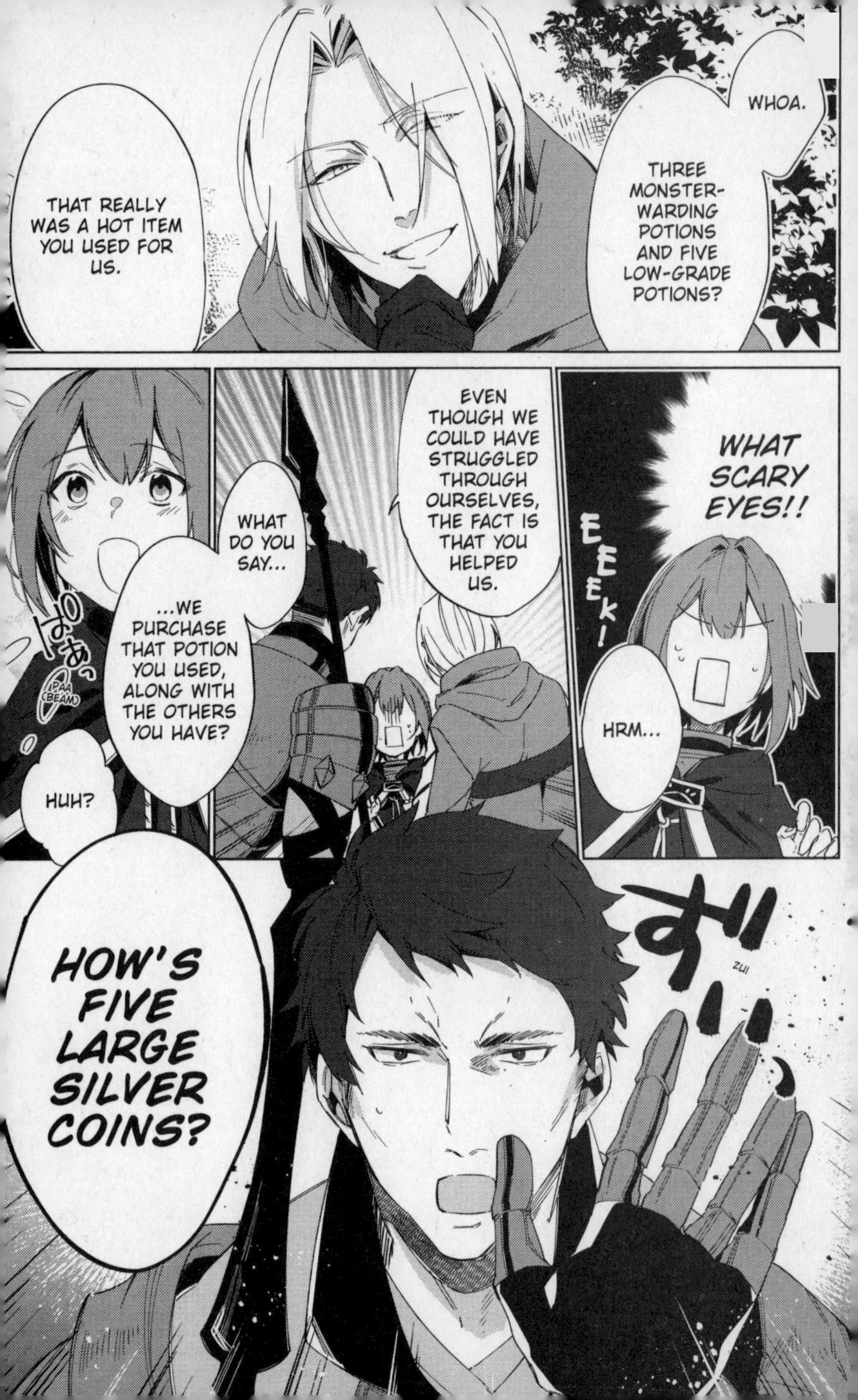
WHOA.
THREE MONSTER-WARDING POTIONS AND FIVE LOW-GRADE POTIONS?
THAT REALLY WAS A HOT ITEM YOU USED FOR US.
WHAT SCARY EYES!!
EEEK!
HRM...
EVEN THOUGH WE COULD HAVE STRUGGLED THROUGH OURSELVES, THE FACT IS THAT YOU HELPED US.
WHAT DO YOU SAY...
...WE PURCHASE THAT POTION YOU USED, ALONG WITH THE OTHERS YOU HAVE?
ぱあっ
PAA (BEAM)
HUH?
ずい
ZUI
HOW'S FIVE LARGE SILVER COINS?

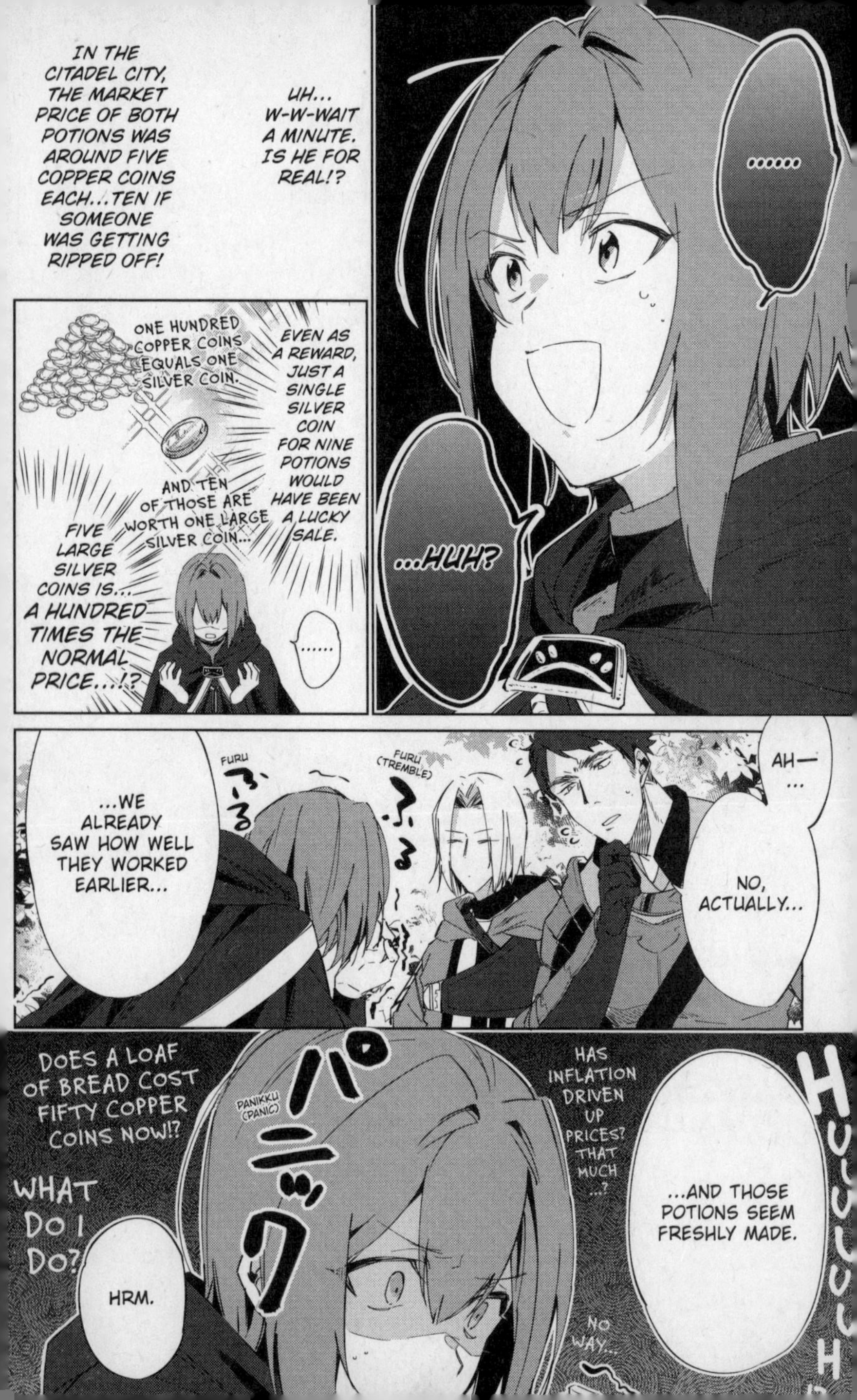
......
...HUH?
UH... W-W-WAIT A MINUTE. IS HE FOR REAL!?
IN THE CITADEL CITY, THE MARKET PRICE OF BOTH POTIONS WAS AROUND FIVE COPPER COINS EACH...TEN IF SOMEONE WAS GETTING RIPPED OFF!
EVEN AS A REWARD, JUST A SINGLE SILVER COIN FOR NINE POTIONS WOULD HAVE BEEN A LUCKY SALE.
ONE HUNDRED COPPER COINS EQUALS ONE SILVER COIN.
AND TEN OF THOSE ARE WORTH ONE LARGE SILVER COIN...
FIVE LARGE SILVER COINS IS... A HUNDRED TIMES THE NORMAL PRICE...!?
......
AH— ...
NO, ACTUALLY...
ふる
FURU (TREMBLE)
ふる
FURU
...WE ALREADY SAW HOW WELL THEY WORKED EARLIER...
...AND THOSE POTIONS SEEM FRESHLY MADE.
HAS INFLATION DRIVEN UP PRICES? THAT MUCH ...?
NO WAY...
パニック
PANIKKU (PANIC)
DOES A LOAF OF BREAD COST FIFTY COPPER COINS NOW!?
WHAT DO I DO?
HRM.

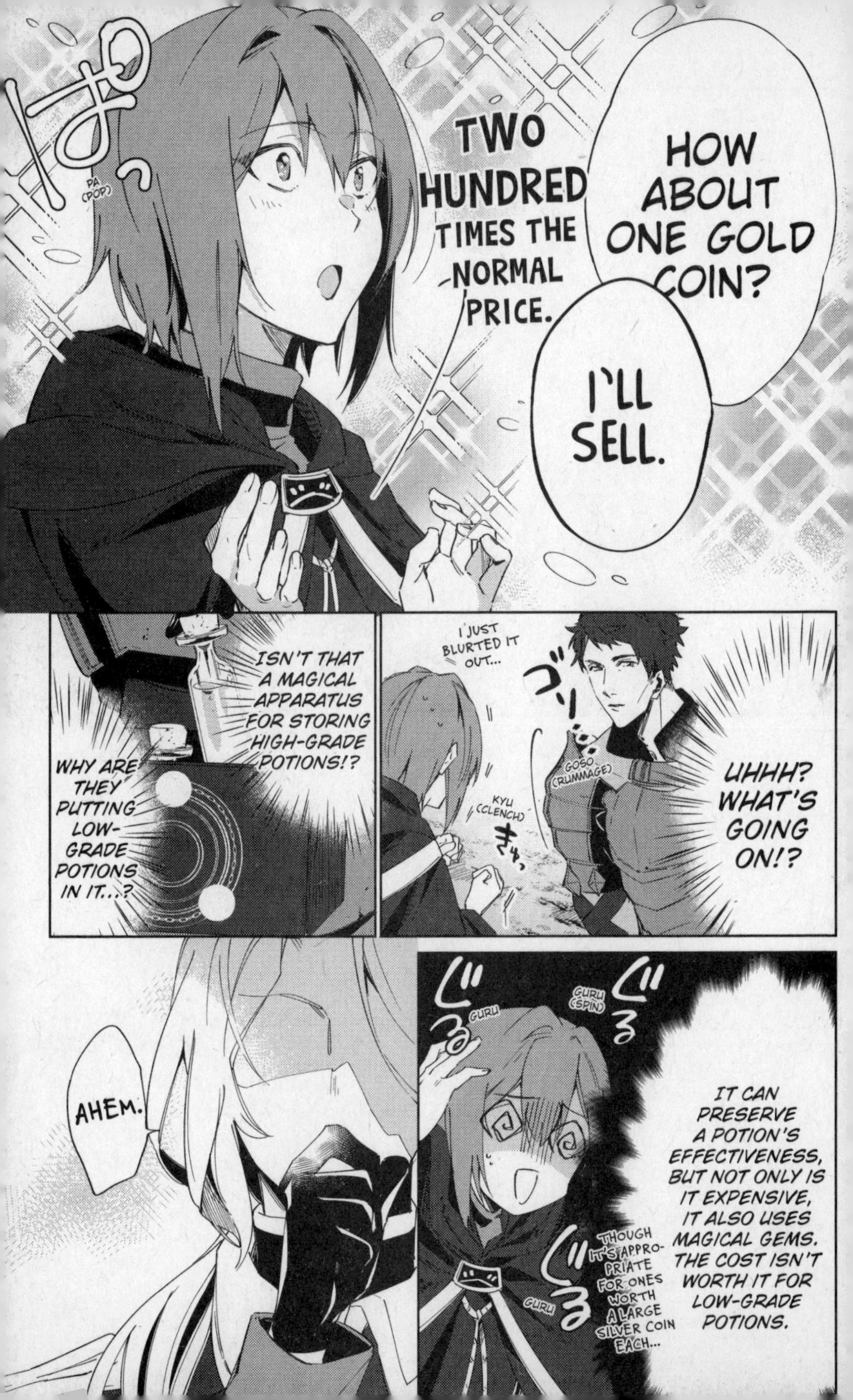
HOW ABOUT ONE GOLD COIN?
TWO HUNDRED TIMES THE NORMAL PRICE.
I'LL SELL.
PA (POP)
UHHH? WHAT'S GOING ON!?
I JUST BLURTED IT OUT...
GOSO (RUMMAGE)
KYU (CLENCH)
ISN'T THAT A MAGICAL APPARATUS FOR STORING HIGH-GRADE POTIONS!?
WHY ARE THEY PUTTING LOW-GRADE POTIONS IN IT...?
GURU (SPIN)
GURU
IT CAN PRESERVE A POTION'S EFFECTIVENESS, BUT NOT ONLY IS IT EXPENSIVE, IT ALSO USES MAGICAL GEMS. THE COST ISN'T WORTH IT FOR LOW-GRADE POTIONS.
THOUGH IT'S APPROPRIATE FOR ONES WORTH A LARGE SILVER COIN EACH...
GURU
AHEM.

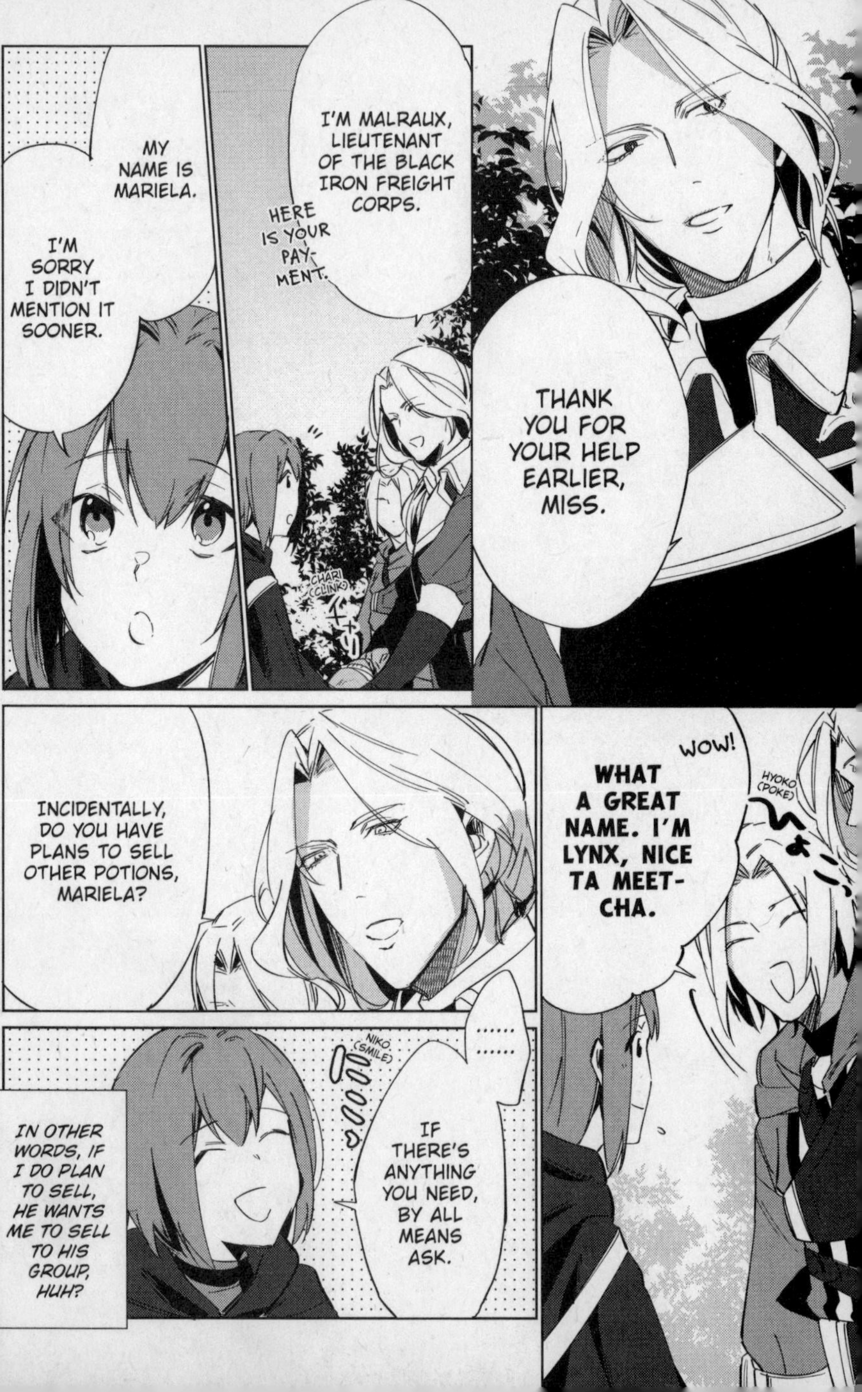
THANK YOU FOR YOUR HELP EARLIER, MISS.
I'M MALRAUX, LIEUTENANT OF THE BLACK IRON FREIGHT CORPS.
HERE IS YOUR PAY-MENT.
CHARI (CLINK)
MY NAME IS MARIELA.
I'M SORRY I DIDN'T MENTION IT SOONER.
WOW!
WHAT A GREAT NAME. I'M LYNX, NICE TA MEET-CHA.
HYOKO (POKE)
INCIDENTALLY, DO YOU HAVE PLANS TO SELL OTHER POTIONS, MARIELA?
......
......
NIKO (SMILE)
IF THERE'S ANYTHING YOU NEED, BY ALL MEANS ASK.
IN OTHER WORDS, IF I DO PLAN TO SELL, HE WANTS ME TO SELL TO HIS GROUP, HUH?

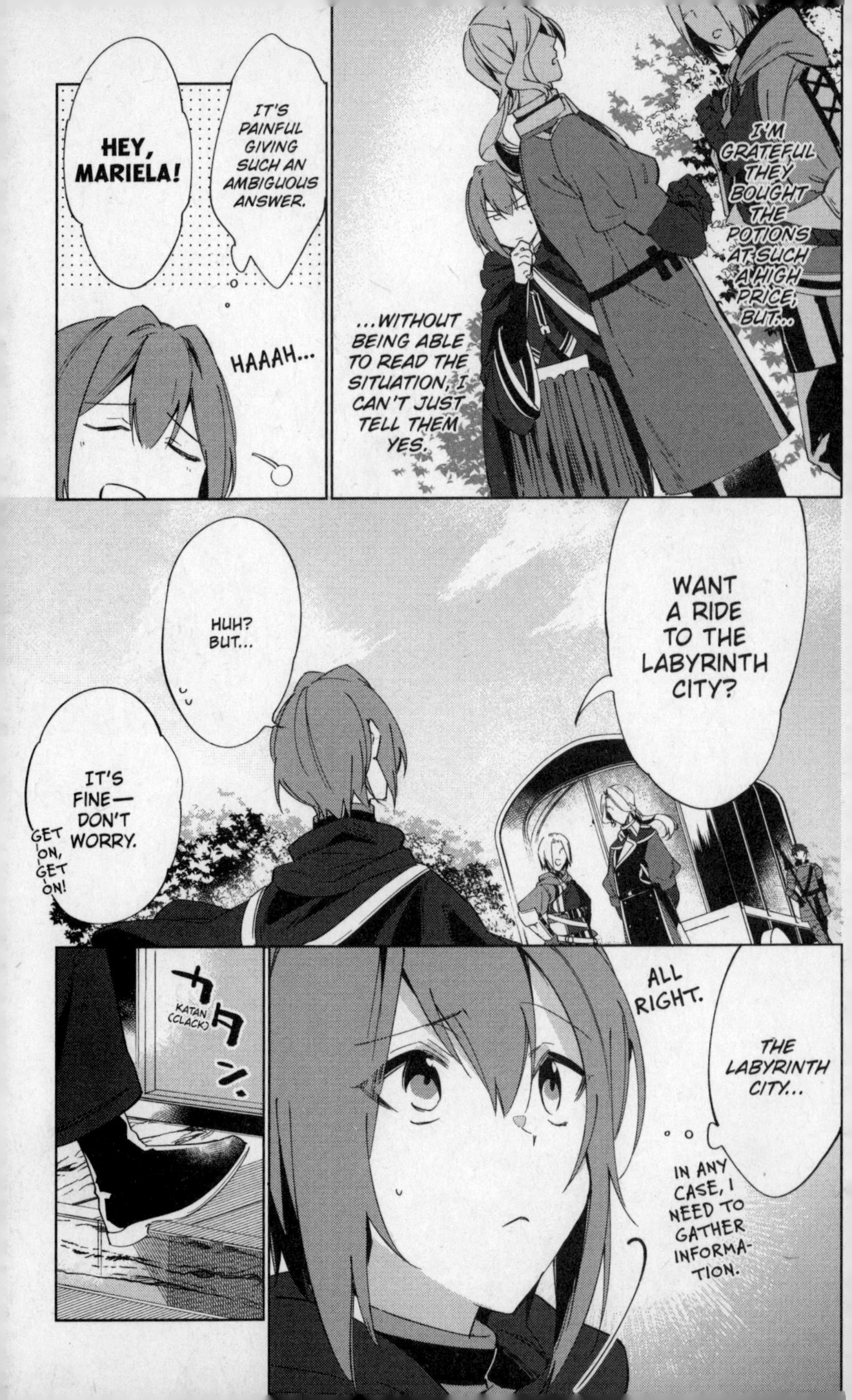
I'M GRATEFUL THEY BOUGHT THE POTIONS AT SUCH A HIGH PRICE, BUT...
...WITHOUT BEING ABLE TO READ THE SITUATION, I CAN'T JUST TELL THEM YES.
IT'S PAINFUL GIVING SUCH AN AMBIGUOUS ANSWER.
HEY, MARIELA!
HAAAH...
WANT A RIDE TO THE LABYRINTH CITY?
HUH? BUT...
IT'S FINE—DON'T WORRY.
GET ON, GET ON!
THE LABYRINTH CITY...
IN ANY CASE, I NEED TO GATHER INFORMATION.
ALL RIGHT.
KATAN (CLACK)

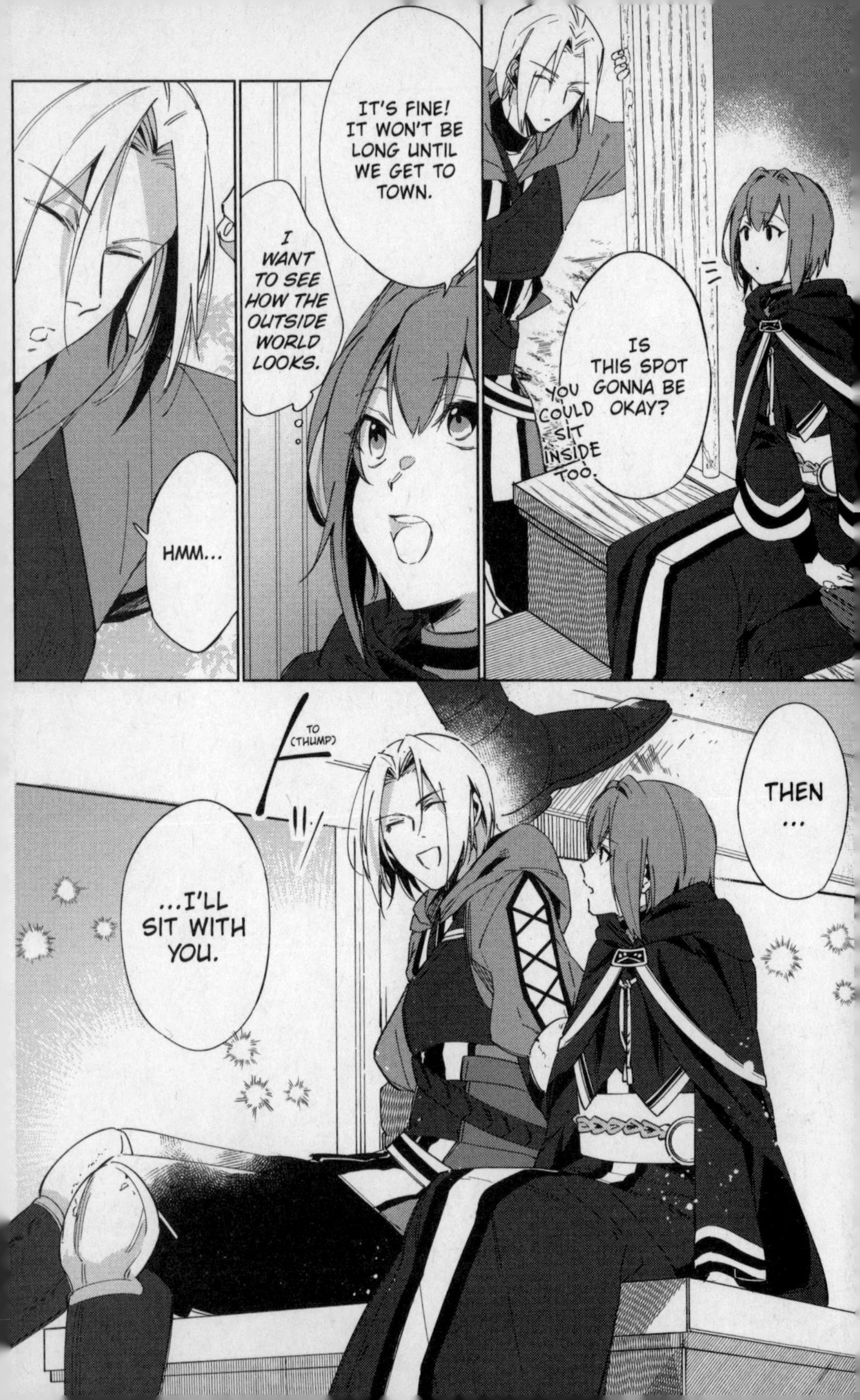
IS THIS SPOT GONNA BE OKAY?
YOU COULD SIT INSIDE TOO.
IT'S FINE! IT WON'T BE LONG UNTIL WE GET TO TOWN.
I WANT TO SEE HOW THE OUTSIDE WORLD LOOKS.
HMM...
THEN...
TO (THUMP)
...I'LL SIT WITH YOU.

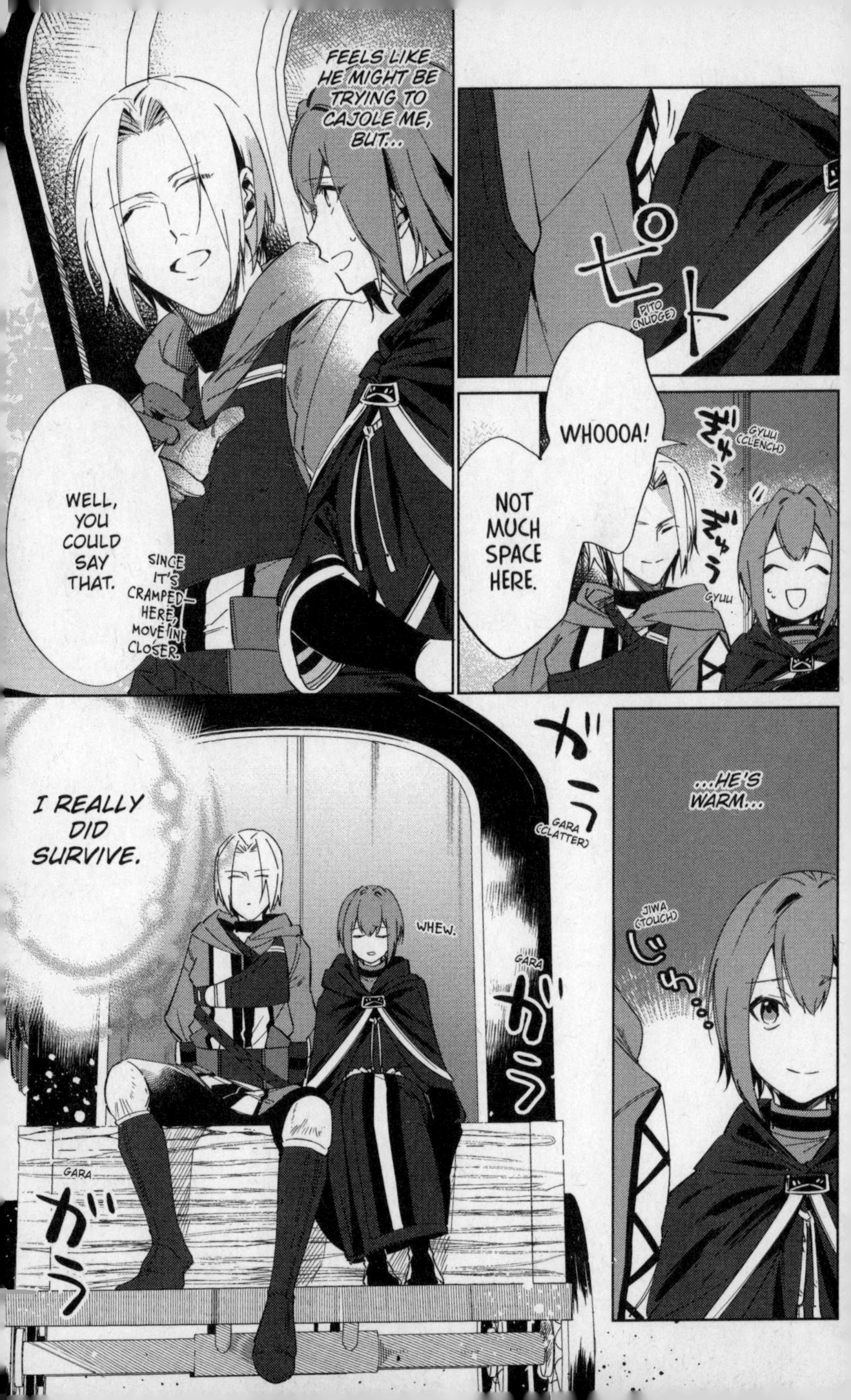

ピト
PITO (NUDGE)
WHOOOA!
NOT MUCH SPACE HERE.
ぎゅう ぎゅう
GYUU (CLENCH)
GYUU
FEELS LIKE HE MIGHT BE TRYING TO CAJOLE ME, BUT...
WELL, YOU COULD SAY THAT.
SINCE IT'S CRAMPED HERE, MOVE IN CLOSER.
...HE'S WARM...
じわ…
JIWA (TOUCH)
ガラ
GARA (CLATTER)
I REALLY DID SURVIVE.
WHEW.
ガラ
GARA
ガラ
GARA

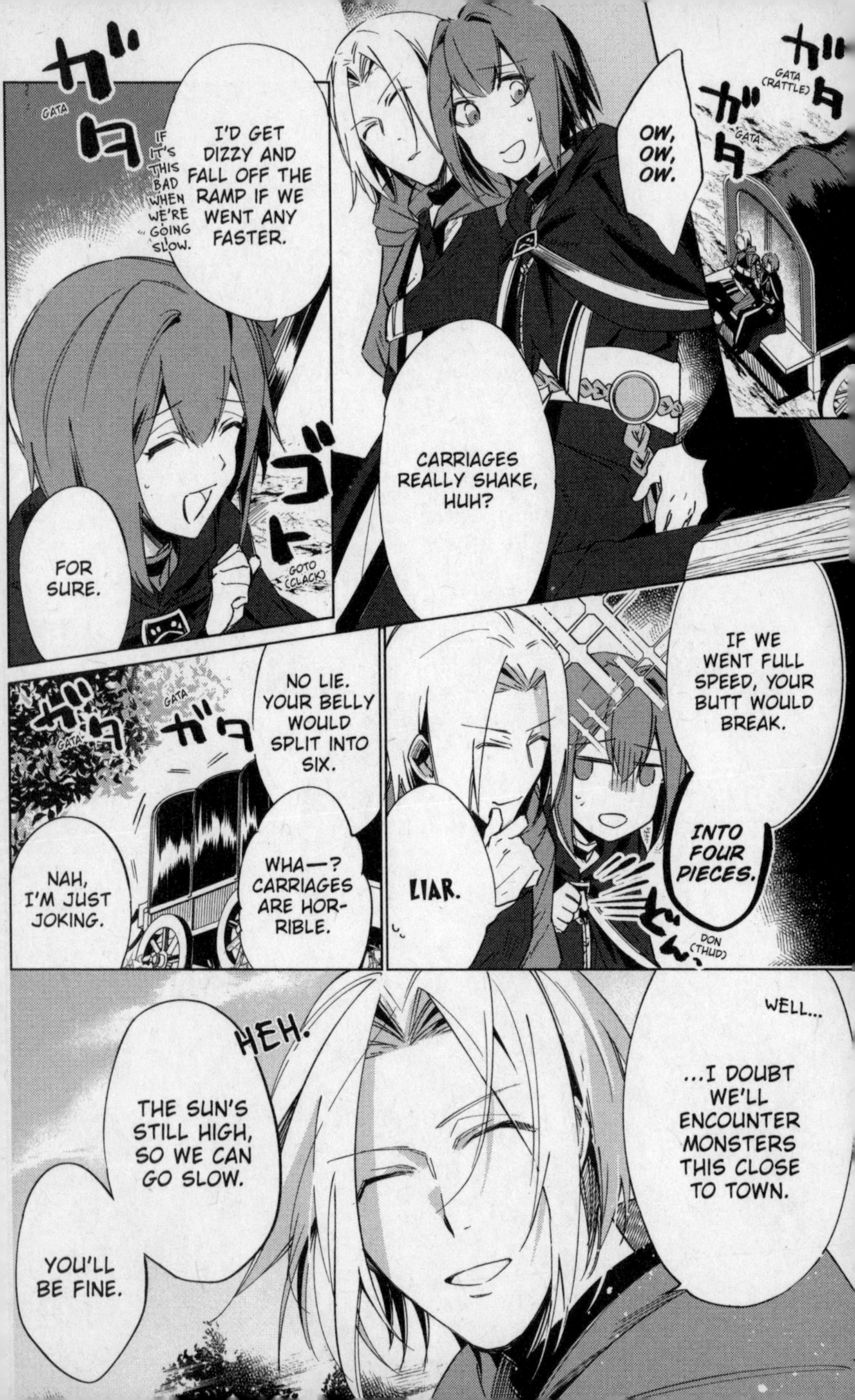
GATA (RATTLE)
GATA
OW, OW, OW.
CARRIAGES REALLY SHAKE, HUH?
GATA
I'D GET DIZZY AND FALL OFF THE RAMP IF WE WENT ANY FASTER.
IF IT'S THIS BAD WHEN WE'RE GOING SLOW.
GOTO (CLACK)
FOR SURE.
IF WE WENT FULL SPEED, YOUR BUTT WOULD BREAK.
INTO FOUR PIECES.
DON (THUD)
LIAR.
GATA
GATA
NO LIE. YOUR BELLY WOULD SPLIT INTO SIX.
WHA—? CARRIAGES ARE HOR-RIBLE.
NAH, I'M JUST JOKING.
WELL...
...I DOUBT WE'LL ENCOUNTER MONSTERS THIS CLOSE TO TOWN.
HEH.
THE SUN'S STILL HIGH, SO WE CAN GO SLOW.
YOU'LL BE FINE.

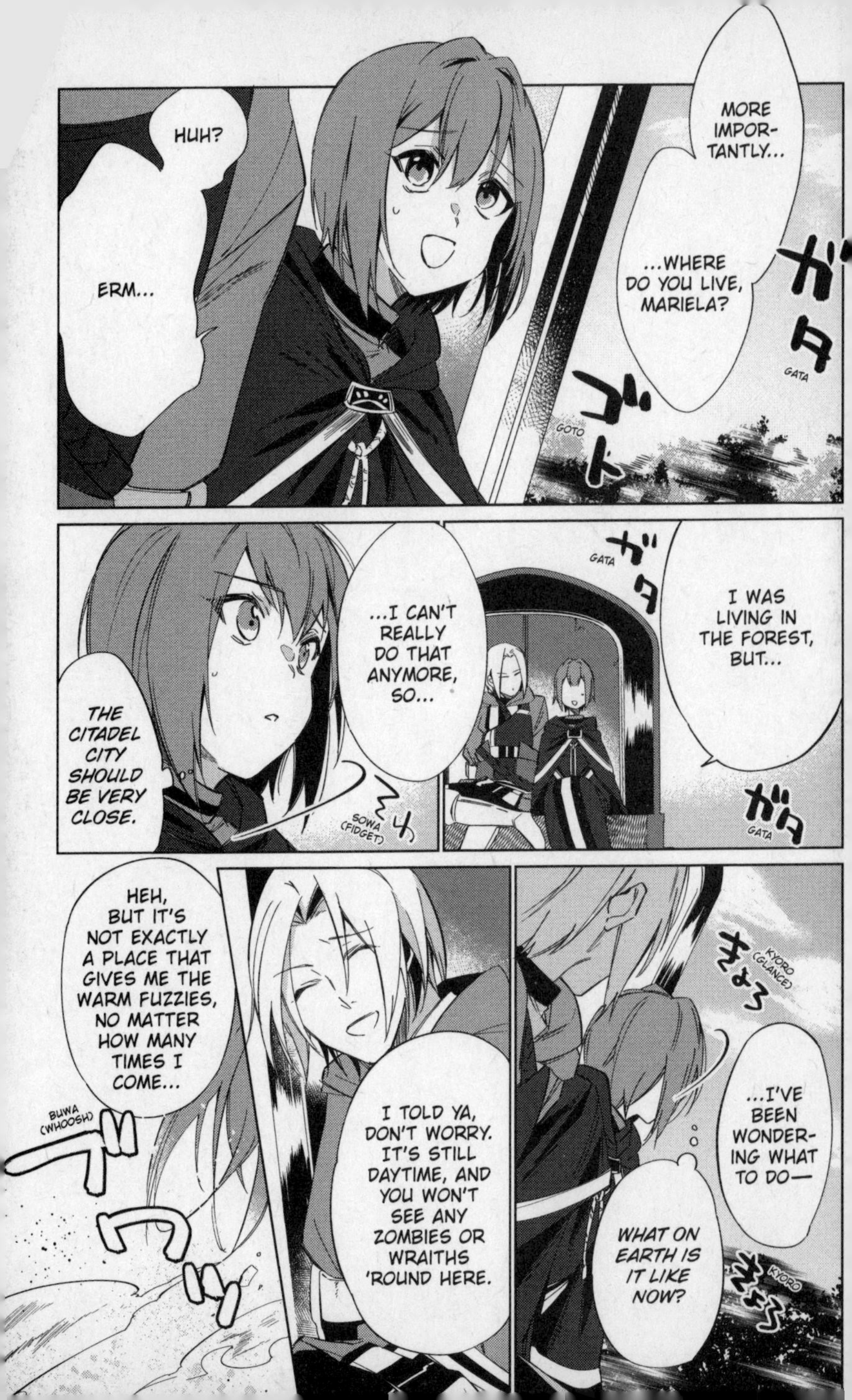
MORE IMPORTANTLY...
...WHERE DO YOU LIVE, MARIELA?
GATA
GOTO
HUH?
ERM...
GATA
I WAS LIVING IN THE FOREST, BUT...
GATA
...I CAN'T REALLY DO THAT ANYMORE, SO...
THE CITADEL CITY SHOULD BE VERY CLOSE.
SOWA (FIDGET)
KYORO (GLANCE)
...I'VE BEEN WONDERING WHAT TO DO—
WHAT ON EARTH IS IT LIKE NOW?
KYORO
HEH, BUT IT'S NOT EXACTLY A PLACE THAT GIVES ME THE WARM FUZZIES, NO MATTER HOW MANY TIMES I COME...
I TOLD YA, DON'T WORRY. IT'S STILL DAYTIME, AND YOU WON'T SEE ANY ZOMBIES OR WRAITHS 'ROUND HERE.
BUWA (WHOOSH)

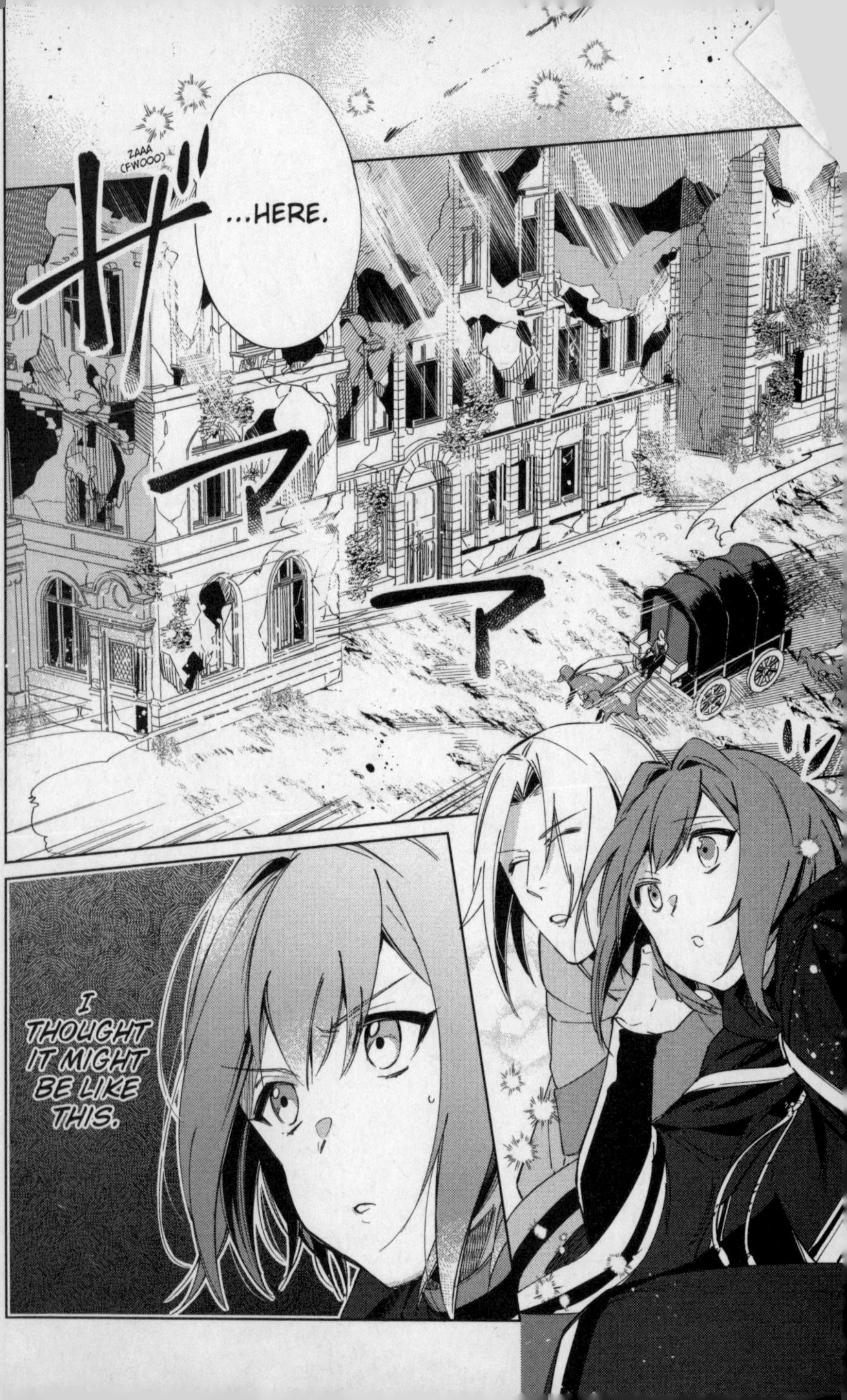
...HERE.
ZAAA (FWOOO)
I THOUGHT IT MIGHT BE LIKE THIS.

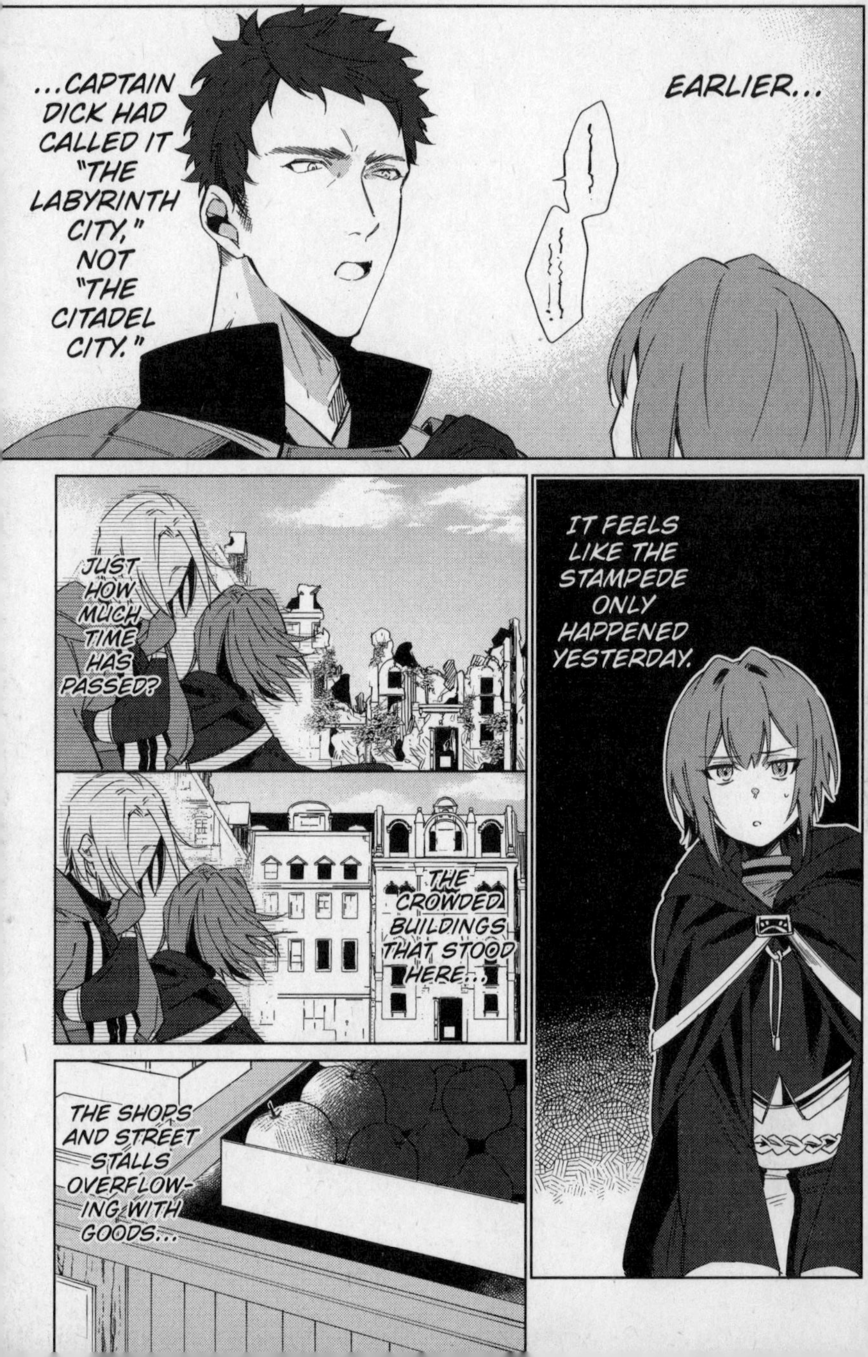
EARLIER...
......
...CAPTAIN DICK HAD CALLED IT "THE LABYRINTH CITY," NOT "THE CITADEL CITY."
IT FEELS LIKE THE STAMPEDE ONLY HAPPENED YESTERDAY.
JUST HOW MUCH TIME HAS PASSED?
THE CROWDED BUILDINGS THAT STOOD HERE...
THE SHOPS AND STREET STALLS OVERFLOWING WITH GOODS...

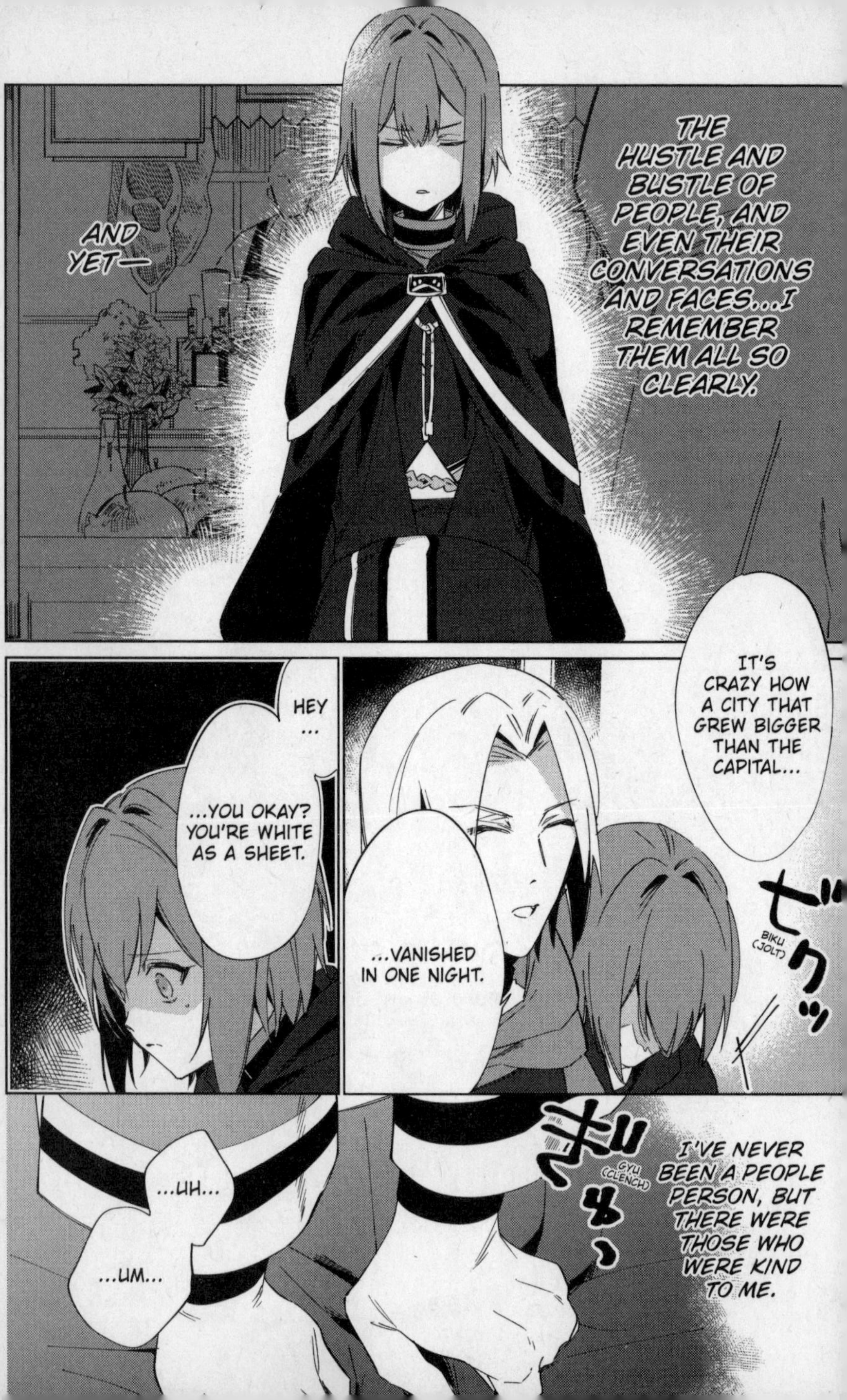
THE HUSTLE AND BUSTLE OF PEOPLE, AND EVEN THEIR CONVERSATIONS AND FACES...I REMEMBER THEM ALL SO CLEARLY.
AND YET—
IT'S CRAZY HOW A CITY THAT GREW BIGGER THAN THE CAPITAL...
...VANISHED IN ONE NIGHT.
BIKU (JOLT)
HEY ...
...YOU OKAY? YOU'RE WHITE AS A SHEET.
I'VE NEVER BEEN A PEOPLE PERSON, BUT THERE WERE THOSE WHO WERE KIND TO ME.
GYU (CLENCH)
...UH...
...UM...

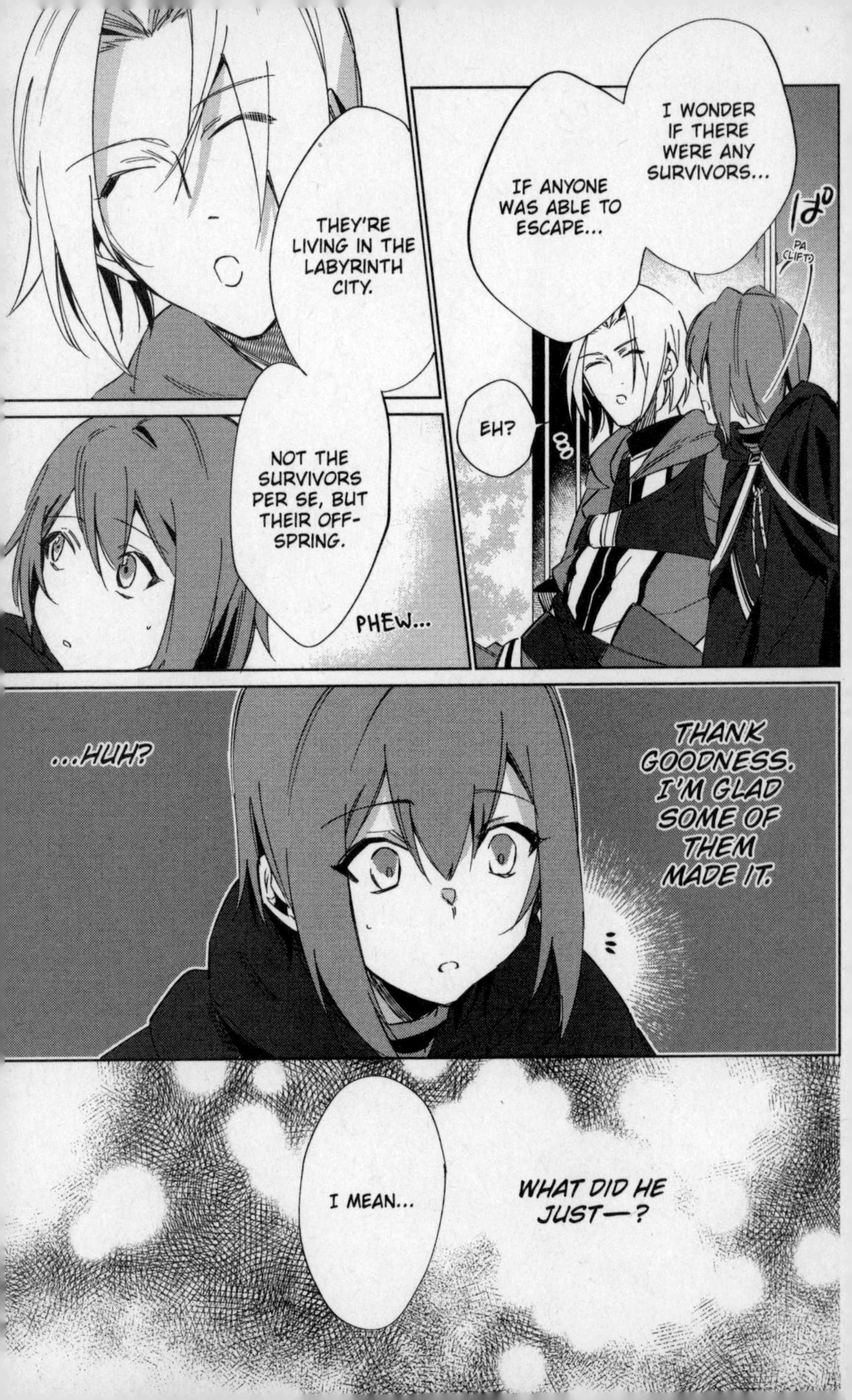
I WONDER IF THERE WERE ANY SURVIVORS...
IF ANYONE WAS ABLE TO ESCAPE...
ぱっ
PA (LIFT)
EH?
THEY'RE LIVING IN THE LABYRINTH CITY.
NOT THE SURVIVORS PER SE, BUT THEIR OFF-SPRING.
PHEW...
THANK GOODNESS. I'M GLAD SOME OF THEM MADE IT.
...HUH?
WHAT DID HE JUST—?
I MEAN...

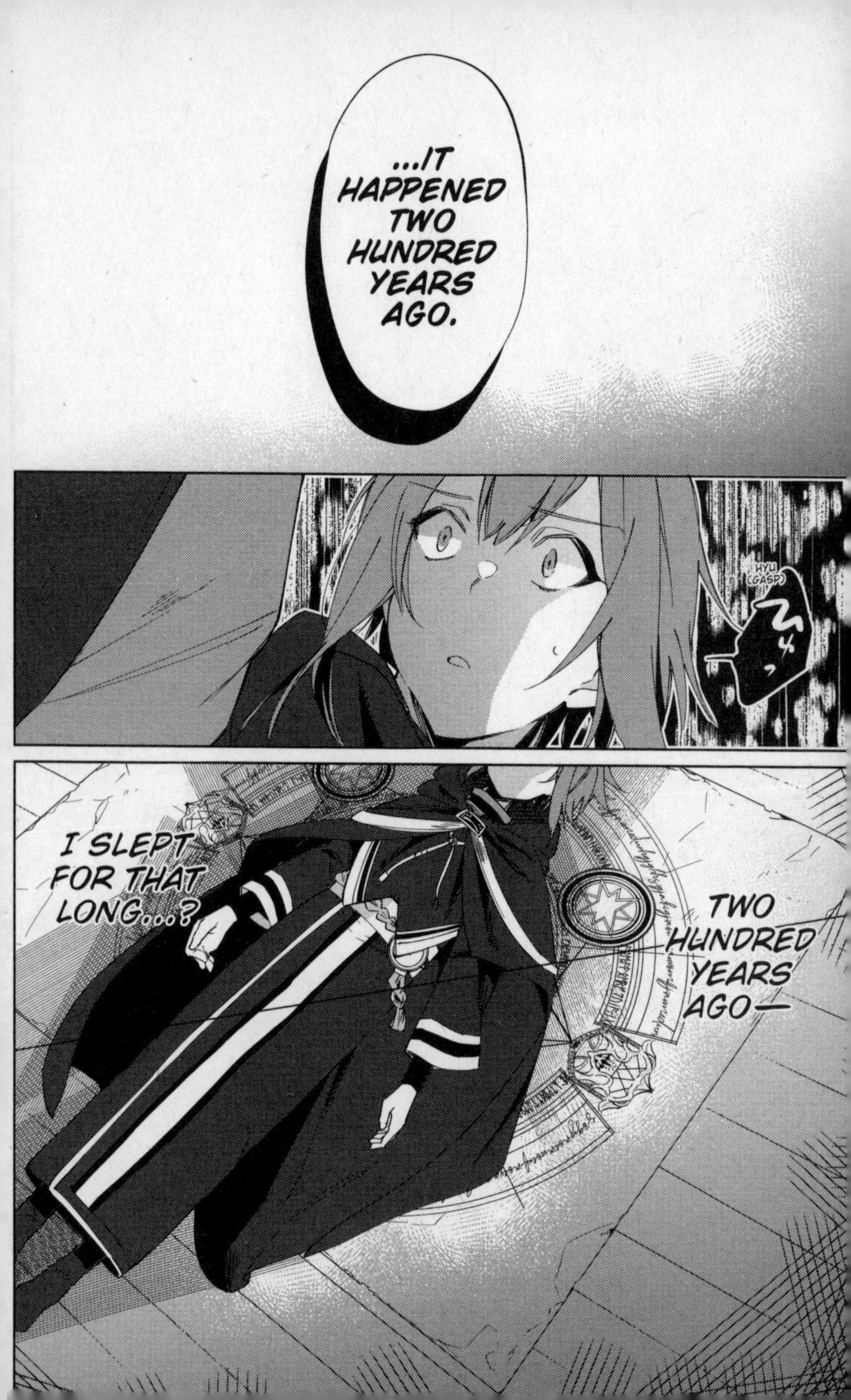
...IT HAPPENED TWO HUNDRED YEARS AGO.
HYU (GASP)
TWO HUNDRED YEARS AGO—
I SLEPT FOR THAT LONG...?

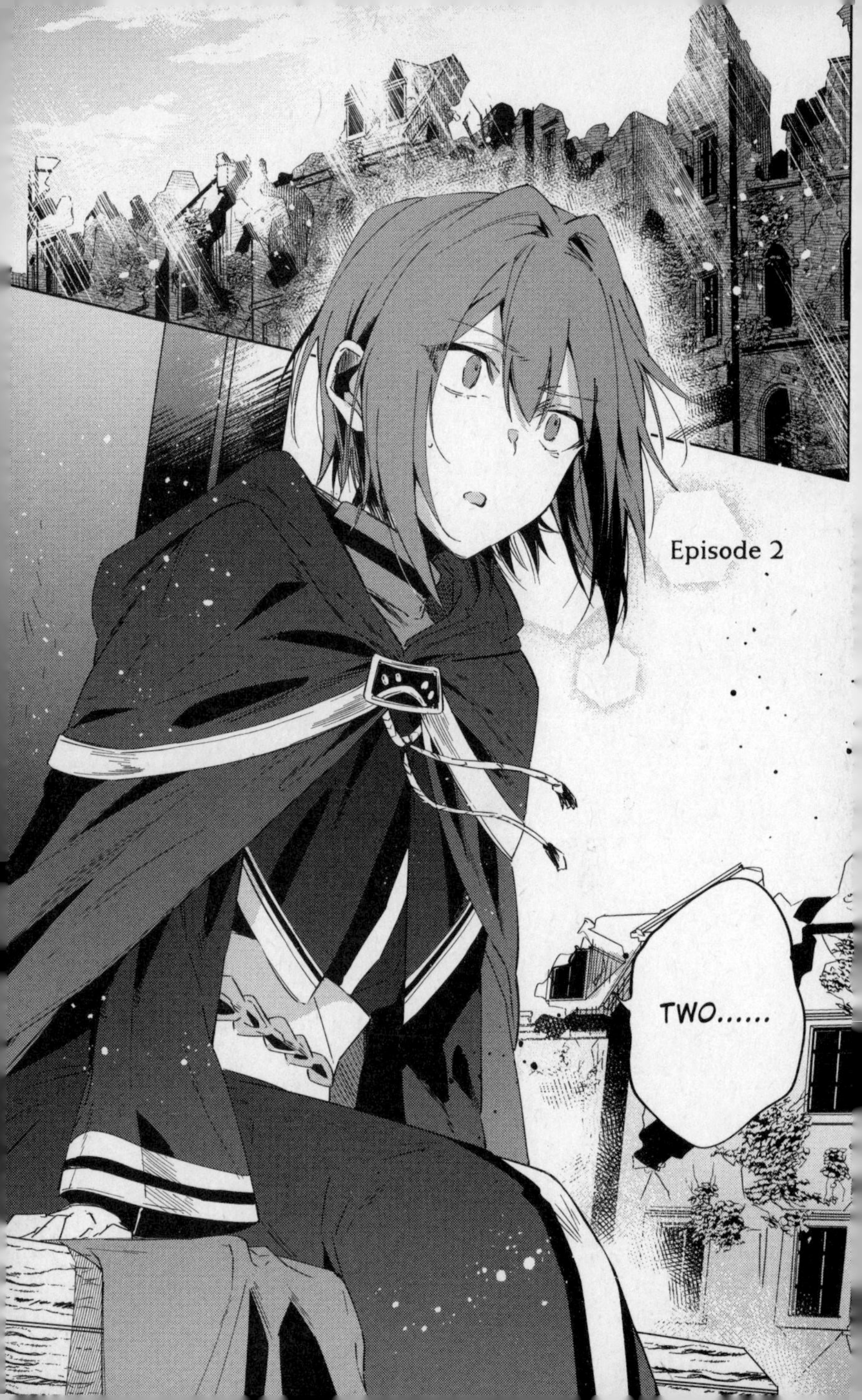
Episode 2
TWO......

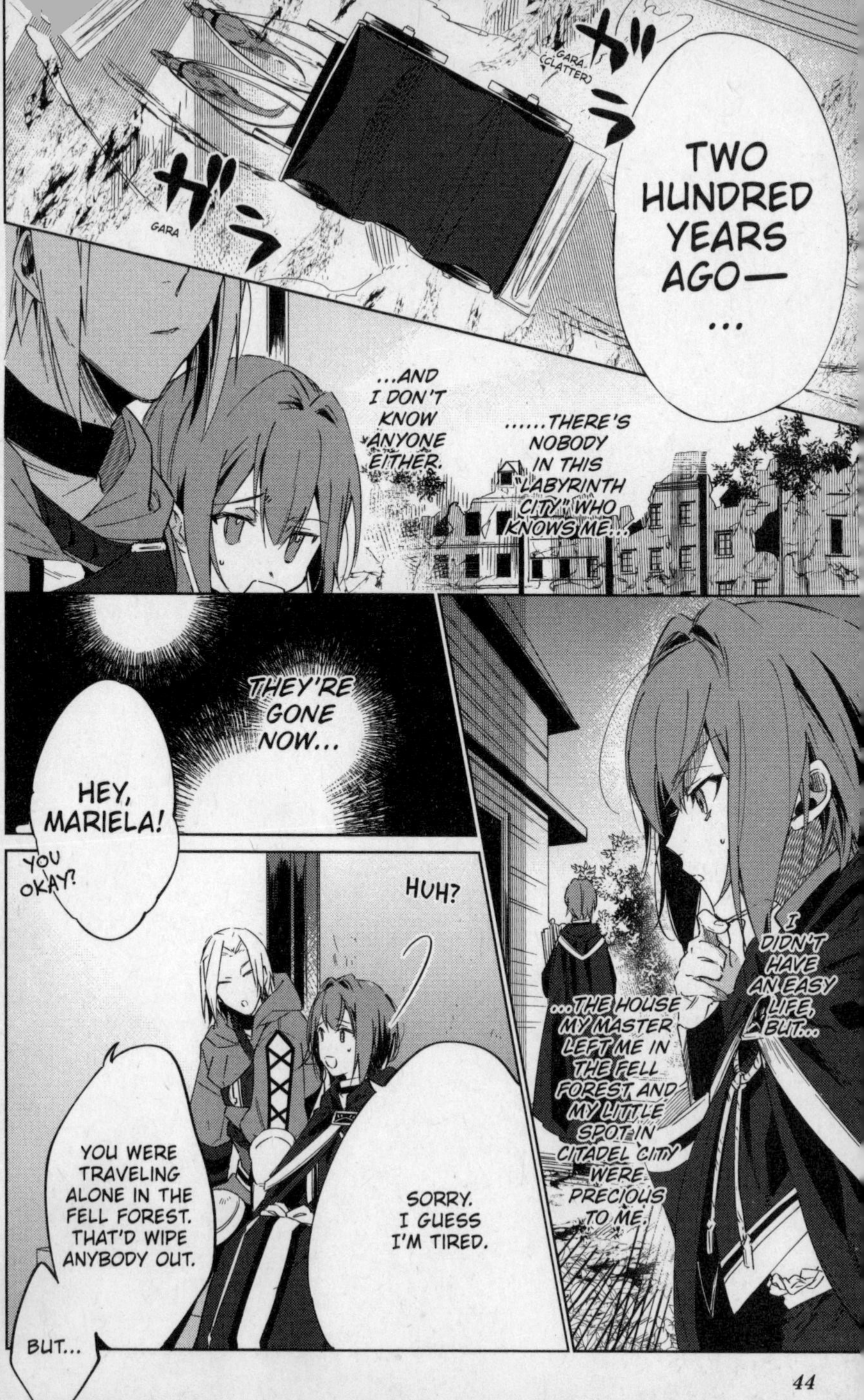
GARA (CLATTER)
TWO HUNDRED YEARS AGO— ...
GARA
......THERE'S NOBODY IN THIS "LABYRINTH CITY" WHO KNOWS ME...
...AND I DON'T KNOW ANYONE EITHER.
I DIDN'T HAVE AN EASY LIFE, BUT...
...THE HOUSE MY MASTER LEFT ME IN THE FELL FOREST AND MY LITTLE SPOT IN CITADEL CITY WERE PRECIOUS TO ME.
THEY'RE GONE NOW...
HEY, MARIELA!
YOU OKAY?
HUH?
SORRY. I GUESS I'M TIRED.
YOU WERE TRAVELING ALONE IN THE FELL FOREST. THAT'D WIPE ANYBODY OUT.
BUT...

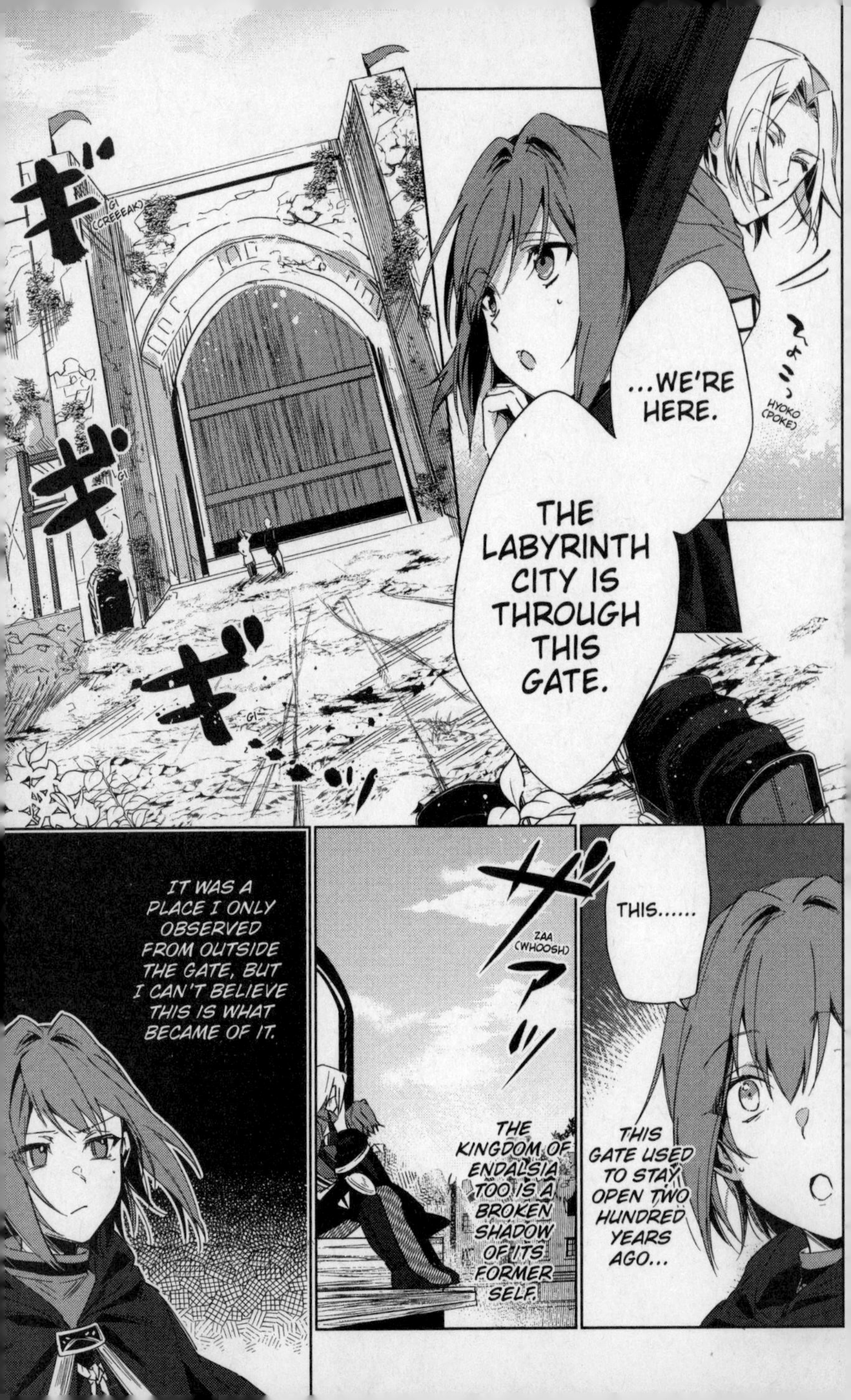
HYOKO (POKE)
...WE'RE HERE.
THE LABYRINTH CITY IS THROUGH THIS GATE.
GI (CREEEAK)
GI
GI
THIS......
THIS GATE USED TO STAY OPEN TWO HUNDRED YEARS AGO...
ZAA (WHOOSH)
THE KINGDOM OF ENDALSIA TOO IS A BROKEN SHADOW OF ITS FORMER SELF.
IT WAS A PLACE I ONLY OBSERVED FROM OUTSIDE THE GATE, BUT I CAN'T BELIEVE THIS IS WHAT BECAME OF IT.

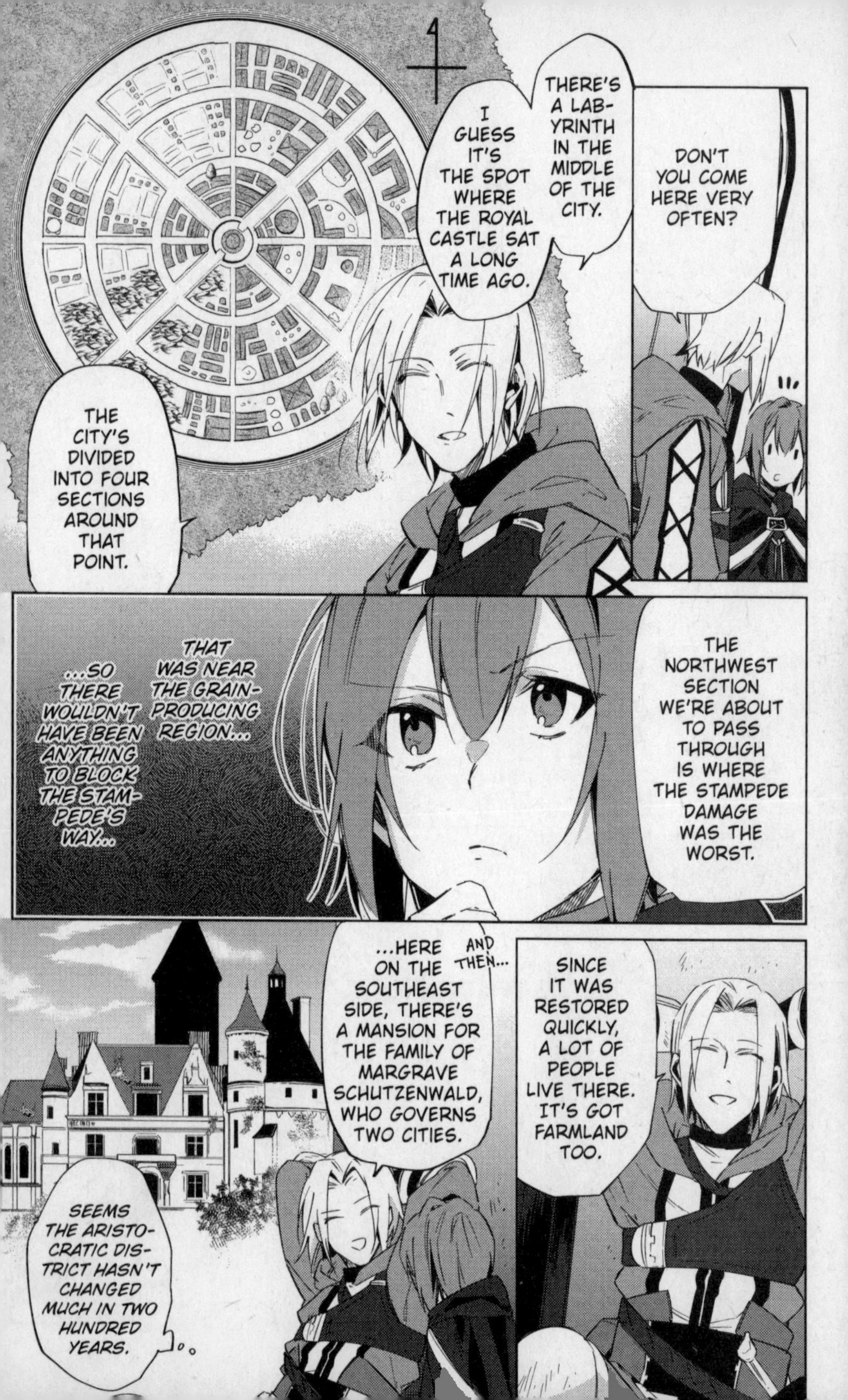
DON'T YOU COME HERE VERY OFTEN?
THERE'S A LAB-YRINTH IN THE MIDDLE OF THE CITY.
I GUESS IT'S THE SPOT WHERE THE ROYAL CASTLE SAT A LONG TIME AGO.
THE CITY'S DIVIDED INTO FOUR SECTIONS AROUND THAT POINT.
THE NORTHWEST SECTION WE'RE ABOUT TO PASS THROUGH IS WHERE THE STAMPEDE DAMAGE WAS THE WORST.
THAT WAS NEAR THE GRAIN-PRODUCING REGION...
...SO THERE WOULDN'T HAVE BEEN ANYTHING TO BLOCK THE STAM-PEDE'S WAY...
SINCE IT WAS RESTORED QUICKLY, A LOT OF PEOPLE LIVE THERE. IT'S GOT FARMLAND TOO.
AND THEN...
...HERE ON THE SOUTHEAST SIDE, THERE'S A MANSION FOR THE FAMILY OF MARGRAVE SCHUTZENWALD, WHO GOVERNS TWO CITIES.
SEEMS THE ARISTO-CRATIC DIS-TRICT HASN'T CHANGED MUCH IN TWO HUNDRED YEARS.

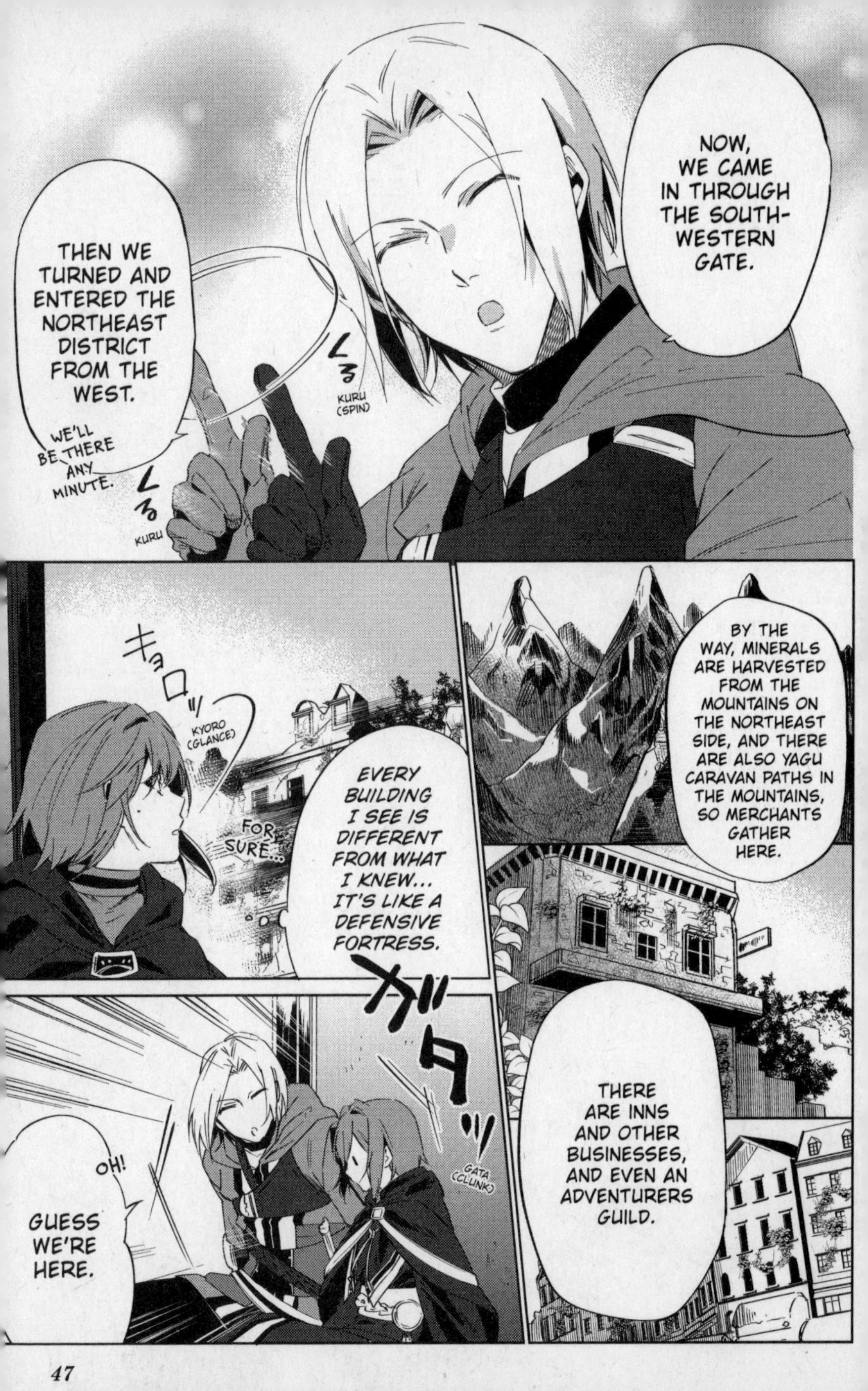
NOW, WE CAME IN THROUGH THE SOUTH-WESTERN GATE.
くる
KURU (SPIN)
THEN WE TURNED AND ENTERED THE NORTHEAST DISTRICT FROM THE WEST.
WE'LL BE THERE ANY MINUTE.
くる
KURU
BY THE WAY, MINERALS ARE HARVESTED FROM THE MOUNTAINS ON THE NORTHEAST SIDE, AND THERE ARE ALSO YAGU CARAVAN PATHS IN THE MOUNTAINS, SO MERCHANTS GATHER HERE.
キョロッ
KYORO (GLANCE)
EVERY BUILDING I SEE IS DIFFERENT FROM WHAT I KNEW... IT'S LIKE A DEFENSIVE FORTRESS.
FOR SURE...
THERE ARE INNS AND OTHER BUSINESSES, AND EVEN AN ADVENTURERS GUILD.
ガタッ
GATA (CLLINK)
OH!
GUESS WE'RE HERE.

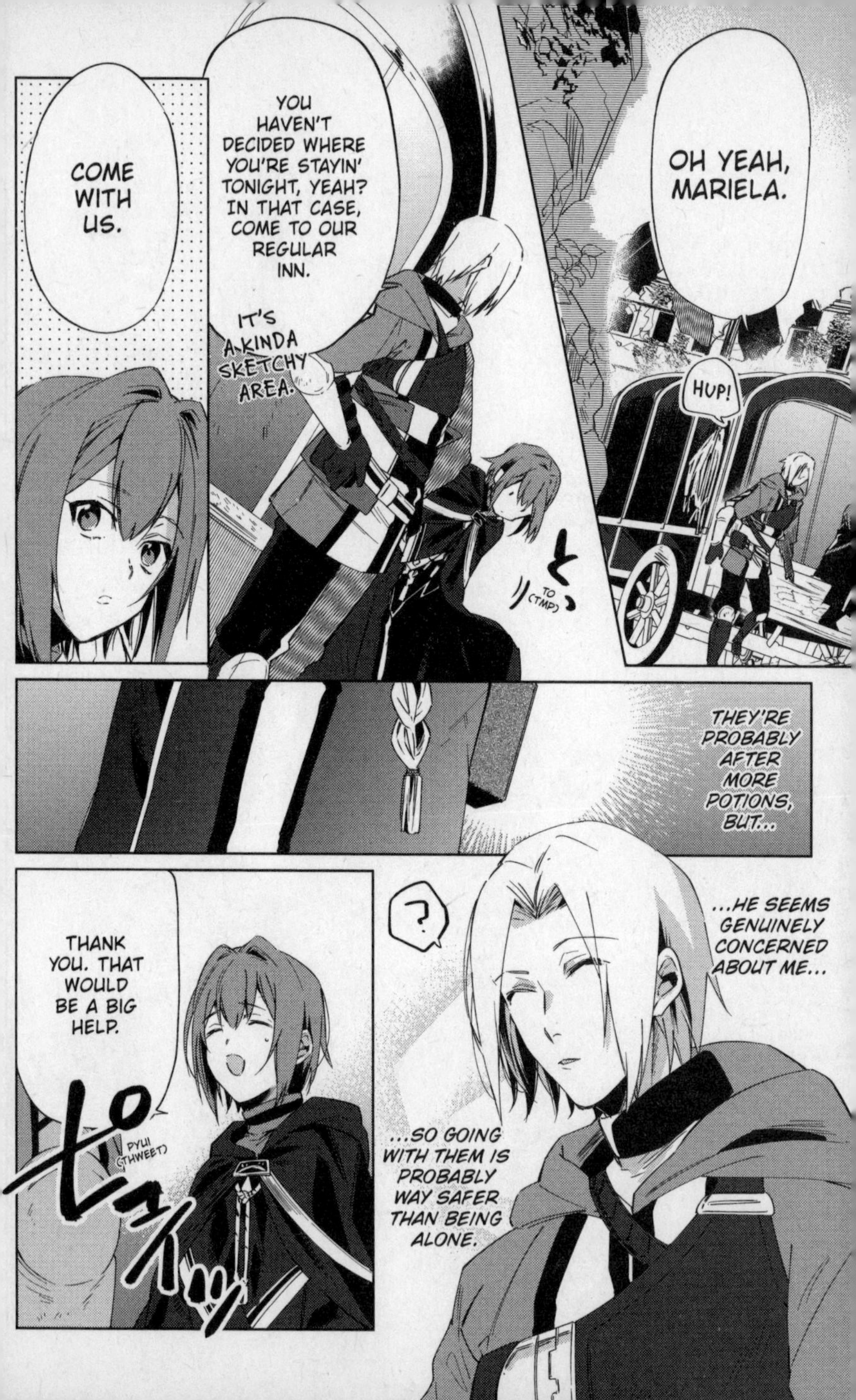
OH YEAH, MARIELA.
HUP!
YOU HAVEN'T DECIDED WHERE YOU'RE STAYIN' TONIGHT, YEAH? IN THAT CASE, COME TO OUR REGULAR INN.
IT'S A KINDA SKETCHY AREA.
TO (TMP)
COME WITH US.
THEY'RE PROBABLY AFTER MORE POTIONS, BUT...
?
...HE SEEMS GENUINELY CONCERNED ABOUT ME...
...SO GOING WITH THEM IS PROBABLY WAY SAFER THAN BEING ALONE.
THANK YOU. THAT WOULD BE A BIG HELP.
PYUI (THWEET)

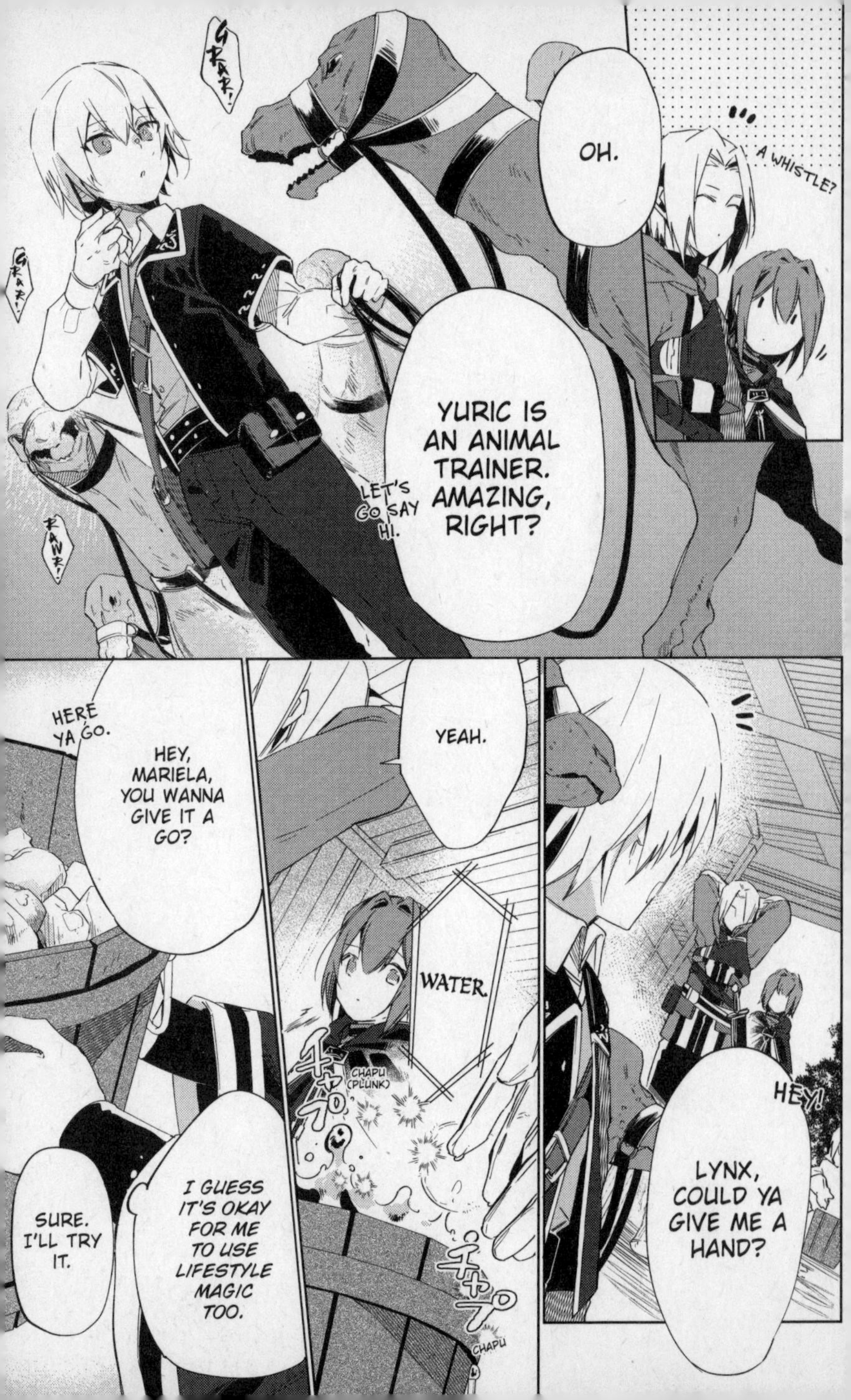
...!
OH.
A WHISTLE?
YURIC IS AN ANIMAL TRAINER. AMAZING, RIGHT?
LET'S GO SAY HI.
GRAR!
GRAR!
RAWR!
HEY!
LYNX, COULD YA GIVE ME A HAND?
YEAH.
WATER.
チャプ
CHAPU (PLUNK)
チャプ
CHAPU
HERE YA GO.
HEY, MARIELA, YOU WANNA GIVE IT A GO?
I GUESS IT'S OKAY FOR ME TO USE LIFESTYLE MAGIC TOO.
SURE. I'LL TRY IT.

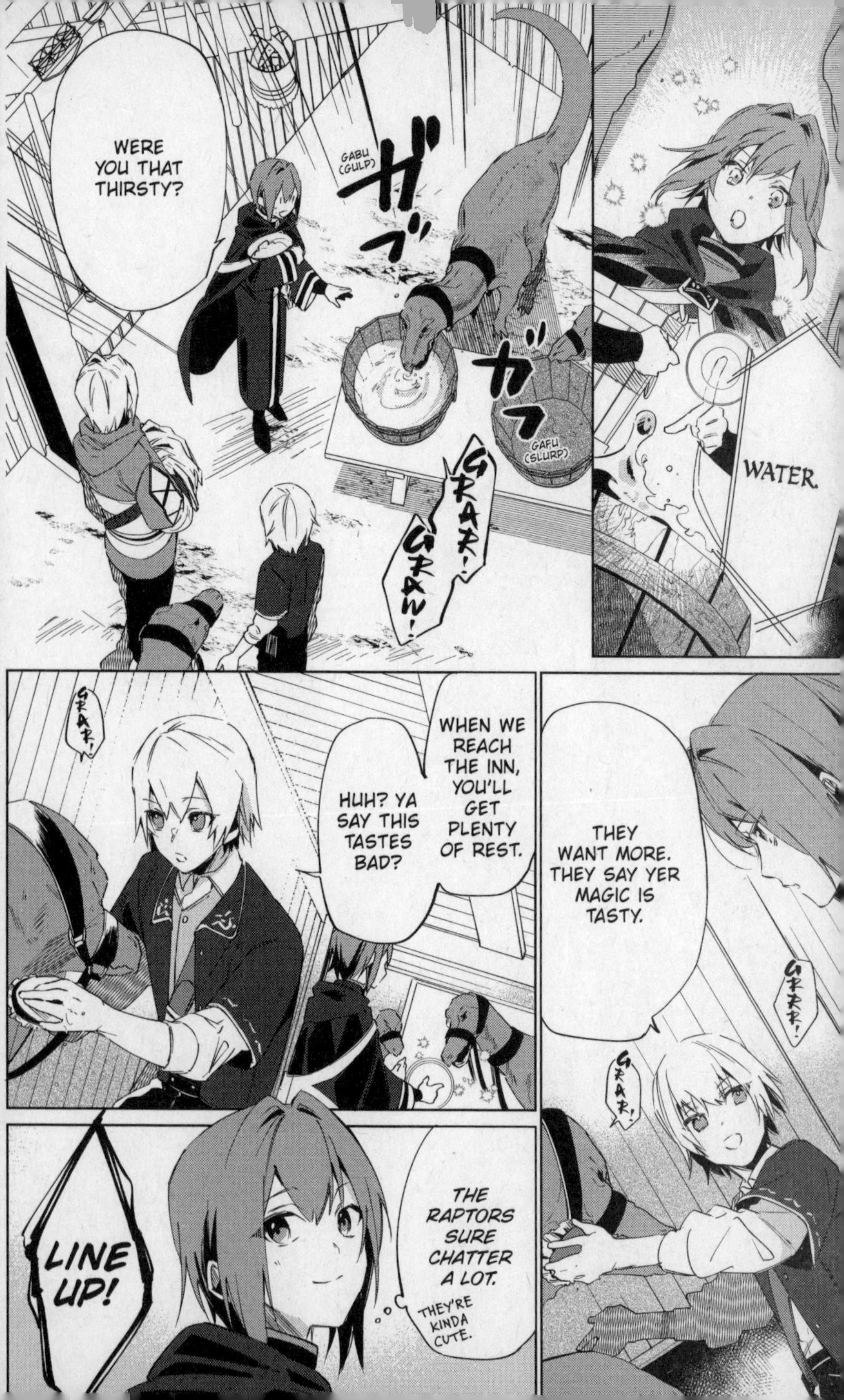
WATER.
GABU (GULP)
WERE YOU THAT THIRSTY?
GAFU (SLURP)
GRAR!
GRAW!
THEY WANT MORE. THEY SAY YER MAGIC IS TASTY.
GRRRR!
GRAR!
WHEN WE REACH THE INN, YOU'LL GET PLENTY OF REST.
HUH? YA SAY THIS TASTES BAD?
GRAR!
THE RAPTORS SURE CHATTER A LOT.
THEY'RE KINDA CUTE.
LINE UP!

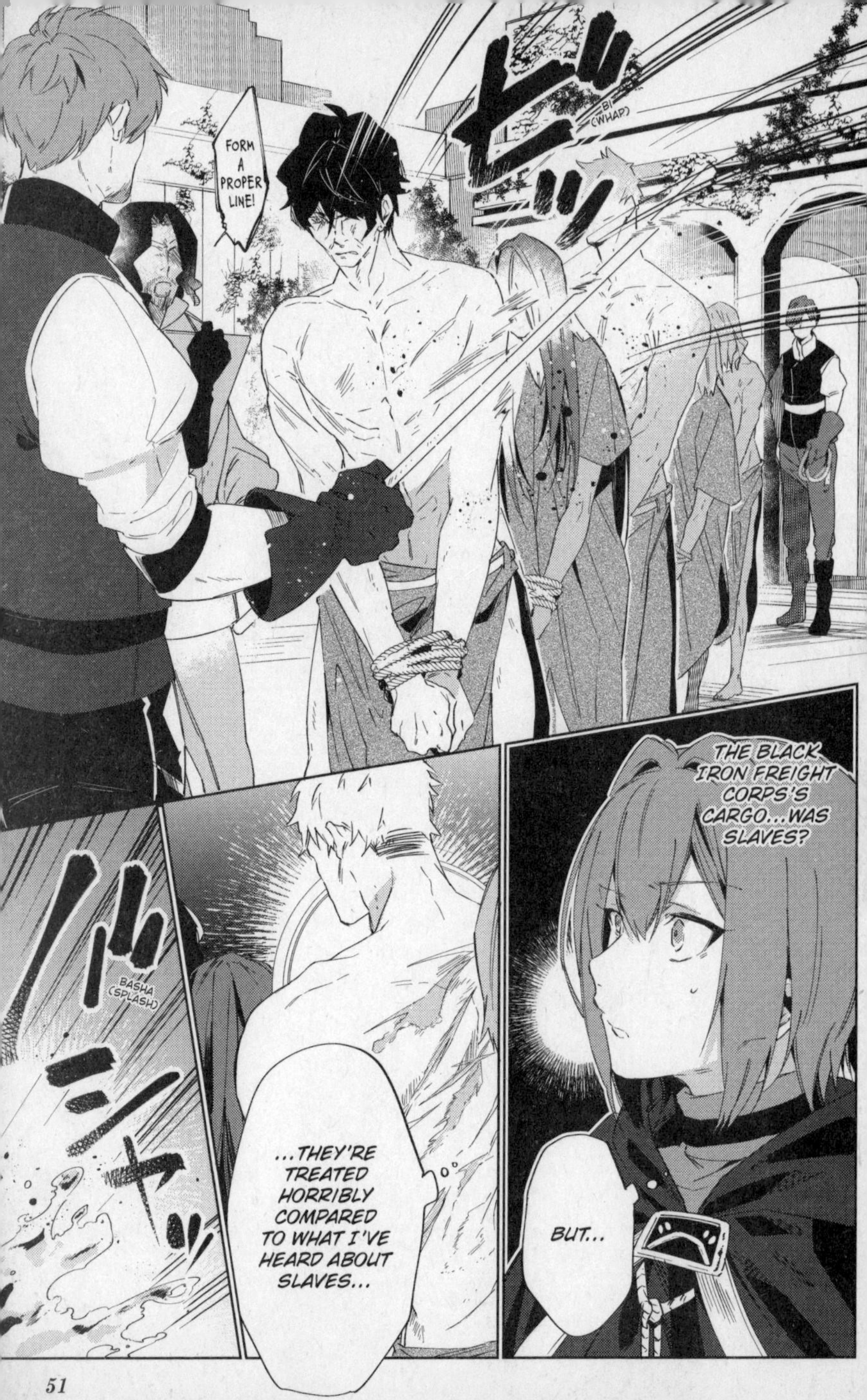
BI (WHAP)
FORM A PROPER LINE!
THE BLACK IRON FREIGHT CORPS'S CARGO...WAS SLAVES?
BUT...
...THEY'RE TREATED HORRIBLY COMPARED TO WHAT I'VE HEARD ABOUT SLAVES...
BASHA (SPLASH)

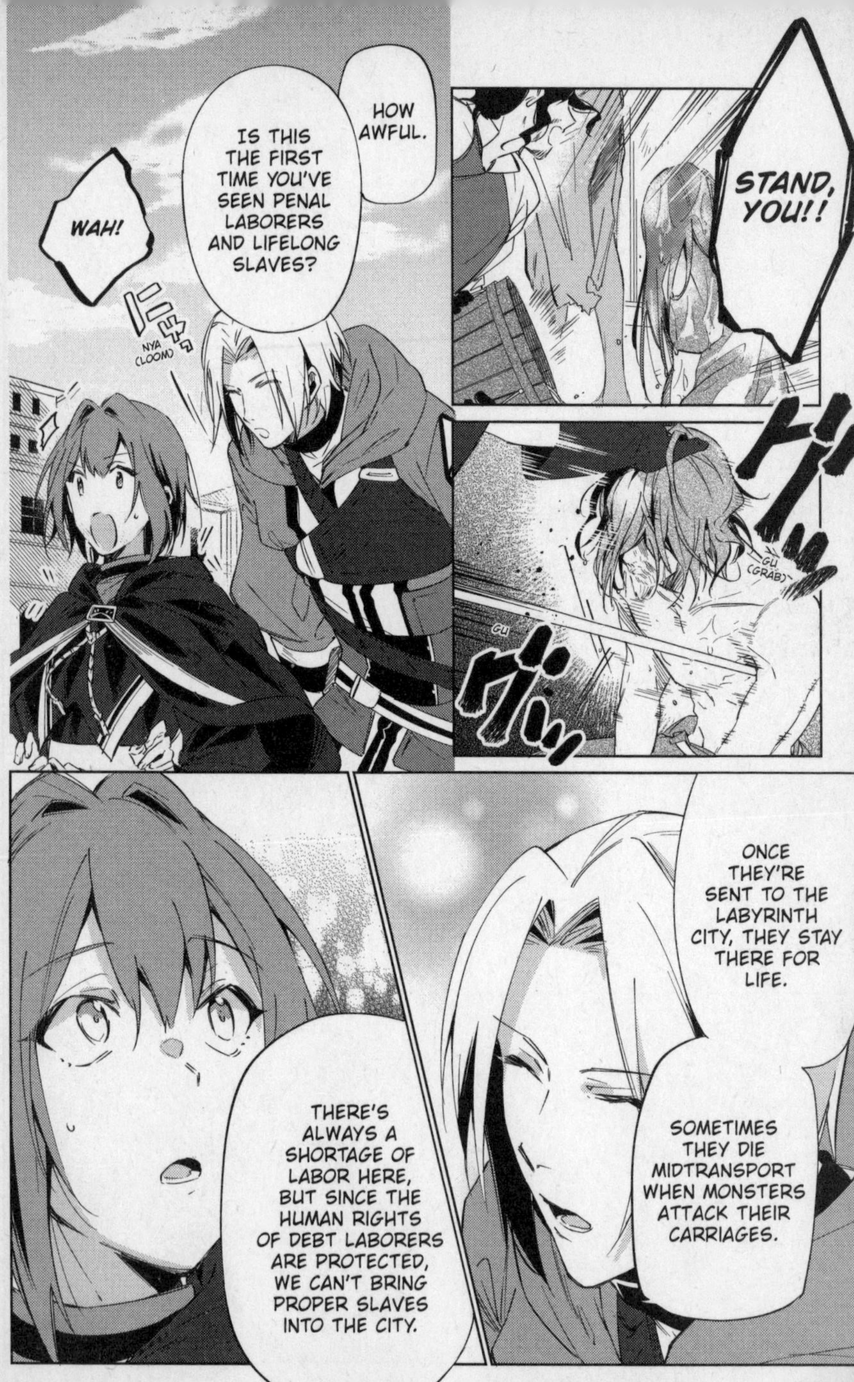
STAND, YOU!!
GU (GRAB)
GU
HOW AWFUL.
IS THIS THE FIRST TIME YOU'VE SEEN PENAL LABORERS AND LIFELONG SLAVES?
WAH!
NYA (LOOM)
ONCE THEY'RE SENT TO THE LABYRINTH CITY, THEY STAY THERE FOR LIFE.
SOMETIMES THEY DIE MIDTRANSPORT WHEN MONSTERS ATTACK THEIR CARRIAGES.
THERE'S ALWAYS A SHORTAGE OF LABOR HERE, BUT SINCE THE HUMAN RIGHTS OF DEBT LABORERS ARE PROTECTED, WE CAN'T BRING PROPER SLAVES INTO THE CITY.

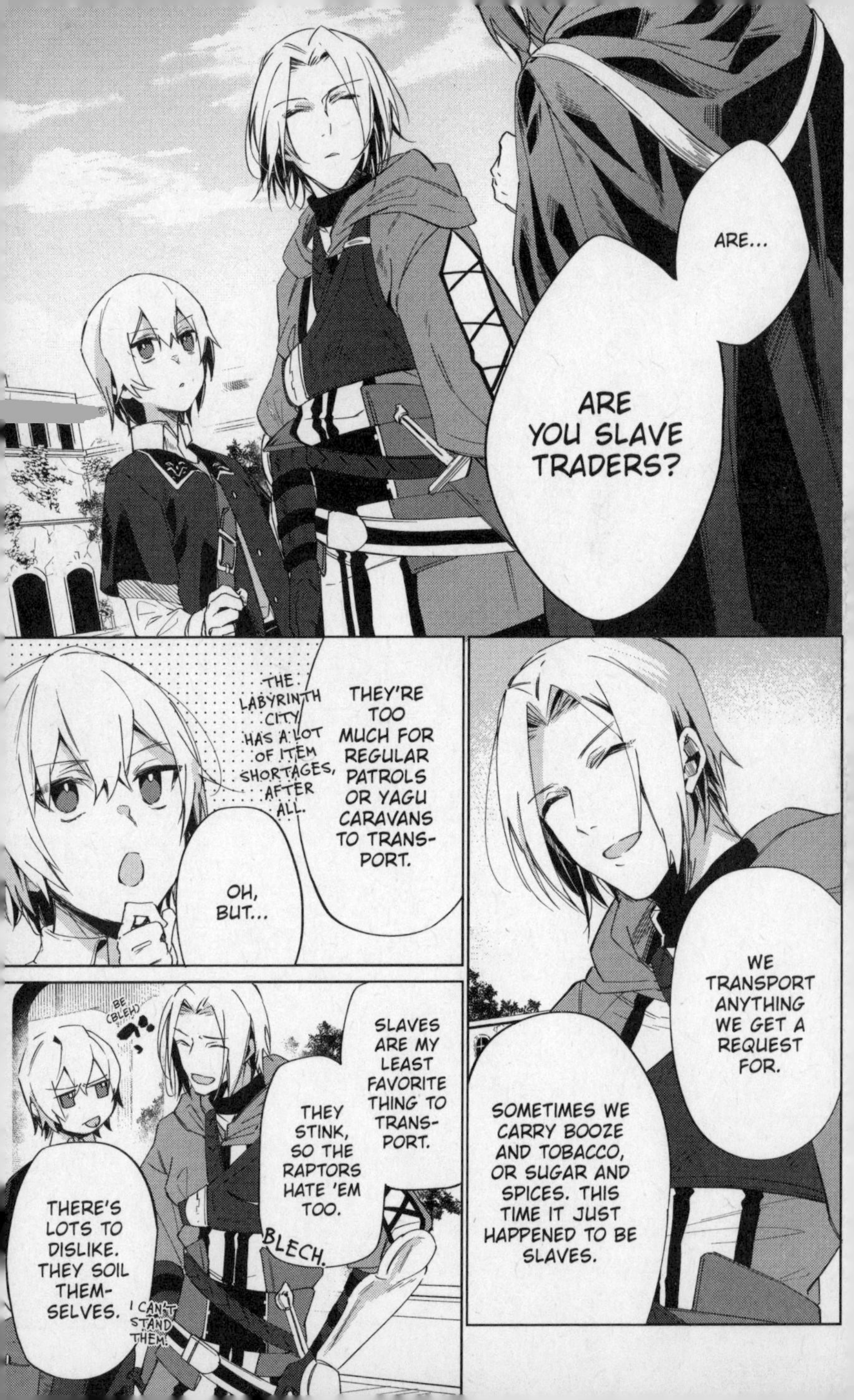
ARE...
ARE YOU SLAVE TRADERS?
WE TRANSPORT ANYTHING WE GET A REQUEST FOR.
SOMETIMES WE CARRY BOOZE AND TOBACCO, OR SUGAR AND SPICES. THIS TIME IT JUST HAPPENED TO BE SLAVES.
THEY'RE TOO MUCH FOR REGULAR PATROLS OR YAGU CARAVANS TO TRANSPORT.
THE LABYRINTH CITY HAS A LOT OF ITEM SHORTAGES, AFTER ALL.
OH, BUT...
SLAVES ARE MY LEAST FAVORITE THING TO TRANSPORT.
THEY STINK, SO THE RAPTORS HATE 'EM TOO.
BLECH.
BE (BLEH)
THERE'S LOTS TO DISLIKE. THEY SOIL THEMSELVES.
I CAN'T STAND THEM.

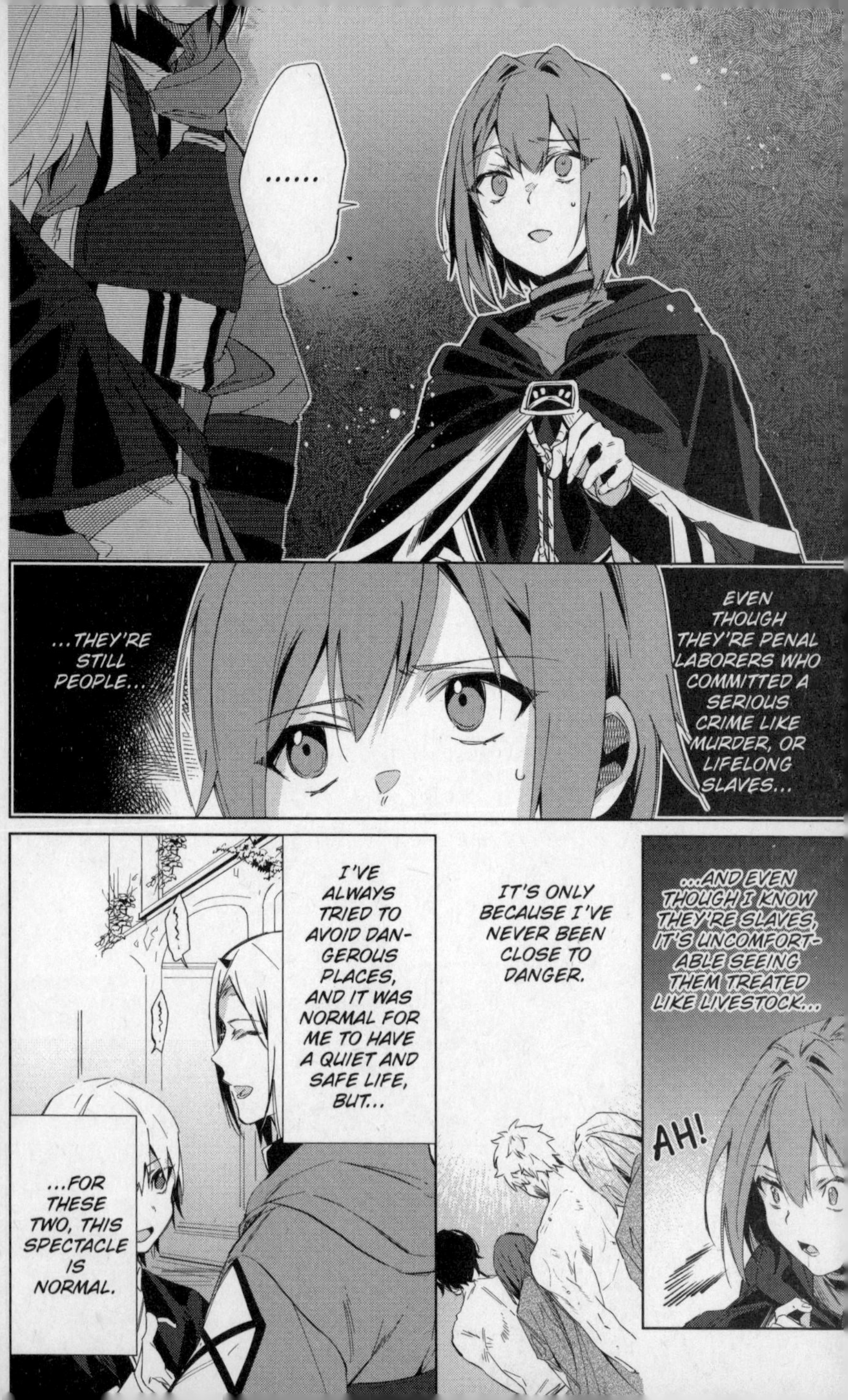
......
EVEN THOUGH THEY'RE PENAL LABORERS WHO COMMITTED A SERIOUS CRIME LIKE MURDER, OR LIFELONG SLAVES...
...THEY'RE STILL PEOPLE...
...AND EVEN THOUGH I KNOW THEY'RE SLAVES, IT'S UNCOMFORT-ABLE SEEING THEM TREATED LIKE LIVESTOCK...
AH!
IT'S ONLY BECAUSE I'VE NEVER BEEN CLOSE TO DANGER.
I'VE ALWAYS TRIED TO AVOID DAN-GEROUS PLACES, AND IT WAS NORMAL FOR ME TO HAVE A QUIET AND SAFE LIFE, BUT...
...FOR THESE TWO, THIS SPECTACLE IS NORMAL.

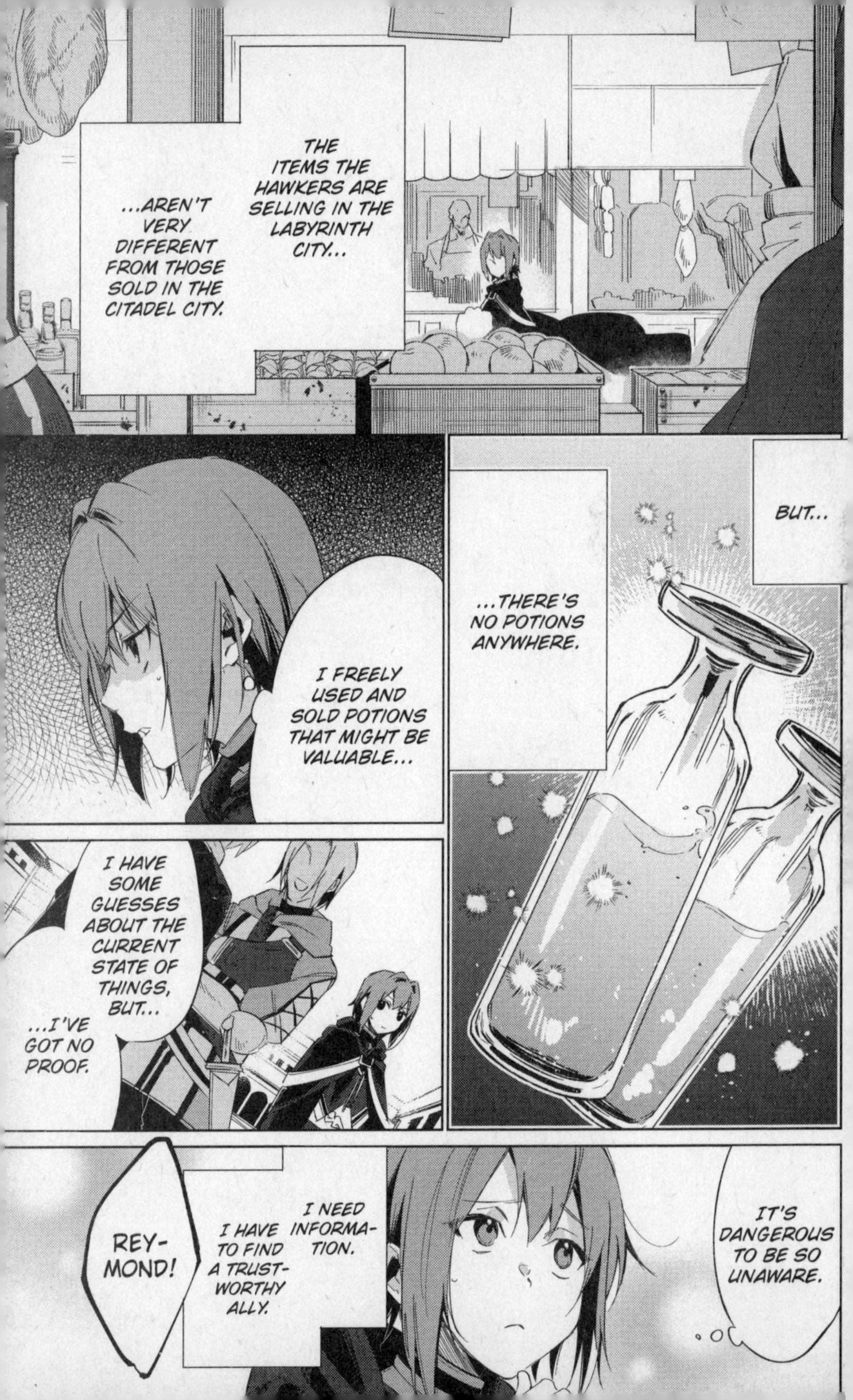
THE ITEMS THE HAWKERS ARE SELLING IN THE LABYRINTH CITY...
...AREN'T VERY DIFFERENT FROM THOSE SOLD IN THE CITADEL CITY.
BUT...
...THERE'S NO POTIONS ANYWHERE.
I FREELY USED AND SOLD POTIONS THAT MIGHT BE VALUABLE...
I HAVE SOME GUESSES ABOUT THE CURRENT STATE OF THINGS, BUT...
...I'VE GOT NO PROOF.
IT'S DANGEROUS TO BE SO UNAWARE.
I NEED INFORMA-TION.
I HAVE TO FIND A TRUST-WORTHY ALLY.
REY-MOND!

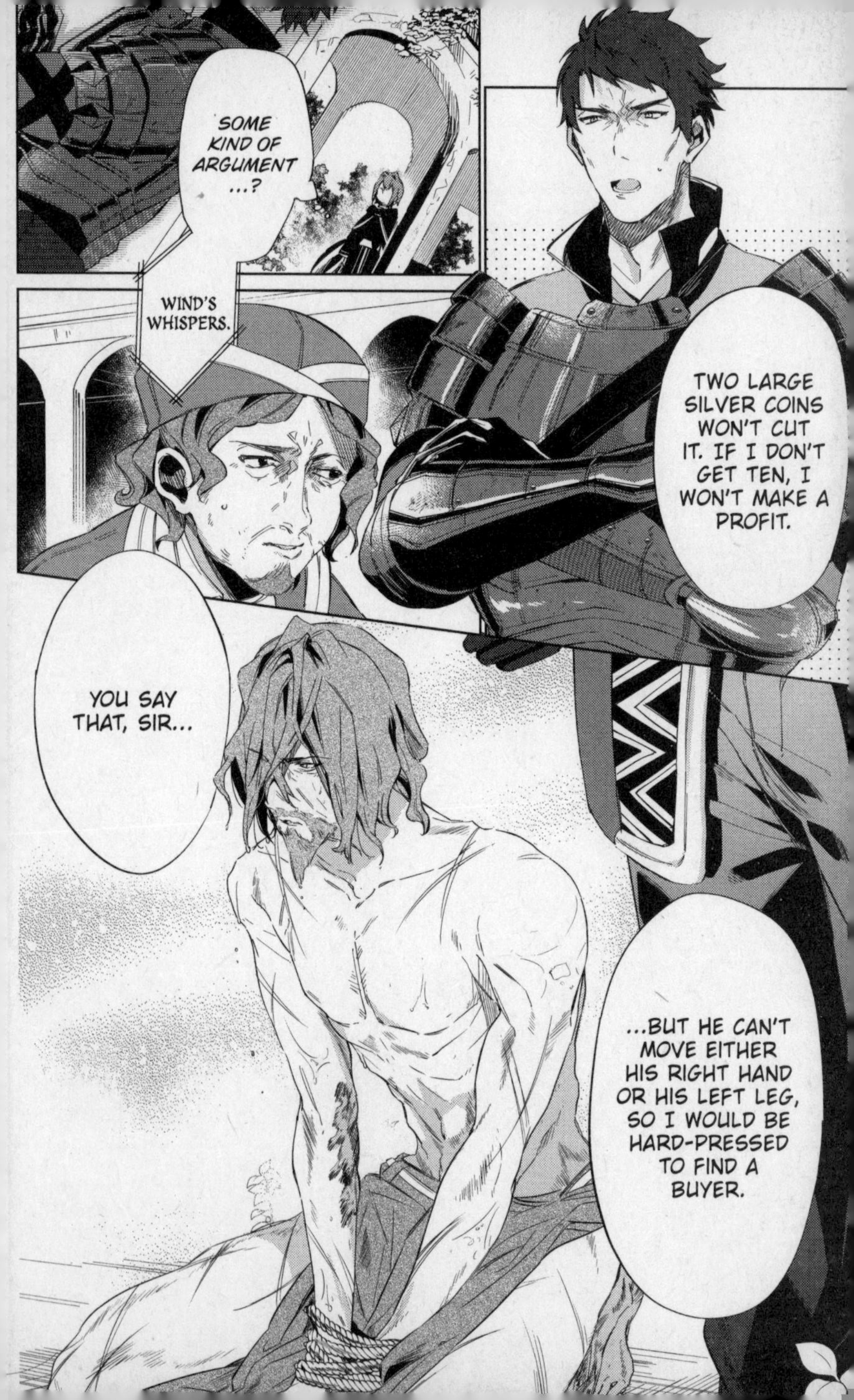
TWO LARGE SILVER COINS WON'T CUT IT. IF I DON'T GET TEN, I WON'T MAKE A PROFIT.
SOME KIND OF ARGUMENT ...?
WIND'S WHISPERS.
YOU SAY THAT, SIR...
...BUT HE CAN'T MOVE EITHER HIS RIGHT HAND OR HIS LEFT LEG, SO I WOULD BE HARD-PRESSED TO FIND A BUYER.

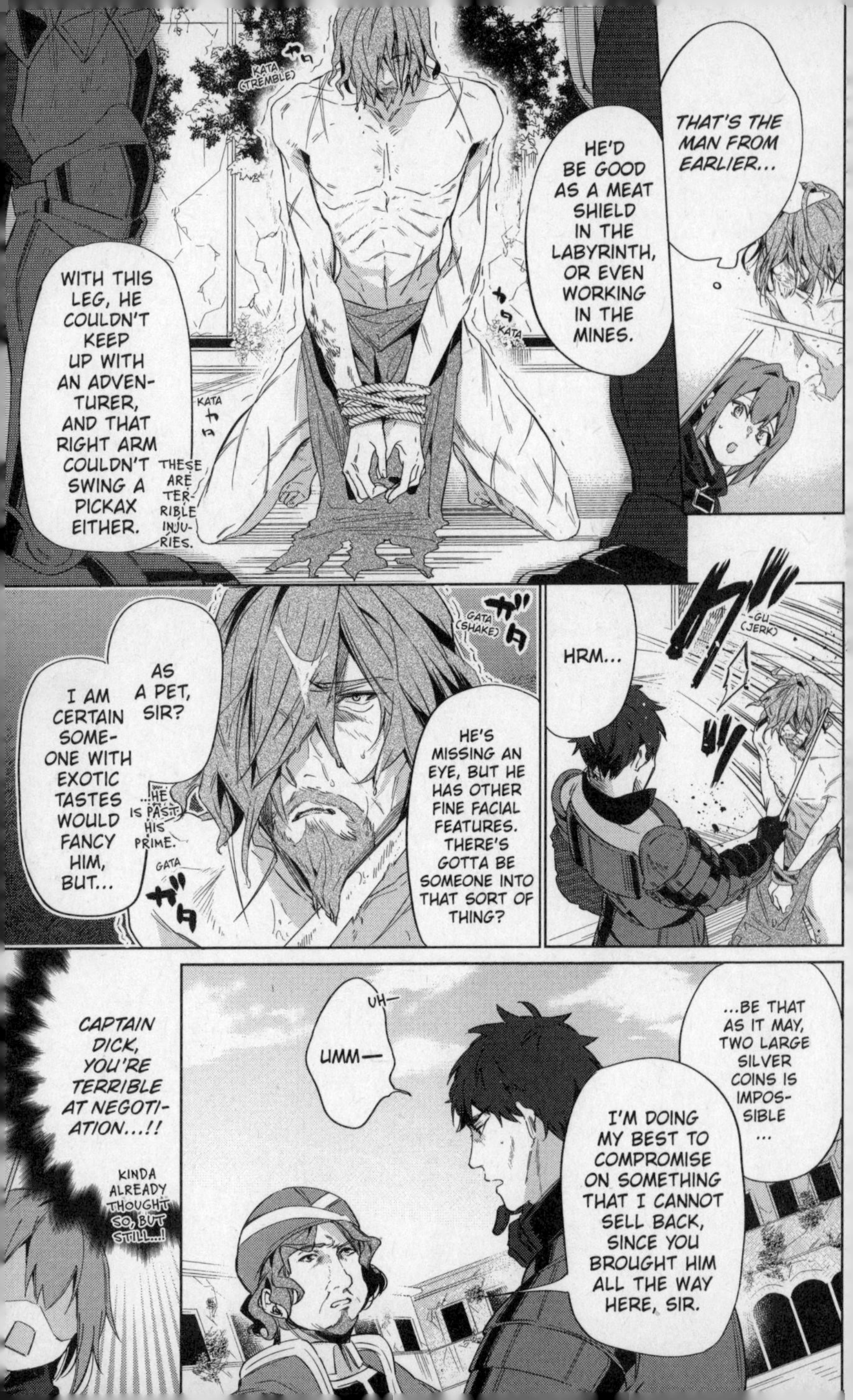
THAT'S THE MAN FROM EARLIER...
HE'D BE GOOD AS A MEAT SHIELD IN THE LABYRINTH, OR EVEN WORKING IN THE MINES.
KATA (TREMBLE)
KATA
KATA
WITH THIS LEG, HE COULDN'T KEEP UP WITH AN ADVENTURER, AND THAT RIGHT ARM COULDN'T SWING A PICKAX EITHER.
THESE ARE TERRIBLE INJURIES.
-GU (JERK)
HRM...
GATA (SHAKE)
HE'S MISSING AN EYE, BUT HE HAS OTHER FINE FACIAL FEATURES. THERE'S GOTTA BE SOMEONE INTO THAT SORT OF THING?
AS A PET, SIR?
I AM CERTAIN SOMEONE WITH EXOTIC TASTES WOULD FANCY HIM, BUT...
...HE IS PAST HIS PRIME.
GATA
...BE THAT AS IT MAY, TWO LARGE SILVER COINS IS IMPOSSIBLE...
I'M DOING MY BEST TO COMPROMISE ON SOMETHING THAT I CANNOT SELL BACK, SINCE YOU BROUGHT HIM ALL THE WAY HERE, SIR.
UH—
UMM—
CAPTAIN DICK, YOU'RE TERRIBLE AT NEGOTIATION...!!
KINDA ALREADY THOUGHT SO, BUT STILL...!

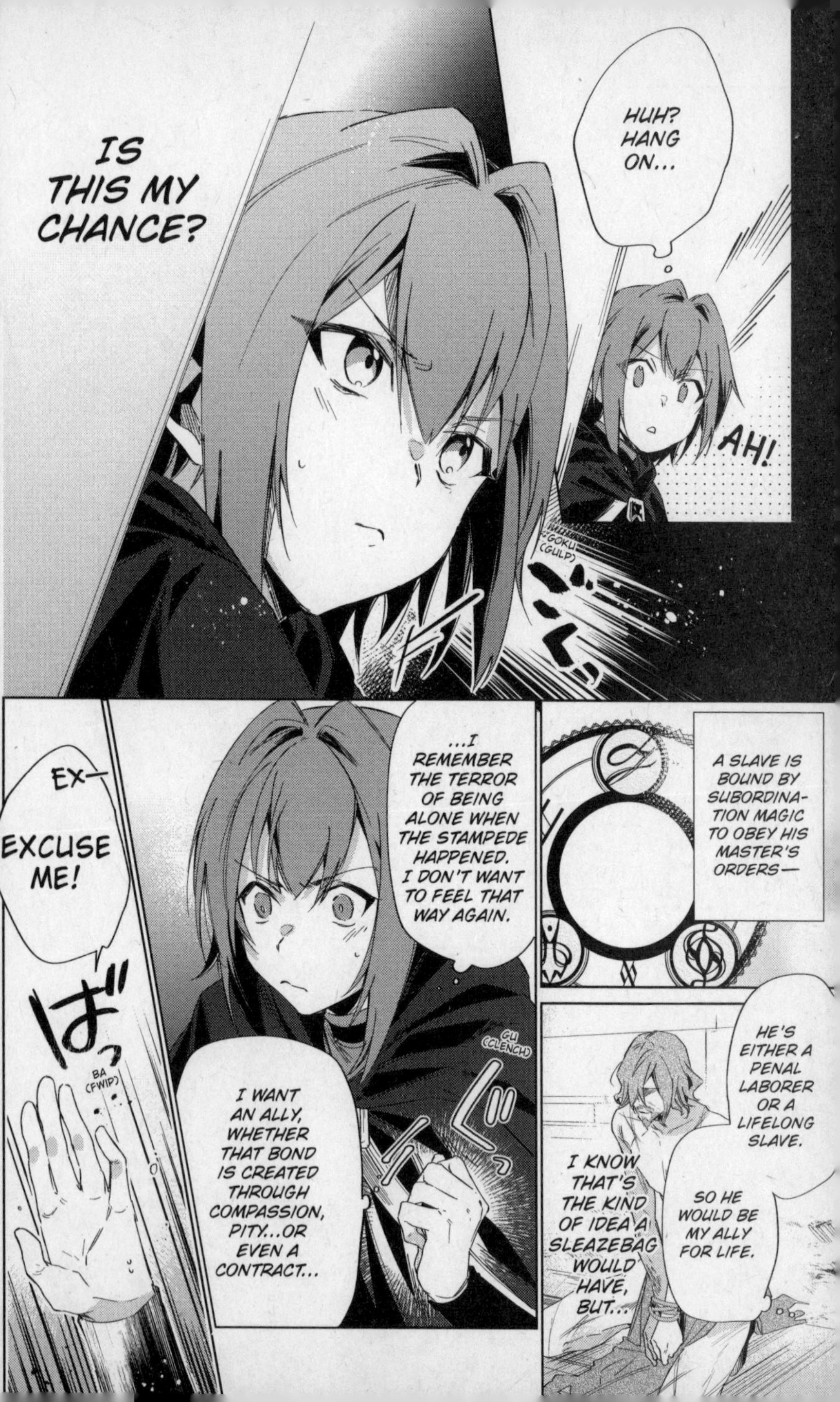
HUH? HANG ON...
AH!
GOKU (GULP)
IS THIS MY CHANCE?
A SLAVE IS BOUND BY SUBORDINATION MAGIC TO OBEY HIS MASTER'S ORDERS—
HE'S EITHER A PENAL LABORER OR A LIFELONG SLAVE.
SO HE WOULD BE MY ALLY FOR LIFE.
I KNOW THAT'S THE KIND OF IDEA A SLEAZEBAG WOULD HAVE, BUT...
...I REMEMBER THE TERROR OF BEING ALONE WHEN THE STAMPEDE HAPPENED. I DON'T WANT TO FEEL THAT WAY AGAIN.
GU (CLENCH)
I WANT AN ALLY, WHETHER THAT BOND IS CREATED THROUGH COMPASSION, PITY...OR EVEN A CONTRACT...
EX— EXCUSE ME!
BA (FWIP)

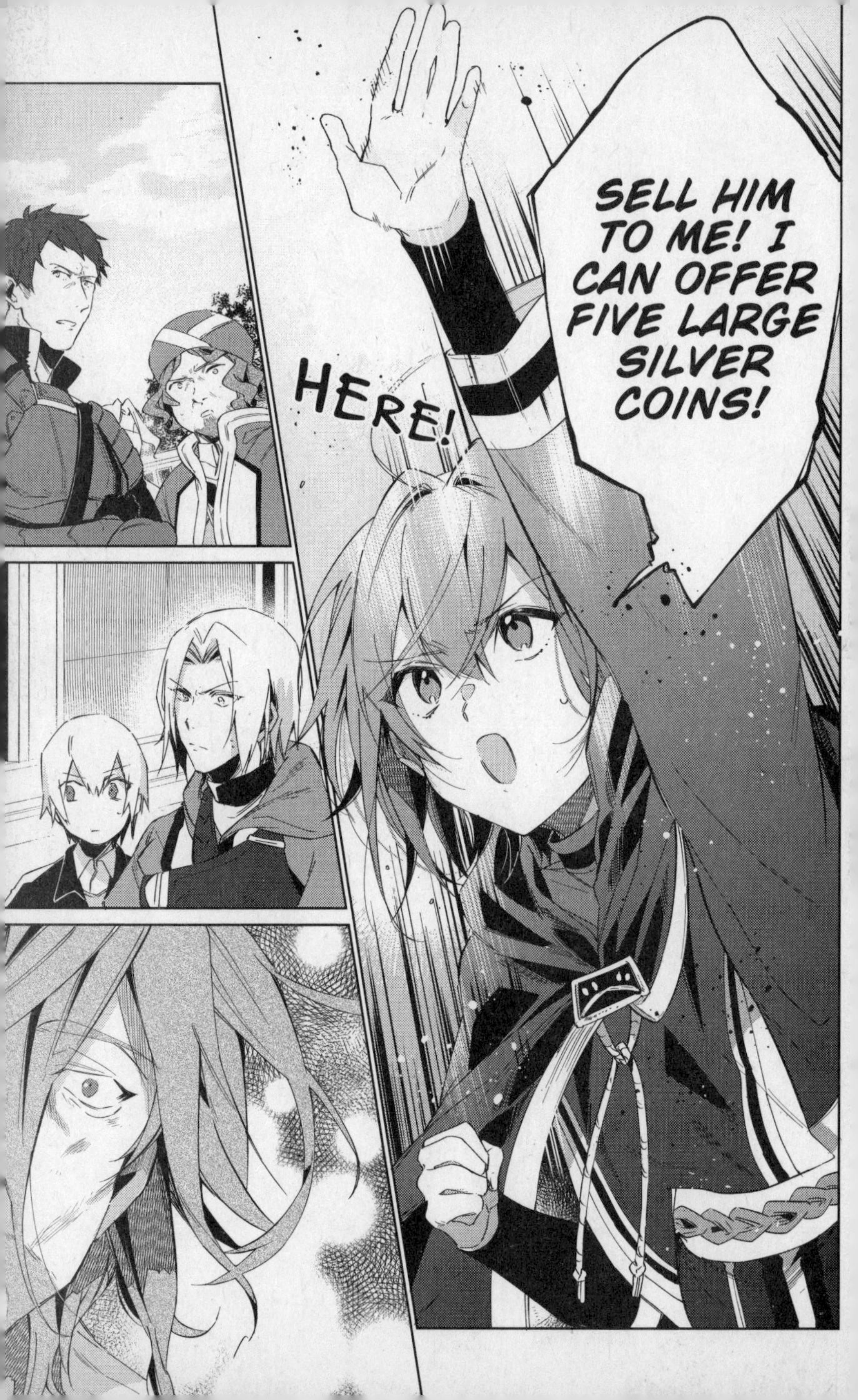
HERE!
SELL HIM TO ME! I CAN OFFER FIVE LARGE SILVER COINS!

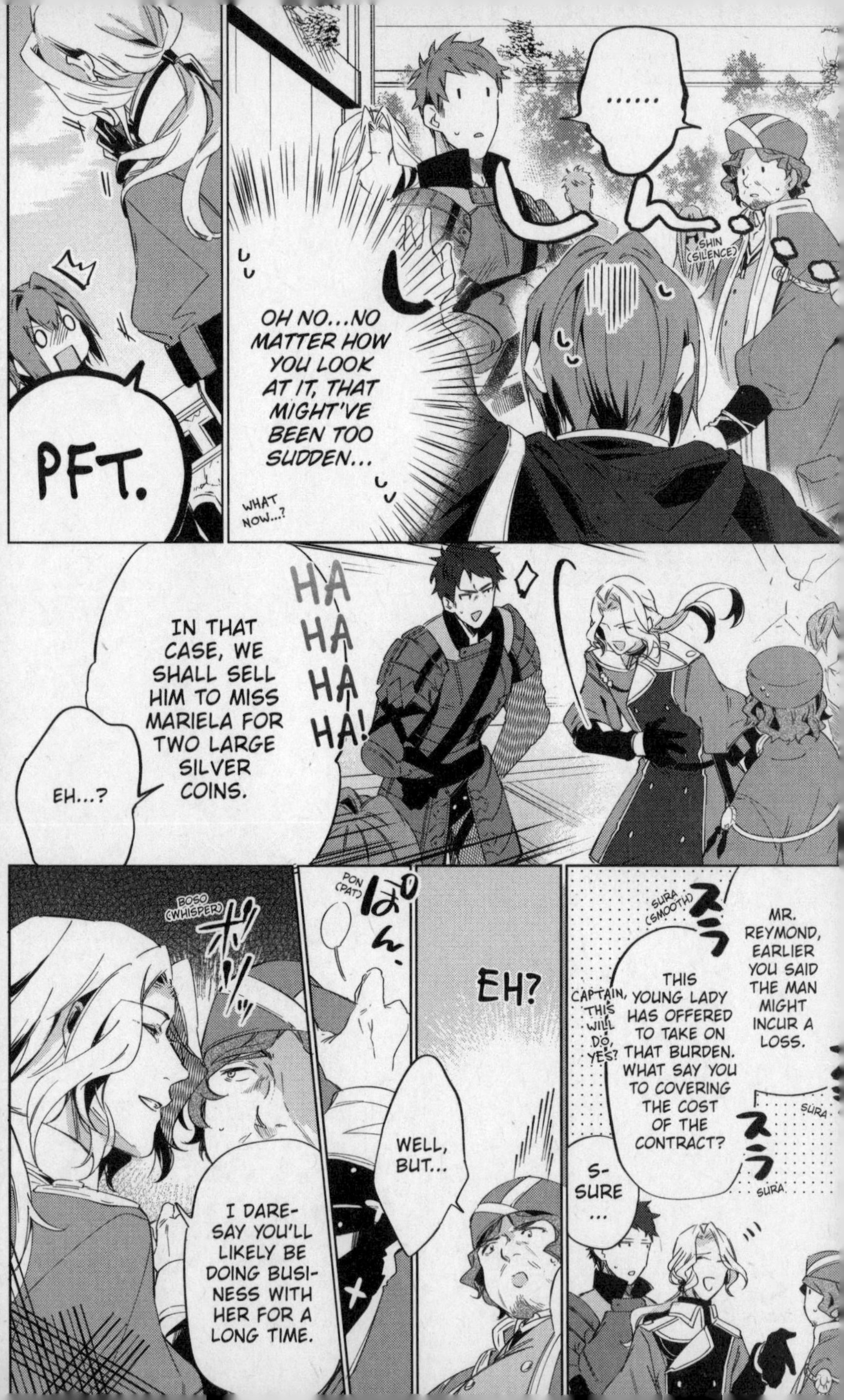
......
SHIN (SILENCE)
OH NO...NO MATTER HOW YOU LOOK AT IT, THAT MIGHT'VE BEEN TOO SUDDEN...
WHAT NOW...?
PFT.
HA HA HA HA!
IN THAT CASE, WE SHALL SELL HIM TO MISS MARIELA FOR TWO LARGE SILVER COINS.
EH...?
SURA (SMOOTH)
MR. REYMOND, EARLIER YOU SAID THE MAN MIGHT INCUR A LOSS.
THIS YOUNG LADY HAS OFFERED TO TAKE ON THAT BURDEN. WHAT SAY YOU TO COVERING THE COST OF THE CONTRACT?
CAPTAIN, THIS WILL DO, YES?
SURA
SURA
S-SURE...
EH?
PON (PAT)
WELL, BUT...
BOSO (WHISPER)
I DARESAY YOU'LL LIKELY BE DOING BUSINESS WITH HER FOR A LONG TIME.

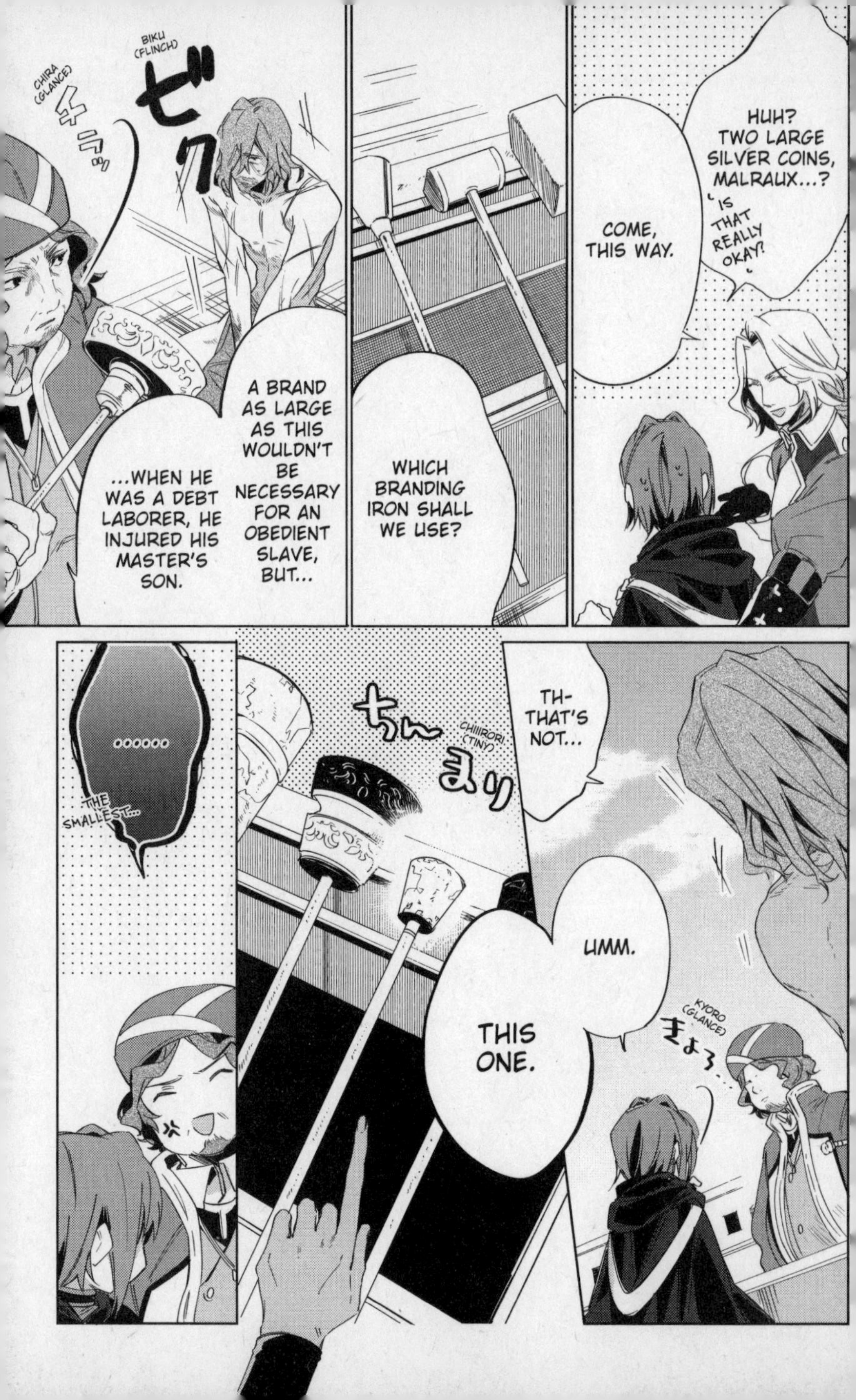
HUH? TWO LARGE SILVER COINS, MALRAUX...?
IS THAT REALLY OKAY?
COME, THIS WAY.
WHICH BRANDING IRON SHALL WE USE?
BIKU (FLINCH)
CHIRA (GLANCE)
A BRAND AS LARGE AS THIS WOULDN'T BE NECESSARY FOR AN OBEDIENT SLAVE, BUT...
...WHEN HE WAS A DEBT LABORER, HE INJURED HIS MASTER'S SON.
TH-THAT'S NOT...
UMM.
THIS ONE.
KYORO (GLANCE)
CHIIIRORI (TINY)
oooooo
THE SMALLEST...

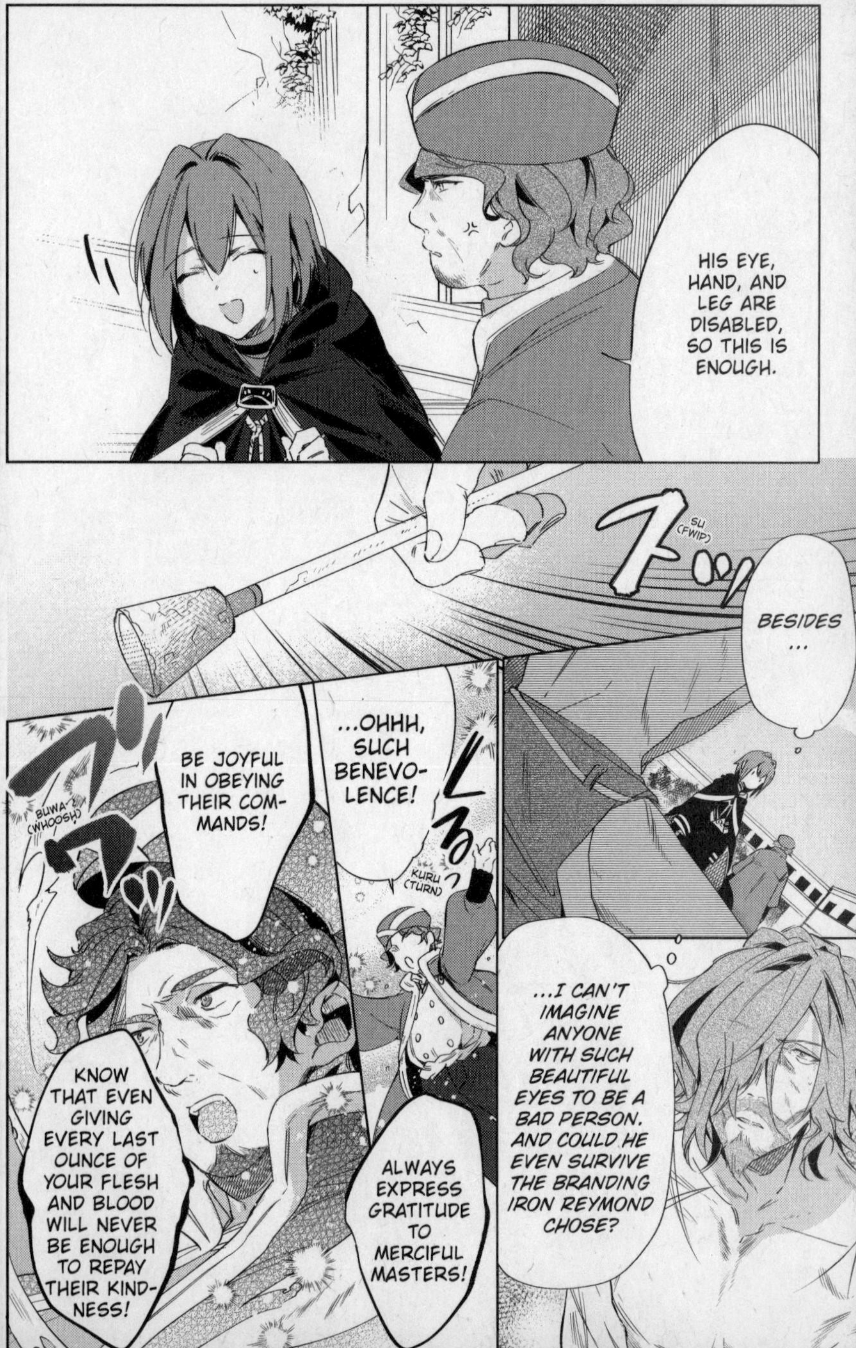
HIS EYE, HAND, AND LEG ARE DISABLED, SO THIS IS ENOUGH.
SU (FWIP)
BESIDES...
...I CAN'T IMAGINE ANYONE WITH SUCH BEAUTIFUL EYES TO BE A BAD PERSON. AND COULD HE EVEN SURVIVE THE BRANDING IRON REYMOND CHOSE?
...OHHH, SUCH BENEVO-LENCE!
KURU (TURN)
BE JOYFUL IN OBEYING THEIR COM-MANDS!
BUWA (WHOOSH)
ALWAYS EXPRESS GRATITUDE TO MERCIFUL MASTERS!
KNOW THAT EVEN GIVING EVERY LAST OUNCE OF YOUR FLESH AND BLOOD WILL NEVER BE ENOUGH TO REPAY THEIR KIND-NESS!

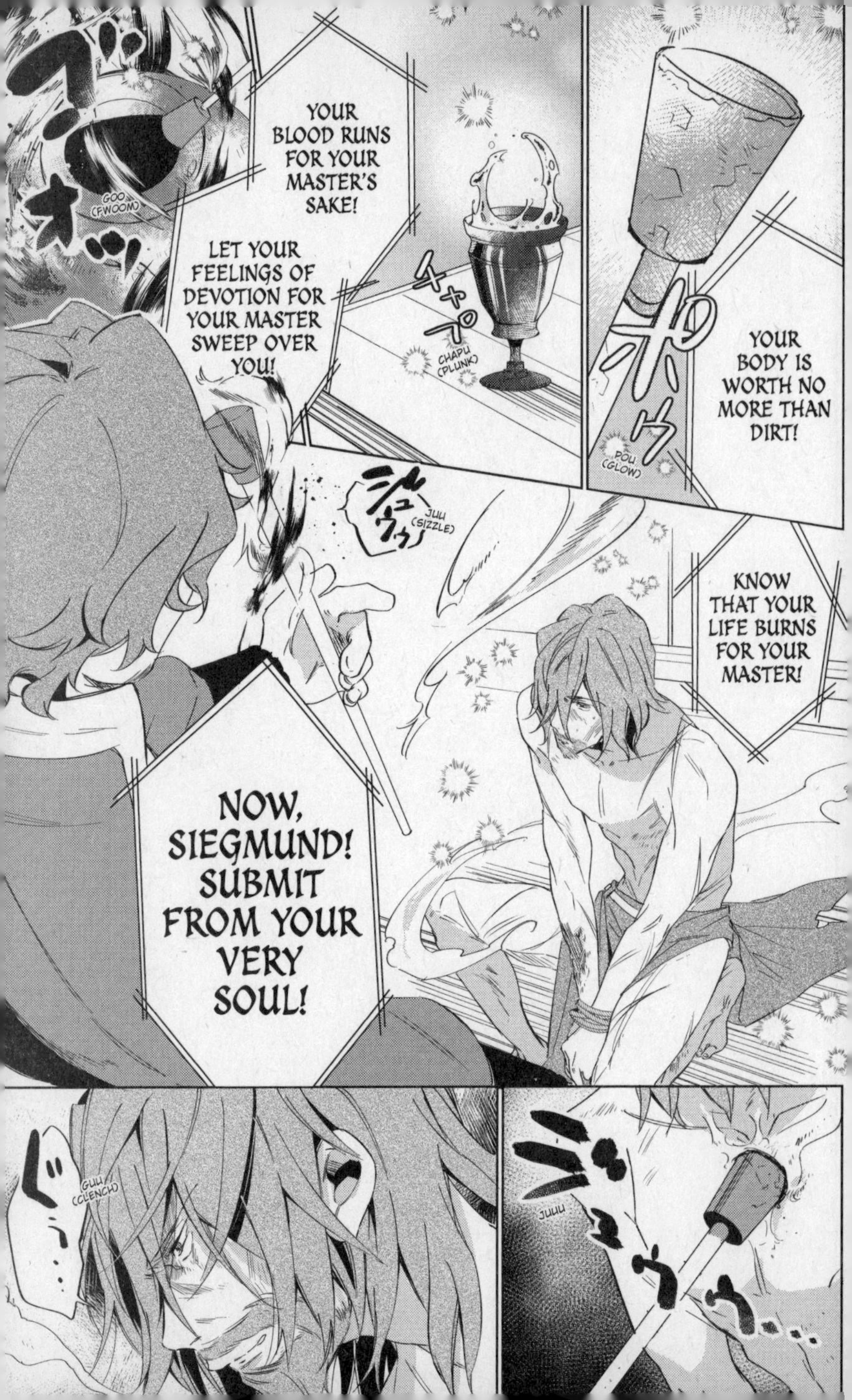
POU (GLOW)
YOUR BODY IS WORTH NO MORE THAN DIRT!
YOUR BLOOD RUNS FOR YOUR MASTER'S SAKE!
CHAPU (PLUNK)
GOO (FWOOM)
LET YOUR FEELINGS OF DEVOTION FOR YOUR MASTER SWEEP OVER YOU!
KNOW THAT YOUR LIFE BURNS FOR YOUR MASTER!
JUU (SIZZLE)
NOW, SIEGMUND! SUBMIT FROM YOUR VERY SOUL!
JUUU
GULI (CLENCH)

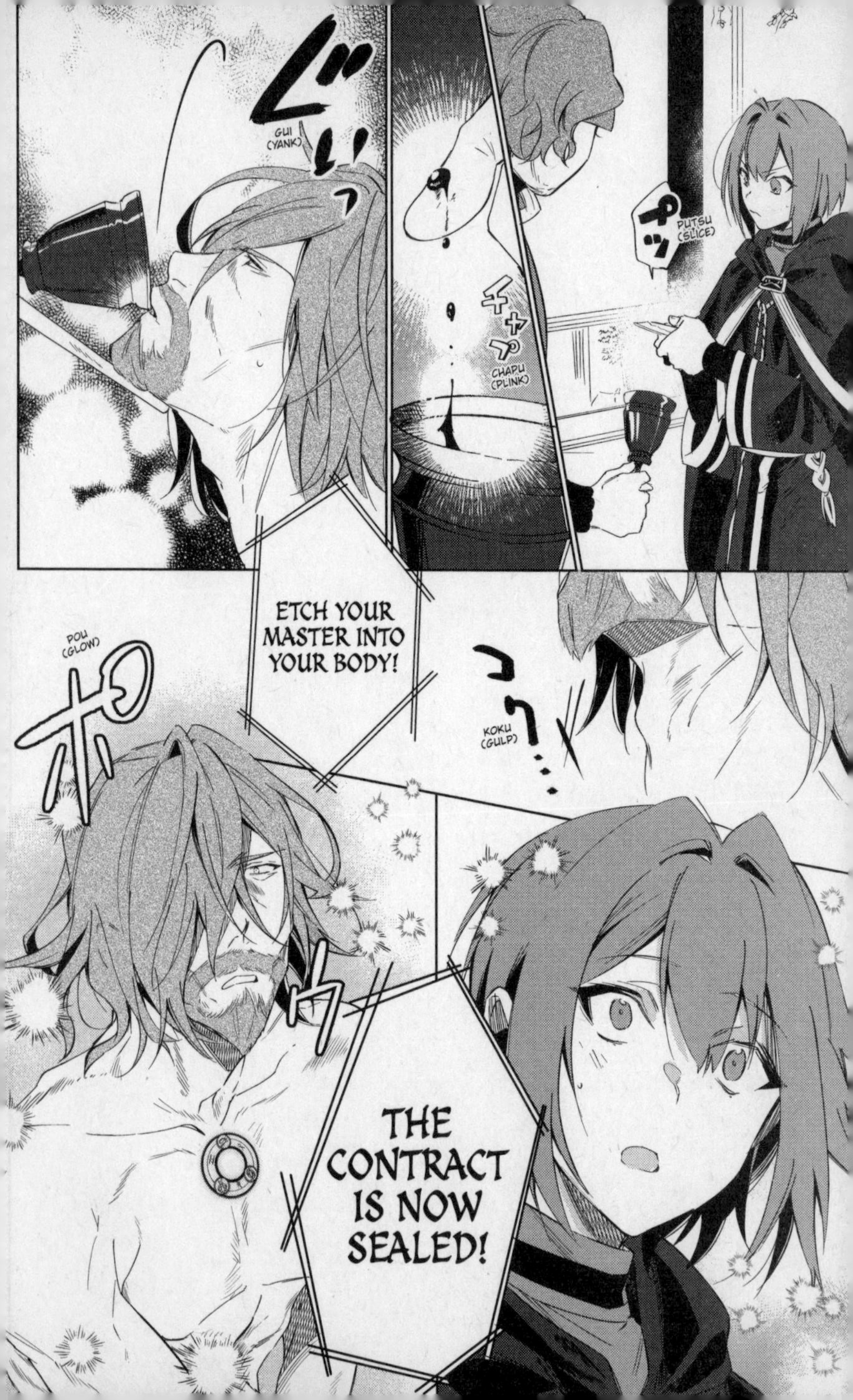
PUTSU (SLICE)
CHAPU (PLINK)
GUI (YANK)
ETCH YOUR MASTER INTO YOUR BODY!
KOKU (GULP)
POU (GLOW)
THE CONTRACT IS NOW SEALED!

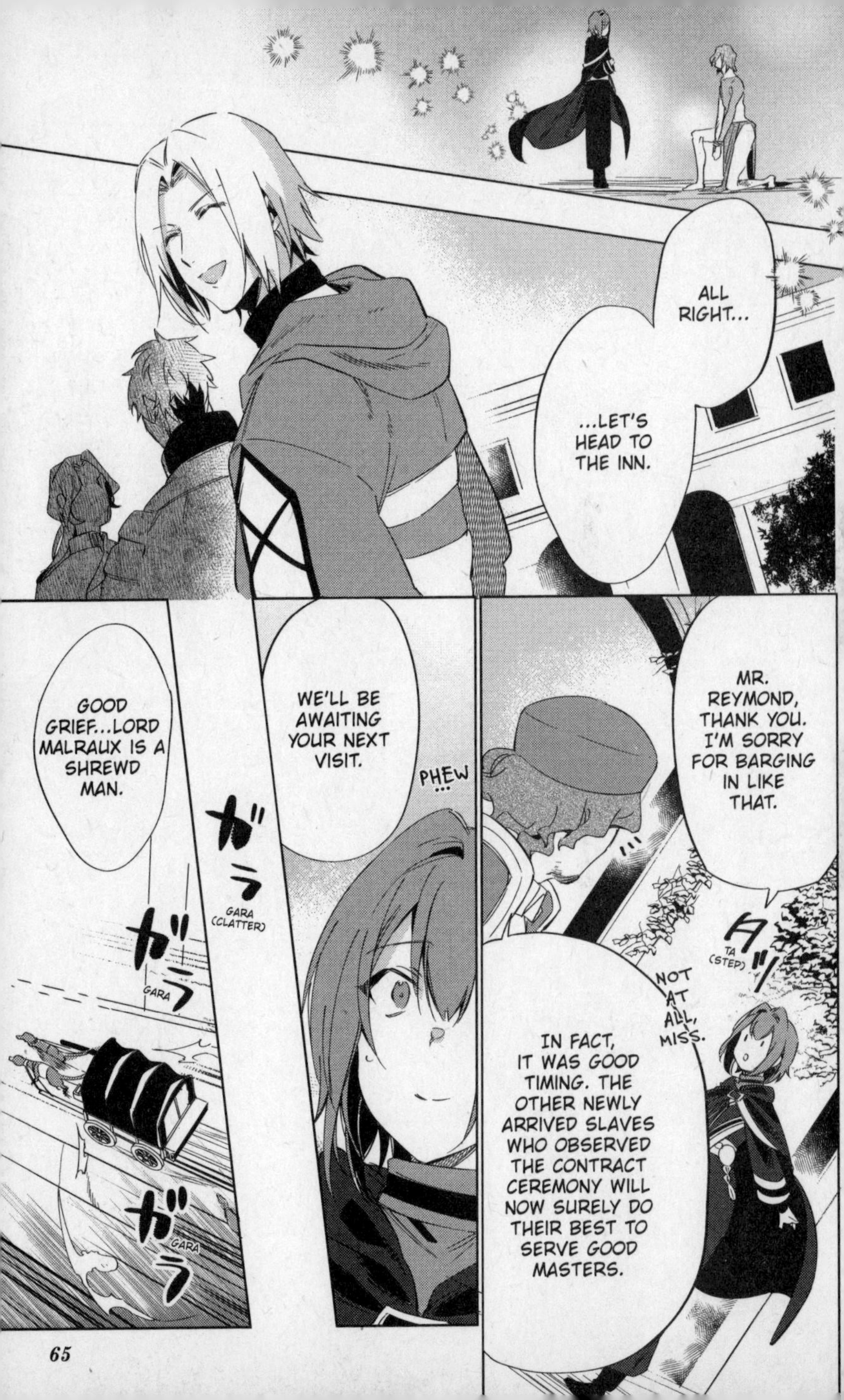
ALL RIGHT...
...LET'S HEAD TO THE INN.
MR. REYMOND, THANK YOU. I'M SORRY FOR BARGING IN LIKE THAT.
タッ
TA (STEP)
NOT AT ALL, MISS.
IN FACT, IT WAS GOOD TIMING. THE OTHER NEWLY ARRIVED SLAVES WHO OBSERVED THE CONTRACT CEREMONY WILL NOW SURELY DO THEIR BEST TO SERVE GOOD MASTERS.
WE'LL BE AWAITING YOUR NEXT VISIT.
PHEW...
ガラ
GARA (CLATTER)
GOOD GRIEF...LORD MALRAUX IS A SHREWD MAN.
ガラ
GARA
ガラ
GARA

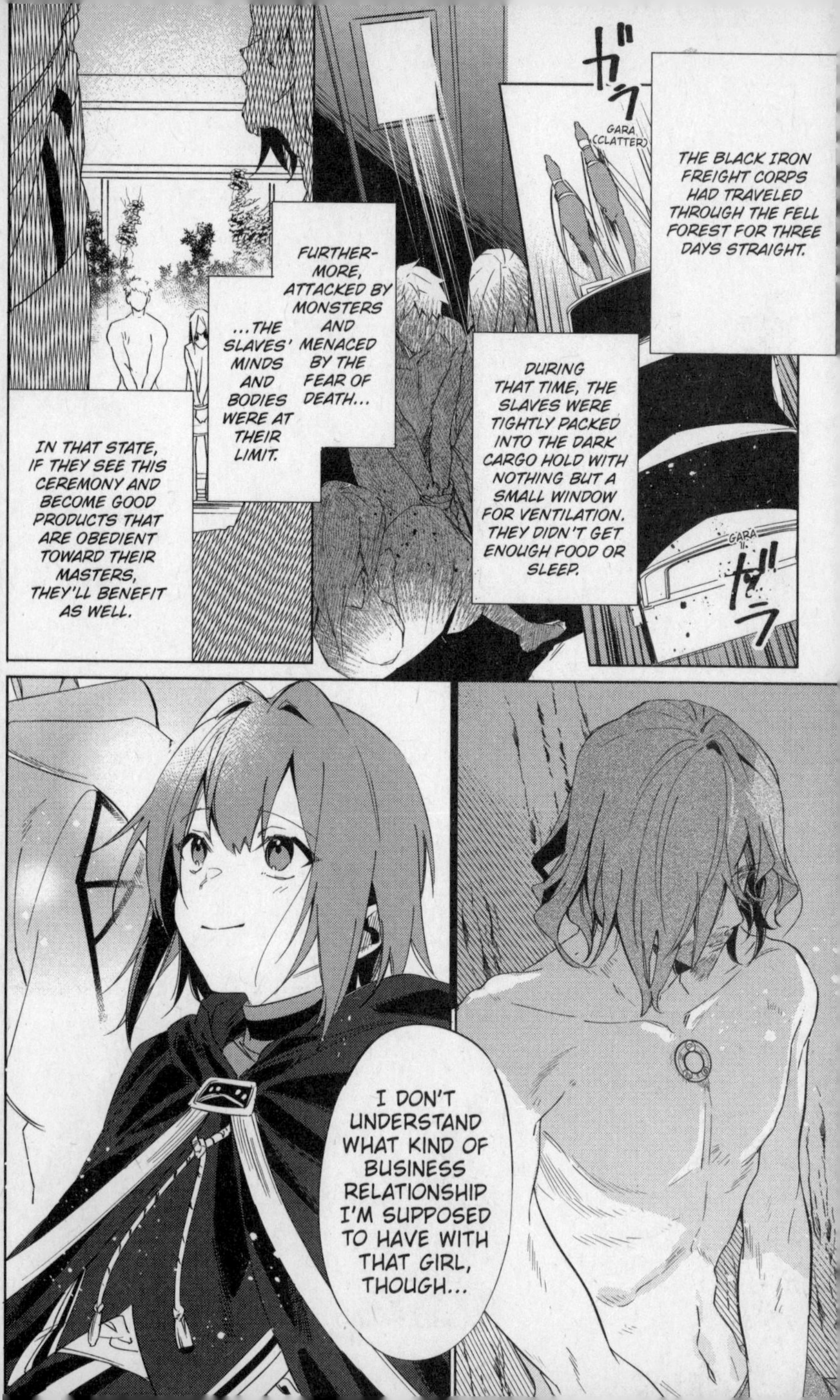
ガラ
GARA (CLATTER)
THE BLACK IRON FREIGHT CORPS HAD TRAVELED THROUGH THE FELL FOREST FOR THREE DAYS STRAIGHT.
DURING THAT TIME, THE SLAVES WERE TIGHTLY PACKED INTO THE DARK CARGO HOLD WITH NOTHING BUT A SMALL WINDOW FOR VENTILATION. THEY DIDN'T GET ENOUGH FOOD OR SLEEP.
GARA
FURTHER-MORE, ATTACKED BY MONSTERS AND MENACED BY THE FEAR OF DEATH...
...THE SLAVES' MINDS AND BODIES WERE AT THEIR LIMIT.
IN THAT STATE, IF THEY SEE THIS CEREMONY AND BECOME GOOD PRODUCTS THAT ARE OBEDIENT TOWARD THEIR MASTERS, THEY'LL BENEFIT AS WELL.
I DON'T UNDERSTAND WHAT KIND OF BUSINESS RELATIONSHIP I'M SUPPOSED TO HAVE WITH THAT GIRL, THOUGH...

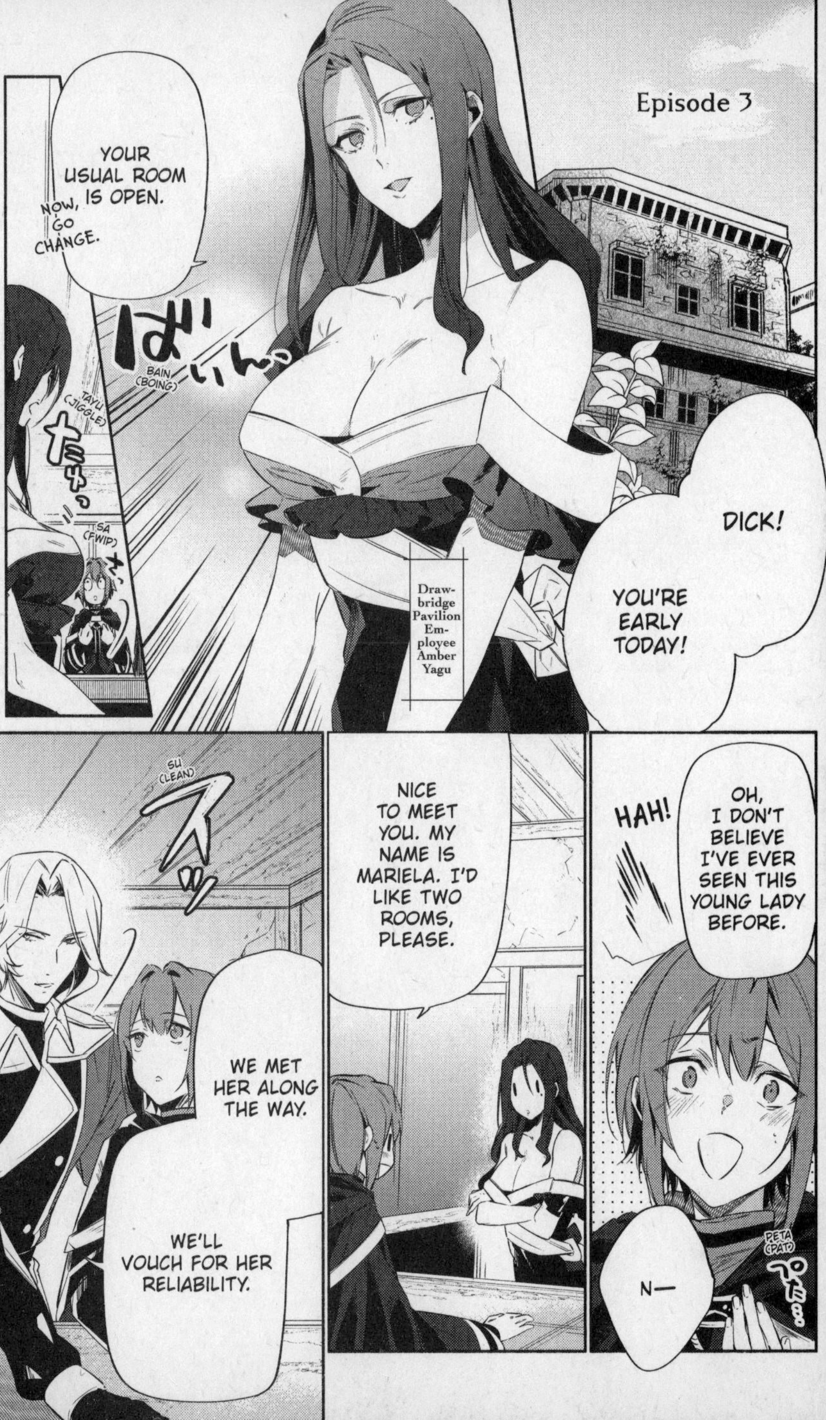
Episode 3
DICK!
YOU'RE EARLY TODAY!
YOUR USUAL ROOM IS OPEN.
NOW, GO CHANGE.
BAIN (BOING)
TAYU (JIGGLE)
SA (FWIP)
Drawbridge Pavilion Employee Amber Yagu
HAH!
OH, I DON'T BELIEVE I'VE EVER SEEN THIS YOUNG LADY BEFORE.
PETA (PAT)
N—
NICE TO MEET YOU. MY NAME IS MARIELA. I'D LIKE TWO ROOMS, PLEASE.
SU (LEAN)
WE MET HER ALONG THE WAY.
WE'LL VOUCH FOR HER RELIABILITY.

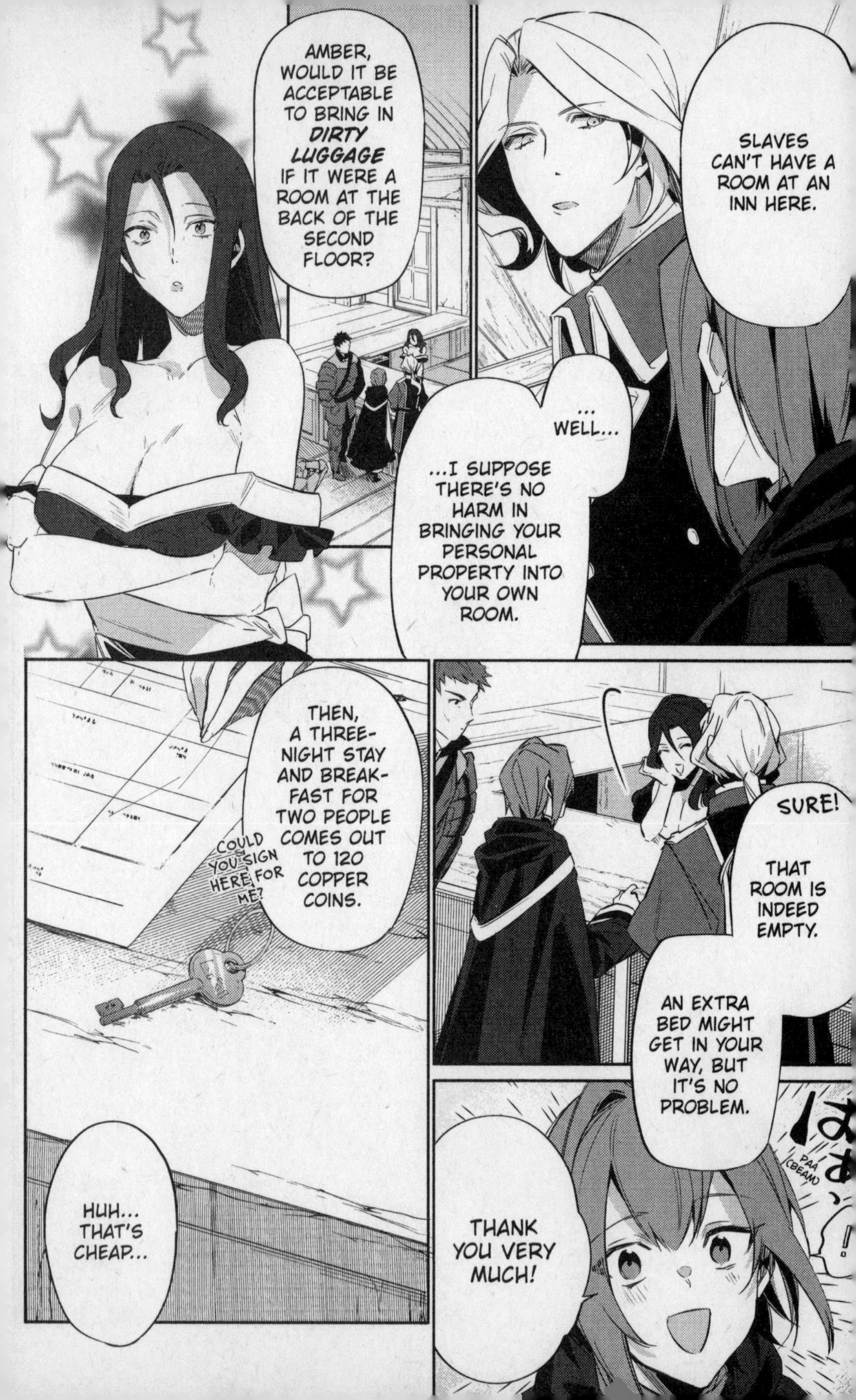
SLAVES CAN'T HAVE A ROOM AT AN INN HERE.
AMBER, WOULD IT BE ACCEPTABLE TO BRING IN *DIRTY LUGGAGE* IF IT WERE A ROOM AT THE BACK OF THE SECOND FLOOR?
... WELL...
...I SUPPOSE THERE'S NO HARM IN BRINGING YOUR PERSONAL PROPERTY INTO YOUR OWN ROOM.
SURE!
THAT ROOM IS INDEED EMPTY.
AN EXTRA BED MIGHT GET IN YOUR WAY, BUT IT'S NO PROBLEM.
THEN, A THREE-NIGHT STAY AND BREAKFAST FOR TWO PEOPLE COMES OUT TO 120 COPPER COINS.
COULD YOU SIGN HERE FOR ME?
PAA (BEAM)
THANK YOU VERY MUCH!
HUH... THAT'S CHEAP...

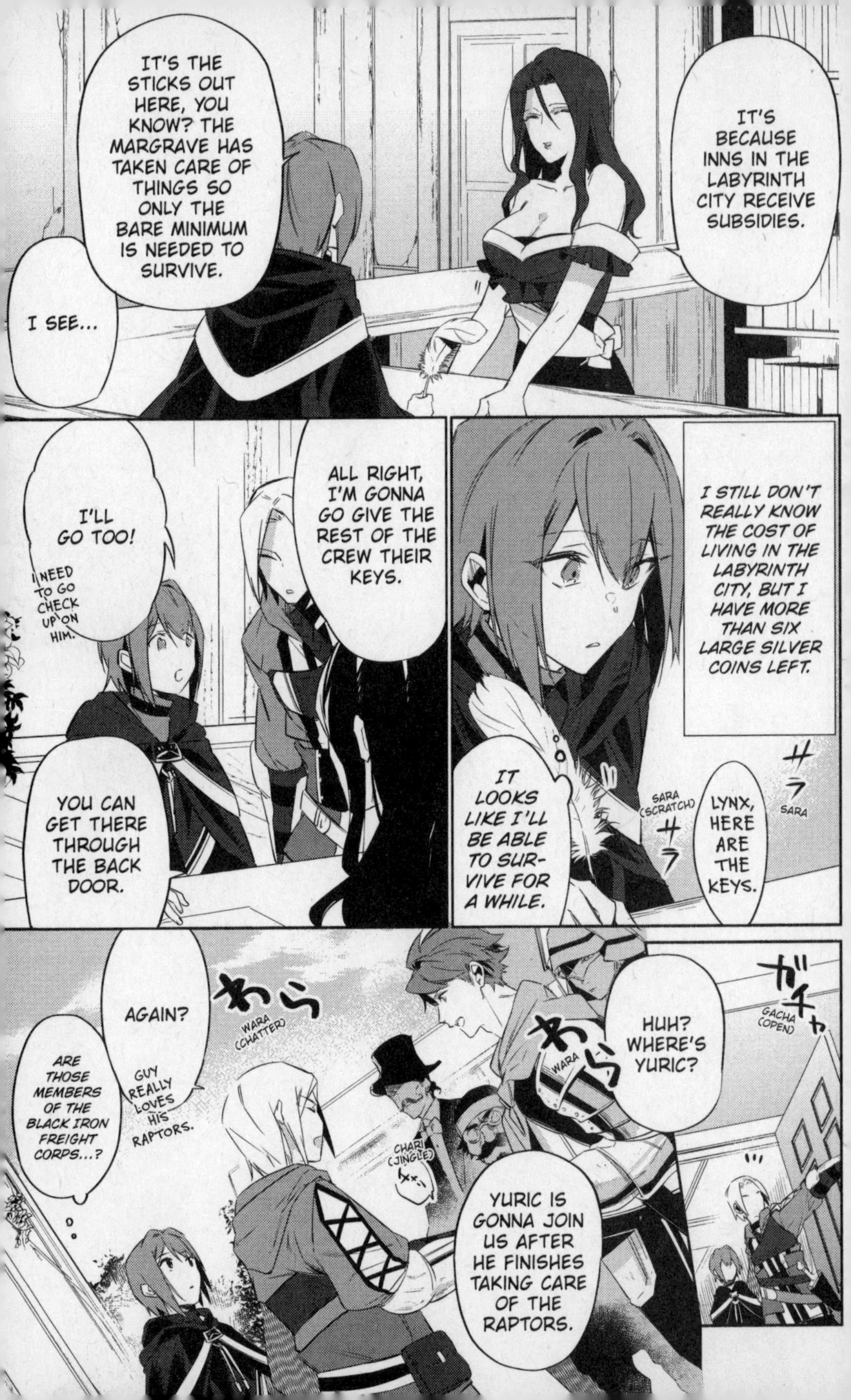
IT'S BECAUSE INNS IN THE LABYRINTH CITY RECEIVE SUBSIDIES.
IT'S THE STICKS OUT HERE, YOU KNOW? THE MARGRAVE HAS TAKEN CARE OF THINGS SO ONLY THE BARE MINIMUM IS NEEDED TO SURVIVE.
I SEE...
I STILL DON'T REALLY KNOW THE COST OF LIVING IN THE LABYRINTH CITY, BUT I HAVE MORE THAN SIX LARGE SILVER COINS LEFT.
SARA
SARA (SCRATCH)
LYNX, HERE ARE THE KEYS.
IT LOOKS LIKE I'LL BE ABLE TO SURVIVE FOR A WHILE.
ALL RIGHT, I'M GONNA GO GIVE THE REST OF THE CREW THEIR KEYS.
I'LL GO TOO!
I NEED TO GO CHECK UP ON HIM.
YOU CAN GET THERE THROUGH THE BACK DOOR.
GACHA (OPEN)
HUH? WHERE'S YURIC?
WARA
YURIC IS GONNA JOIN US AFTER HE FINISHES TAKING CARE OF THE RAPTORS.
WARA (CHATTER)
AGAIN?
GUY REALLY LOVES HIS RAPTORS.
CHARI (JINGLE)
ARE THOSE MEMBERS OF THE BLACK IRON FREIGHT CORPS...?

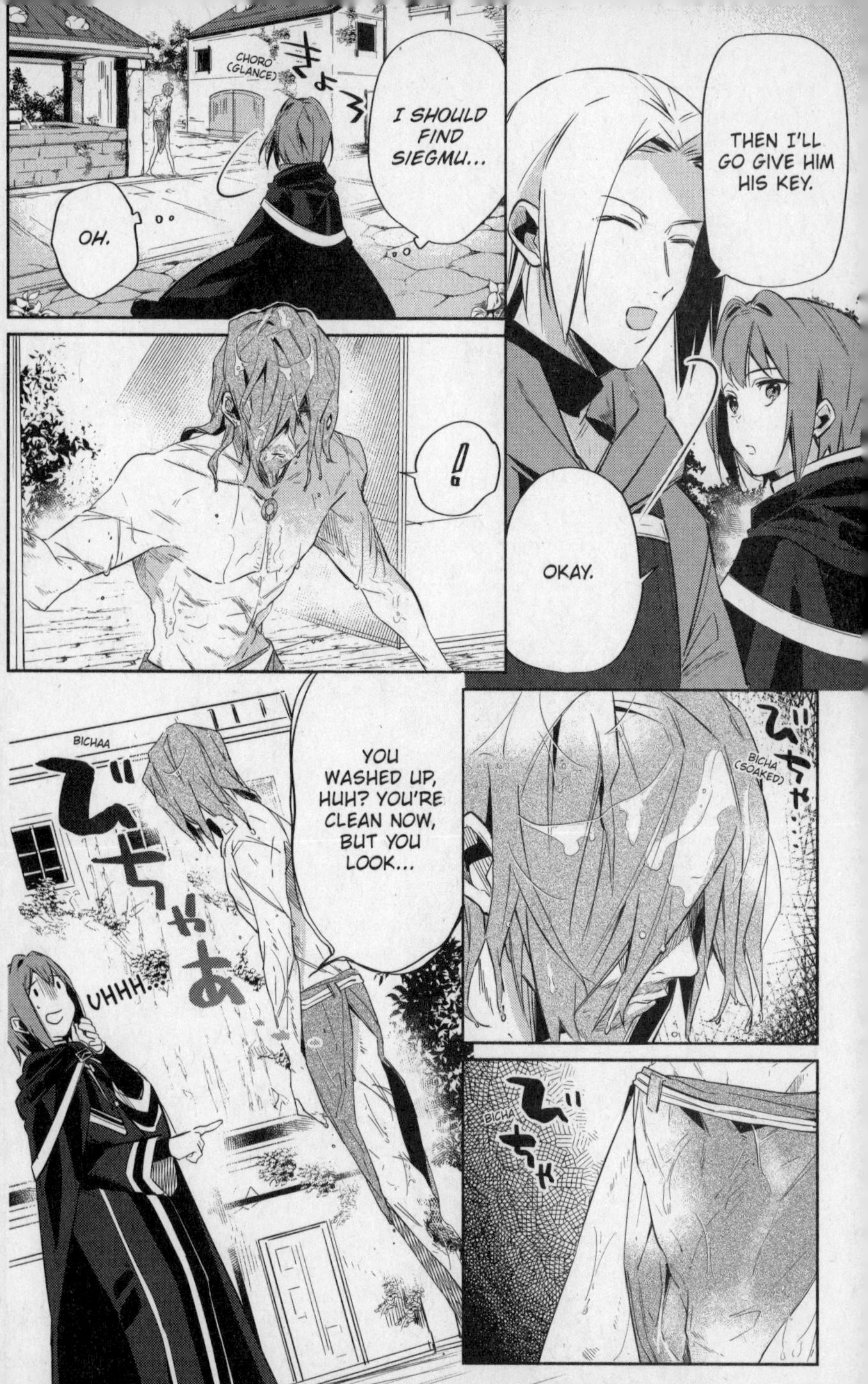
THEN I'LL GO GIVE HIM HIS KEY.
OKAY.
I SHOULD FIND SIEGMU...
CHORO (GLANCE)
OH.
!
BICHA (SOAKED)
BICHA
YOU WASHED UP, HUH? YOU'RE CLEAN NOW, BUT YOU LOOK...
BICHAA
UHHH..

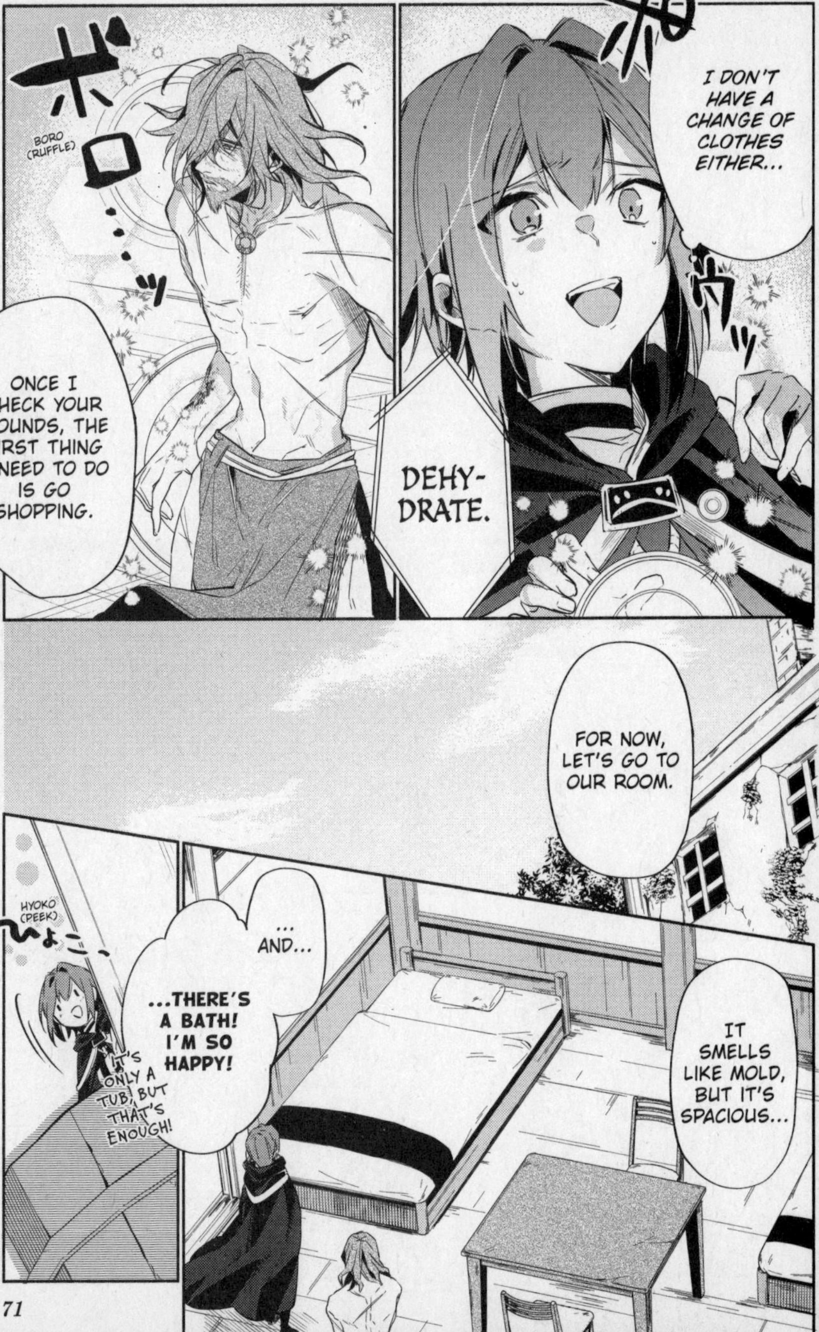
POU (GLOW)
I DON'T HAVE A CHANGE OF CLOTHES EITHER...
DEHY-DRATE.
BORO (RUFFLE)
ONCE I CHECK YOUR WOUNDS, THE FIRST THING I NEED TO DO IS GO SHOPPING.
FOR NOW, LET'S GO TO OUR ROOM.
IT SMELLS LIKE MOLD, BUT IT'S SPACIOUS...
... AND...
...THERE'S A BATH! I'M SO HAPPY!
HYOKO (PEEK)
IT'S ONLY A TUB, BUT THAT'S ENOUGH!

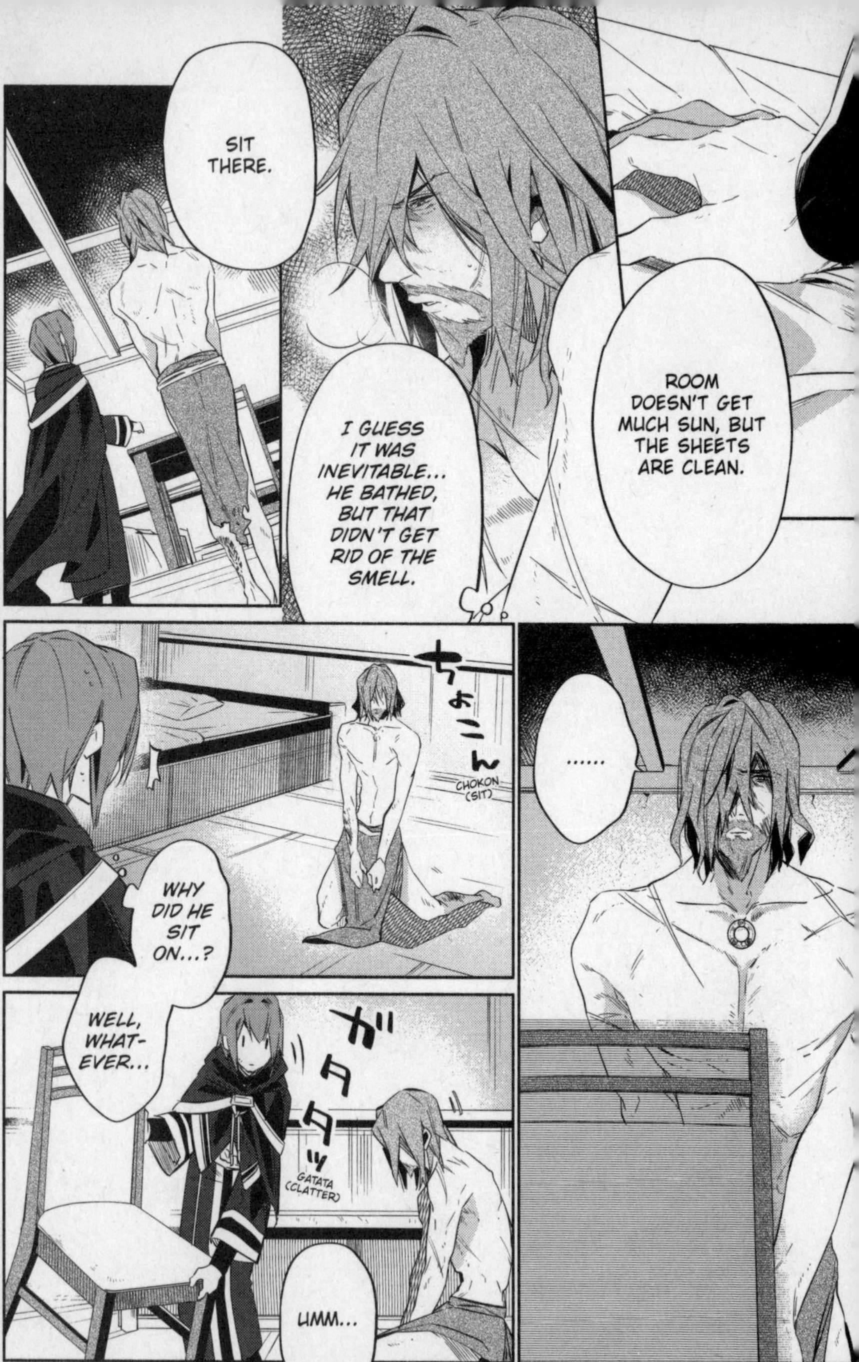
ROOM DOESN'T GET MUCH SUN, BUT THE SHEETS ARE CLEAN.
I GUESS IT WAS INEVITABLE... HE BATHED, BUT THAT DIDN'T GET RID OF THE SMELL.
SIT THERE.
......
ちょこん
CHOKON (SIT)
WHY DID HE SIT ON...?
WELL, WHAT-EVER...
ガタタッ
GATATA (CLATTER)
UMM...

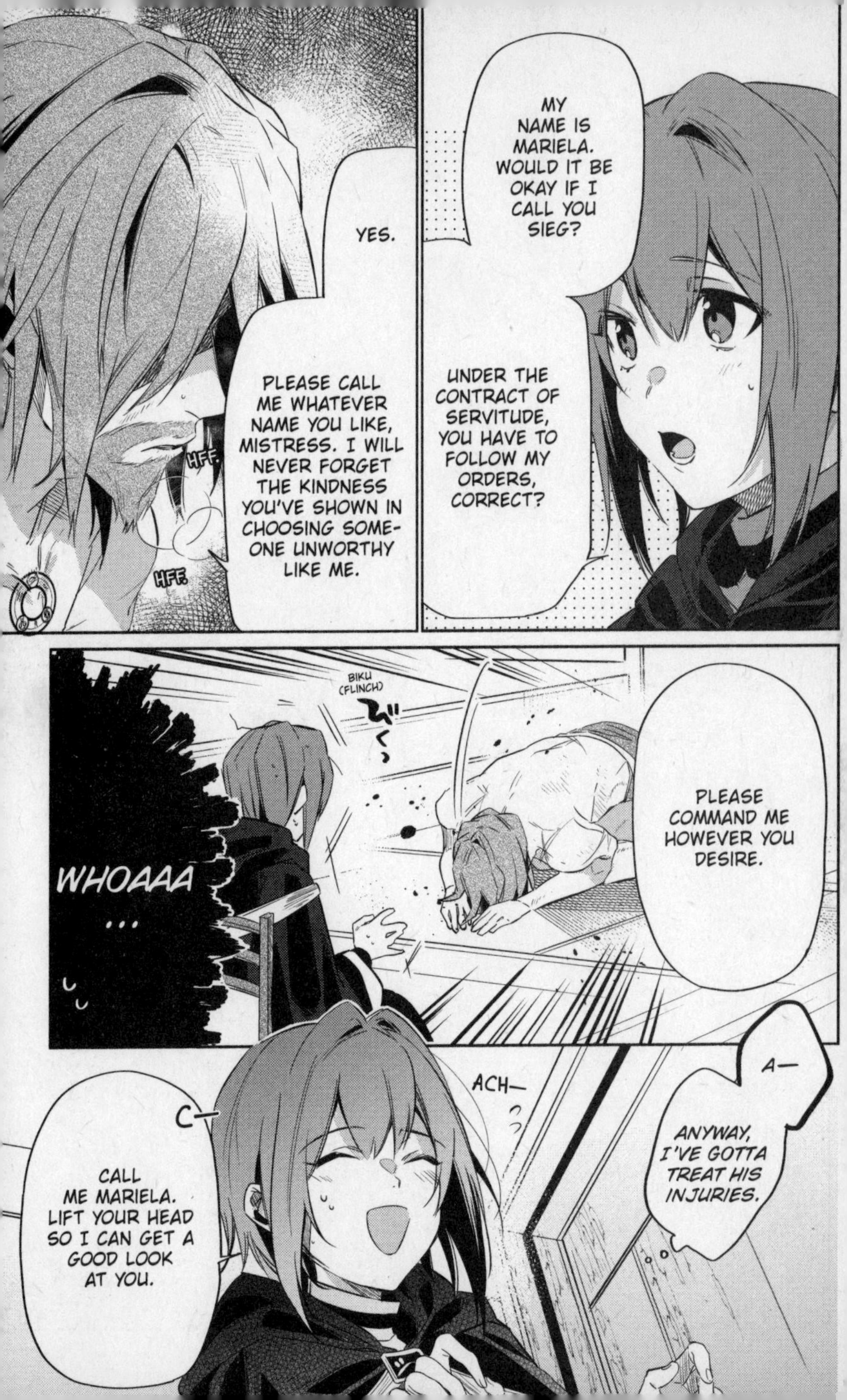
MY NAME IS MARIELA. WOULD IT BE OKAY IF I CALL YOU SIEG?
UNDER THE CONTRACT OF SERVITUDE, YOU HAVE TO FOLLOW MY ORDERS, CORRECT?
YES.
PLEASE CALL ME WHATEVER NAME YOU LIKE, MISTRESS. I WILL NEVER FORGET THE KINDNESS YOU'VE SHOWN IN CHOOSING SOME-ONE UNWORTHY LIKE ME.
HFF.
HFF.
PLEASE COMMAND ME HOWEVER YOU DESIRE.
BIKU (FLINCH)
WHOAAA...
A—
ANYWAY, I'VE GOTTA TREAT HIS INJURIES.
ACH—
C—
CALL ME MARIELA. LIFT YOUR HEAD SO I CAN GET A GOOD LOOK AT YOU.

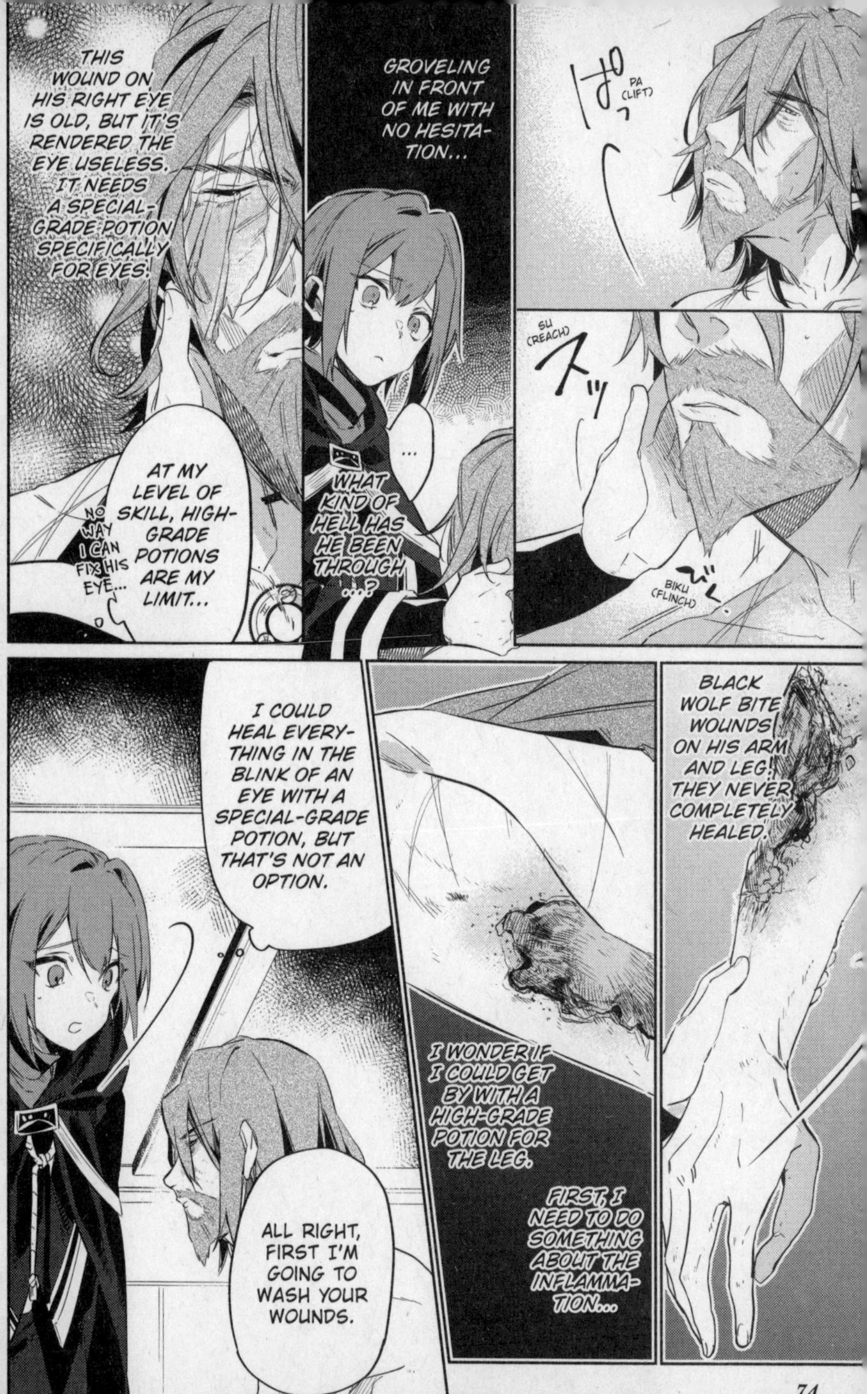
ぱっ
PA (LIFT)
スッ
SU (REACH)
びくっ
BIKU (FLINCH)
GROVELING IN FRONT OF ME WITH NO HESITATION…
…
WHAT KIND OF HELL HAS HE BEEN THROUGH …?
THIS WOUND ON HIS RIGHT EYE IS OLD, BUT IT'S RENDERED THE EYE USELESS. IT NEEDS A SPECIAL-GRADE POTION SPECIFICALLY FOR EYES!
AT MY LEVEL OF SKILL, HIGH-GRADE POTIONS ARE MY LIMIT…
NO WAY I CAN FIX HIS EYE…
BLACK WOLF BITE WOUNDS ON HIS ARM AND LEG! THEY NEVER COMPLETELY HEALED.
I WONDER IF I COULD GET BY WITH A HIGH-GRADE POTION FOR THE LEG.
FIRST, I NEED TO DO SOMETHING ABOUT THE INFLAMMATION…
I COULD HEAL EVERYTHING IN THE BLINK OF AN EYE WITH A SPECIAL-GRADE POTION, BUT THAT'S NOT AN OPTION.
ALL RIGHT, FIRST I'M GOING TO WASH YOUR WOUNDS.

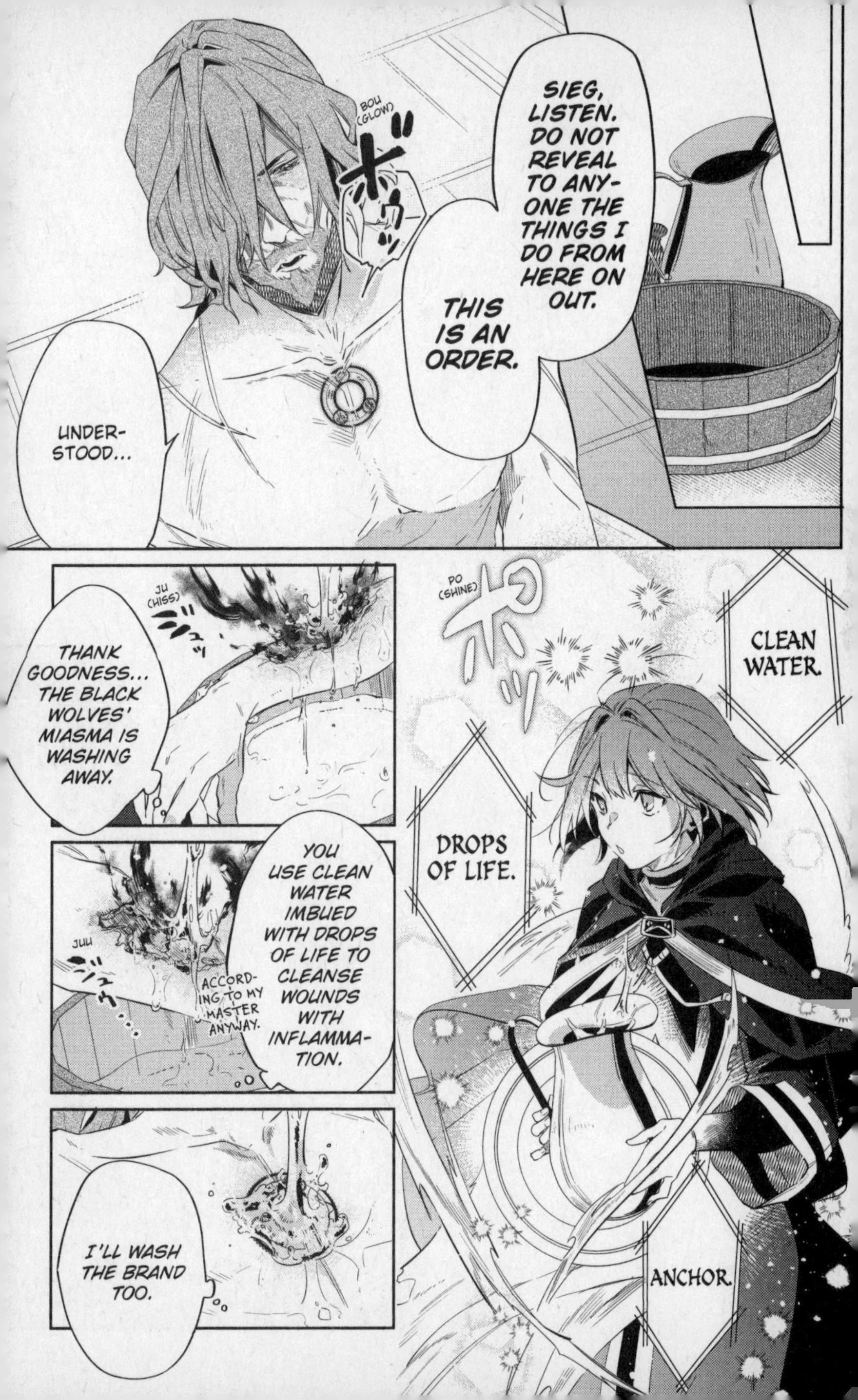
SIEG, LISTEN. DO NOT REVEAL TO ANYONE THE THINGS I DO FROM HERE ON OUT.
THIS IS AN ORDER.
BOU (GLOW)
UNDERSTOOD...
PO (SHINE)
CLEAN WATER.
DROPS OF LIFE.
ANCHOR.
JU (HISS)
THANK GOODNESS... THE BLACK WOLVES' MIASMA IS WASHING AWAY.
YOU USE CLEAN WATER IMBUED WITH DROPS OF LIFE TO CLEANSE WOUNDS WITH INFLAMMATION.
ACCORDING TO MY MASTER ANYWAY.
JUU
I'LL WASH THE BRAND TOO.

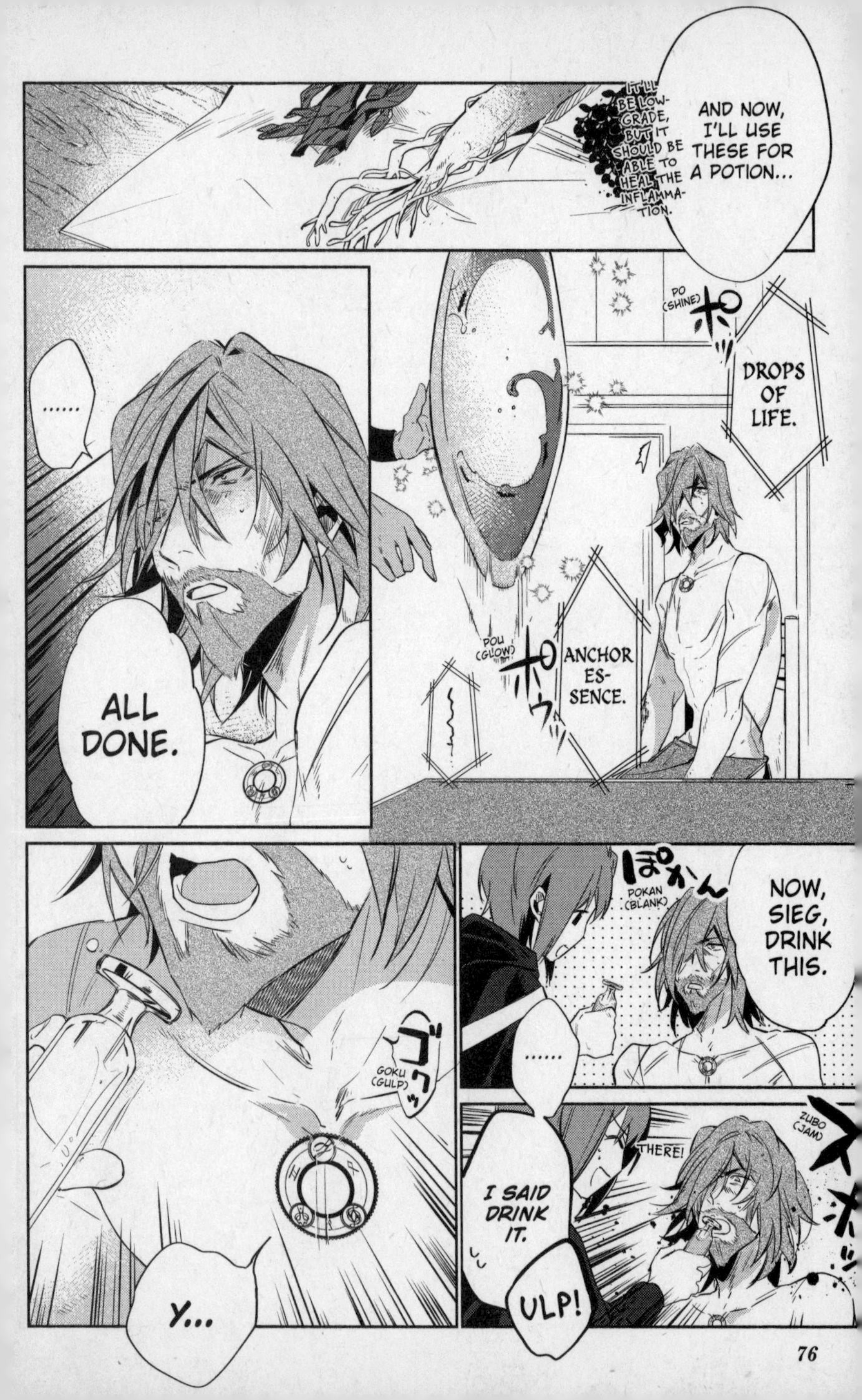
AND NOW, I'LL USE THESE FOR A POTION...
IT'LL BE LOW-GRADE, BUT IT SHOULD BE ABLE TO HEAL THE INFLAMMATION.
PO (SHINE)
DROPS OF LIFE.
POU (GLOW)
ANCHOR ESSENCE.
......
ALL DONE.
ぽかん
POKAN (BLANK)
NOW, SIEG, DRINK THIS.
......
ZUBO (JAM)
THERE!
I SAID DRINK IT.
ULP!
GOKU (GULP)
Y...

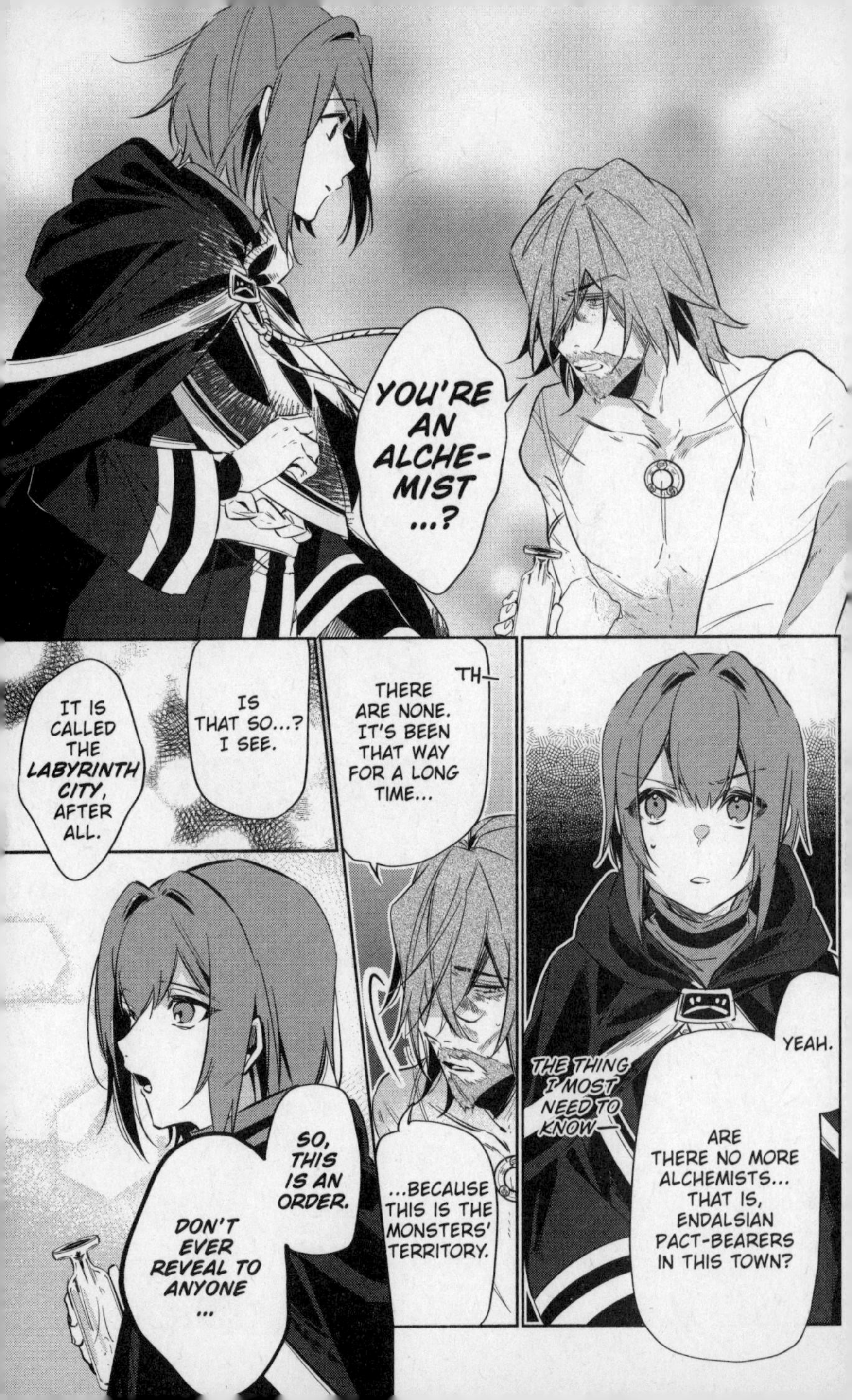
YOU'RE AN ALCHEMIST ...?
YEAH.
THE THING I MOST NEED TO KNOW—
ARE THERE NO MORE ALCHEMISTS... THAT IS, ENDALSIAN PACT-BEARERS IN THIS TOWN?
TH—
THERE ARE NONE. IT'S BEEN THAT WAY FOR A LONG TIME...
IS THAT SO...? I SEE.
IT IS CALLED THE LABYRINTH CITY, AFTER ALL.
...BECAUSE THIS IS THE MONSTERS' TERRITORY.
SO, THIS IS AN ORDER.
DON'T EVER REVEAL TO ANYONE ...

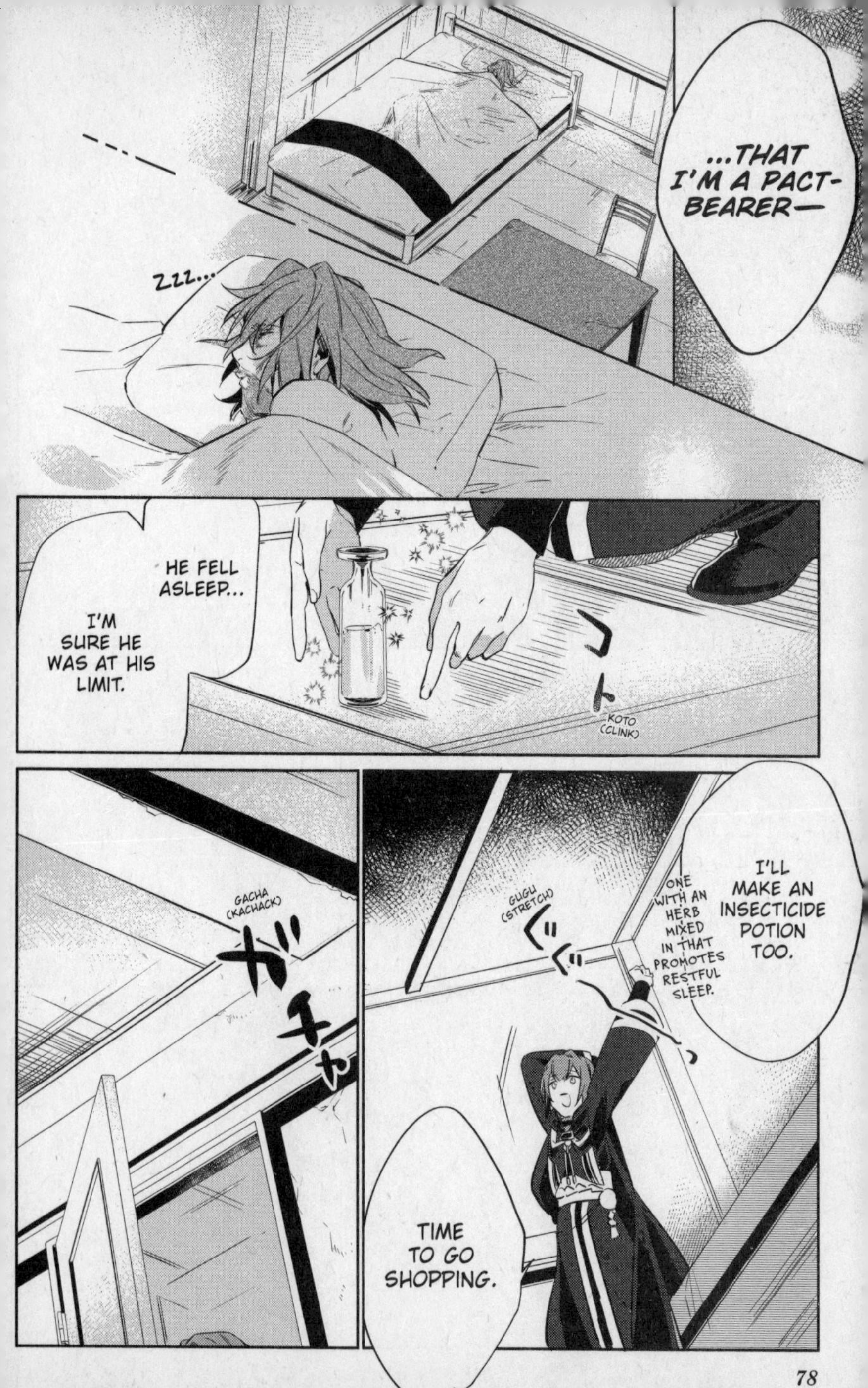
...THAT I'M A PACT-BEARER—
ZZZ...
HE FELL ASLEEP...
I'M SURE HE WAS AT HIS LIMIT.
コト
KOTO (CLINK)
I'LL MAKE AN INSECTICIDE POTION TOO.
ONE WITH AN HERB MIXED IN THAT PROMOTES RESTFUL SLEEP.
ぐぐ
GUGU (STRETCH)
TIME TO GO SHOPPING.
ガチャ
GACHA (KACHACK)

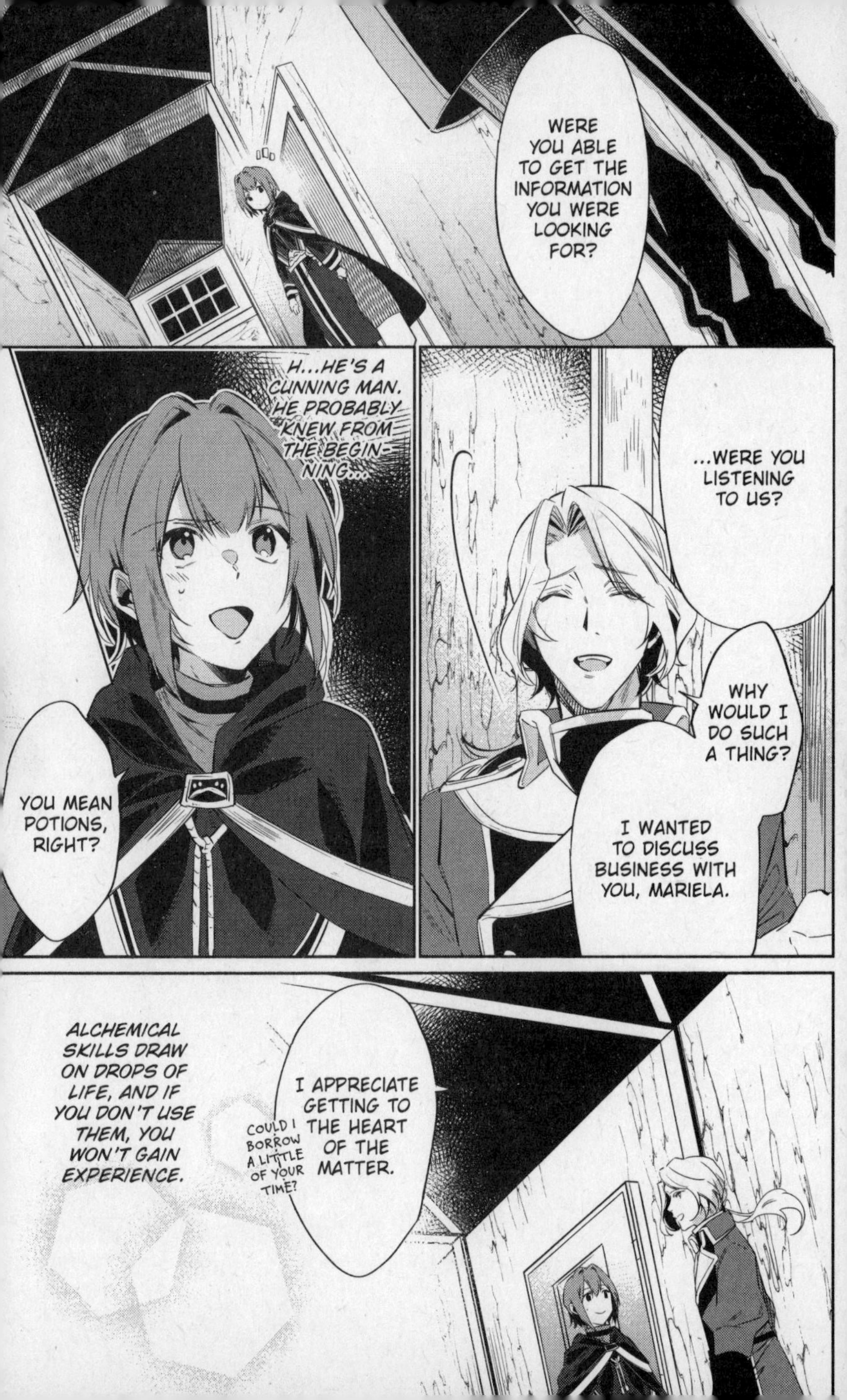
WERE YOU ABLE TO GET THE INFORMATION YOU WERE LOOKING FOR?
...WERE YOU LISTENING TO US?
WHY WOULD I DO SUCH A THING?
I WANTED TO DISCUSS BUSINESS WITH YOU, MARIELA.
H...HE'S A CUNNING MAN. HE PROBABLY KNEW FROM THE BEGIN-NING...
YOU MEAN POTIONS, RIGHT?
I APPRECIATE GETTING TO THE HEART OF THE MATTER.
COULD I BORROW A LITTLE OF YOUR TIME?
ALCHEMICAL SKILLS DRAW ON DROPS OF LIFE, AND IF YOU DON'T USE THEM, YOU WON'T GAIN EXPERIENCE.

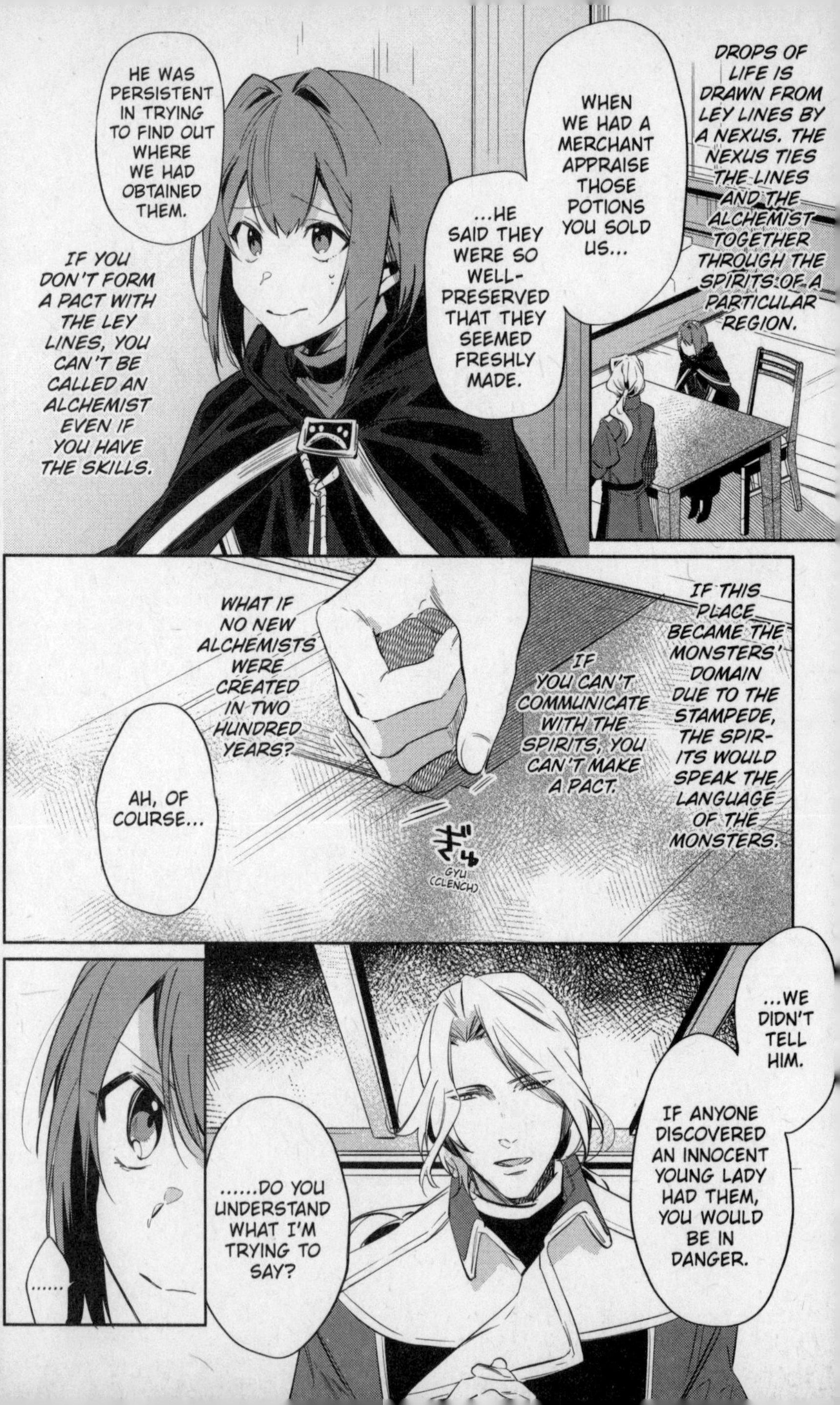
DROPS OF LIFE IS DRAWN FROM LEY LINES BY A NEXUS. THE NEXUS TIES THE LINES AND THE ALCHEMIST TOGETHER THROUGH THE SPIRITS OF A PARTICULAR REGION.
WHEN WE HAD A MERCHANT APPRAISE THOSE POTIONS YOU SOLD US...
...HE SAID THEY WERE SO WELL-PRESERVED THAT THEY SEEMED FRESHLY MADE.
HE WAS PERSISTENT IN TRYING TO FIND OUT WHERE WE HAD OBTAINED THEM.
IF YOU DON'T FORM A PACT WITH THE LEY LINES, YOU CAN'T BE CALLED AN ALCHEMIST EVEN IF YOU HAVE THE SKILLS.
IF THIS PLACE BECAME THE MONSTERS' DOMAIN DUE TO THE STAMPEDE, THE SPIRITS WOULD SPEAK THE LANGUAGE OF THE MONSTERS.
IF YOU CAN'T COMMUNICATE WITH THE SPIRITS, YOU CAN'T MAKE A PACT.
WHAT IF NO NEW ALCHEMISTS WERE CREATED IN TWO HUNDRED YEARS?
AH, OF COURSE...
ぎゅ
GYU (CLENCH)
...WE DIDN'T TELL HIM.
IF ANYONE DISCOVERED AN INNOCENT YOUNG LADY HAD THEM, YOU WOULD BE IN DANGER.
......DO YOU UNDERSTAND WHAT I'M TRYING TO SAY?
......

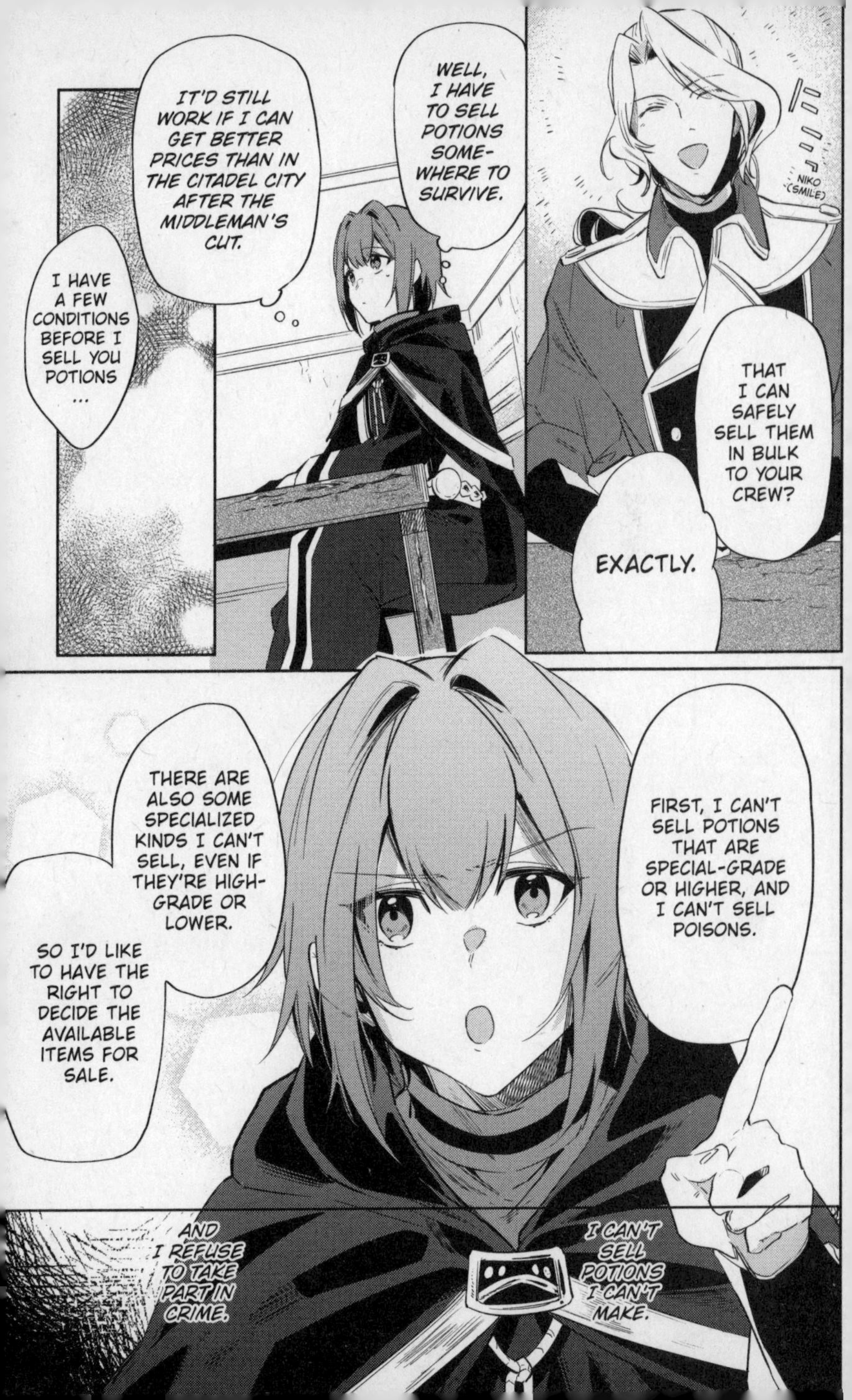
NIKO (SMILE)
THAT I CAN SAFELY SELL THEM IN BULK TO YOUR CREW?
EXACTLY.
WELL, I HAVE TO SELL POTIONS SOME-WHERE TO SURVIVE.
IT'D STILL WORK IF I CAN GET BETTER PRICES THAN IN THE CITADEL CITY AFTER THE MIDDLEMAN'S CUT.
I HAVE A FEW CONDITIONS BEFORE I SELL YOU POTIONS ...
FIRST, I CAN'T SELL POTIONS THAT ARE SPECIAL-GRADE OR HIGHER, AND I CAN'T SELL POISONS.
THERE ARE ALSO SOME SPECIALIZED KINDS I CAN'T SELL, EVEN IF THEY'RE HIGH-GRADE OR LOWER.
SO I'D LIKE TO HAVE THE RIGHT TO DECIDE THE AVAILABLE ITEMS FOR SALE.
I CAN'T SELL POTIONS I CAN'T MAKE.
AND I REFUSE TO TAKE PART IN CRIME.

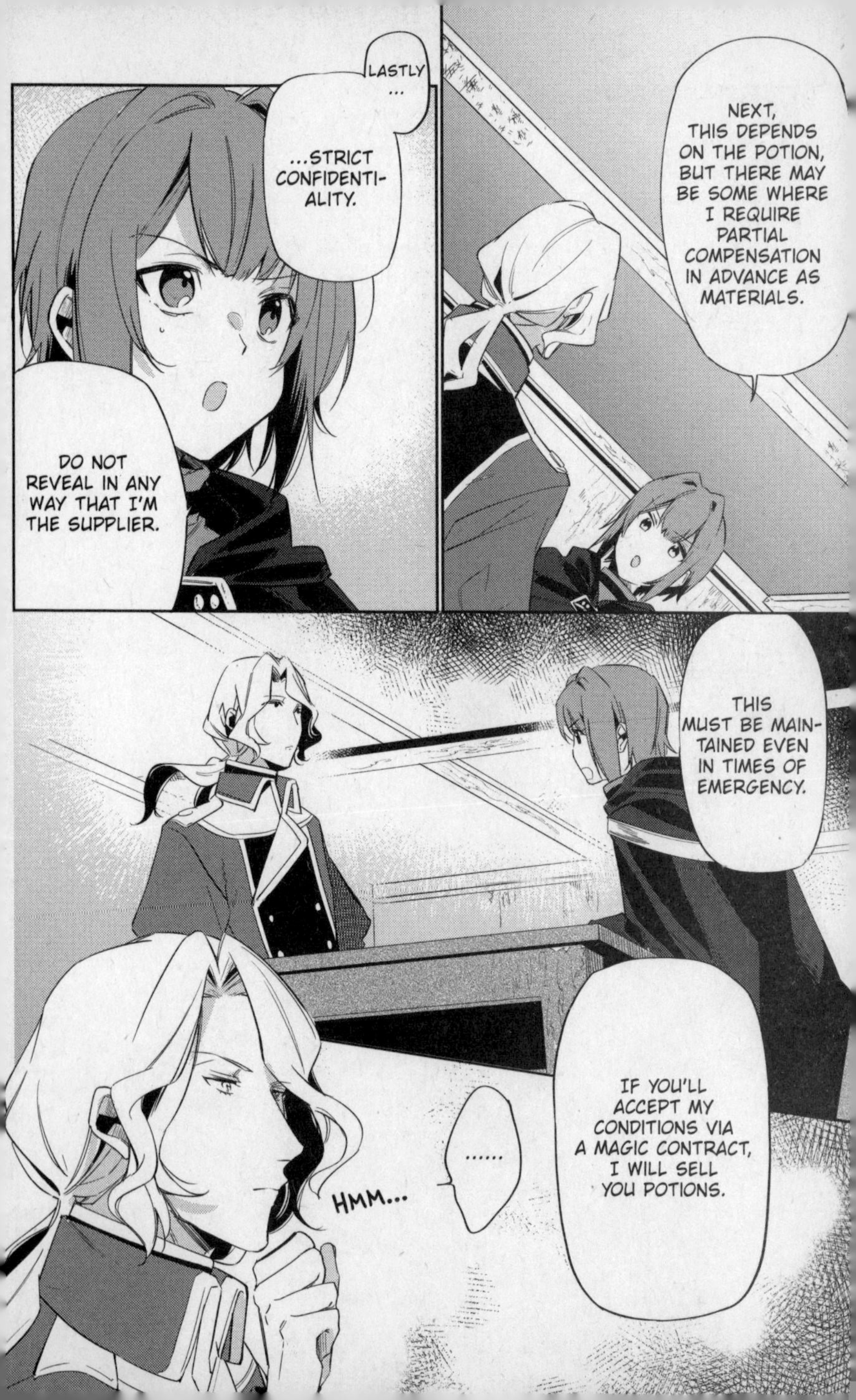
NEXT, THIS DEPENDS ON THE POTION, BUT THERE MAY BE SOME WHERE I REQUIRE PARTIAL COMPENSATION IN ADVANCE AS MATERIALS.
LASTLY...
...STRICT CONFIDENTIALITY.
DO NOT REVEAL IN ANY WAY THAT I'M THE SUPPLIER.
THIS MUST BE MAINTAINED EVEN IN TIMES OF EMERGENCY.
IF YOU'LL ACCEPT MY CONDITIONS VIA A MAGIC CONTRACT, I WILL SELL YOU POTIONS.
......
HMM...

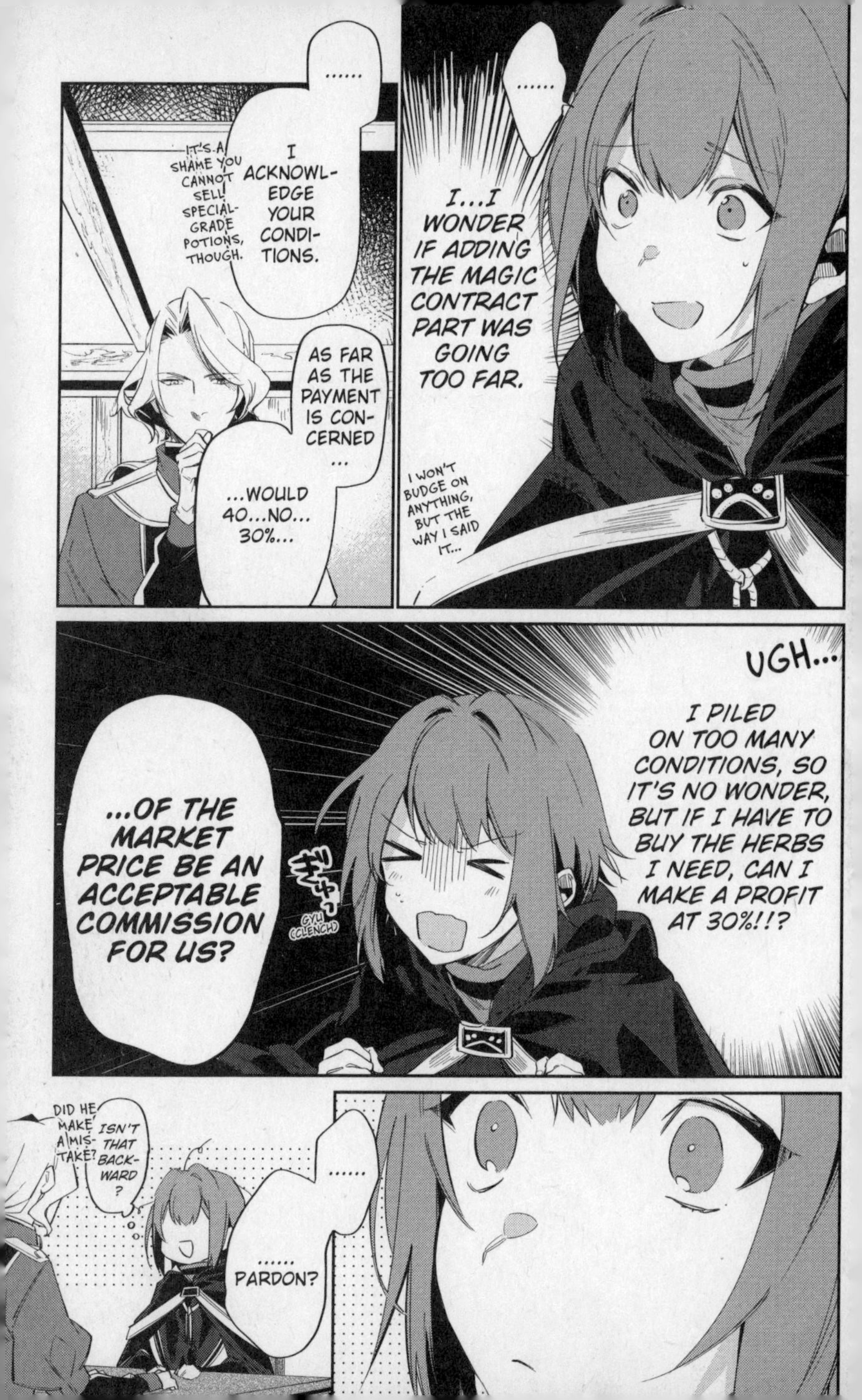
......
I...I WONDER IF ADDING THE MAGIC CONTRACT PART WAS GOING TOO FAR.
I WON'T BUDGE ON ANYTHING, BUT THE WAY I SAID IT...
......
I ACKNOWLEDGE YOUR CONDITIONS.
IT'S A SHAME YOU CANNOT SELL SPECIAL-GRADE POTIONS, THOUGH.
AS FAR AS THE PAYMENT IS CONCERNED...
...WOULD 40...NO... 30%...
UGH...
I PILED ON TOO MANY CONDITIONS, SO IT'S NO WONDER, BUT IF I HAVE TO BUY THE HERBS I NEED, CAN I MAKE A PROFIT AT 30%!!?
...OF THE MARKET PRICE BE AN ACCEPTABLE COMMISSION FOR US?
ぎゅっ
GYU (CLENCH)
......
...... PARDON?
ISN'T THAT BACKWARD?
DID HE MAKE A MISTAKE?

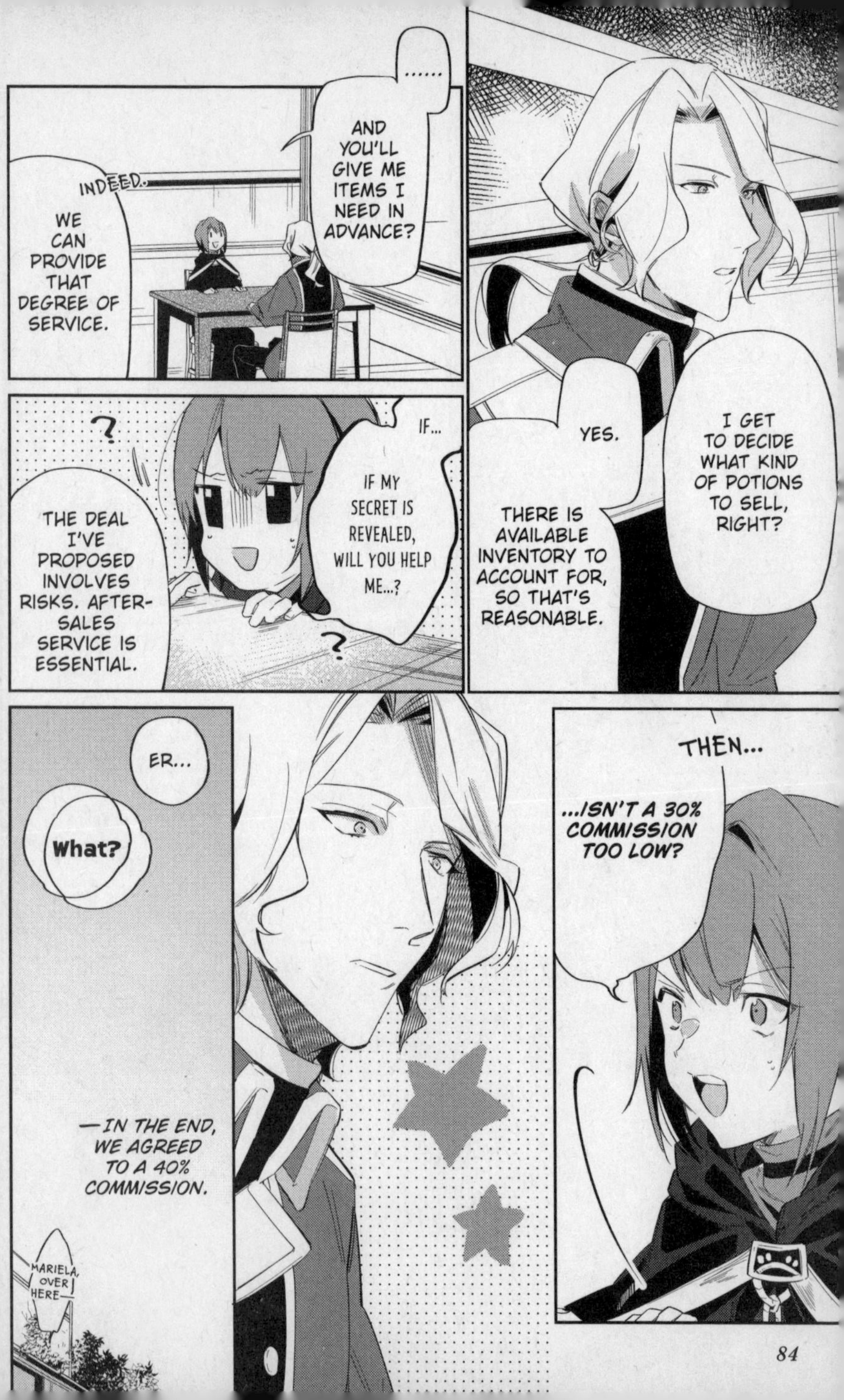
I GET TO DECIDE WHAT KIND OF POTIONS TO SELL, RIGHT?
YES.
THERE IS AVAILABLE INVENTORY TO ACCOUNT FOR, SO THAT'S REASONABLE.
......
AND YOU'LL GIVE ME ITEMS I NEED IN ADVANCE?
INDEED.
WE CAN PROVIDE THAT DEGREE OF SERVICE.
IF...
IF MY SECRET IS REVEALED, WILL YOU HELP ME...?
THE DEAL I'VE PROPOSED INVOLVES RISKS. AFTER-SALES SERVICE IS ESSENTIAL.
THEN...
...ISN'T A 30% COMMISSION TOO LOW?
ER...
What?
—IN THE END, WE AGREED TO A 40% COMMISSION.
MARIELA, OVER HERE—

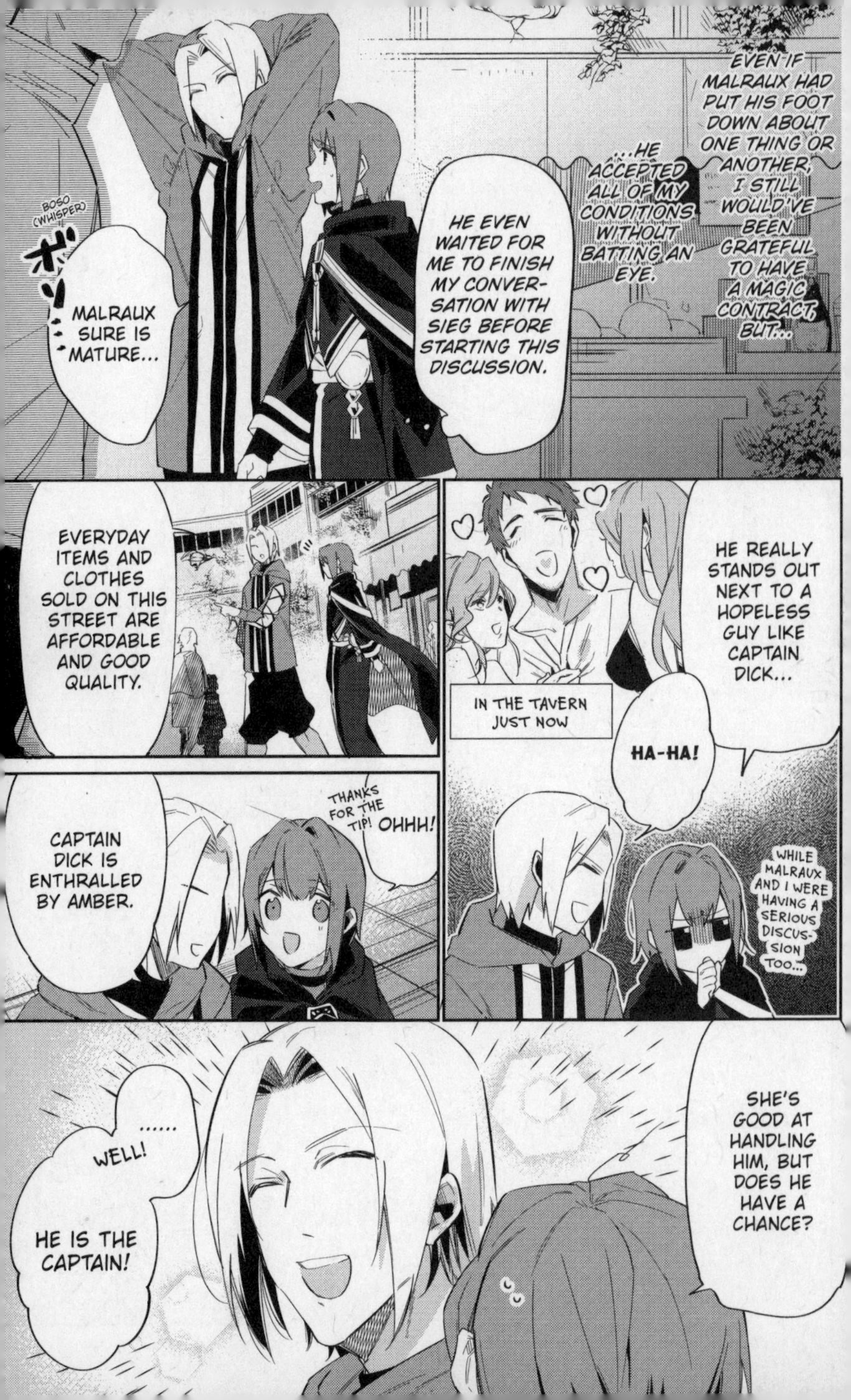
EVEN IF MALRAUX HAD PUT HIS FOOT DOWN ABOUT ONE THING OR ANOTHER, I STILL WOULD'VE BEEN GRATEFUL TO HAVE A MAGIC CONTRACT, BUT...
...HE ACCEPTED ALL OF MY CONDITIONS WITHOUT BATTING AN EYE.
HE EVEN WAITED FOR ME TO FINISH MY CONVER-SATION WITH SIEG BEFORE STARTING THIS DISCUSSION.
BOSO (WHISPER)
MALRAUX SURE IS MATURE...
HE REALLY STANDS OUT NEXT TO A HOPELESS GUY LIKE CAPTAIN DICK...
IN THE TAVERN JUST NOW
HA-HA!
WHILE MALRAUX AND I WERE HAVING A SERIOUS DISCUS-SION TOO...
EVERYDAY ITEMS AND CLOTHES SOLD ON THIS STREET ARE AFFORDABLE AND GOOD QUALITY.
OHHH!
THANKS FOR THE TIP!
CAPTAIN DICK IS ENTHRALLED BY AMBER.
SHE'S GOOD AT HANDLING HIM, BUT DOES HE HAVE A CHANCE?
......
WELL!
HE IS THE CAPTAIN!

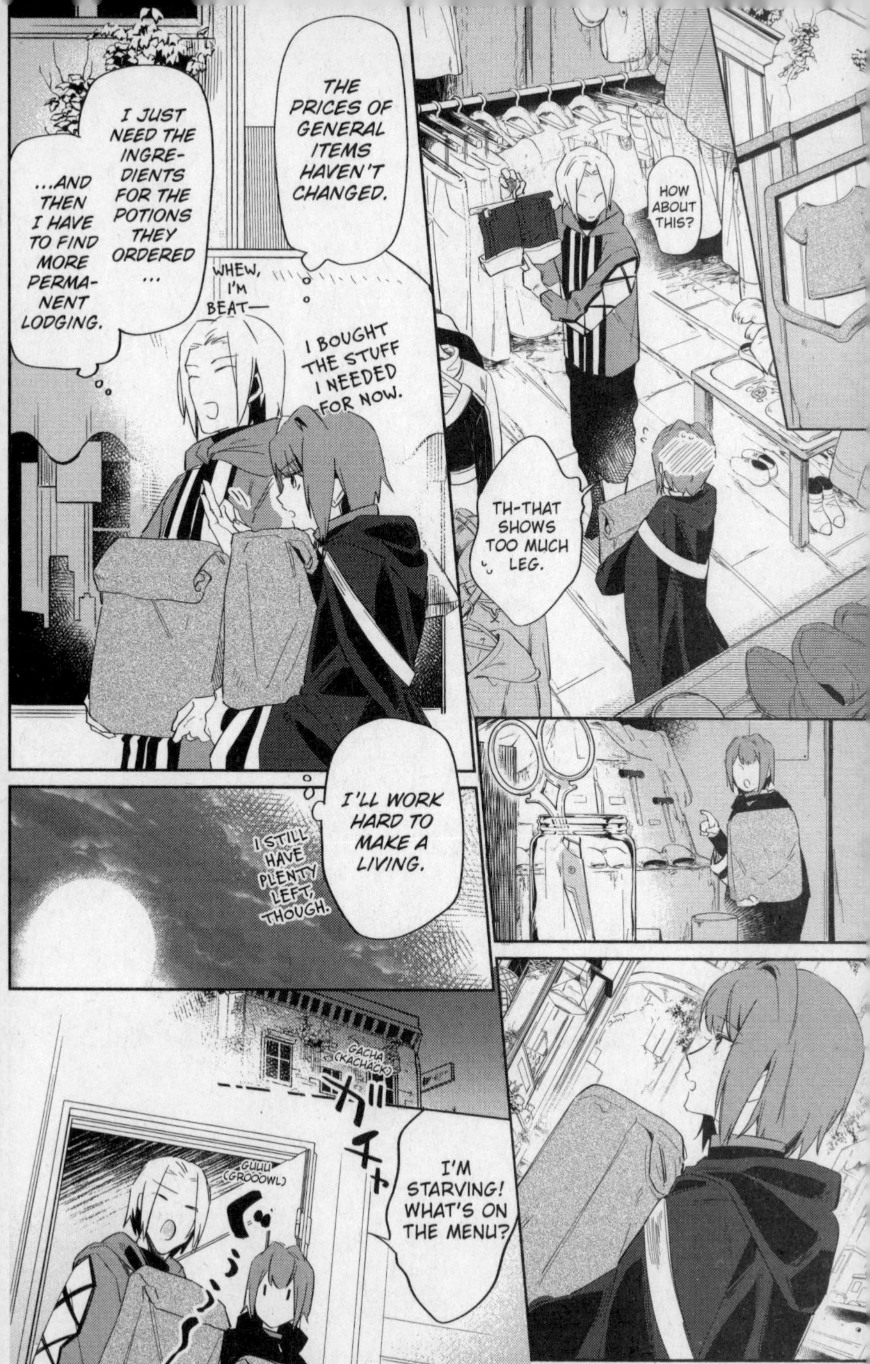
HOW ABOUT THIS?
TH-THAT SHOWS TOO MUCH LEG.
THE PRICES OF GENERAL ITEMS HAVEN'T CHANGED.
I JUST NEED THE INGREDIENTS FOR THE POTIONS THEY ORDERED...
...AND THEN I HAVE TO FIND MORE PERMANENT LODGING.
WHEW, I'M BEAT—
I BOUGHT THE STUFF I NEEDED FOR NOW.
I'LL WORK HARD TO MAKE A LIVING.
I STILL HAVE PLENTY LEFT, THOUGH.
GACHA (KACHACK)
I'M STARVING! WHAT'S ON THE MENU?
GUUU (GROOOWL)

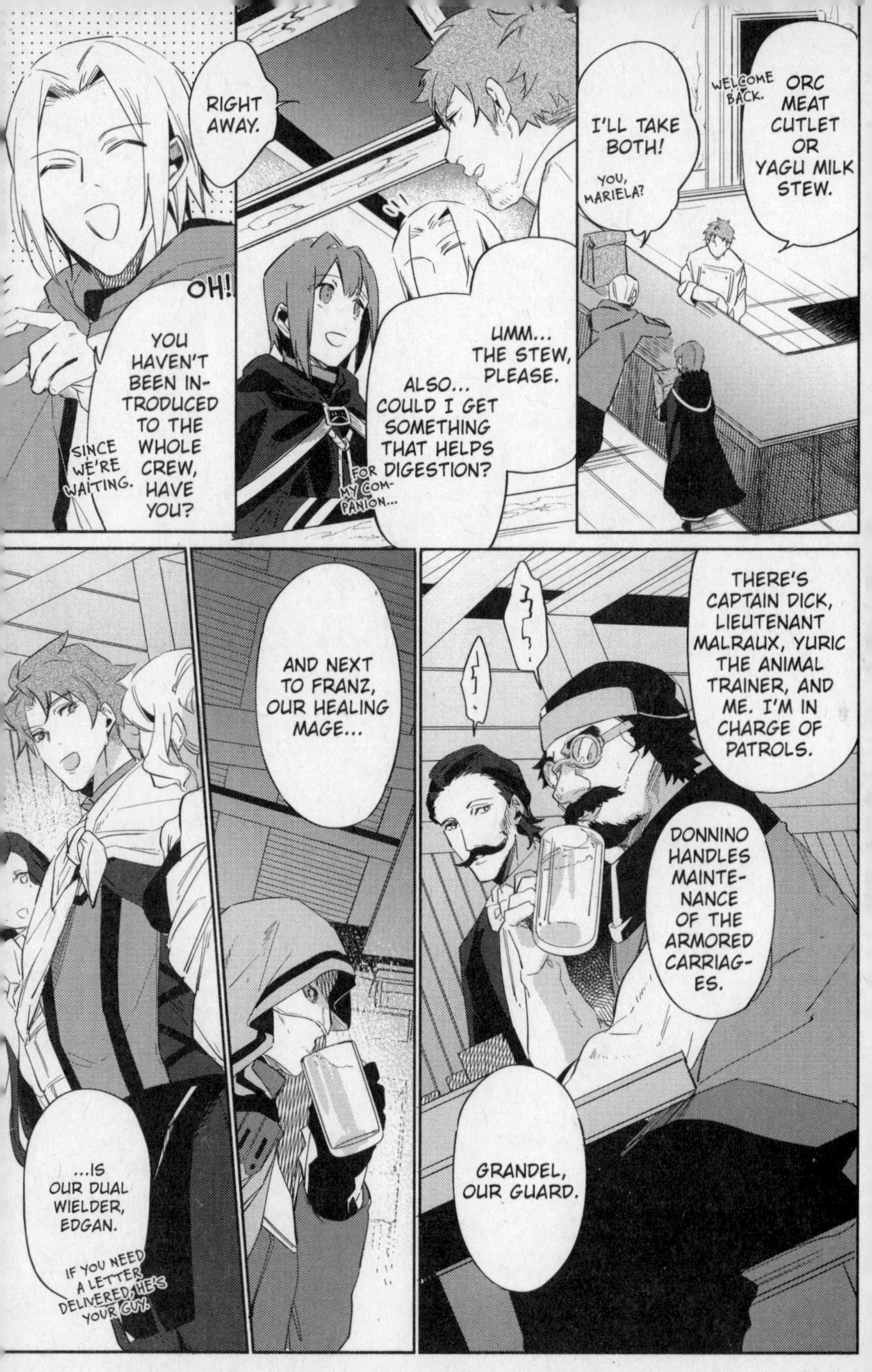
WELCOME BACK.
ORC MEAT CUTLET OR YAGU MILK STEW.
I'LL TAKE BOTH!
YOU, MARIELA?
UMM... THE STEW, PLEASE.
ALSO... COULD I GET SOMETHING THAT HELPS DIGESTION?
FOR MY COMPANION...
RIGHT AWAY.
OH!
YOU HAVEN'T BEEN INTRODUCED TO THE WHOLE CREW, HAVE YOU?
SINCE WE'RE WAITING.
THERE'S CAPTAIN DICK, LIEUTENANT MALRAUX, YURIC THE ANIMAL TRAINER, AND ME. I'M IN CHARGE OF PATROLS.
DONNINO HANDLES MAINTENANCE OF THE ARMORED CARRIAGES.
GRANDEL, OUR GUARD.
AND NEXT TO FRANZ, OUR HEALING MAGE...
...IS OUR DUAL WIELDER, EDGAN.
IF YOU NEED A LETTER DELIVERED, HE'S YOUR GUY.

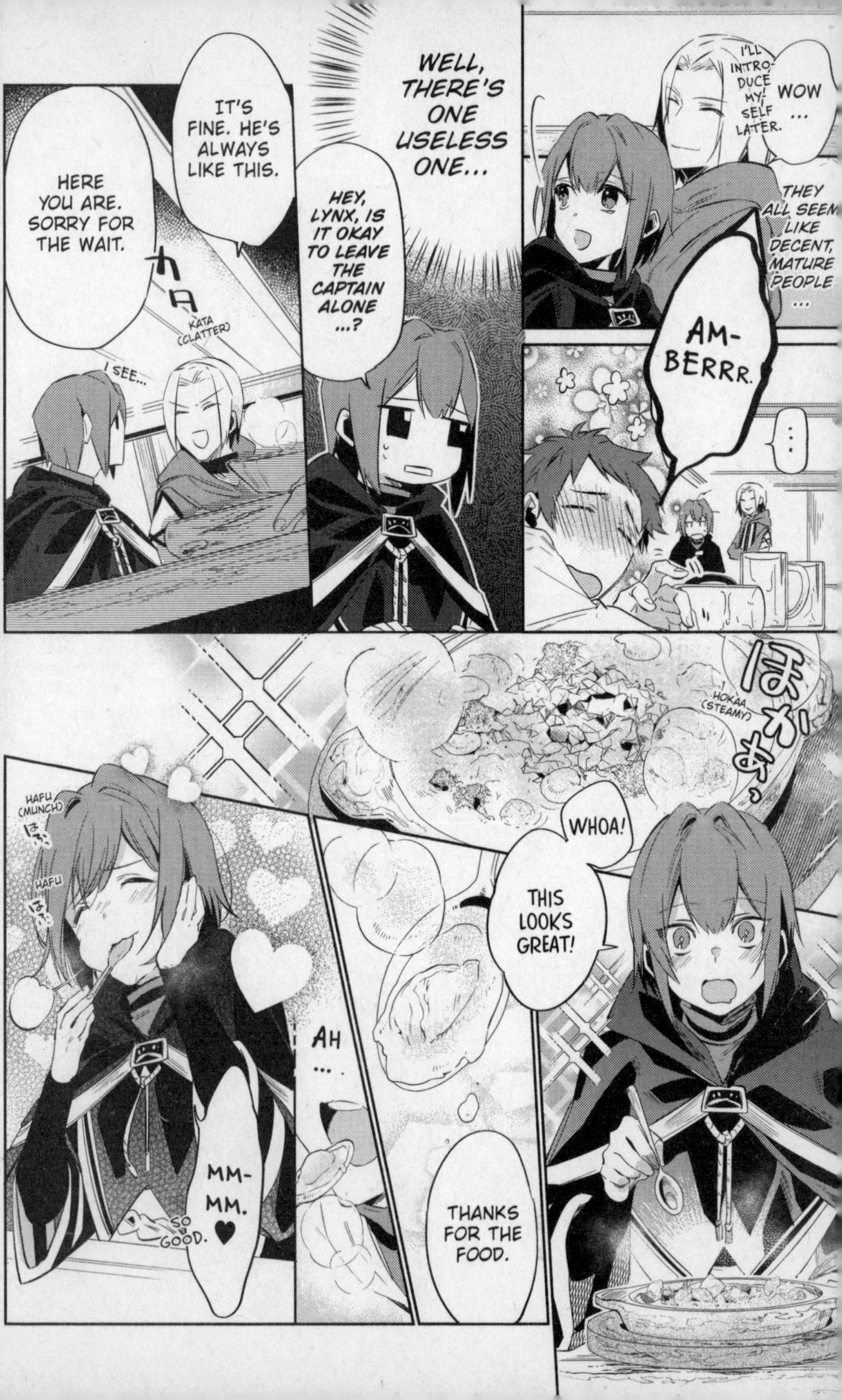

I'LL INTRODUCE MYSELF LATER.
WOW ...
THEY ALL SEEM LIKE DECENT, MATURE PEOPLE ...
AM-BERRR.
...
WELL, THERE'S ONE USELESS ONE...
HEY, LYNX, IS IT OKAY TO LEAVE THE CAPTAIN ALONE ...?
IT'S FINE. HE'S ALWAYS LIKE THIS.
I SEE...
カタ
KATA (CLATTER)
HERE YOU ARE. SORRY FOR THE WAIT.
ほかぁ
HOKAA (STEAMY)
WHOA!
THIS LOOKS GREAT!
THANKS FOR THE FOOD.
AH ...
HAFU (MUNCH) はふ
HAFU はふ
MM-MM. ♥
SO GOOD.

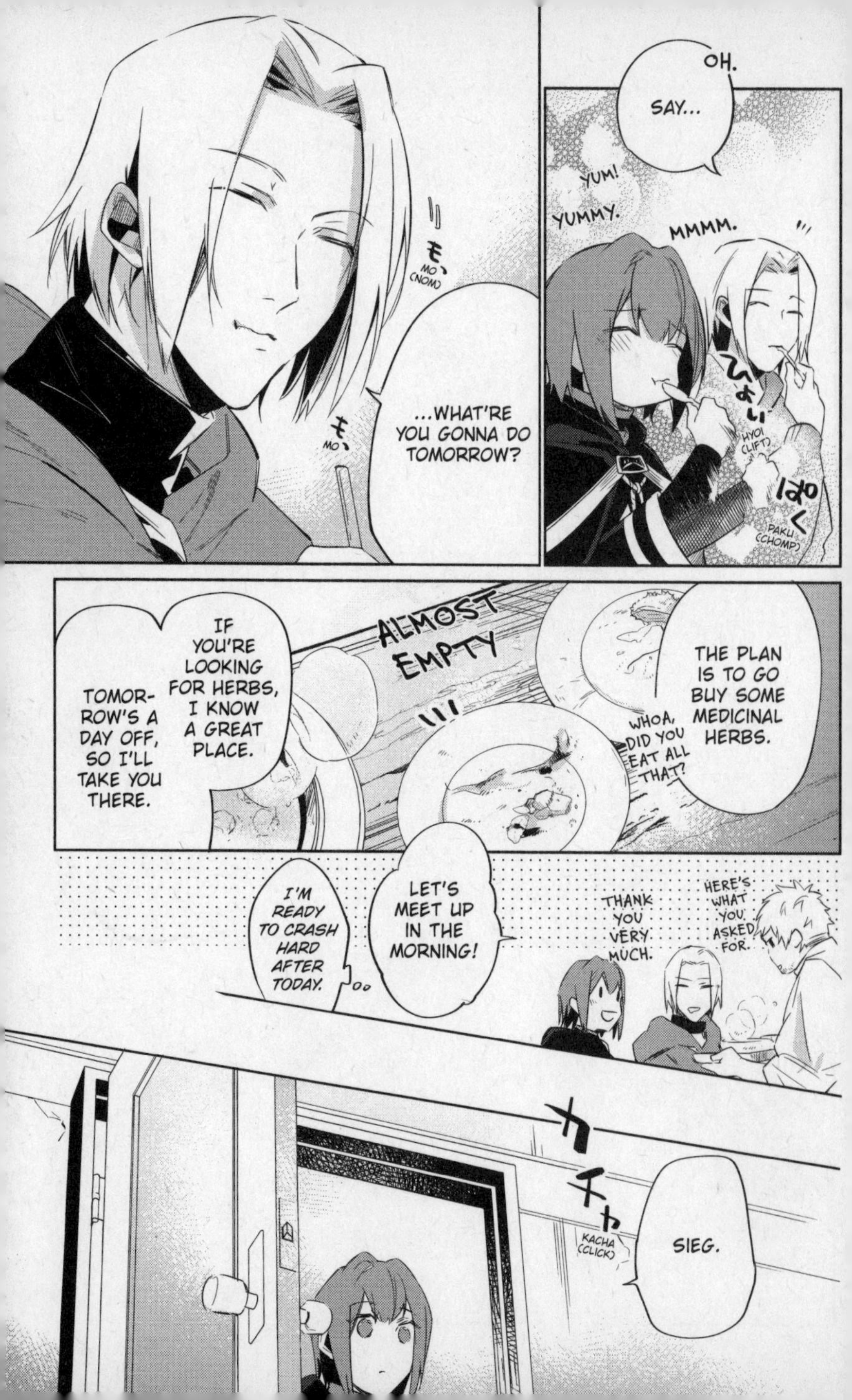
OH.
SAY...
YUM!
YUMMY.
MMMM.
ひょい
HYOI (LIFT)
ぱく
PAKU (CHOMP)
も
MO (NOM)
も
MO
...WHAT'RE YOU GONNA DO TOMORROW?
THE PLAN IS TO GO BUY SOME MEDICINAL HERBS.
WHOA, DID YOU EAT ALL THAT?
ALMOST EMPTY
IF YOU'RE LOOKING FOR HERBS, I KNOW A GREAT PLACE.
TOMORROW'S A DAY OFF, SO I'LL TAKE YOU THERE.
HERE'S WHAT YOU ASKED FOR.
THANK YOU VERY MUCH.
LET'S MEET UP IN THE MORNING!
I'M READY TO CRASH HARD AFTER TODAY.
カチャ
KACHA (CLICK)
SIEG.

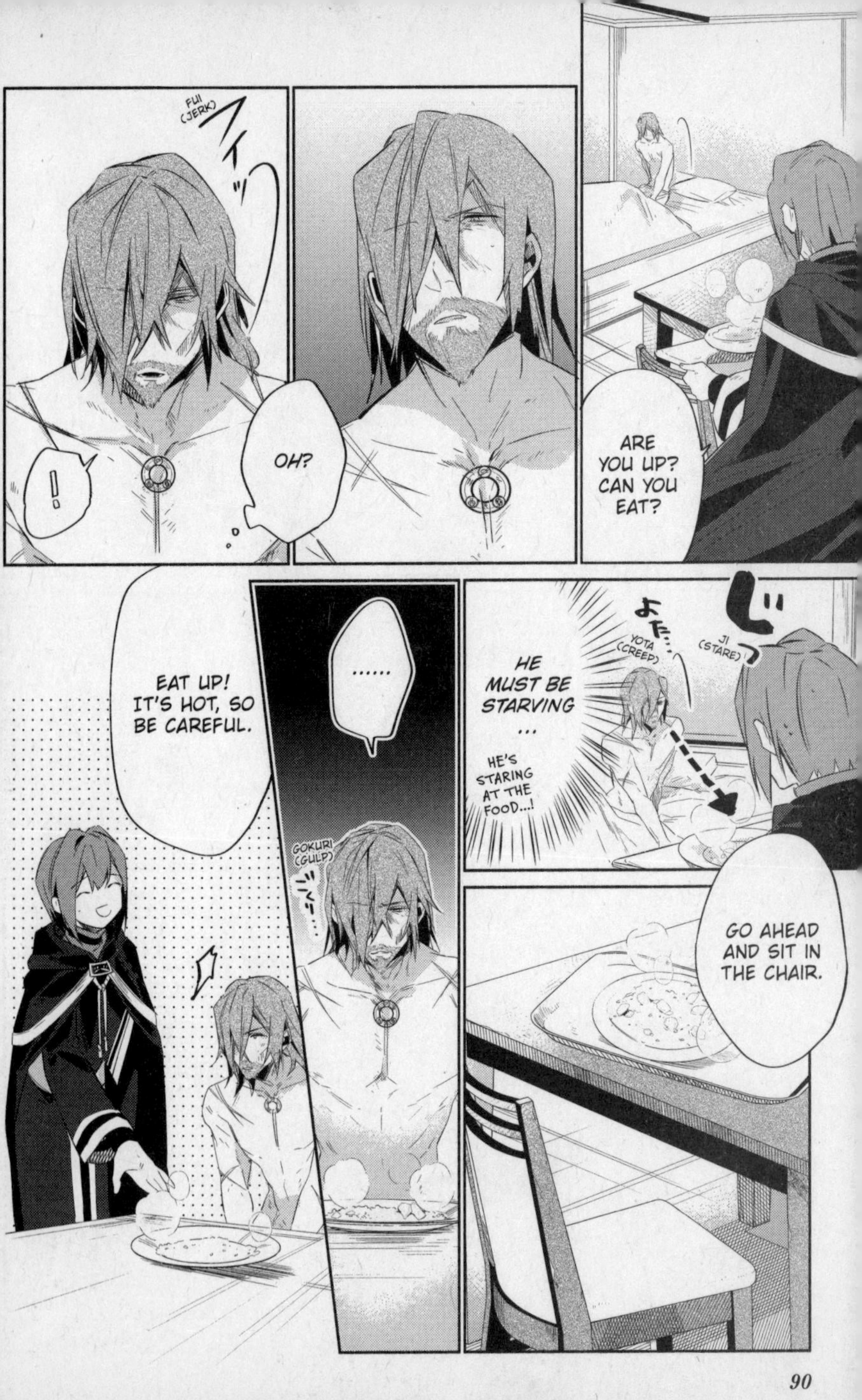
ARE YOU UP? CAN YOU EAT?
OH?
FUI (JERK)
!
JI (STARE)
YOTA (CREEP)
HE MUST BE STARVING...
HE'S STARING AT THE FOOD...!
GO AHEAD AND SIT IN THE CHAIR.
......
GOKURI (GULP)
EAT UP! IT'S HOT, SO BE CAREFUL.

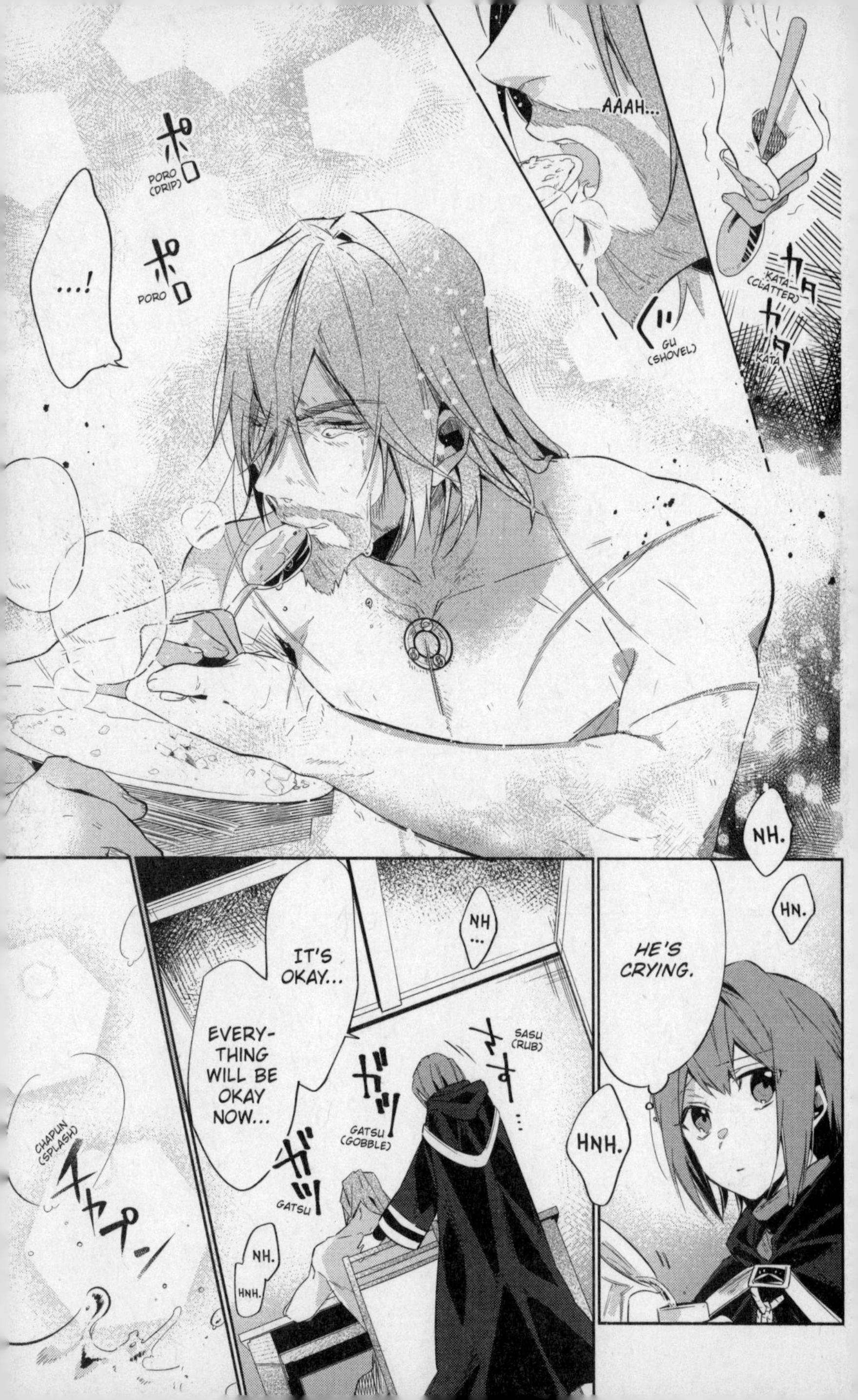
AAAH...
KATA (CLATTER)
KATA
GU (SHOVEL)
PORO (DRIP)
PORO
...!
NH.
HN.
HE'S CRYING.
HNH.
NH ...
IT'S OKAY...
EVERY-THING WILL BE OKAY NOW...
SASU (RUB)
GATSU (GOBBLE)
GATSU
NH.
HNH.
CHAPUN (SPLASH)

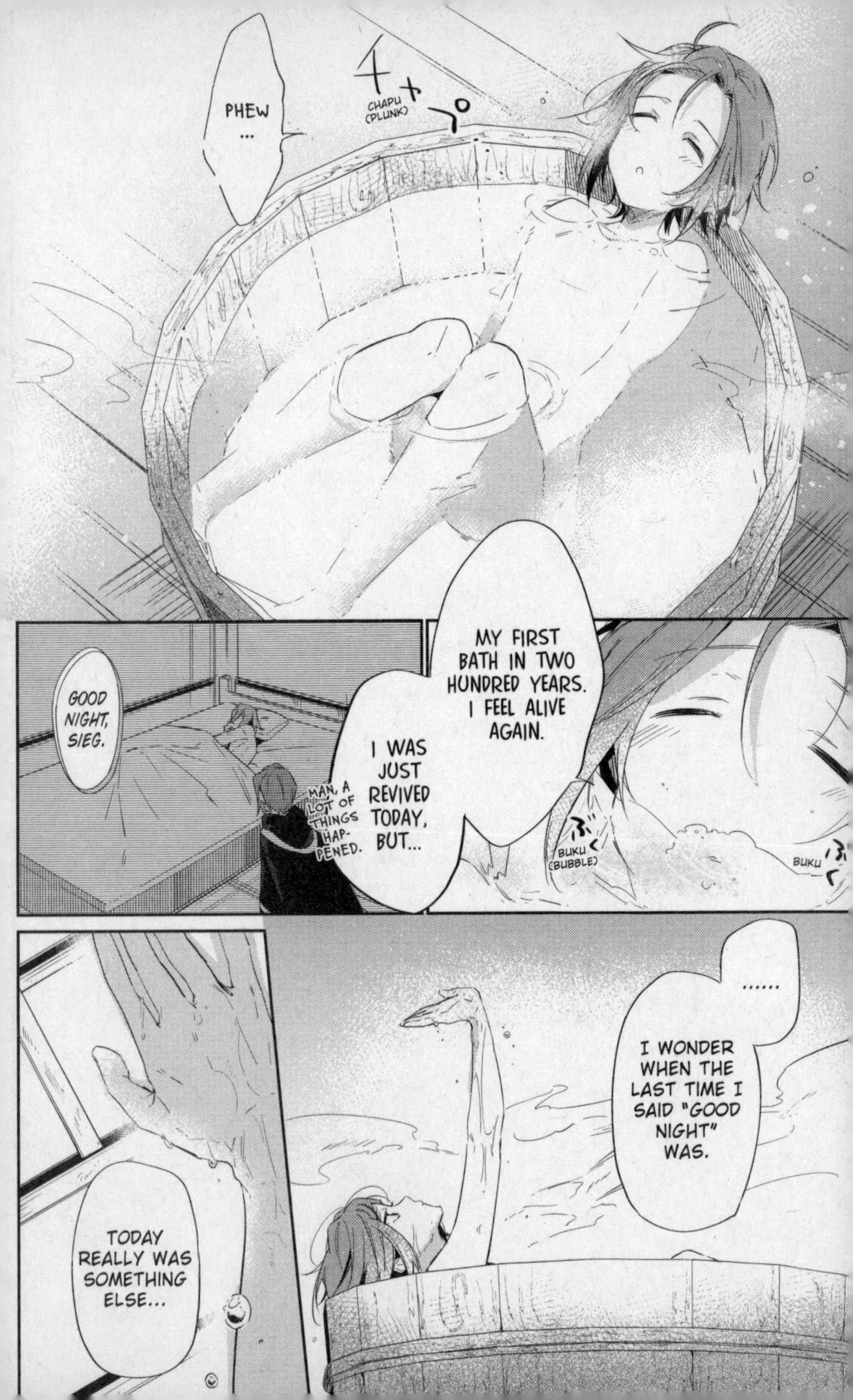
PHEW...
CHAPU (PLUNK)
MY FIRST BATH IN TWO HUNDRED YEARS. I FEEL ALIVE AGAIN.
BUKU (BUBBLE)
BUKU
I WAS JUST REVIVED TODAY, BUT...
MAN, A LOT OF THINGS HAP-PENED.
GOOD NIGHT, SIEG.
......
I WONDER WHEN THE LAST TIME I SAID "GOOD NIGHT" WAS.
TODAY REALLY WAS SOMETHING ELSE...

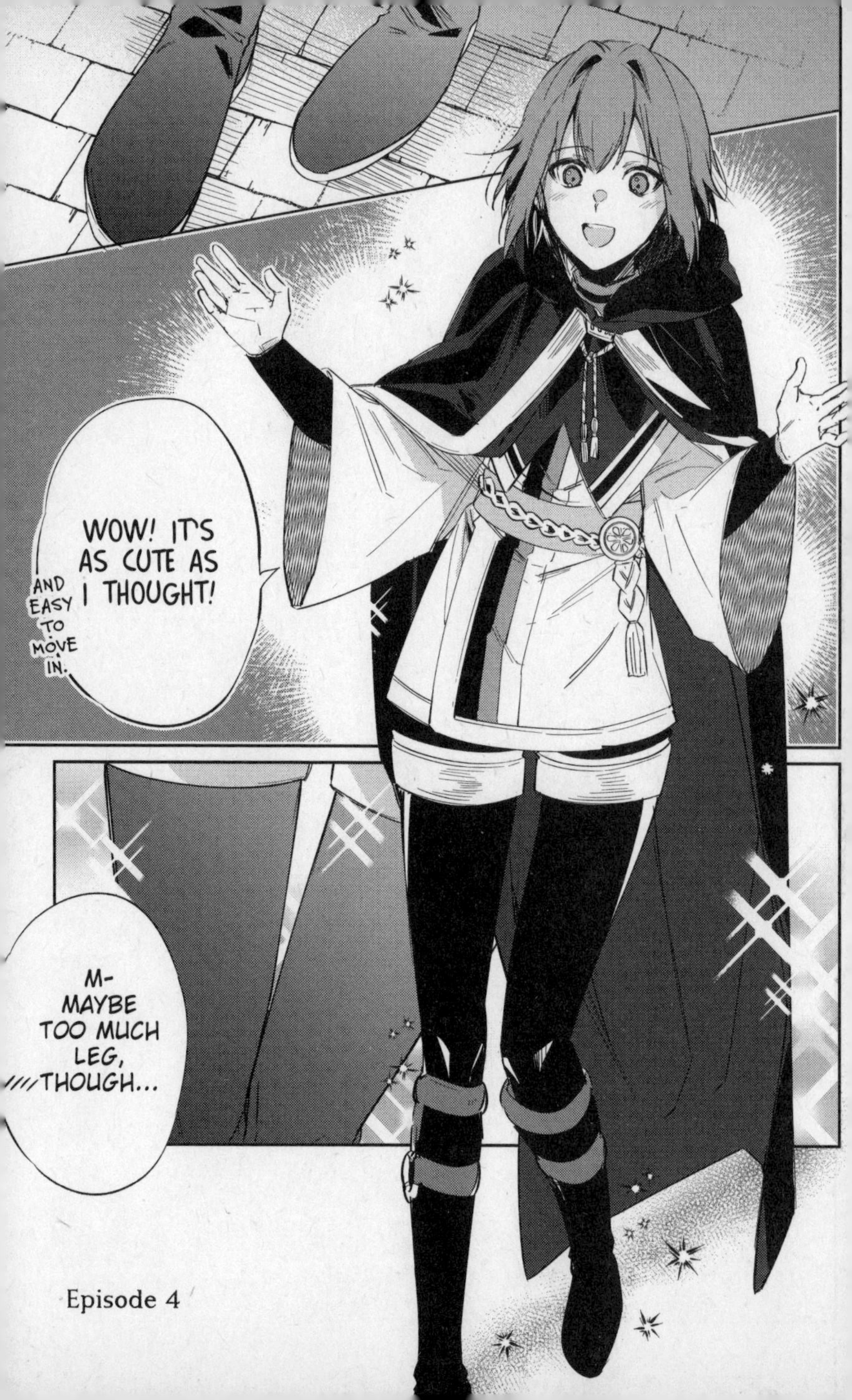
WOW! IT'S AS CUTE AS I THOUGHT!
AND EASY TO MOVE IN.
M-MAYBE TOO MUCH LEG, THOUGH...

Episode 4

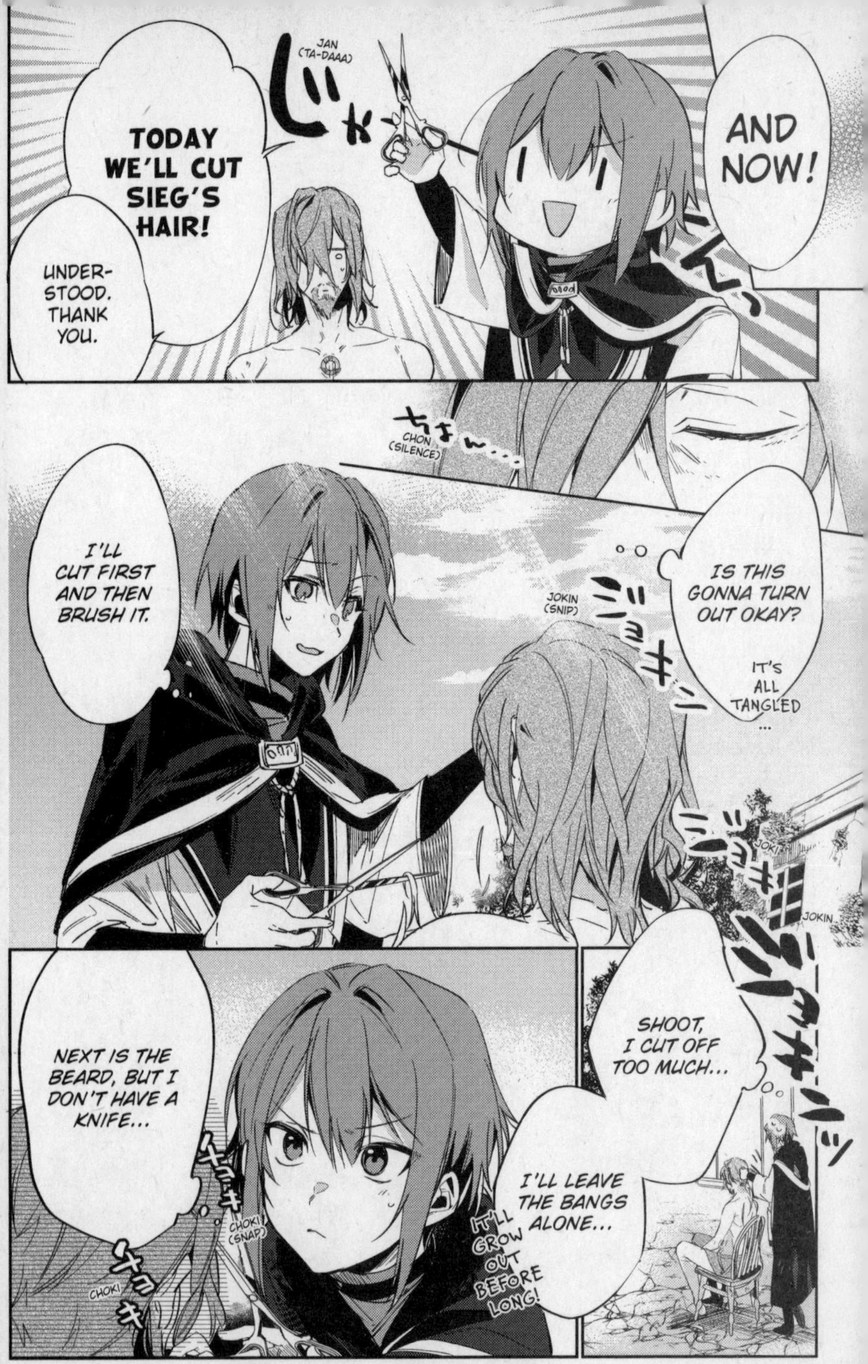
AND NOW!
JAN (TA-DAAA)
TODAY WE'LL CUT SIEG'S HAIR!
UNDER-STOOD. THANK YOU.
CHON (SILENCE)
IS THIS GONNA TURN OUT OKAY?
IT'S ALL TANGLED...
JOKIN (SNIP)
I'LL CUT FIRST AND THEN BRUSH IT.
JOKI
JOKIN
SHOOT, I CUT OFF TOO MUCH...
I'LL LEAVE THE BANGS ALONE...
IT'LL GROW OUT BEFORE LONG!
NEXT IS THE BEARD, BUT I DON'T HAVE A KNIFE...
CHOKI (SNAP)
CHOKI

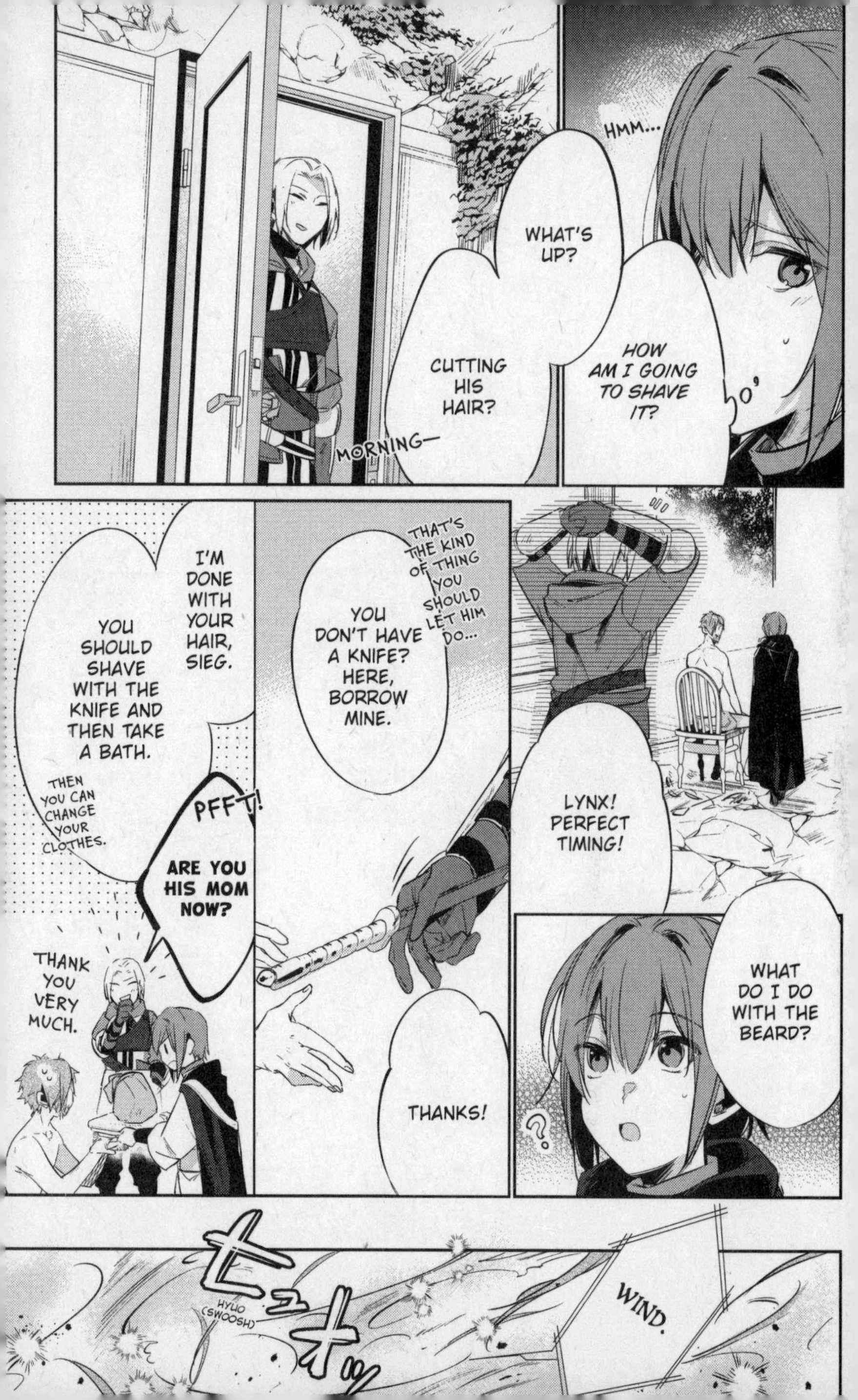
HMM...
HOW AM I GOING TO SHAVE IT?
WHAT'S UP?
CUTTING HIS HAIR?
MORNING—
LYNX! PERFECT TIMING!
WHAT DO I DO WITH THE BEARD?
THAT'S THE KIND OF THING YOU SHOULD LET HIM DO...
YOU DON'T HAVE A KNIFE? HERE, BORROW MINE.
THANKS!
I'M DONE WITH YOUR HAIR, SIEG.
YOU SHOULD SHAVE WITH THE KNIFE AND THEN TAKE A BATH.
THEN YOU CAN CHANGE YOUR CLOTHES.
PFFT!
ARE YOU HIS MOM NOW?
THANK YOU VERY MUCH.
WIND.
HYUO (SWOOSH)

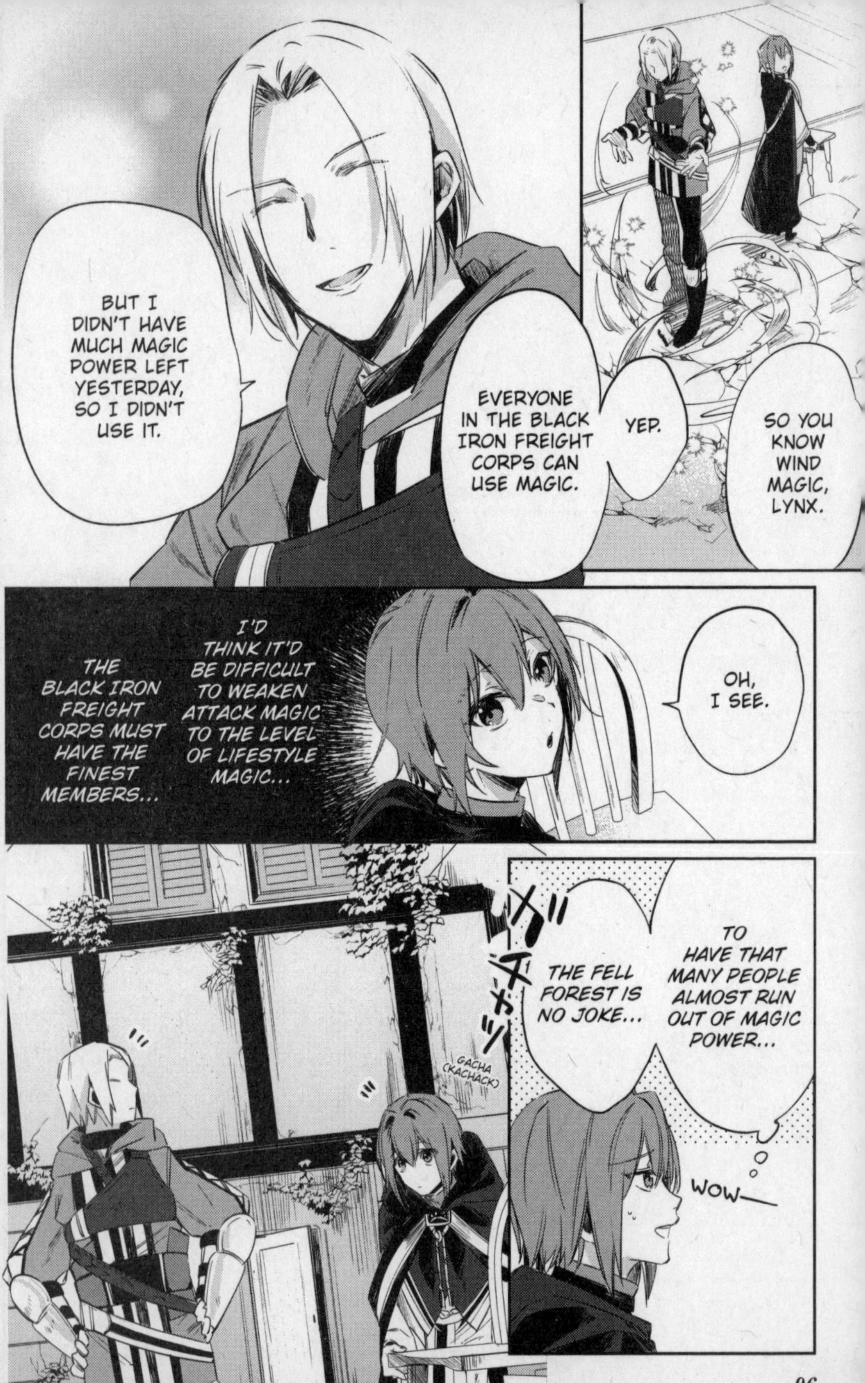
SO YOU KNOW WIND MAGIC, LYNX.
YEP.
EVERYONE IN THE BLACK IRON FREIGHT CORPS CAN USE MAGIC.
BUT I DIDN'T HAVE MUCH MAGIC POWER LEFT YESTERDAY, SO I DIDN'T USE IT.
OH, I SEE.
I'D THINK IT'D BE DIFFICULT TO WEAKEN ATTACK MAGIC TO THE LEVEL OF LIFESTYLE MAGIC...
THE BLACK IRON FREIGHT CORPS MUST HAVE THE FINEST MEMBERS...
TO HAVE THAT MANY PEOPLE ALMOST RUN OUT OF MAGIC POWER...
THE FELL FOREST IS NO JOKE...
WOW—
GACHA (KACHACK)

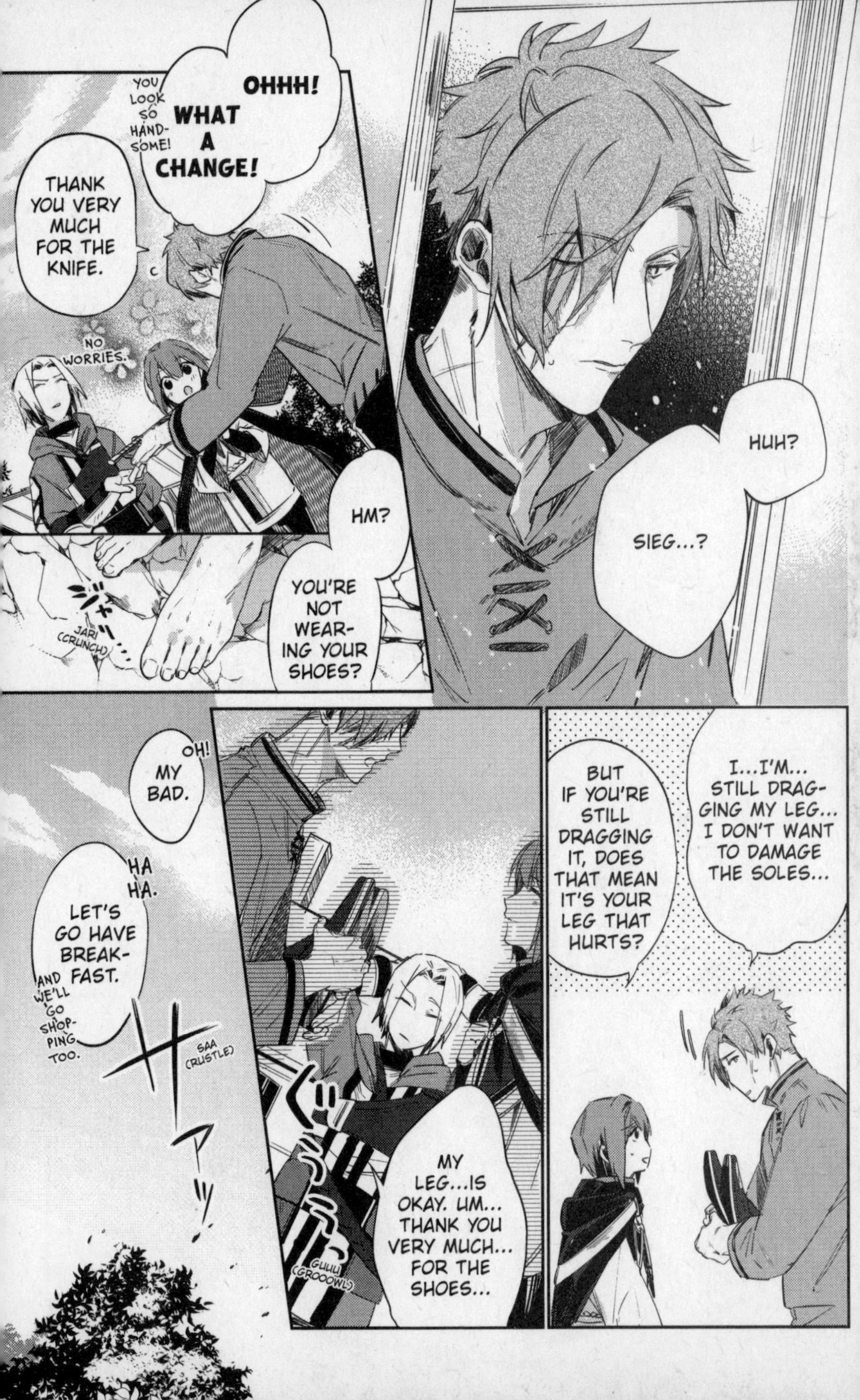
HUH?
SIEG...?
OHHH! WHAT A CHANGE!
YOU LOOK SO HAND-SOME!
THANK YOU VERY MUCH FOR THE KNIFE.
NO WORRIES.
HM?
YOU'RE NOT WEAR-ING YOUR SHOES?
JARI (CRUNCH)
I...I'M... STILL DRAG-GING MY LEG... I DON'T WANT TO DAMAGE THE SOLES...
BUT IF YOU'RE STILL DRAGGING IT, DOES THAT MEAN IT'S YOUR LEG THAT HURTS?
MY LEG...IS OKAY. UM... THANK YOU VERY MUCH... FOR THE SHOES...
GUUU (GROOOWL)
OH! MY BAD.
HA HA.
LET'S GO HAVE BREAK-FAST.
AND WE'LL GO SHOP-PING TOO.
SAA (RUSTLE)

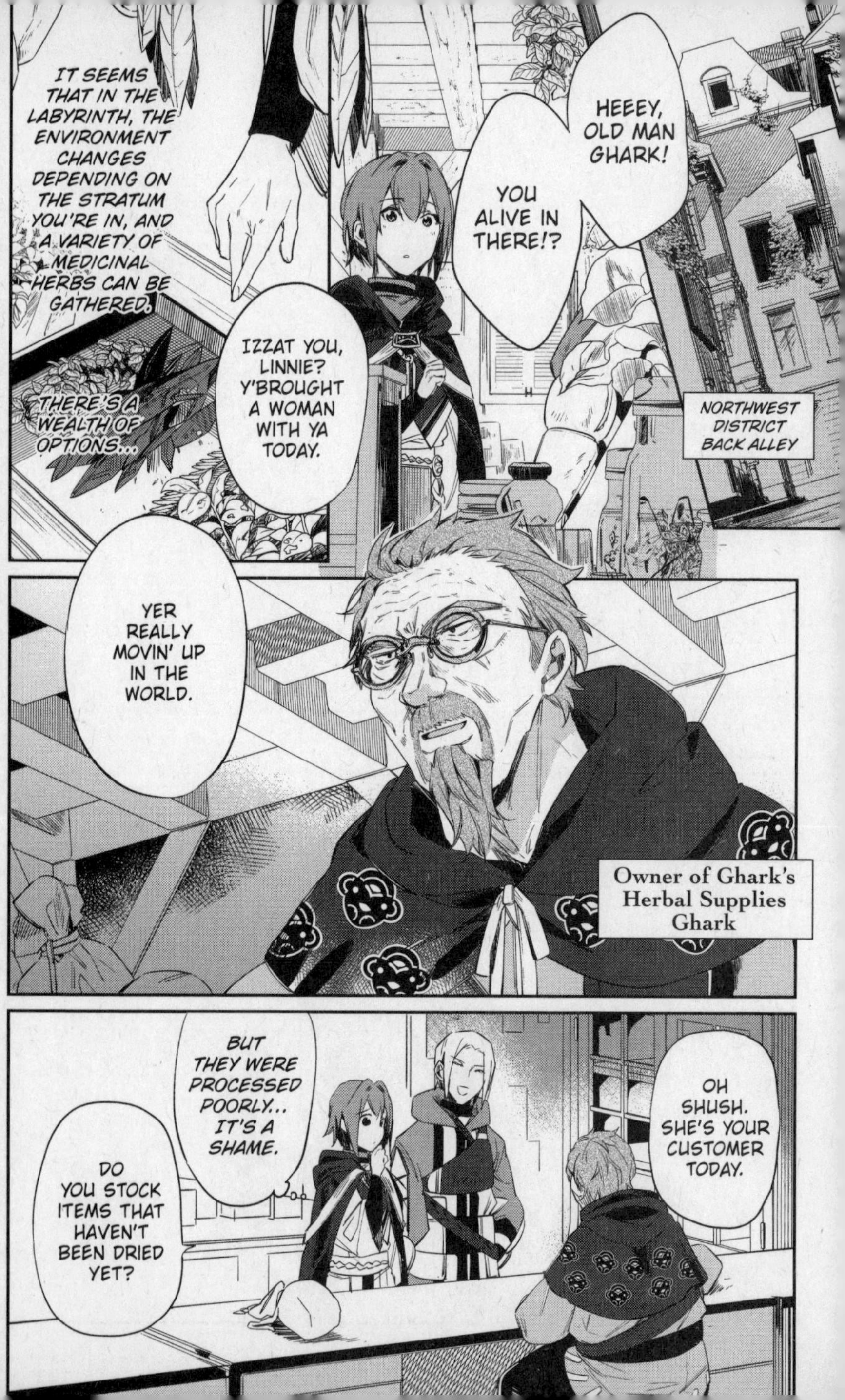
NORTHWEST DISTRICT BACK ALLEY
HEEEY, OLD MAN GHARK!
YOU ALIVE IN THERE!?
IZZAT YOU, LINNIE? Y'BROUGHT A WOMAN WITH YA TODAY.
IT SEEMS THAT IN THE LABYRINTH, THE ENVIRONMENT CHANGES DEPENDING ON THE STRATUM YOU'RE IN, AND A VARIETY OF MEDICINAL HERBS CAN BE GATHERED.
THERE'S A WEALTH OF OPTIONS...
YER REALLY MOVIN' UP IN THE WORLD.
Owner of Ghark's Herbal Supplies Ghark
OH SHUSH. SHE'S YOUR CUSTOMER TODAY.
BUT THEY WERE PROCESSED POORLY... IT'S A SHAME.
DO YOU STOCK ITEMS THAT HAVEN'T BEEN DRIED YET?

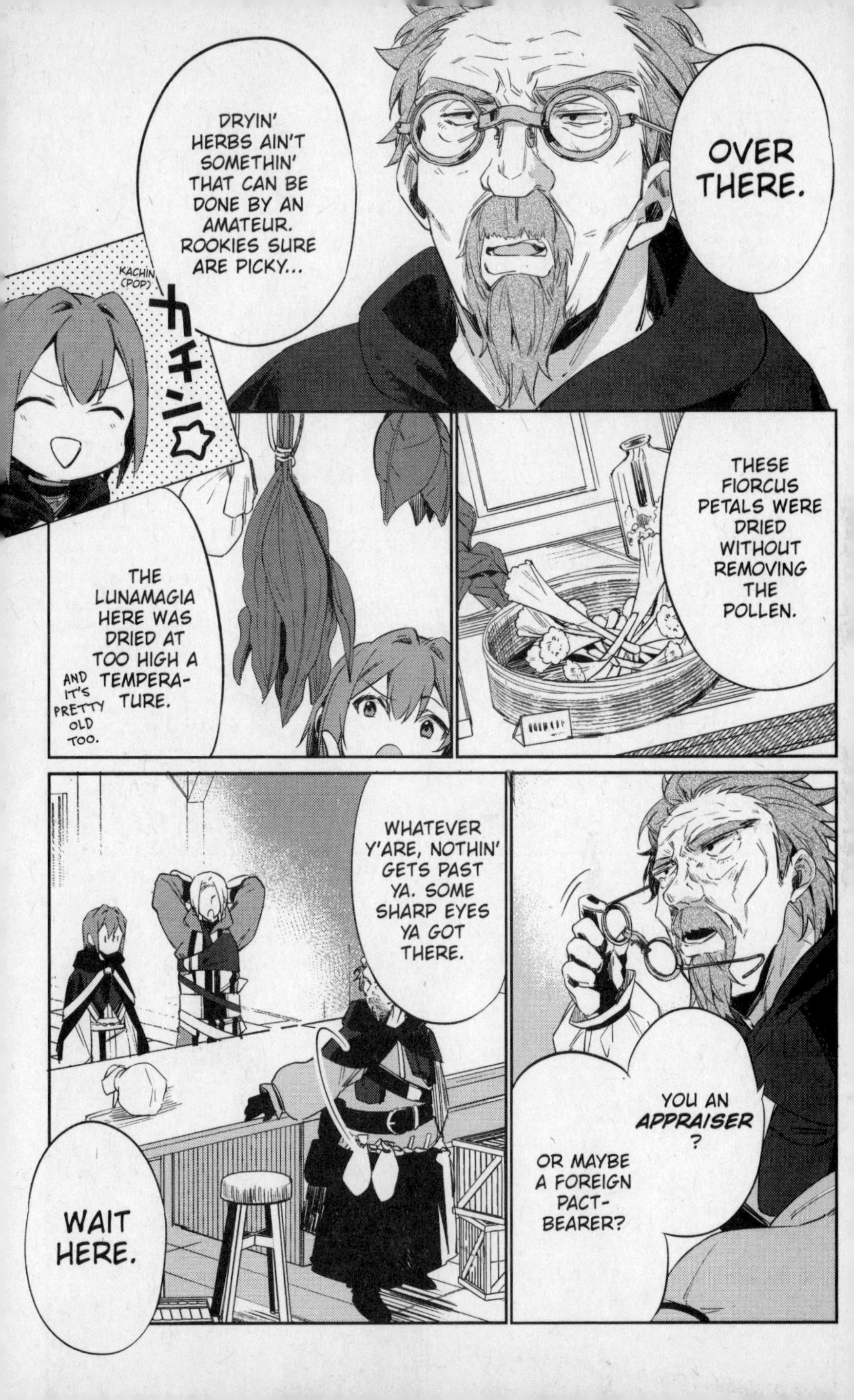

OVER THERE.
DRYIN' HERBS AIN'T SOMETHIN' THAT CAN BE DONE BY AN AMATEUR. ROOKIES SURE ARE PICKY...
カチン
KACHIN (POP)
THESE FIORCUS PETALS WERE DRIED WITHOUT REMOVING THE POLLEN.
THE LUNAMAGIA HERE WAS DRIED AT TOO HIGH A TEMPERA-TURE.
AND IT'S PRETTY OLD TOO.
YOU AN *APPRAISER*?
OR MAYBE A FOREIGN PACT-BEARER?
WHATEVER Y'ARE, NOTHIN' GETS PAST YA. SOME SHARP EYES YA GOT THERE.
WAIT HERE.

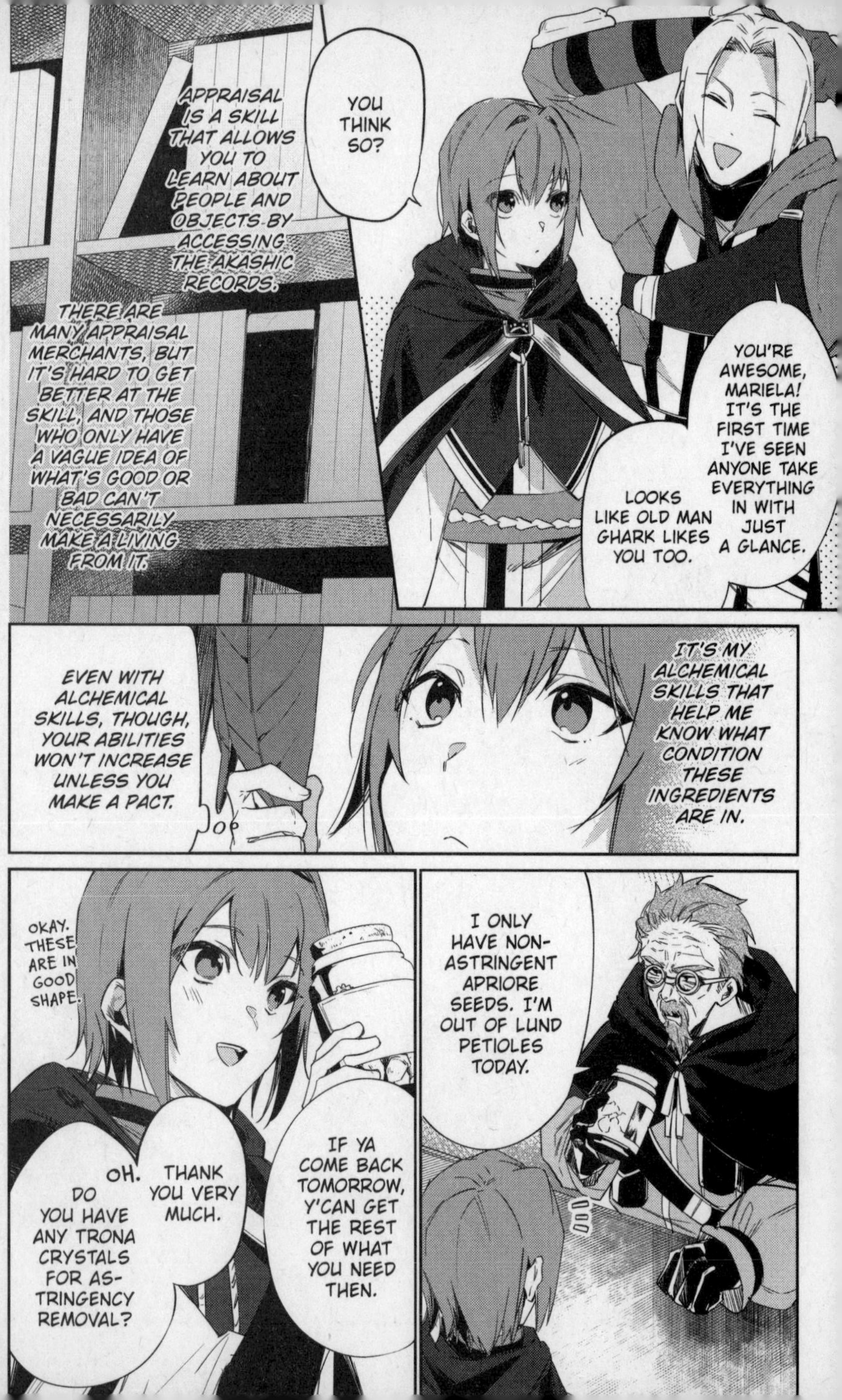
YOU'RE AWESOME, MARIELA! IT'S THE FIRST TIME I'VE SEEN ANYONE TAKE EVERYTHING IN WITH JUST A GLANCE.
LOOKS LIKE OLD MAN GHARK LIKES YOU TOO.
YOU THINK SO?
APPRAISAL IS A SKILL THAT ALLOWS YOU TO LEARN ABOUT PEOPLE AND OBJECTS BY ACCESSING THE AKASHIC RECORDS.
THERE ARE MANY APPRAISAL MERCHANTS, BUT IT'S HARD TO GET BETTER AT THE SKILL, AND THOSE WHO ONLY HAVE A VAGUE IDEA OF WHAT'S GOOD OR BAD CAN'T NECESSARILY MAKE A LIVING FROM IT.
IT'S MY ALCHEMICAL SKILLS THAT HELP ME KNOW WHAT CONDITION THESE INGREDIENTS ARE IN.
EVEN WITH ALCHEMICAL SKILLS, THOUGH, YOUR ABILITIES WON'T INCREASE UNLESS YOU MAKE A PACT.
I ONLY HAVE NON-ASTRINGENT APRIORE SEEDS. I'M OUT OF LUND PETIOLES TODAY.
IF YA COME BACK TOMORROW, Y'CAN GET THE REST OF WHAT YOU NEED THEN.
OKAY. THESE ARE IN GOOD SHAPE.
THANK YOU VERY MUCH.
OH. DO YOU HAVE ANY TRONA CRYSTALS FOR AS-TRINGENCY REMOVAL?

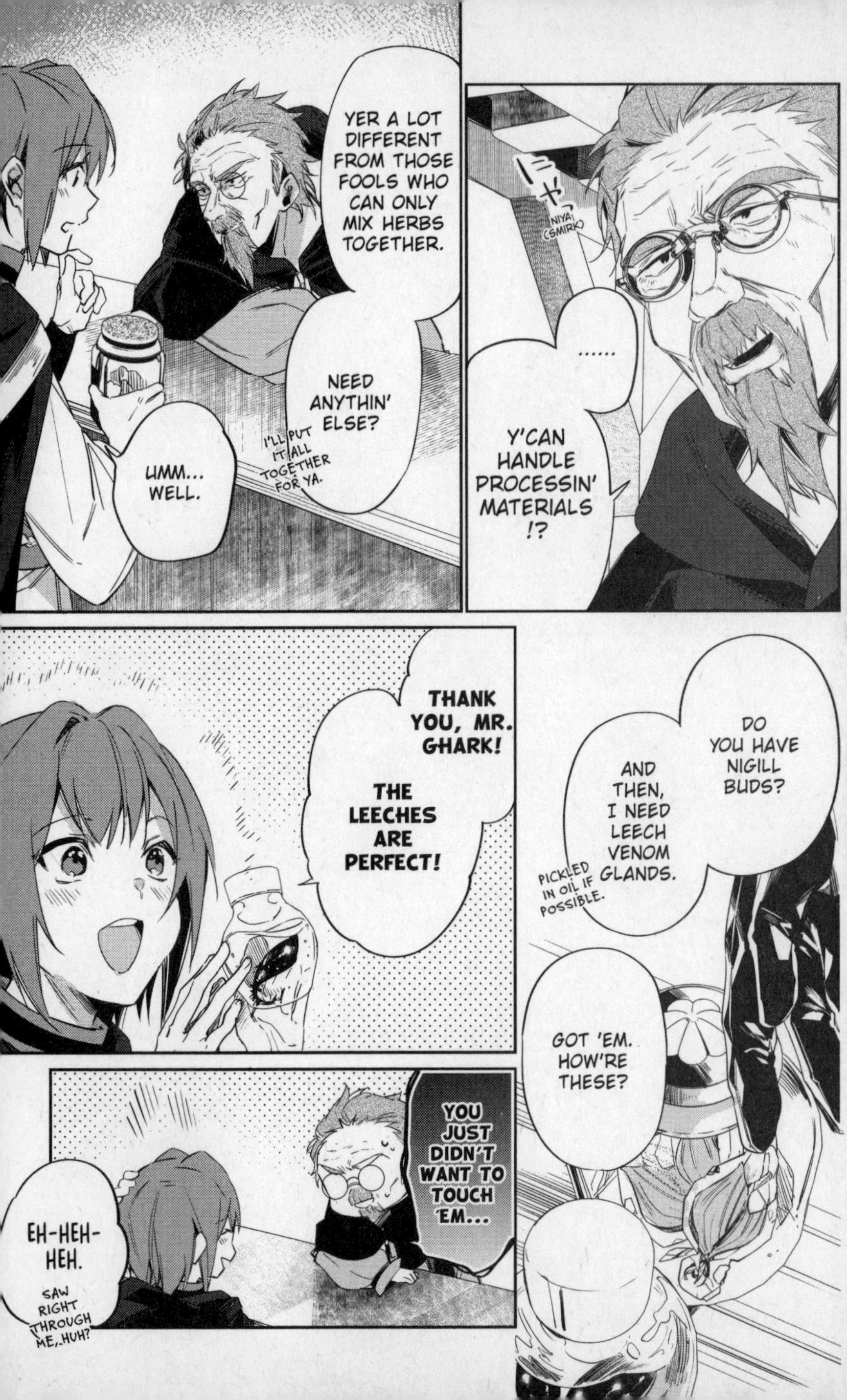
NIYA (SMIRK)
......
Y'CAN HANDLE PROCESSIN' MATERIALS !?
YER A LOT DIFFERENT FROM THOSE FOOLS WHO CAN ONLY MIX HERBS TOGETHER.
NEED ANYTHIN' ELSE?
I'LL PUT IT ALL TOGETHER FOR YA.
UMM... WELL.
DO YOU HAVE NIGILL BUDS?
AND THEN, I NEED LEECH VENOM GLANDS.
PICKLED IN OIL IF POSSIBLE.
GOT 'EM. HOW'RE THESE?
THANK YOU, MR. GHARK!
THE LEECHES ARE PERFECT!
YOU JUST DIDN'T WANT TO TOUCH 'EM...
EH-HEH-HEH.
SAW RIGHT THROUGH ME, HUH?

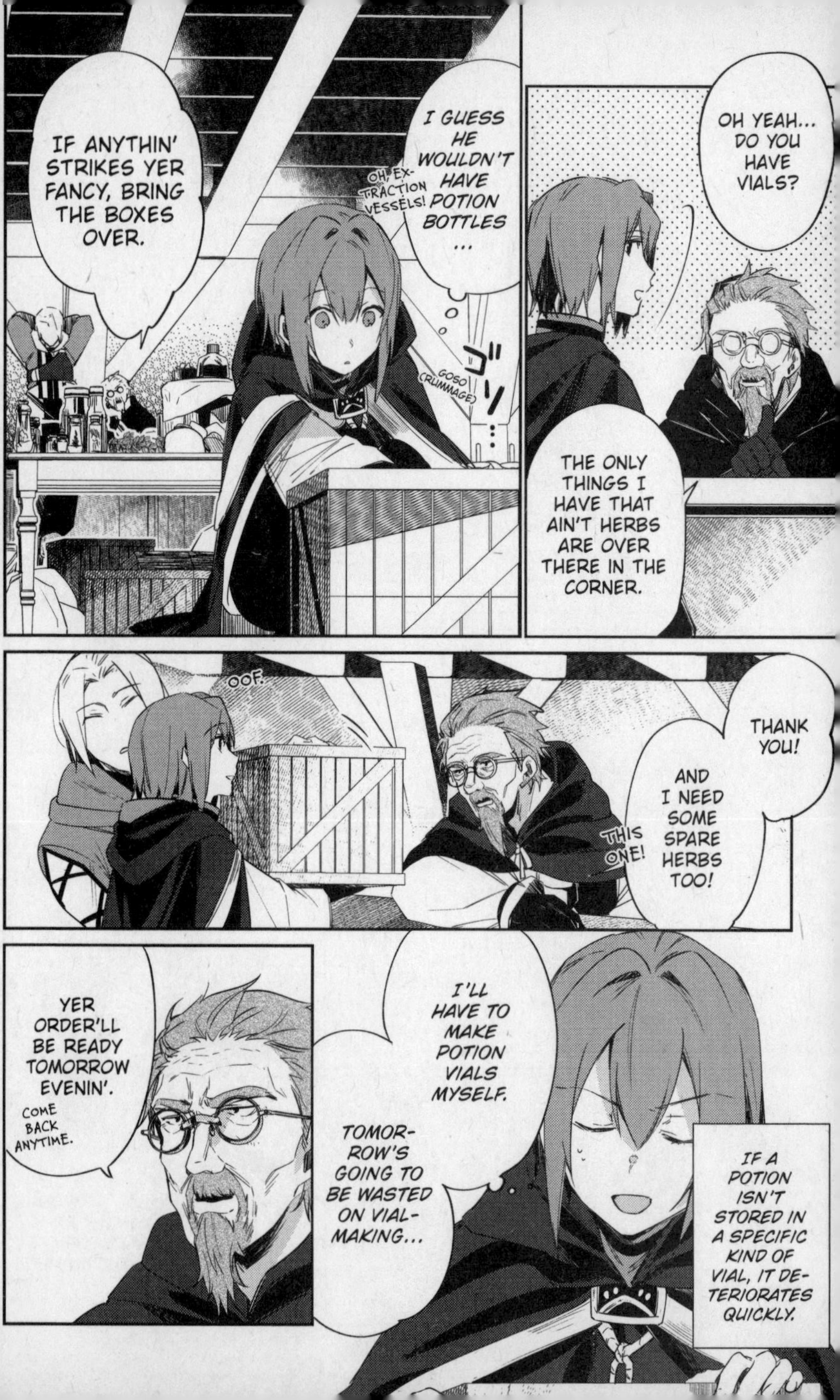
OH YEAH... DO YOU HAVE VIALS?
THE ONLY THINGS I HAVE THAT AIN'T HERBS ARE OVER THERE IN THE CORNER.
I GUESS HE WOULDN'T HAVE POTION BOTTLES...
OH, EXTRACTION VESSELS!
GOSO (RUMMAGE)
IF ANYTHIN' STRIKES YER FANCY, BRING THE BOXES OVER.
THANK YOU!
AND I NEED SOME SPARE HERBS TOO!
THIS ONE!
OOF.
IF A POTION ISN'T STORED IN A SPECIFIC KIND OF VIAL, IT DETERIORATES QUICKLY.
I'LL HAVE TO MAKE POTION VIALS MYSELF.
TOMORROW'S GOING TO BE WASTED ON VIAL-MAKING...
YER ORDER'LL BE READY TOMORROW EVENIN'.
COME BACK ANYTIME.

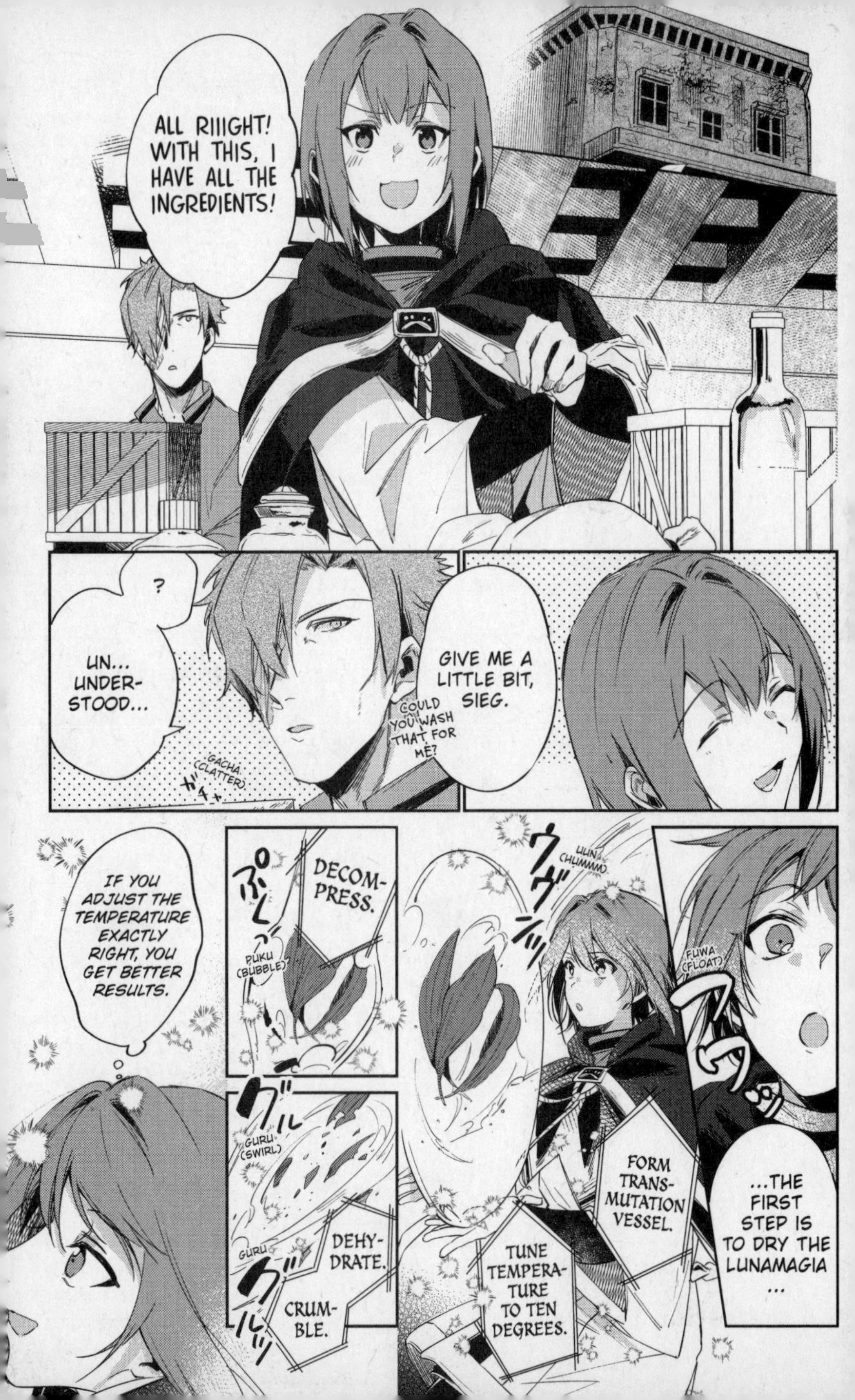
ALL RIIIGHT! WITH THIS, I HAVE ALL THE INGREDIENTS!
GIVE ME A LITTLE BIT, SIEG.
COULD YOU WASH THAT FOR ME?
?
UN... UNDER-STOOD...
GACHA (CLATTER)
FUWA (FLOAT)
...THE FIRST STEP IS TO DRY THE LUNAMAGIA ...
UUN (HUMMM)
FORM TRANS-MUTATION VESSEL.
TUNE TEMPERA-TURE TO TEN DEGREES.
DECOM-PRESS.
PUKU (BUBBLE)
GURU (SWIRL)
DEHY-DRATE.
GURU
CRUM-BLE.
IF YOU ADJUST THE TEMPERATURE EXACTLY RIGHT, YOU GET BETTER RESULTS.

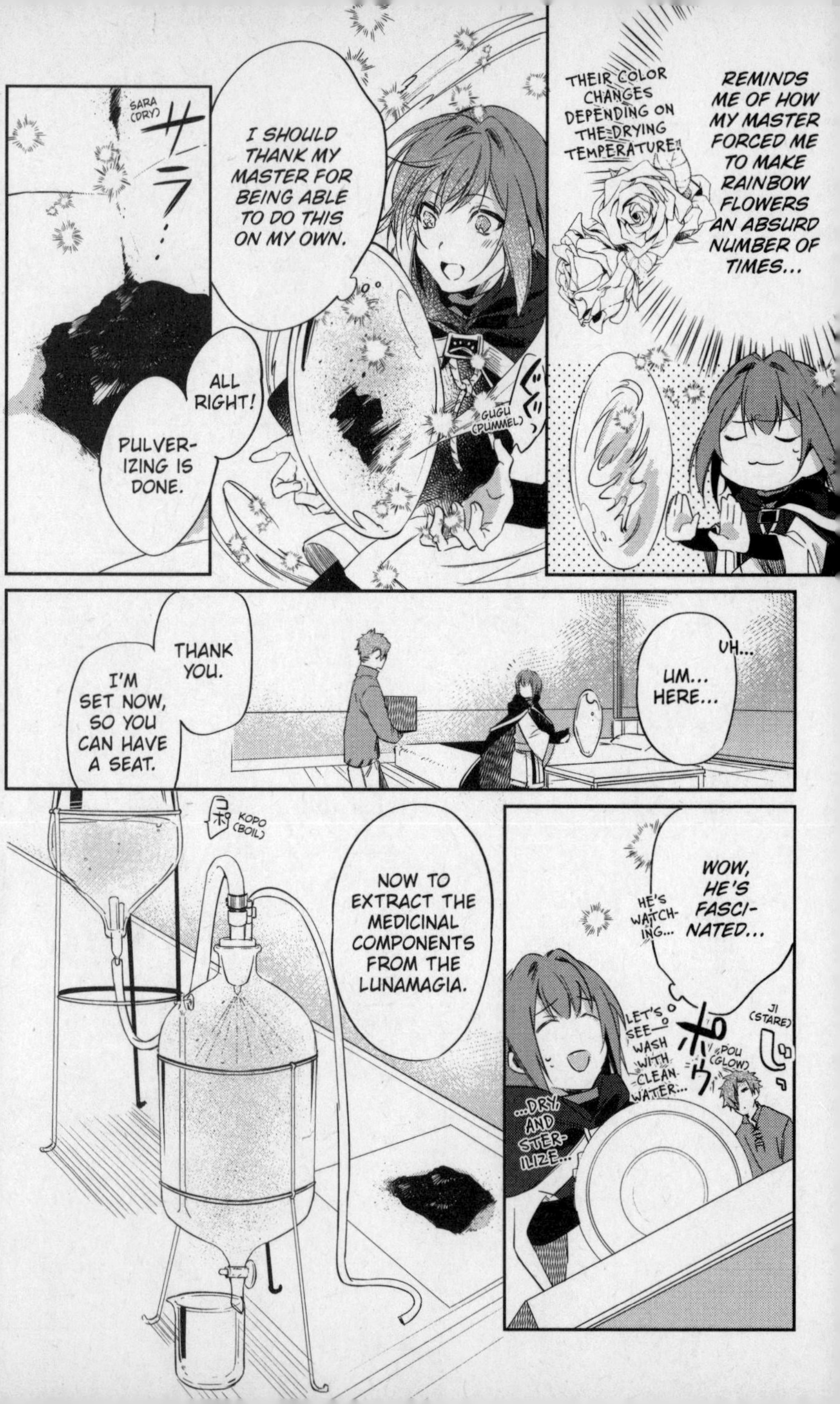
THEIR COLOR CHANGES DEPENDING ON THE DRYING TEMPERATURE!
REMINDS ME OF HOW MY MASTER FORCED ME TO MAKE RAINBOW FLOWERS AN ABSURD NUMBER OF TIMES...
I SHOULD THANK MY MASTER FOR BEING ABLE TO DO THIS ON MY OWN.
GUGU (PUMMEL)
ALL RIGHT!
PULVERIZING IS DONE.
SARA (DRY)
UH...
UM... HERE...
THANK YOU.
I'M SET NOW, SO YOU CAN HAVE A SEAT.
WOW, HE'S FASCINATED...
HE'S WATCHING...
JI (STARE)
POU (GLOW)
LET'S SEE—WASH WITH CLEAN WATER...
...DRY, AND STERILIZE...
KOPO (BOIL)
NOW TO EXTRACT THE MEDICINAL COMPONENTS FROM THE LUNAMAGIA.

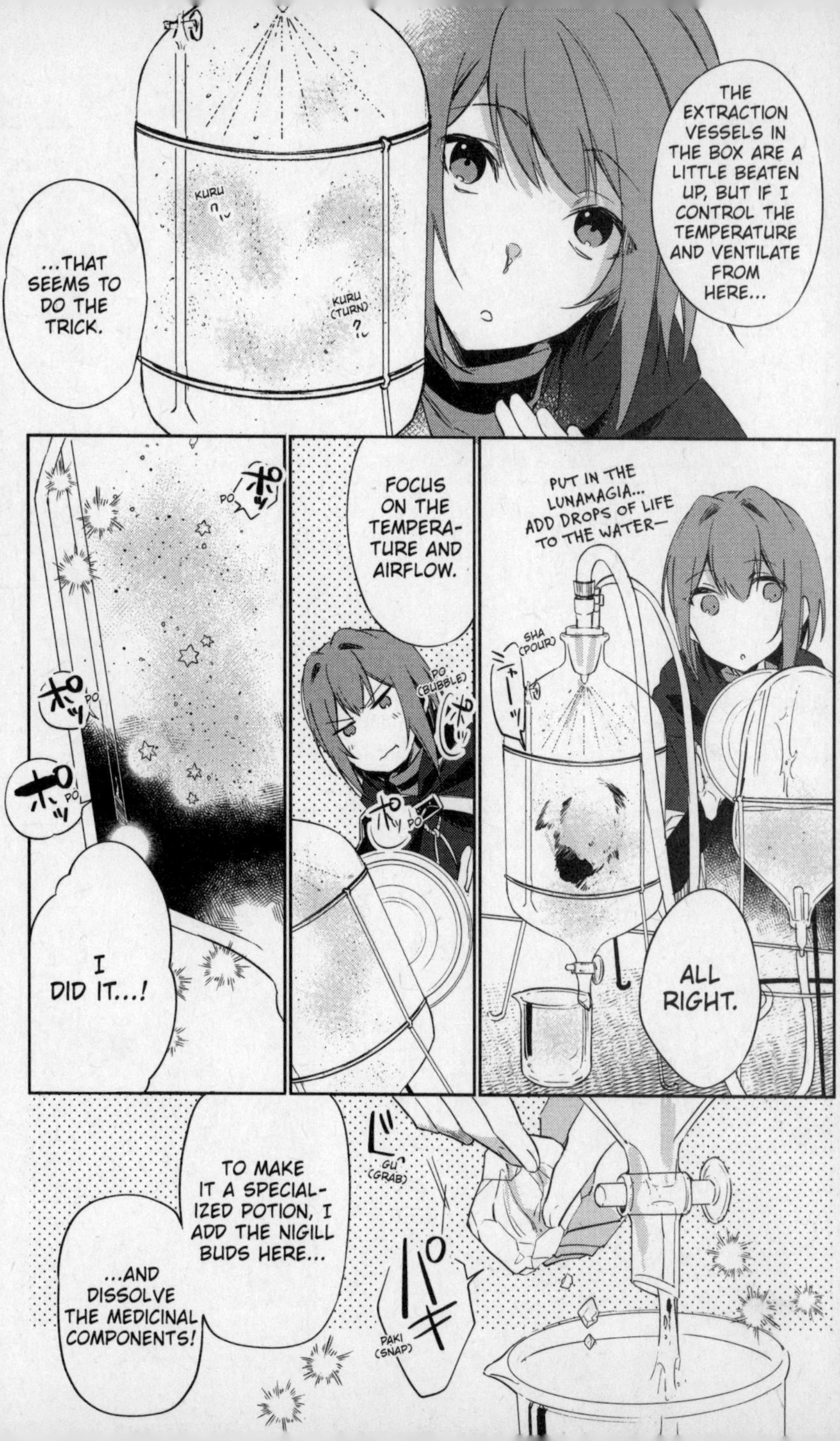

THE EXTRACTION VESSELS IN THE BOX ARE A LITTLE BEATEN UP, BUT IF I CONTROL THE TEMPERATURE AND VENTILATE FROM HERE...
KURU
KURU (TURN)
...THAT SEEMS TO DO THE TRICK.
PUT IN THE LUNAMAGIA... ADD DROPS OF LIFE TO THE WATER—
SHA (POUR)
ALL RIGHT.
FOCUS ON THE TEMPERATURE AND AIRFLOW.
PO (BUBBLE)
PO
PO
PO
PO
I DID IT...!
GU (GRAB)
TO MAKE IT A SPECIALIZED POTION, I ADD THE NIGILL BUDS HERE...
...AND DISSOLVE THE MEDICINAL COMPONENTS!
PAKI (SNAP)

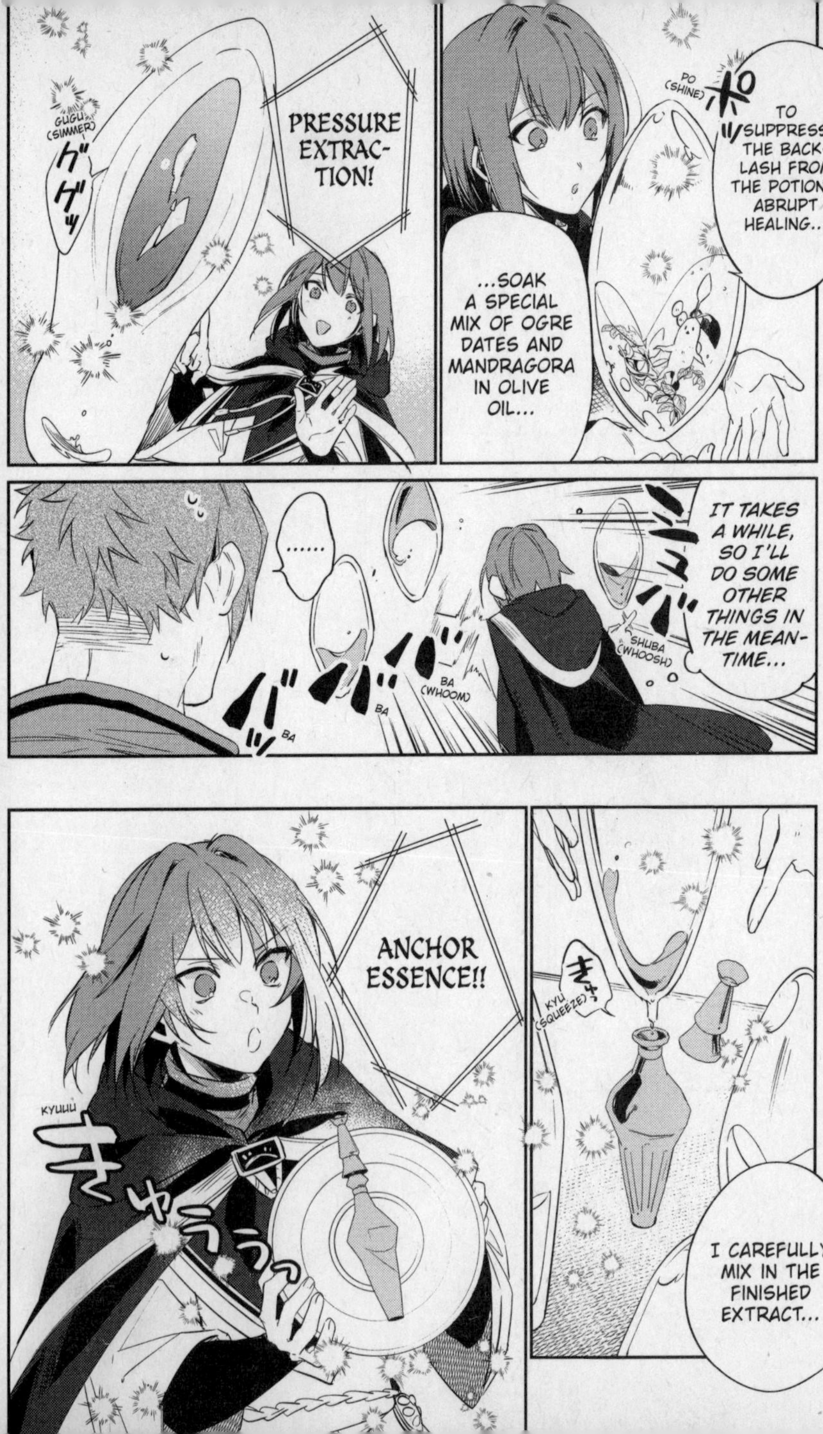
PO (SHINE)
TO SUPPRESS THE BACK-LASH FROM THE POTION'S ABRUPT HEALING...
...SOAK A SPECIAL MIX OF OGRE DATES AND MANDRAGORA IN OLIVE OIL...
GUGU (SIMMER)
PRESSURE EXTRAC-TION!
IT TAKES A WHILE, SO I'LL DO SOME OTHER THINGS IN THE MEAN-TIME...
SHUBA (WHOOSH)
BA (WHOOM)
BA
BA
......
KYU (SQUEEZE)
I CAREFULLY MIX IN THE FINISHED EXTRACT...
ANCHOR ESSENCE!!
KYUUU

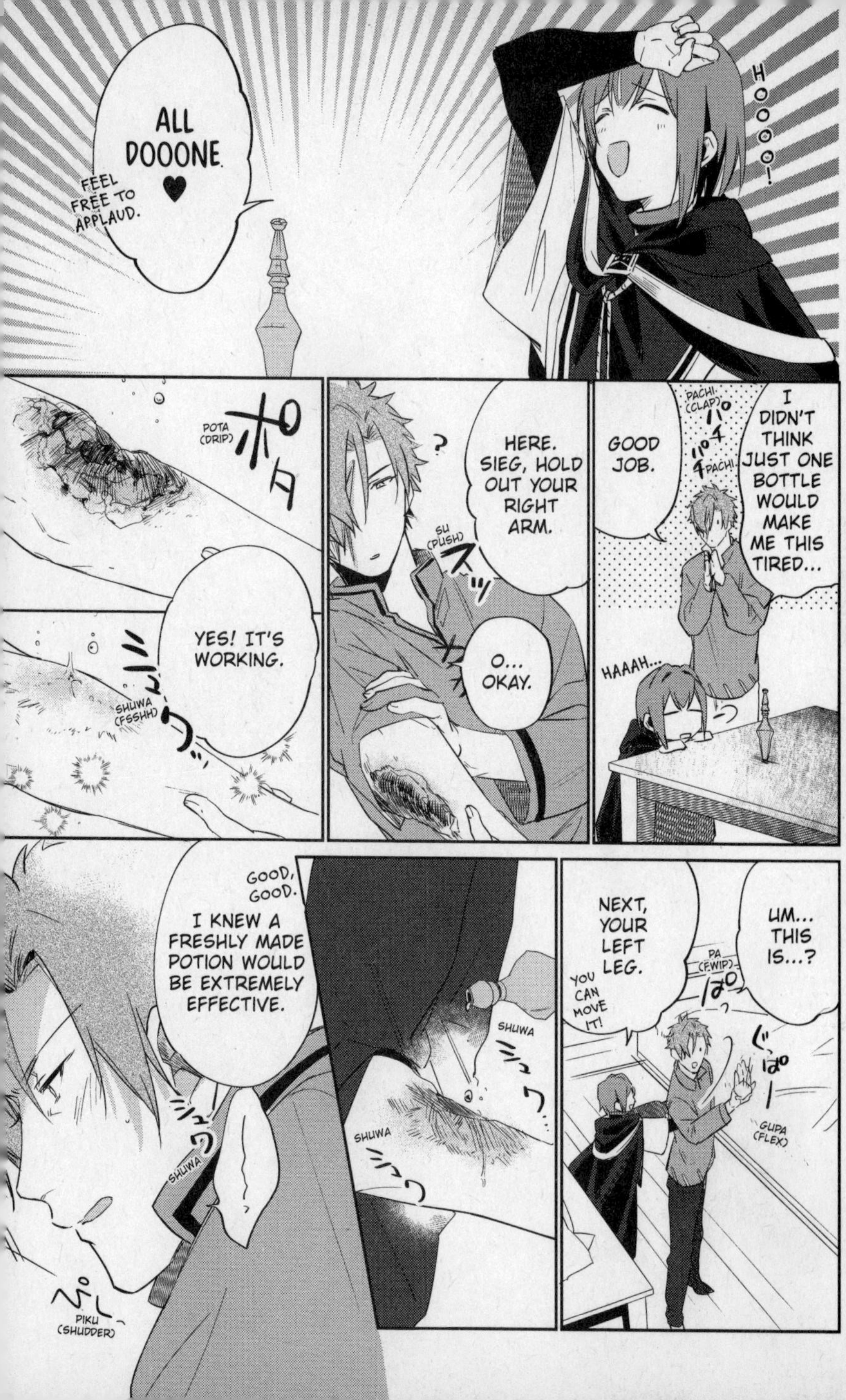
HOOOOO!
ALL DOOONE ♥
FEEL FREE TO APPLAUD.
I DIDN'T THINK JUST ONE BOTTLE WOULD MAKE ME THIS TIRED...
PACHI (CLAP)
PACHI
GOOD JOB.
HAAAH...
HERE. SIEG, HOLD OUT YOUR RIGHT ARM.
?
SU (PUSH)
O... OKAY.
POTA (DRIP)
YES! IT'S WORKING.
SHUWA (FSSHH)
UM... THIS IS...?
PA (FWIP)
NEXT, YOUR LEFT LEG.
YOU CAN MOVE IT!
GUPA (FLEX)
SHUWA
SHUWA
GOOD, GOOD.
I KNEW A FRESHLY MADE POTION WOULD BE EXTREMELY EFFECTIVE.
SHUWA
PIKU (SHUDDER)

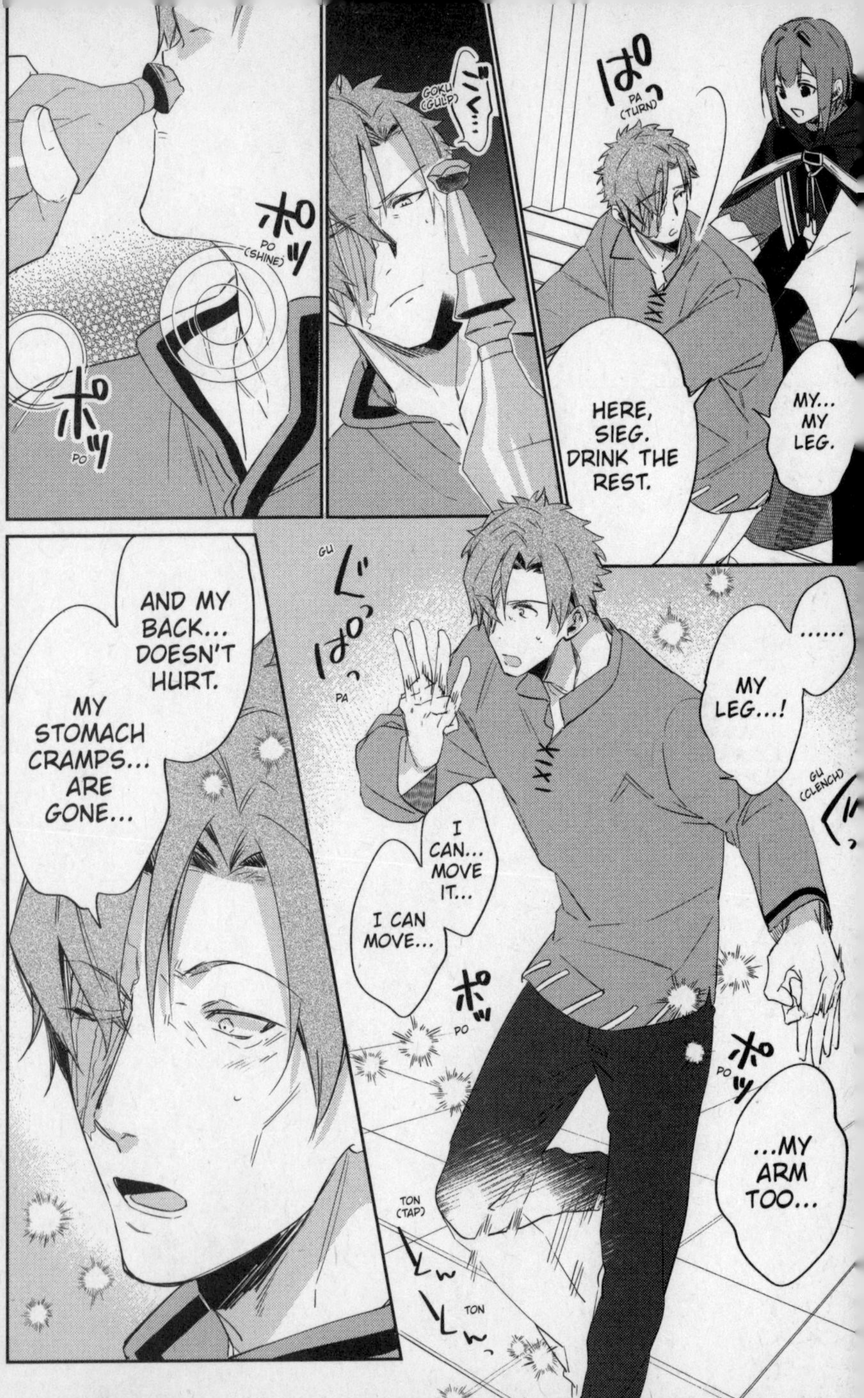
ぱっ
PA (TURN)
HERE, SIEG. DRINK THE REST.
MY... MY LEG.
ゴく…
GOKU (GULP)
ポッ
PO (SHINE)
ポッ
PO
......
MY LEG...!
ぐっ
GU (CLENCH)
ポッ
PO
...MY ARM TOO...
ぐ
GU
ぱっ
PA
I CAN... MOVE IT...
I CAN MOVE...
ポッ
PO
TON (TAP)
とん
とん
TON
AND MY BACK... DOESN'T HURT.
MY STOMACH CRAMPS... ARE GONE...

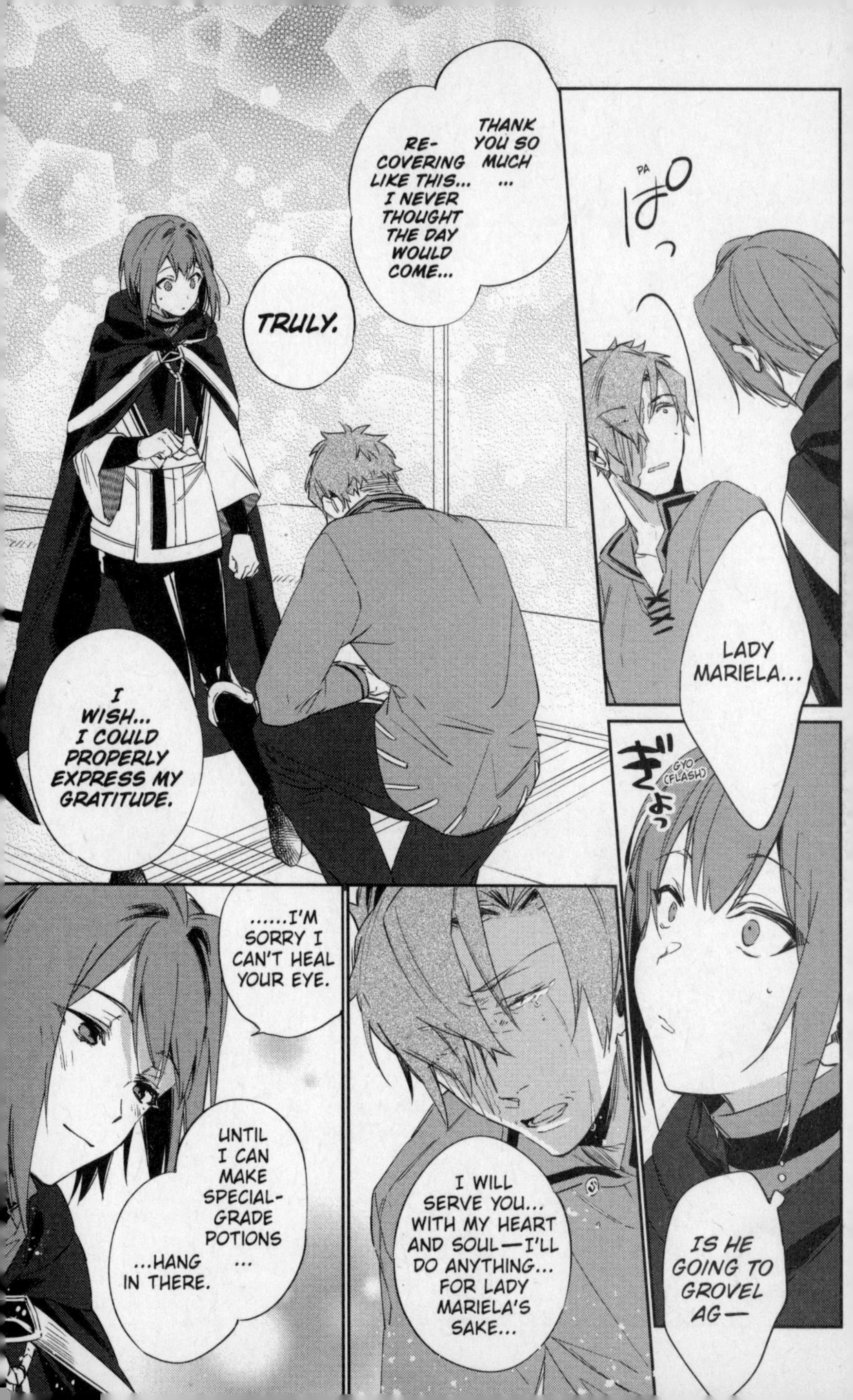

PA
LADY MARIELA...
THANK YOU SO MUCH...
RE-COVERING LIKE THIS... I NEVER THOUGHT THE DAY WOULD COME...
TRULY.
I WISH... I COULD PROPERLY EXPRESS MY GRATITUDE.
GYO (FLASH)
IS HE GOING TO GROVEL AG—
I WILL SERVE YOU... WITH MY HEART AND SOUL—I'LL DO ANYTHING... FOR LADY MARIELA'S SAKE...
......I'M SORRY I CAN'T HEAL YOUR EYE.
UNTIL I CAN MAKE SPECIAL-GRADE POTIONS ...
...HANG IN THERE.

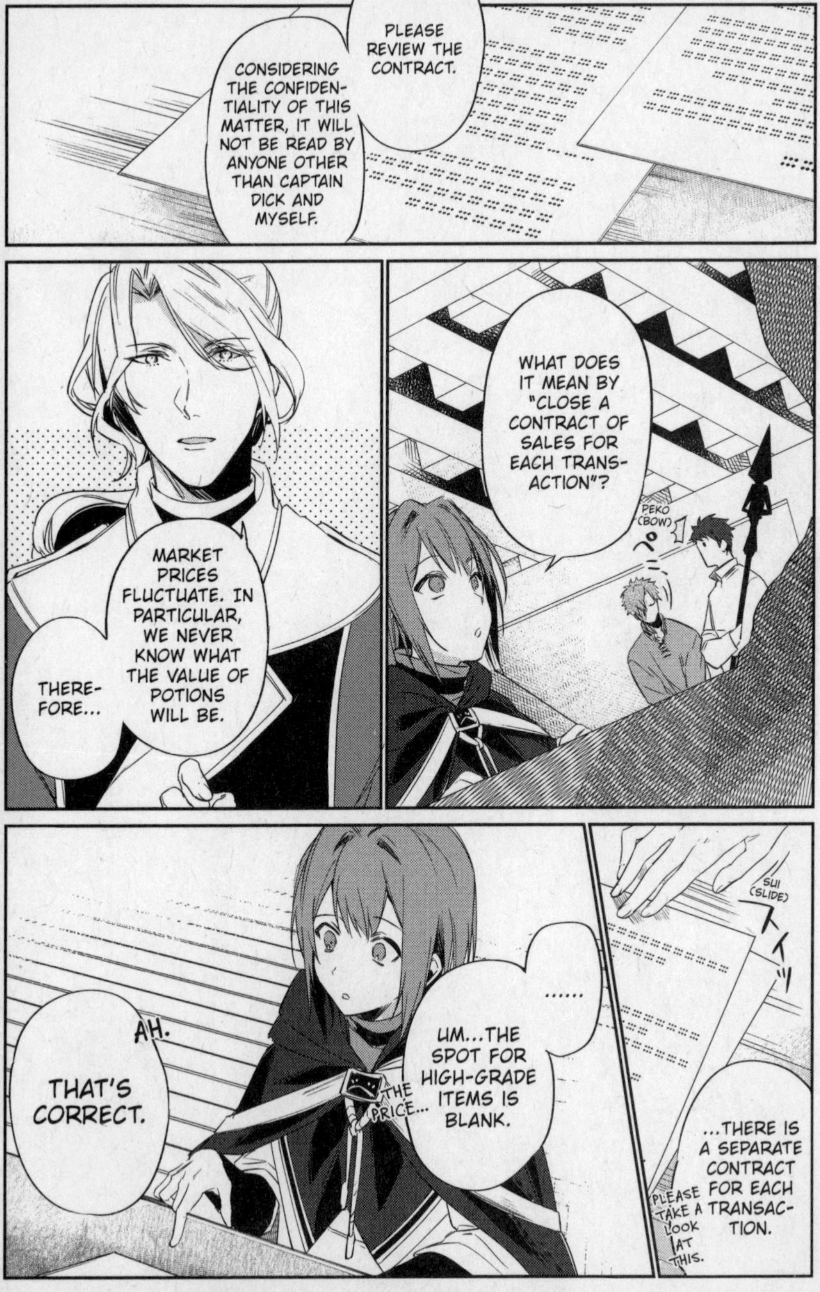
PLEASE REVIEW THE CONTRACT.
CONSIDERING THE CONFIDENTIALITY OF THIS MATTER, IT WILL NOT BE READ BY ANYONE OTHER THAN CAPTAIN DICK AND MYSELF.
WHAT DOES IT MEAN BY "CLOSE A CONTRACT OF SALES FOR EACH TRANSACTION"?
PEKO (BOW)
MARKET PRICES FLUCTUATE. IN PARTICULAR, WE NEVER KNOW WHAT THE VALUE OF POTIONS WILL BE.
THEREFORE...
SUI (SLIDE)
...THERE IS A SEPARATE CONTRACT FOR EACH TRANSACTION.
PLEASE TAKE A LOOK AT THIS.
......
UM...THE SPOT FOR HIGH-GRADE ITEMS IS BLANK.
THE PRICE...
AH.
THAT'S CORRECT.

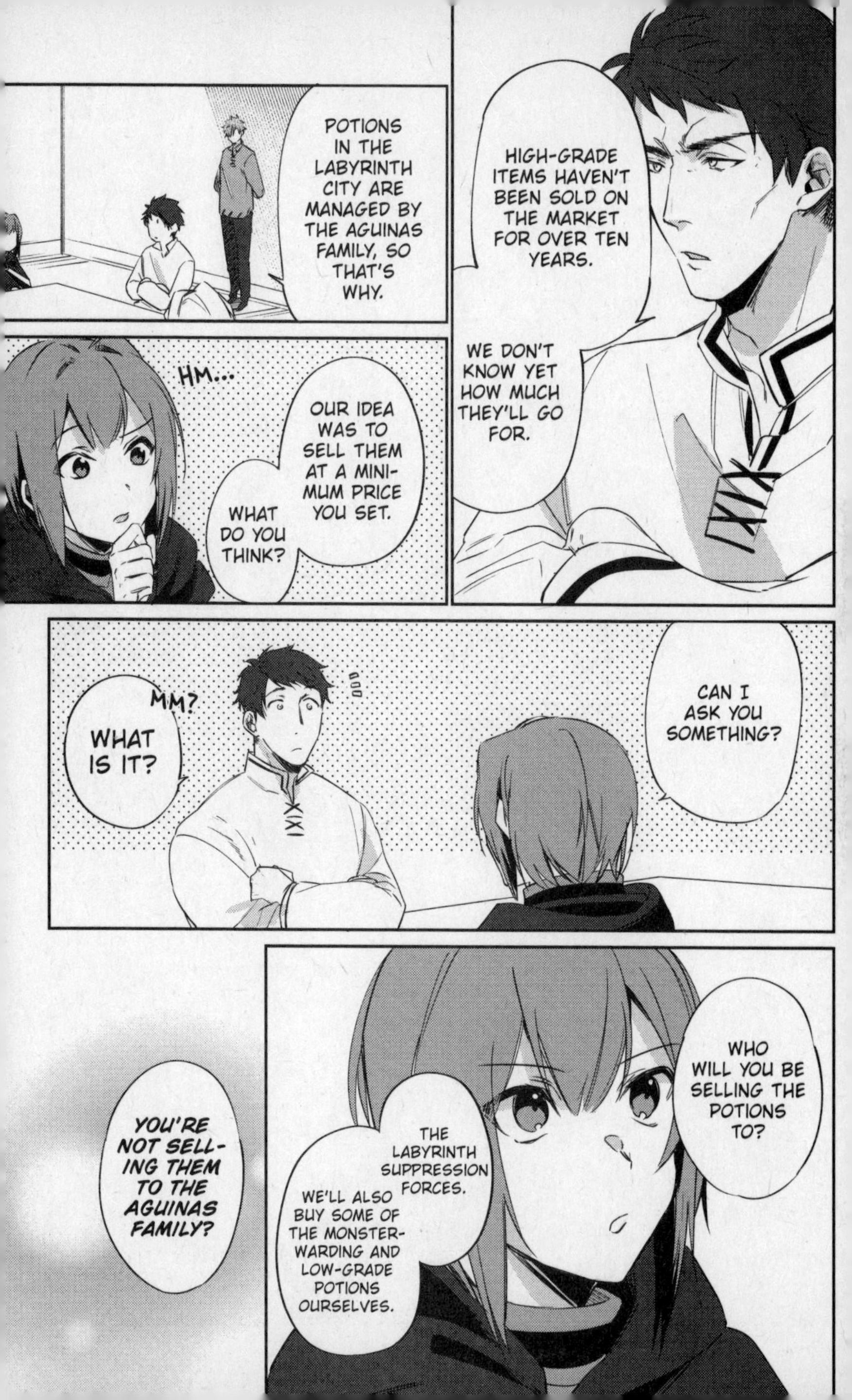
HIGH-GRADE ITEMS HAVEN'T BEEN SOLD ON THE MARKET FOR OVER TEN YEARS.
WE DON'T KNOW YET HOW MUCH THEY'LL GO FOR.
POTIONS IN THE LABYRINTH CITY ARE MANAGED BY THE AGUINAS FAMILY, SO THAT'S WHY.
OUR IDEA WAS TO SELL THEM AT A MINI-MUM PRICE YOU SET.
WHAT DO YOU THINK?
HM...
CAN I ASK YOU SOMETHING?
MM?
WHAT IS IT?
WHO WILL YOU BE SELLING THE POTIONS TO?
THE LABYRINTH SUPPRESSION FORCES.
WE'LL ALSO BUY SOME OF THE MONSTER-WARDING AND LOW-GRADE POTIONS OURSELVES.
YOU'RE NOT SELL-ING THEM TO THE AGUINAS FAMILY?

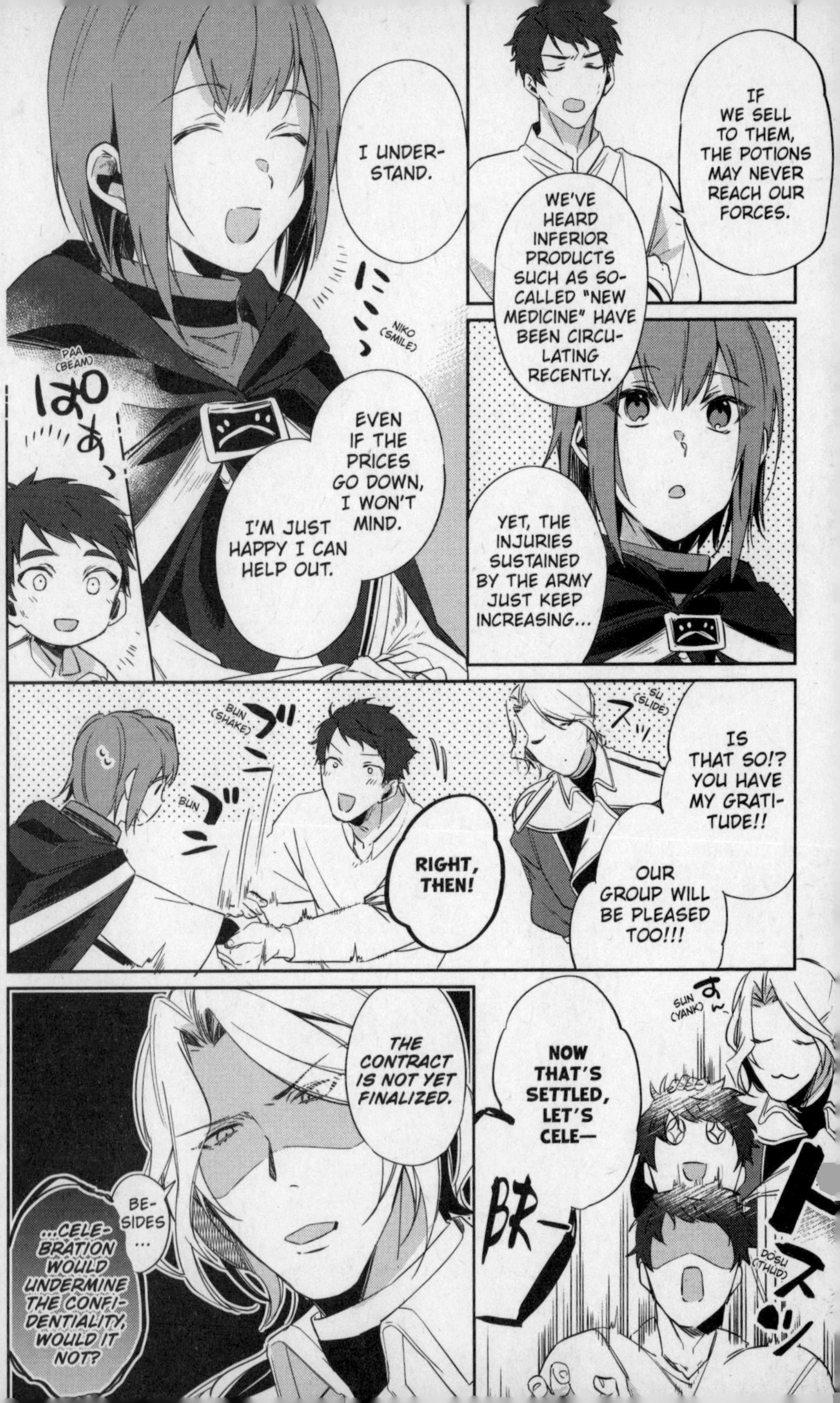
IF WE SELL TO THEM, THE POTIONS MAY NEVER REACH OUR FORCES.
WE'VE HEARD INFERIOR PRODUCTS SUCH AS SO-CALLED "NEW MEDICINE" HAVE BEEN CIRCULATING RECENTLY.
YET, THE INJURIES SUSTAINED BY THE ARMY JUST KEEP INCREASING...
I UNDERSTAND.
NIKO (SMILE)
EVEN IF THE PRICES GO DOWN, I WON'T MIND.
I'M JUST HAPPY I CAN HELP OUT.
PAA (BEAM)
IS THAT SO!? YOU HAVE MY GRATITUDE!!
OUR GROUP WILL BE PLEASED TOO!!!
SU (SLIDE)
RIGHT, THEN!
BUN (SHAKE)
BUN
SUN (YANK)
NOW THAT'S SETTLED, LET'S CELE—
BR—
DOSU (THUD)
THE CONTRACT IS NOT YET FINALIZED.
BESIDES...
...CELEBRATION WOULD UNDERMINE THE CONFIDENTIALITY, WOULD IT NOT?

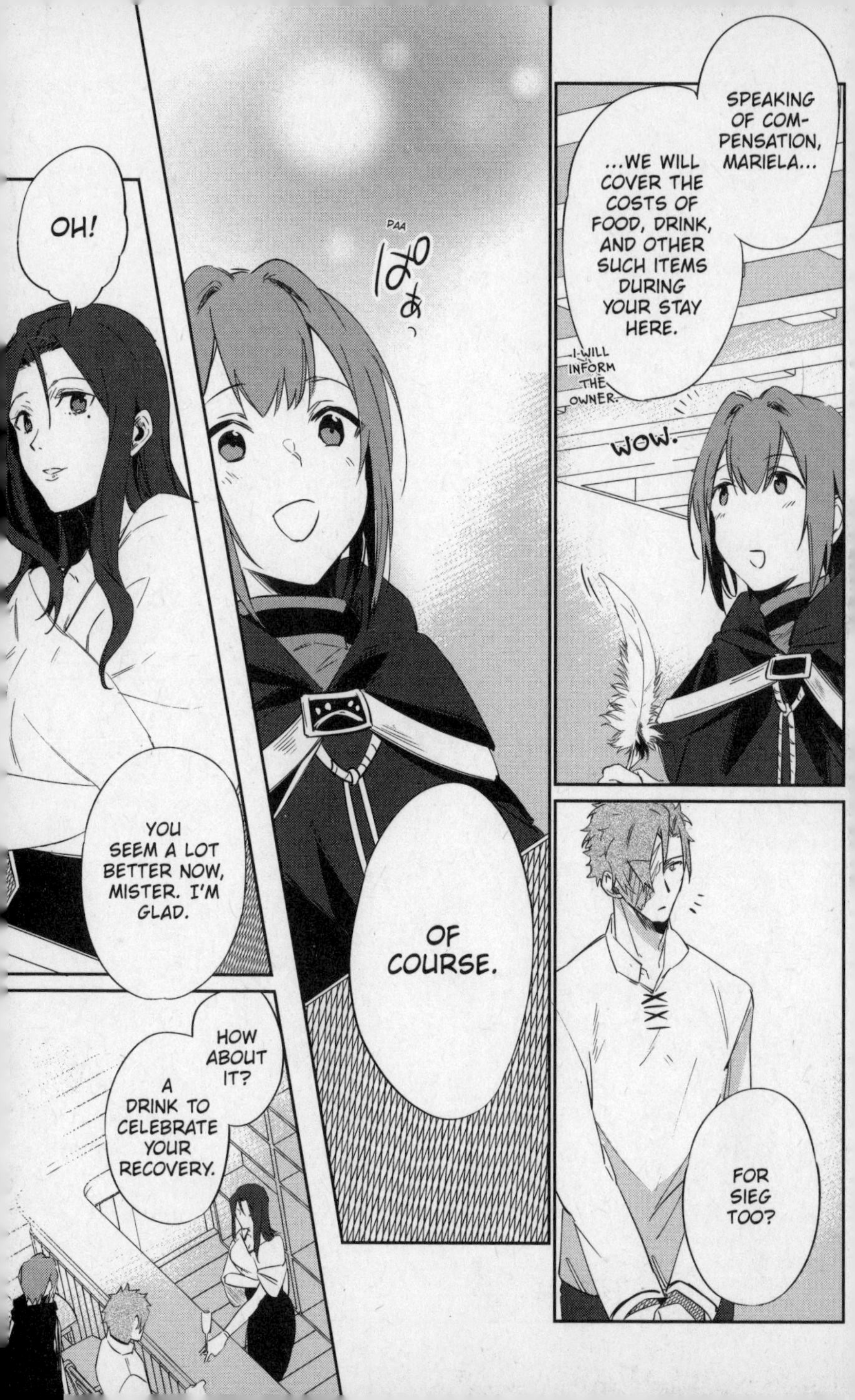
SPEAKING OF COM- PENSATION, MARIELA...
...WE WILL COVER THE COSTS OF FOOD, DRINK, AND OTHER SUCH ITEMS DURING YOUR STAY HERE.
I WILL INFORM THE OWNER.
WOW.
FOR SIEG TOO?
PAA
ぱぁっ
OF COURSE.
OH!
YOU SEEM A LOT BETTER NOW, MISTER. I'M GLAD.
HOW ABOUT IT?
A DRINK TO CELEBRATE YOUR RECOVERY.

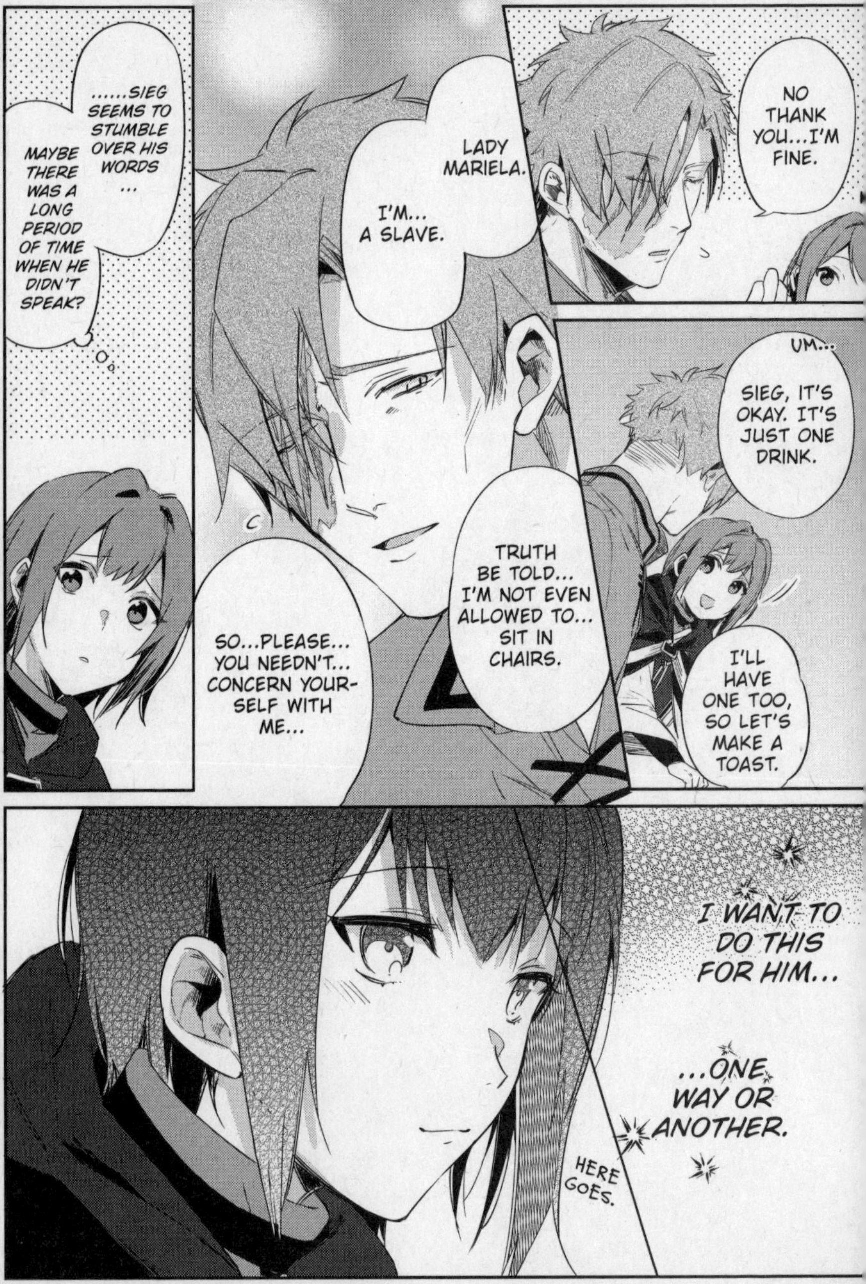
NO THANK YOU...I'M FINE.
UM...
SIEG, IT'S OKAY. IT'S JUST ONE DRINK.
I'LL HAVE ONE TOO, SO LET'S MAKE A TOAST.
LADY MARIELA.
I'M... A SLAVE.
TRUTH BE TOLD... I'M NOT EVEN ALLOWED TO... SIT IN CHAIRS.
SO...PLEASE... YOU NEEDN'T... CONCERN YOURSELF WITH ME...
......SIEG SEEMS TO STUMBLE OVER HIS WORDS ...
MAYBE THERE WAS A LONG PERIOD OF TIME WHEN HE DIDN'T SPEAK?
I WANT TO DO THIS FOR HIM...
...ONE WAY OR ANOTHER.
HERE GOES.

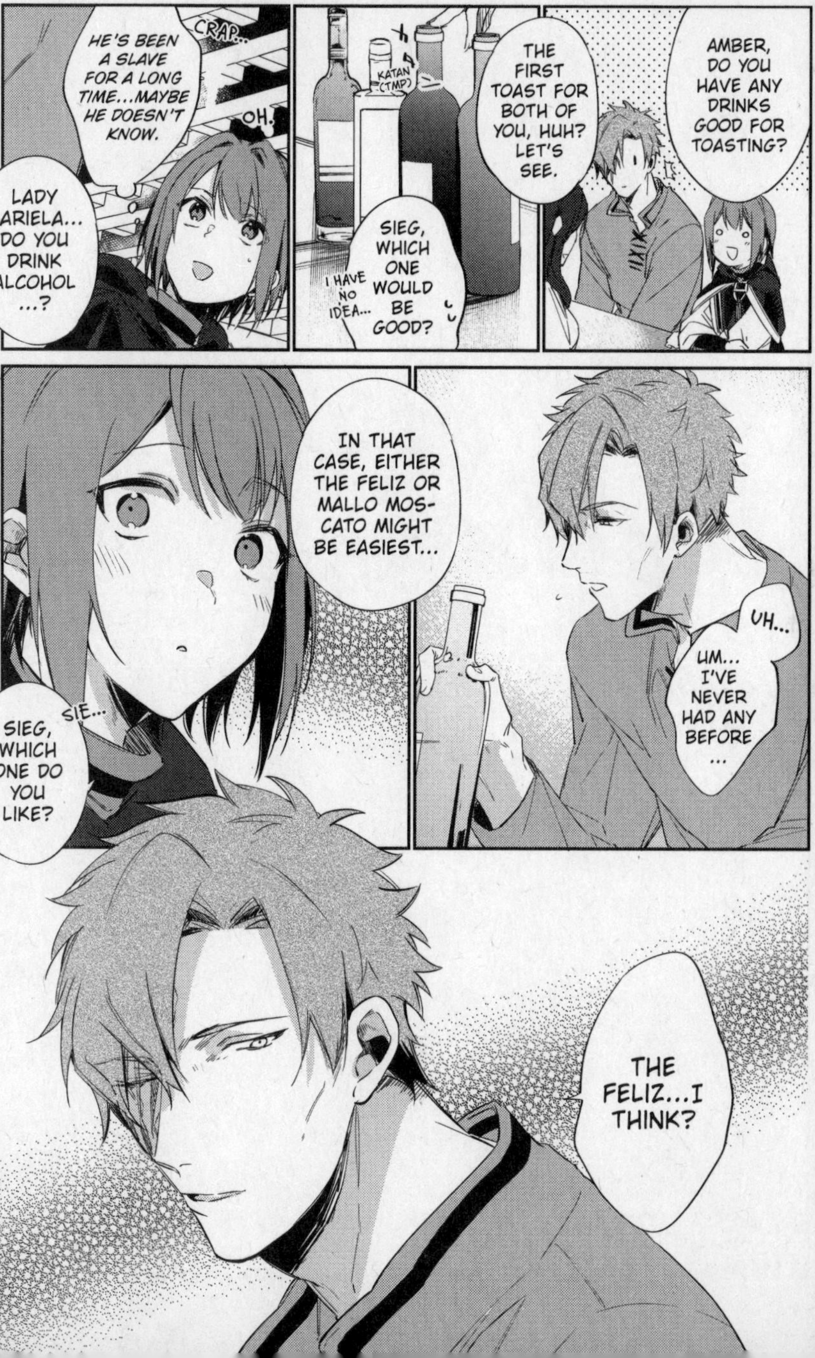
AMBER, DO YOU HAVE ANY DRINKS GOOD FOR TOASTING?
THE FIRST TOAST FOR BOTH OF YOU, HUH? LET'S SEE.
KATAN (TMP)
SIEG, WHICH ONE WOULD BE GOOD?
I HAVE NO IDEA...
CRAP...
HE'S BEEN A SLAVE FOR A LONG TIME...MAYBE HE DOESN'T KNOW.
OH.
LADY MARIELA... DO YOU DRINK ALCOHOL...?
UH...
UM... I'VE NEVER HAD ANY BEFORE...
IN THAT CASE, EITHER THE FELIZ OR MALLO MOSCATO MIGHT BE EASIEST...
SIE...
SIEG, WHICH ONE DO YOU LIKE?
THE FELIZ...I THINK?

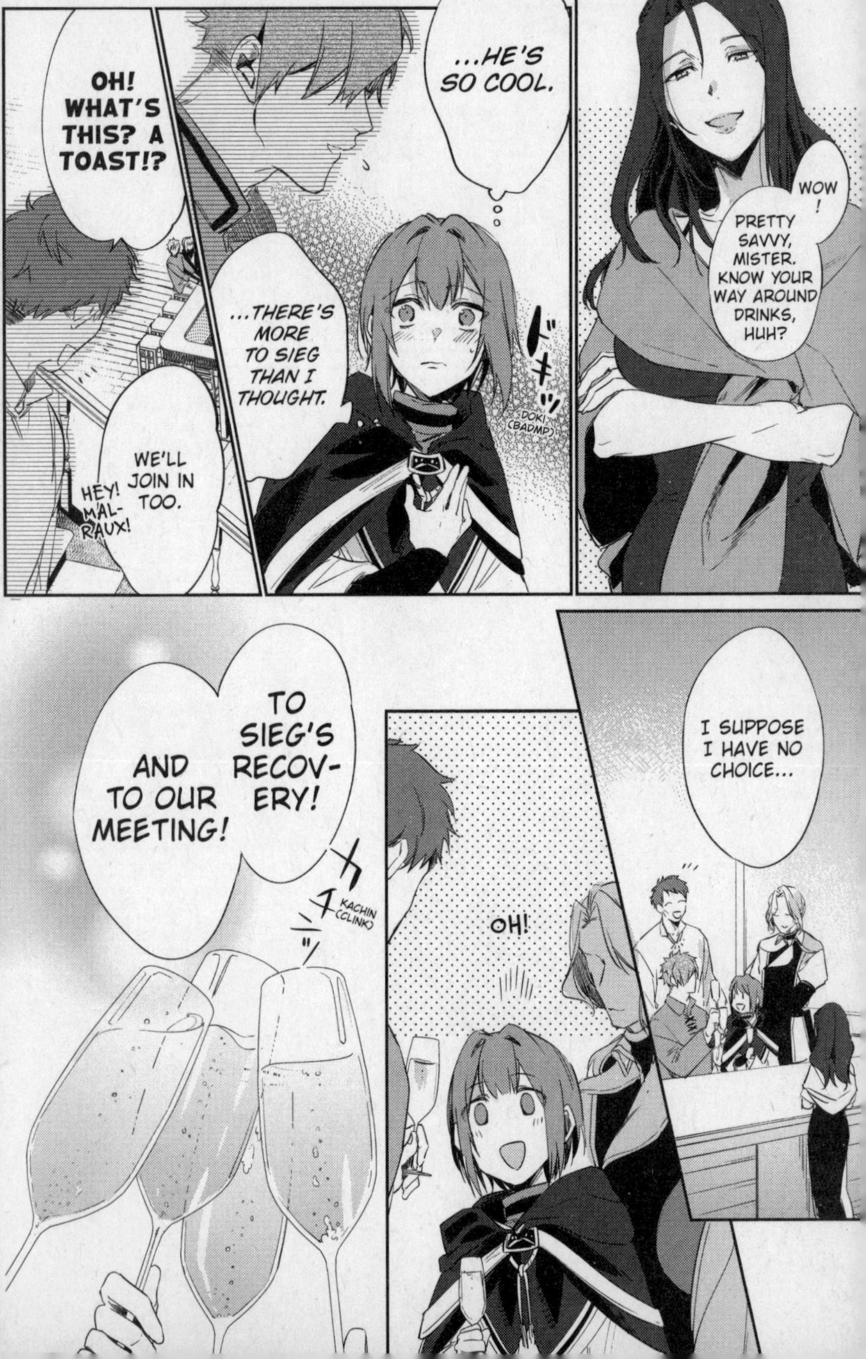
WOW! PRETTY SAVVY, MISTER. KNOW YOUR WAY AROUND DRINKS, HUH?
...HE'S SO COOL.
...THERE'S MORE TO SIEG THAN I THOUGHT.
DOKI (BADMP)
OH! WHAT'S THIS? A TOAST!?
WE'LL JOIN IN TOO.
HEY! MAL-RAUX!
I SUPPOSE I HAVE NO CHOICE...
OH!
TO SIEG'S RECOVERY! AND TO OUR MEETING!
KACHIN (CLINK)

Episode 5

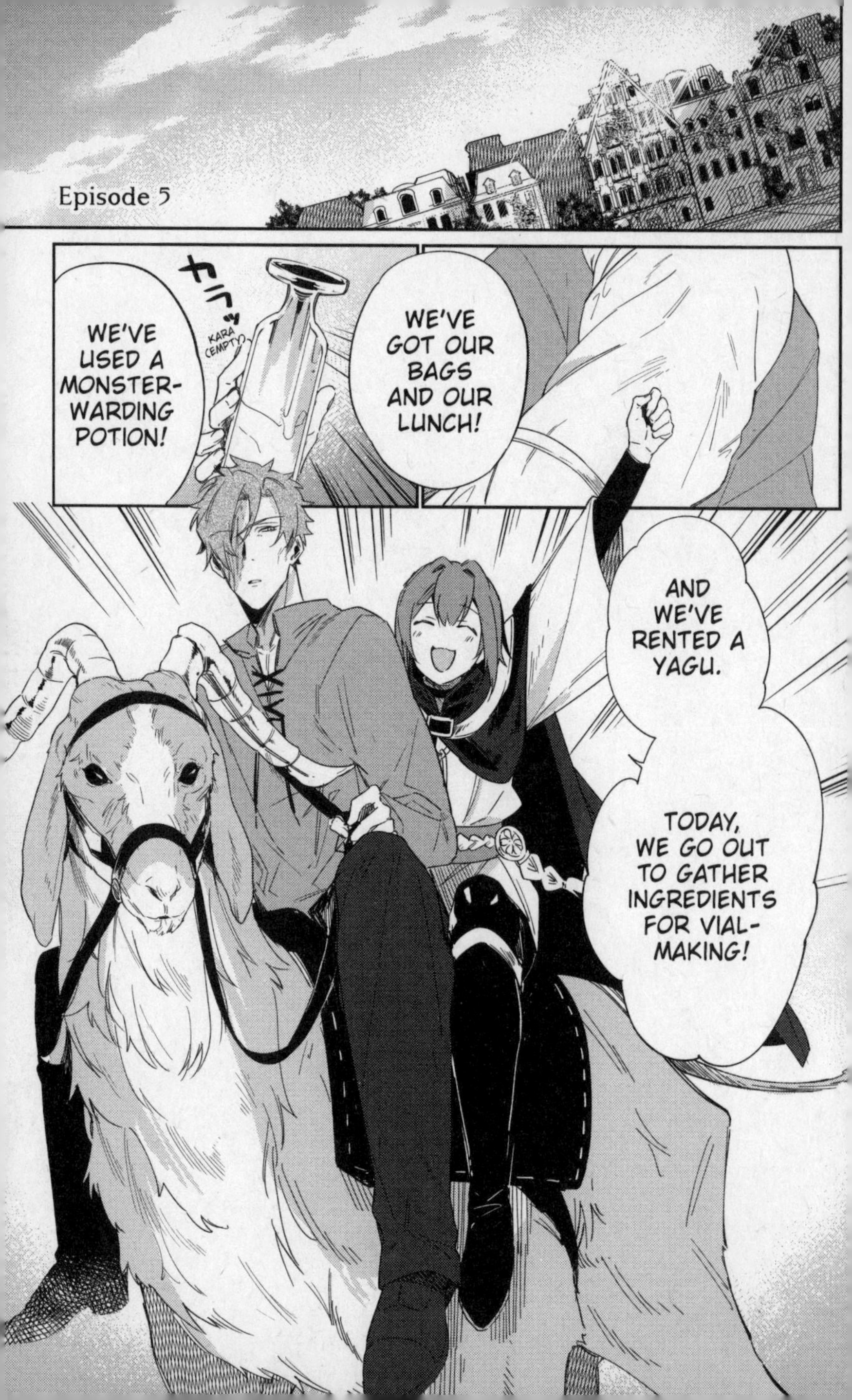
WE'VE GOT OUR BAGS AND OUR LUNCH!
カラッ
KARA (EMPTY)
WE'VE USED A MONSTER-WARDING POTION!
AND WE'VE RENTED A YAGU.
TODAY, WE GO OUT TO GATHER INGREDIENTS FOR VIAL-MAKING!

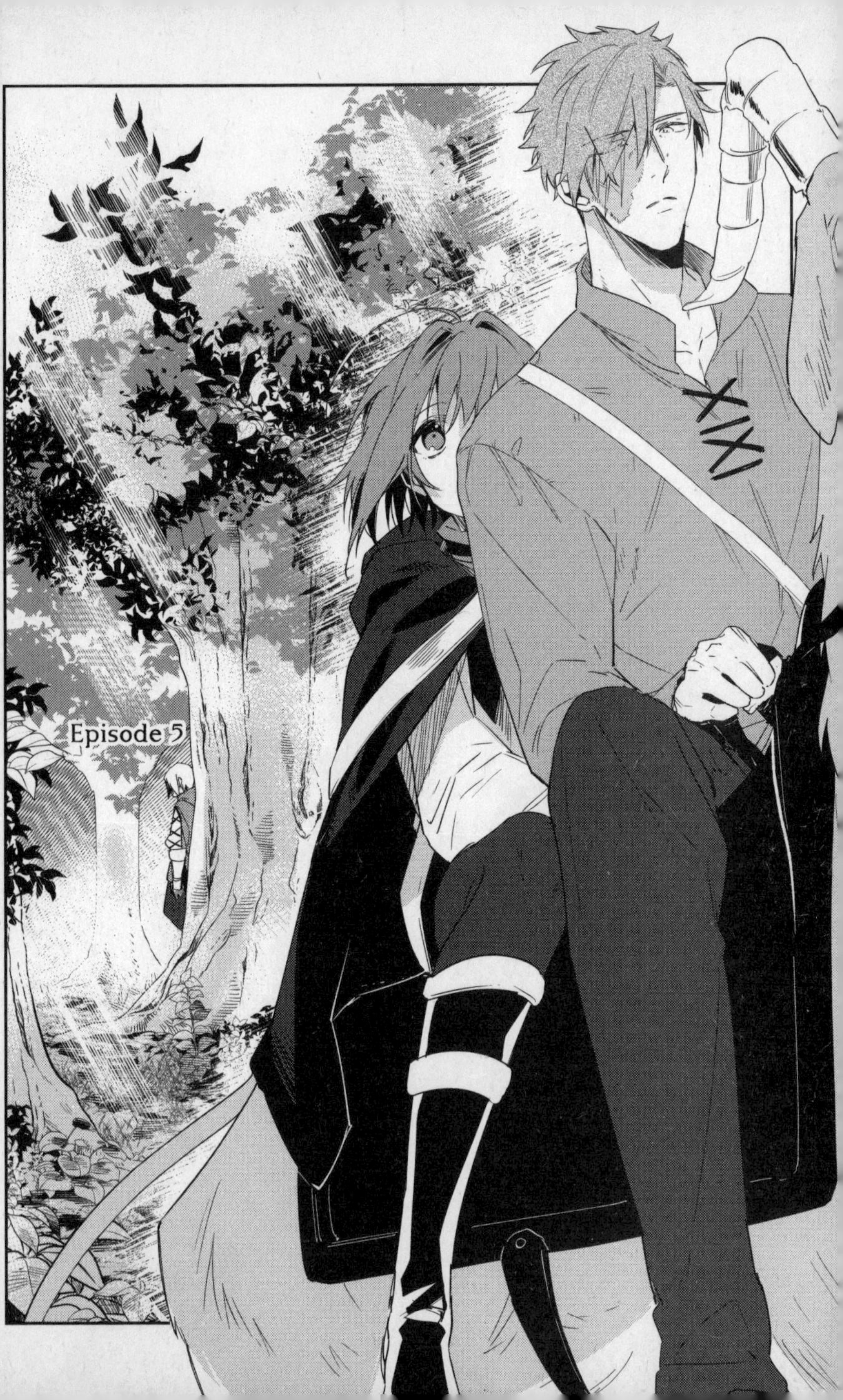
Episode 5

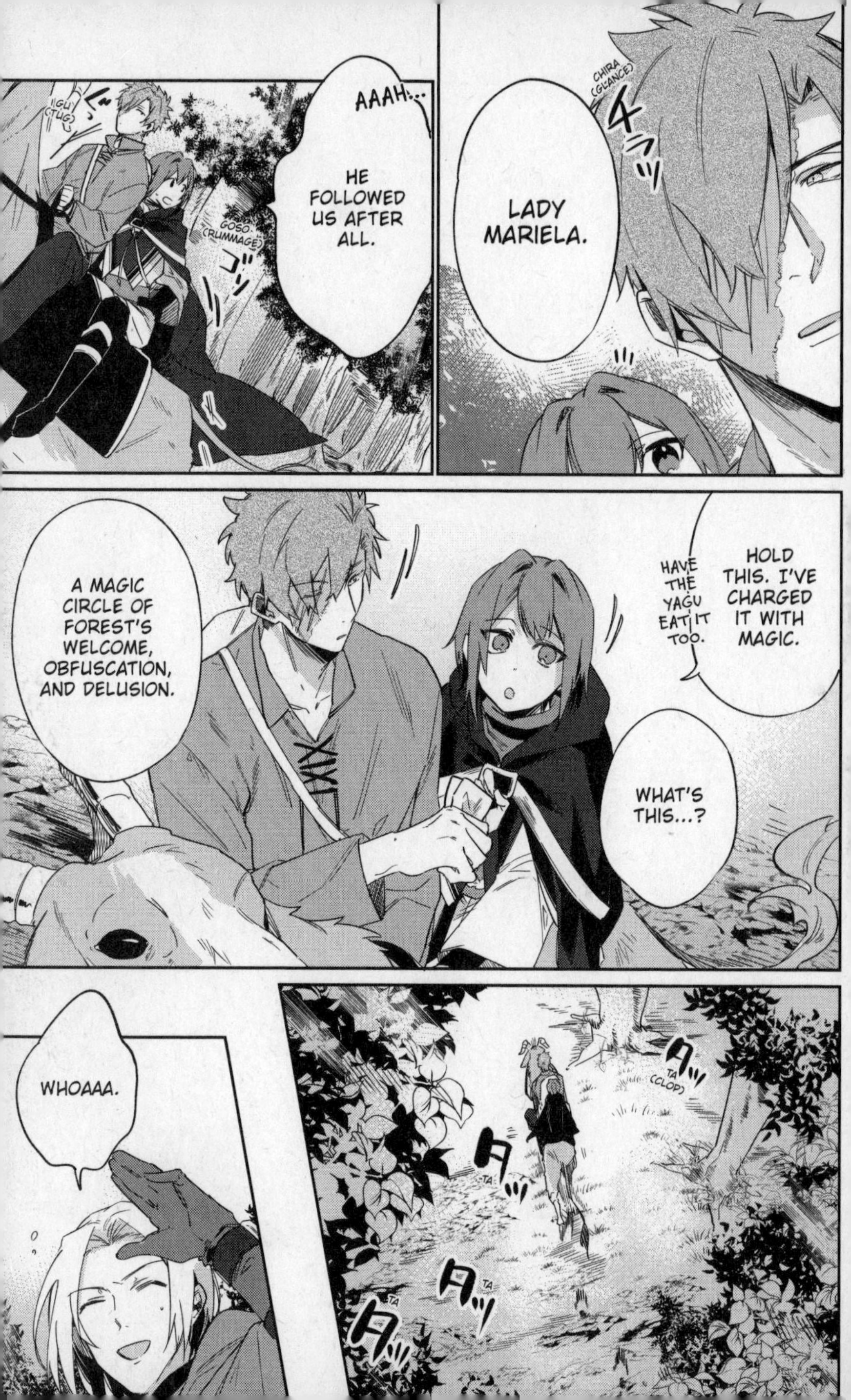
CHIRA (GLANCE)
LADY MARIELA.
AAAH...
HE FOLLOWED US AFTER ALL.
GUI (TUG)
GOSO (RUMMAGE)
HOLD THIS. I'VE CHARGED IT WITH MAGIC.
HAVE THE YAGU EAT IT TOO.
WHAT'S THIS...?
A MAGIC CIRCLE OF FOREST'S WELCOME, OBFUSCATION, AND DELUSION.
TA (CLOP)
TA
TA
TA
WHOAAA.

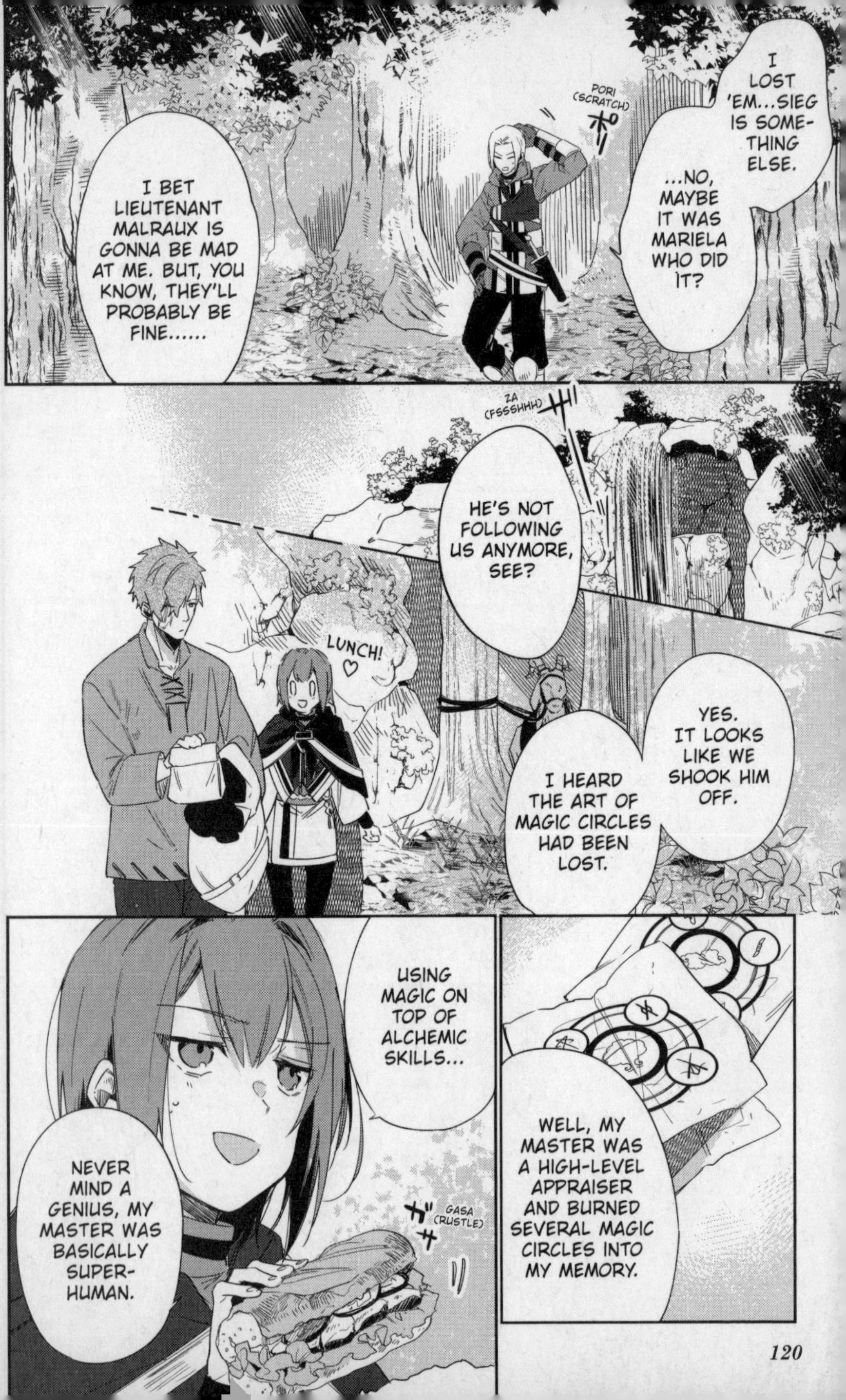
I LOST 'EM...SIEG IS SOME-THING ELSE.
...NO, MAYBE IT WAS MARIELA WHO DID IT?
PORI (SCRATCH)
I BET LIEUTENANT MALRAUX IS GONNA BE MAD AT ME. BUT, YOU KNOW, THEY'LL PROBABLY BE FINE......
ZA (FSSSHHH)
HE'S NOT FOLLOWING US ANYMORE, SEE?
YES. IT LOOKS LIKE WE SHOOK HIM OFF.
I HEARD THE ART OF MAGIC CIRCLES HAD BEEN LOST.
LUNCH! ♡
WELL, MY MASTER WAS A HIGH-LEVEL APPRAISER AND BURNED SEVERAL MAGIC CIRCLES INTO MY MEMORY.
USING MAGIC ON TOP OF ALCHEMIC SKILLS...
NEVER MIND A GENIUS, MY MASTER WAS BASICALLY SUPER-HUMAN.
GASA (RUSTLE)

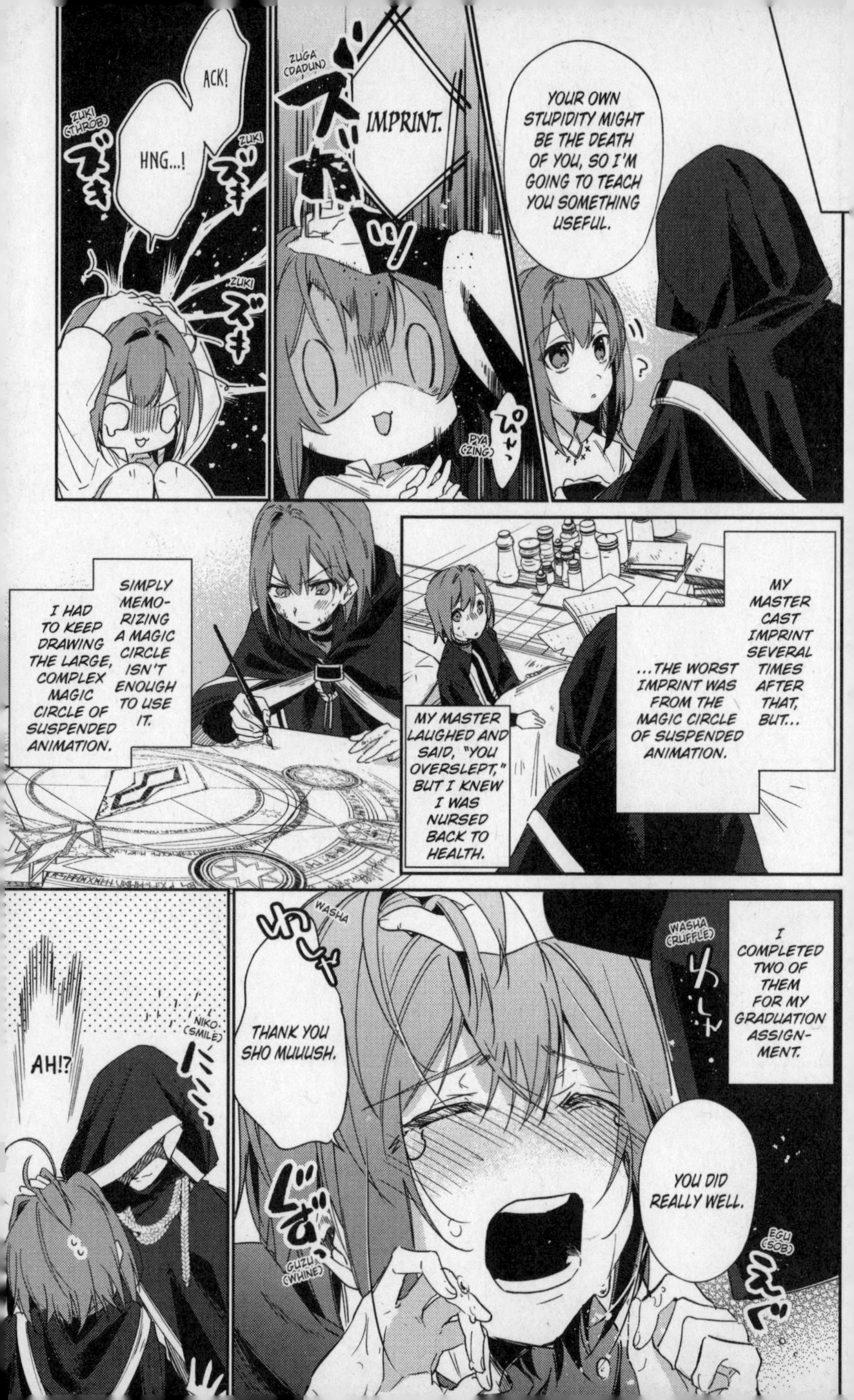
YOUR OWN STUPIDITY MIGHT BE THE DEATH OF YOU, SO I'M GOING TO TEACH YOU SOMETHING USEFUL.
ZUGA (DADUN)
IMPRINT.
PYA (ZING)
ACK!
ZUKI
HNG...!
ZUKI (THROB)
ZUKI
MY MASTER CAST IMPRINT SEVERAL TIMES AFTER THAT, BUT...
...THE WORST IMPRINT WAS FROM THE MAGIC CIRCLE OF SUSPENDED ANIMATION.
MY MASTER LAUGHED AND SAID, "YOU OVERSLEPT," BUT I KNEW I WAS NURSED BACK TO HEALTH.
SIMPLY MEMORIZING A MAGIC CIRCLE ISN'T ENOUGH TO USE IT.
I HAD TO KEEP DRAWING THE LARGE, COMPLEX MAGIC CIRCLE OF SUSPENDED ANIMATION.
I COMPLETED TWO OF THEM FOR MY GRADUATION ASSIGNMENT.
WASHA (RUFFLE)
WASHA
THANK YOU SHO MUUUSH.
YOU DID REALLY WELL.
EGU (SOB)
GUZU (WHINE)
NIKO (SMILE)
AH!?

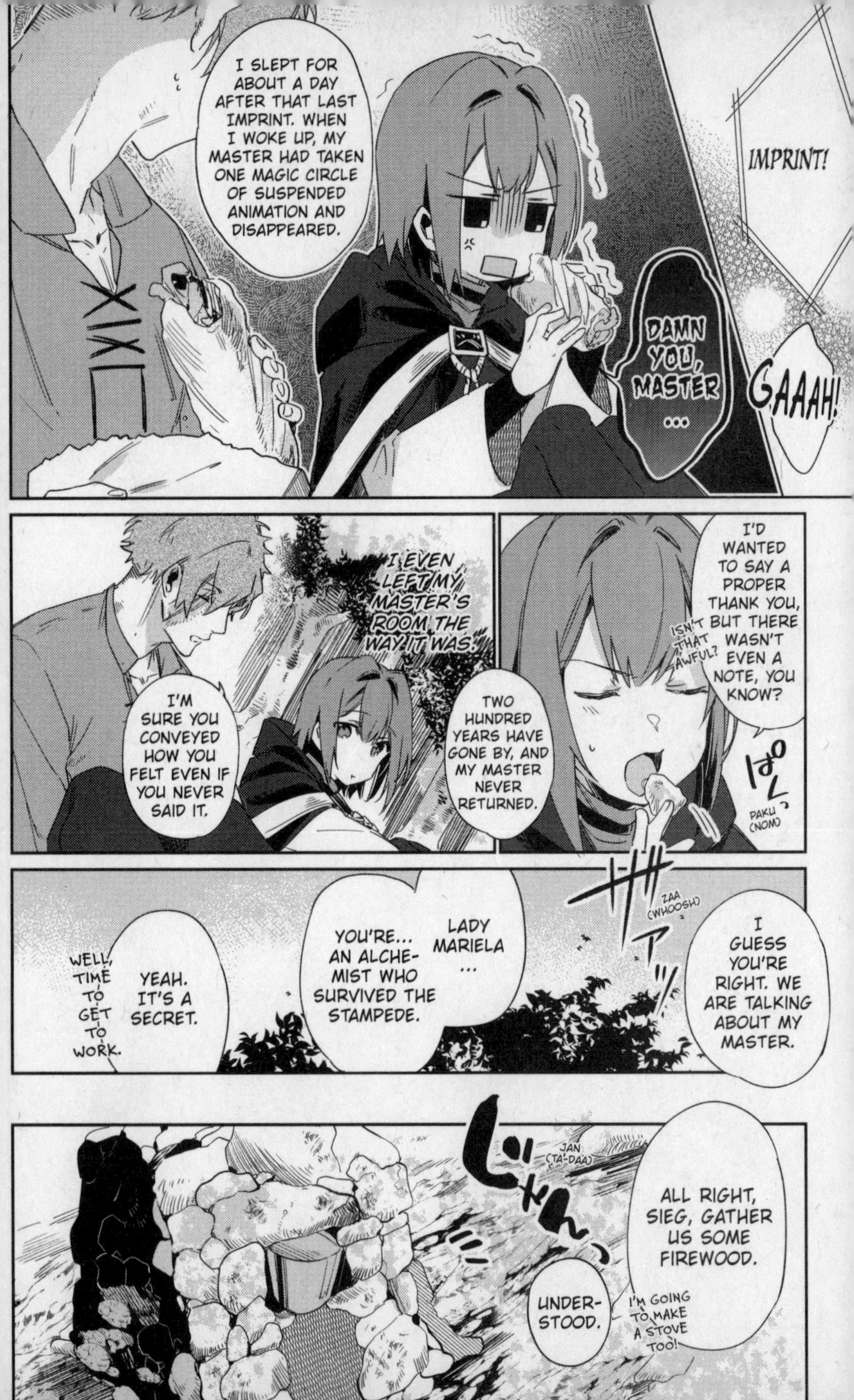

IMPRINT!
I SLEPT FOR ABOUT A DAY AFTER THAT LAST IMPRINT. WHEN I WOKE UP, MY MASTER HAD TAKEN ONE MAGIC CIRCLE OF SUSPENDED ANIMATION AND DISAPPEARED.
DAMN YOU, MASTER...
GAAAH!
I'D WANTED TO SAY A PROPER THANK YOU, BUT THERE WASN'T EVEN A NOTE, YOU KNOW?
ISN'T THAT AWFUL?
PAKU (NOM)
I EVEN LEFT MY MASTER'S ROOM THE WAY IT WAS.
TWO HUNDRED YEARS HAVE GONE BY, AND MY MASTER NEVER RETURNED.
I'M SURE YOU CONVEYED HOW YOU FELT EVEN IF YOU NEVER SAID IT.
ZAA (WHOOSH)
I GUESS YOU'RE RIGHT. WE ARE TALKING ABOUT MY MASTER.
LADY MARIELA...
YOU'RE... AN ALCHEMIST WHO SURVIVED THE STAMPEDE.
YEAH. IT'S A SECRET.
WELL, TIME TO GET TO WORK.
JAN (TA-DAA)
ALL RIGHT, SIEG, GATHER US SOME FIREWOOD.
UNDERSTOOD.
I'M GOING TO MAKE A STOVE TOO!

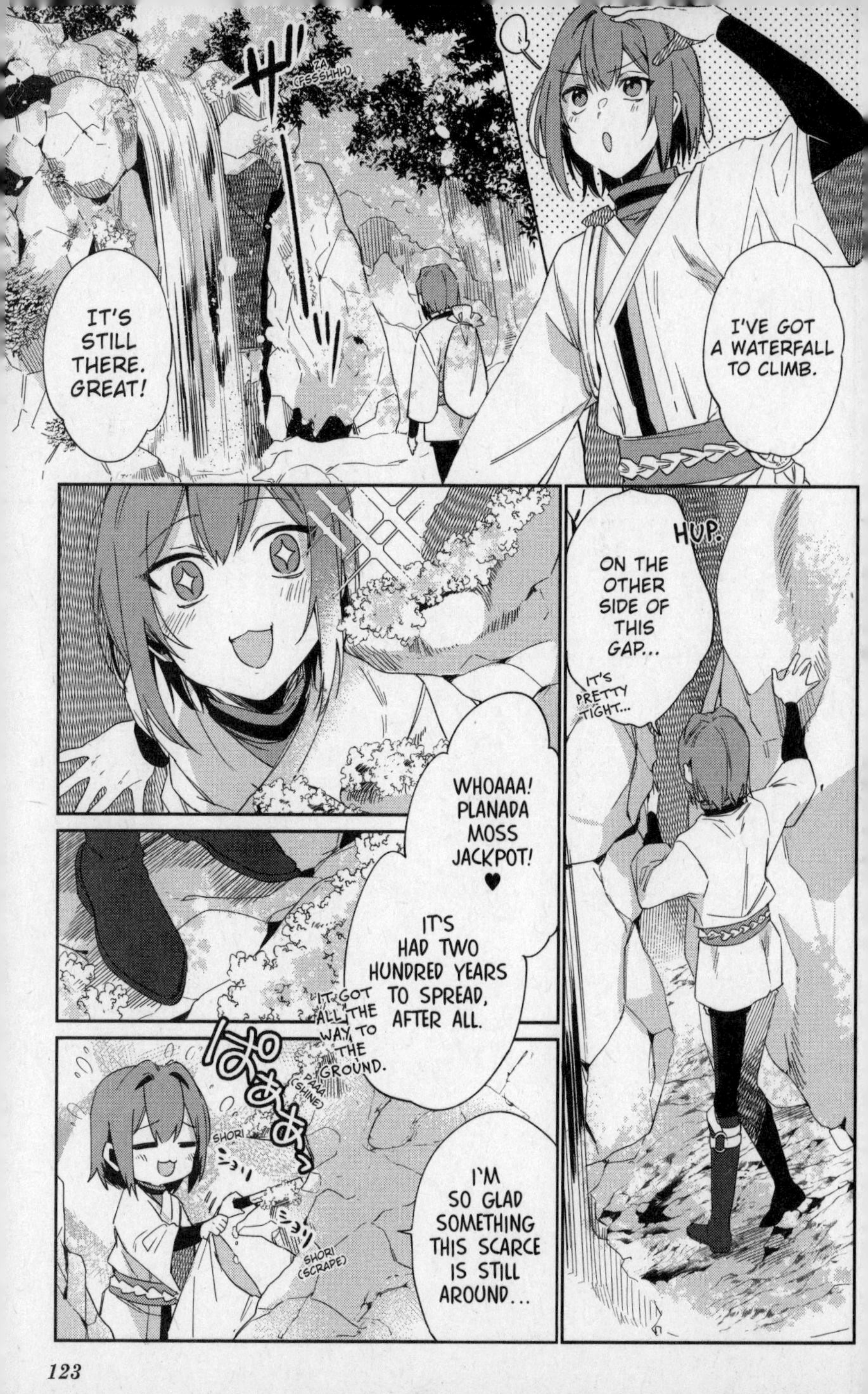
I'VE GOT A WATERFALL TO CLIMB.
ZA (FSSSHHH)
IT'S STILL THERE. GREAT!
HUP.
ON THE OTHER SIDE OF THIS GAP...
IT'S PRETTY TIGHT...
WHOAAA! PLANADA MOSS JACKPOT! ♥
IT'S HAD TWO HUNDRED YEARS TO SPREAD, AFTER ALL.
IT GOT ALL THE WAY TO THE GROUND.
PAAA (SHINE)
SHORI
SHORI (SCRAPE)
I'M SO GLAD SOMETHING THIS SCARCE IS STILL AROUND...

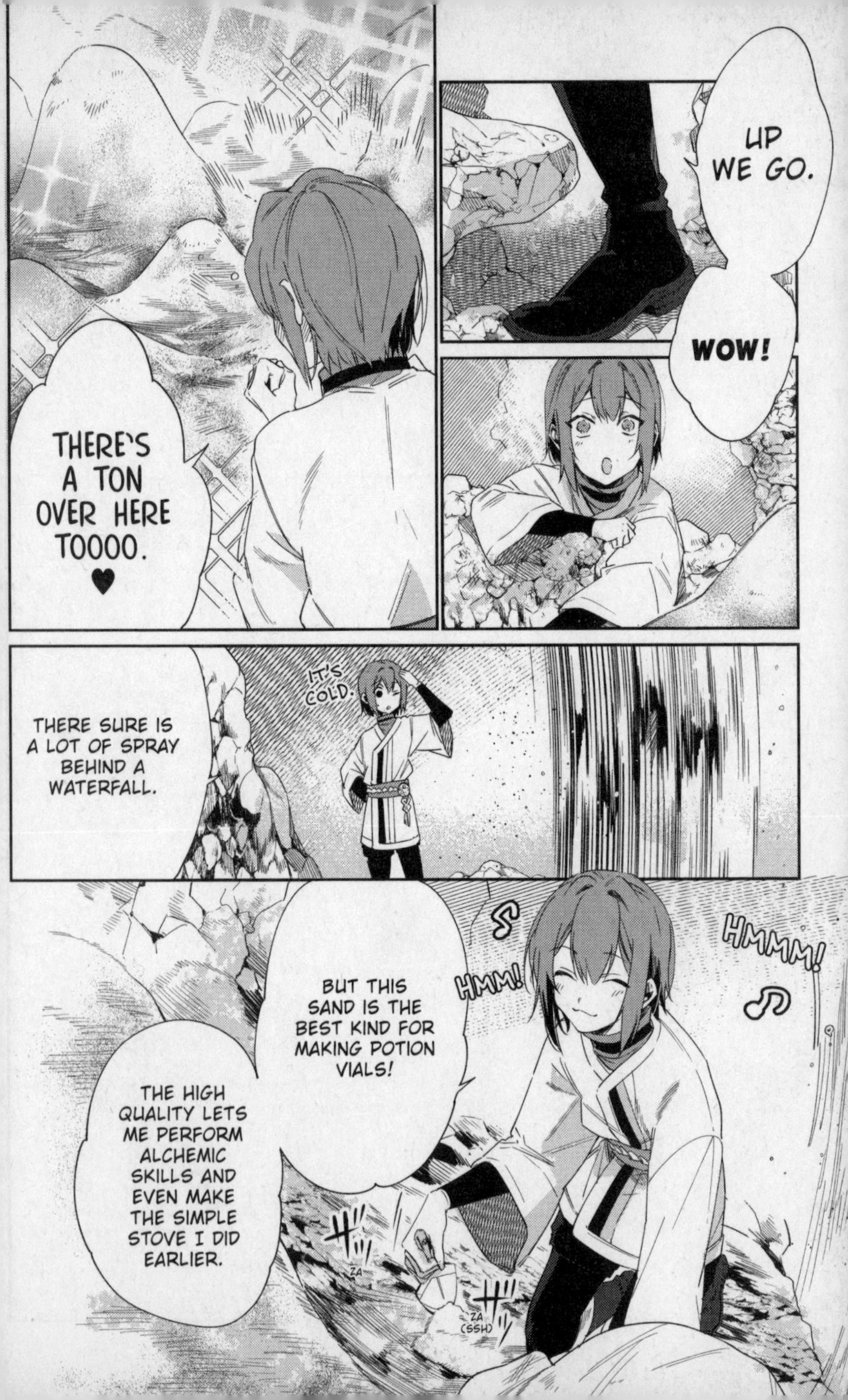
UP WE GO.
WOW!
THERE'S A TON OVER HERE TOOOO. ♥
IT'S COLD.
THERE SURE IS A LOT OF SPRAY BEHIND A WATERFALL.
HMMM!
HMM!
BUT THIS SAND IS THE BEST KIND FOR MAKING POTION VIALS!
THE HIGH QUALITY LETS ME PERFORM ALCHEMIC SKILLS AND EVEN MAKE THE SIMPLE STOVE I DID EARLIER.
ZA (SSH)
ZA

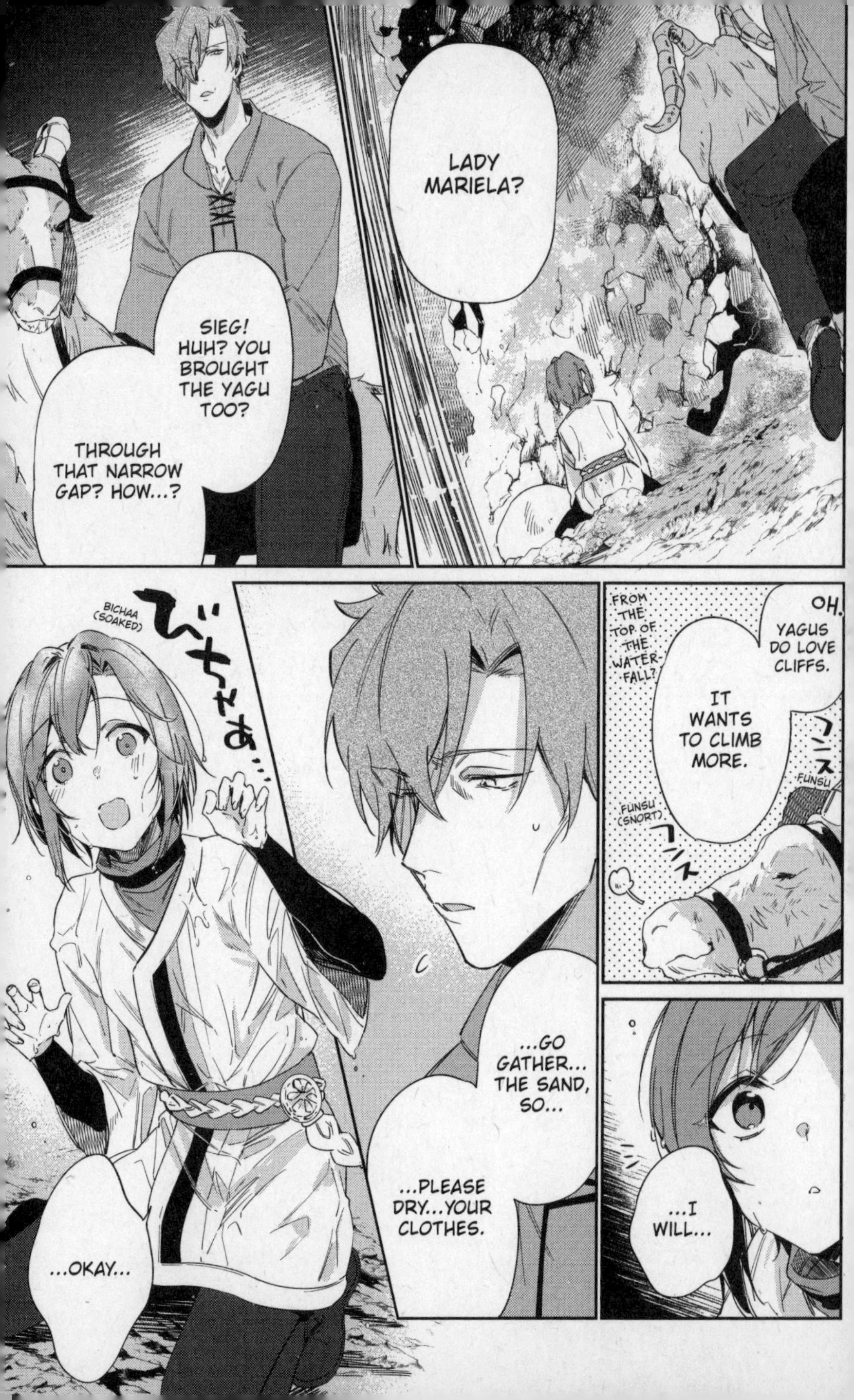
LADY MARIELA?
SIEG! HUH? YOU BROUGHT THE YAGU TOO?
THROUGH THAT NARROW GAP? HOW...?
OH. YAGUS DO LOVE CLIFFS.
FUNSU
IT WANTS TO CLIMB MORE.
FUNSU (SNORT)
FROM THE TOP OF THE WATER-FALL?
...I WILL...
...GO GATHER... THE SAND, SO...
...PLEASE DRY...YOUR CLOTHES.
BICHAA (SOAKED)
...OKAY...

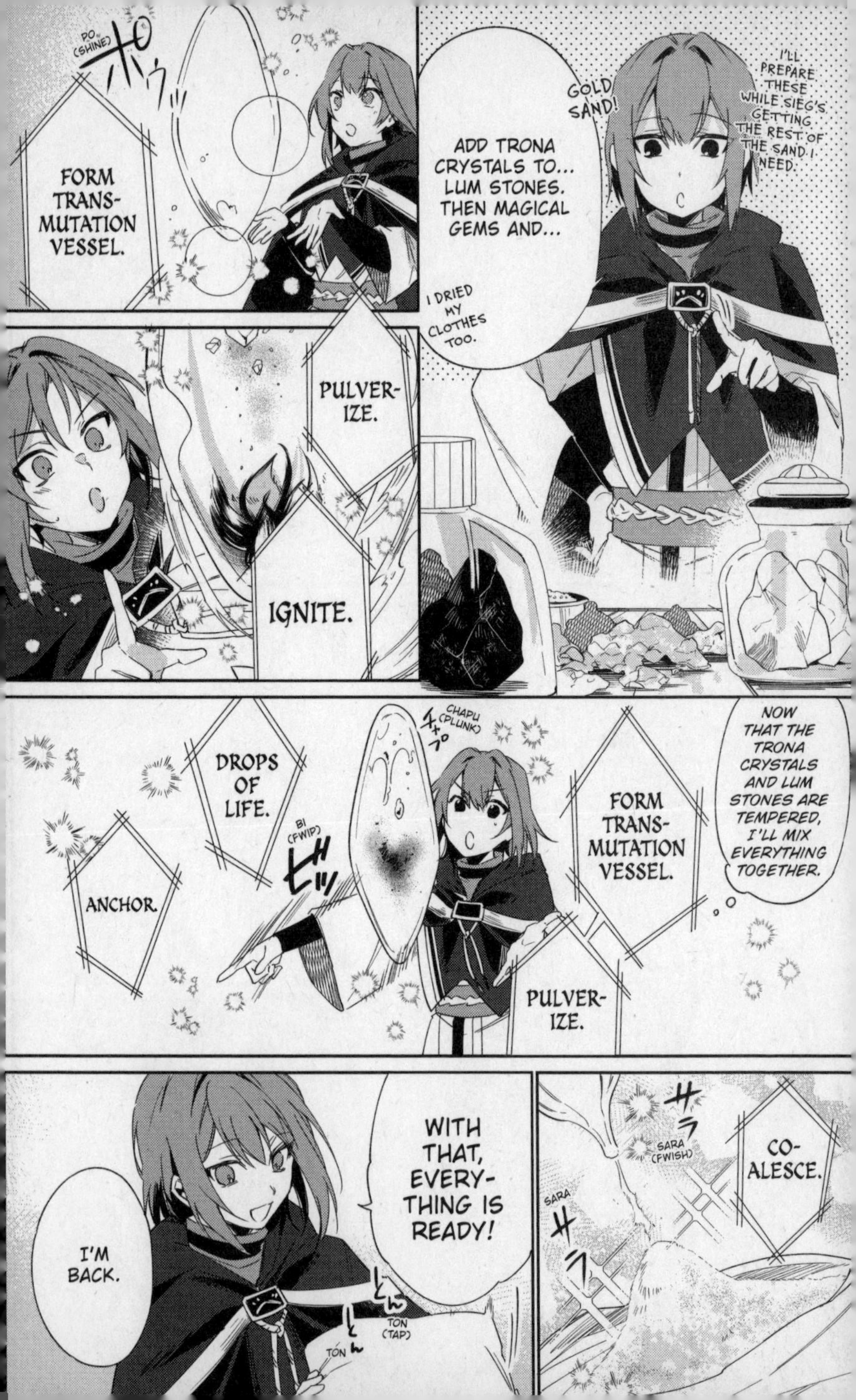
I'LL PREPARE THESE WHILE SIEG'S GETTING THE REST OF THE SAND I NEED.
GOLD SAND!
ADD TRONA CRYSTALS TO... LUM STONES. THEN MAGICAL GEMS AND...
I DRIED MY CLOTHES TOO.
PO (SHINE)
FORM TRANS-MUTATION VESSEL.
PULVER-IZE.
IGNITE.
NOW THAT THE TRONA CRYSTALS AND LUM STONES ARE TEMPERED, I'LL MIX EVERYTHING TOGETHER.
FORM TRANS-MUTATION VESSEL.
CHAPU (PLUNK)
PULVER-IZE.
DROPS OF LIFE.
BI (FWIP)
ANCHOR.
SARA (FWISH)
CO-ALESCE.
SARA
WITH THAT, EVERY-THING IS READY!
TON (TAP)
TON
I'M BACK.

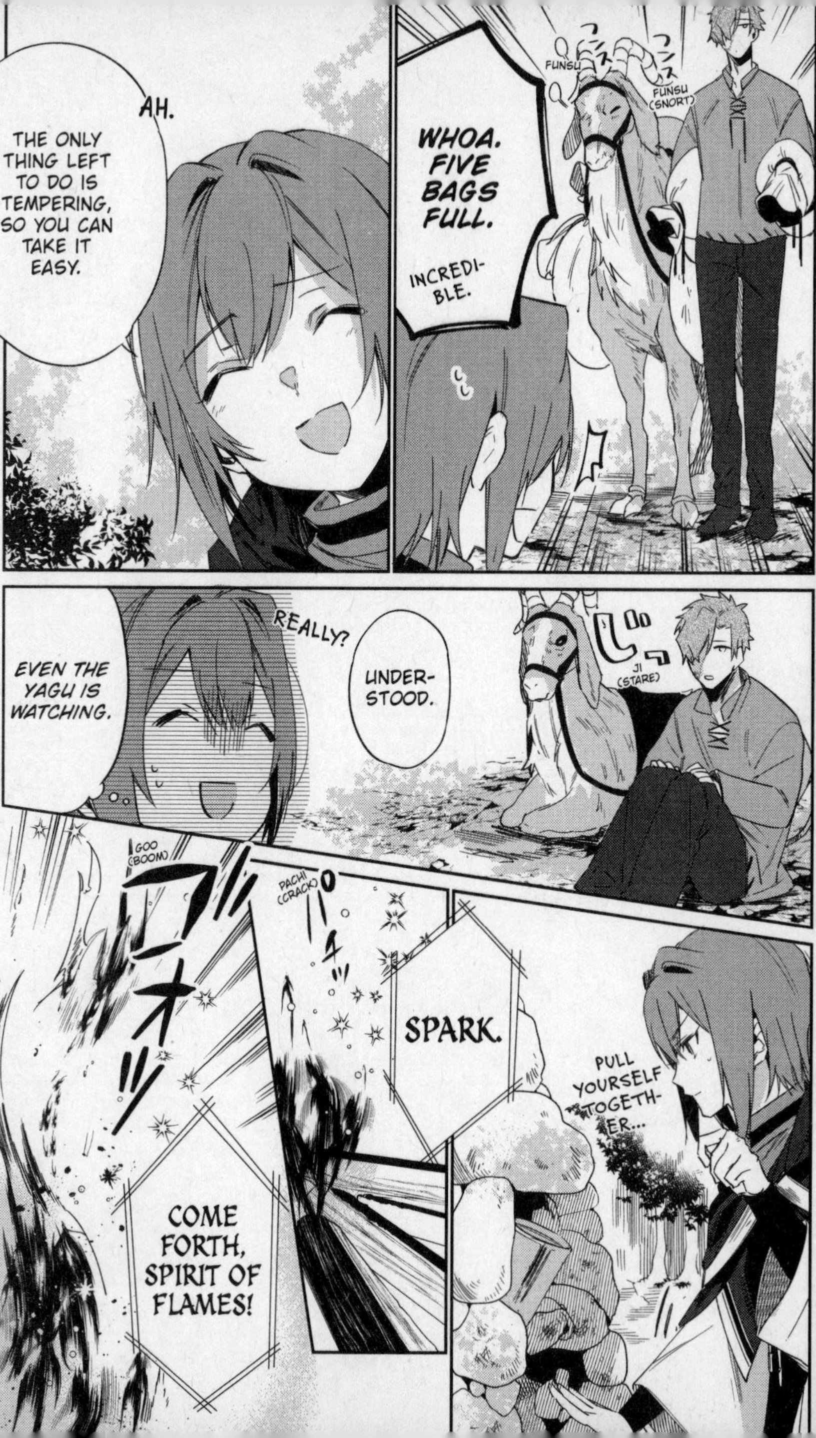

FUNSU
FUNSU (SNORT)
WHOA. FIVE BAGS FULL.
INCREDIBLE.
AH.
THE ONLY THING LEFT TO DO IS TEMPERING, SO YOU CAN TAKE IT EASY.
JI (STARE)
UNDERSTOOD.
REALLY?
EVEN THE YAGU IS WATCHING.
PULL YOURSELF TOGETHER...
SPARK.
PACHI (CRACK)
GOO (BOOM)
COME FORTH, SPIRIT OF FLAMES!

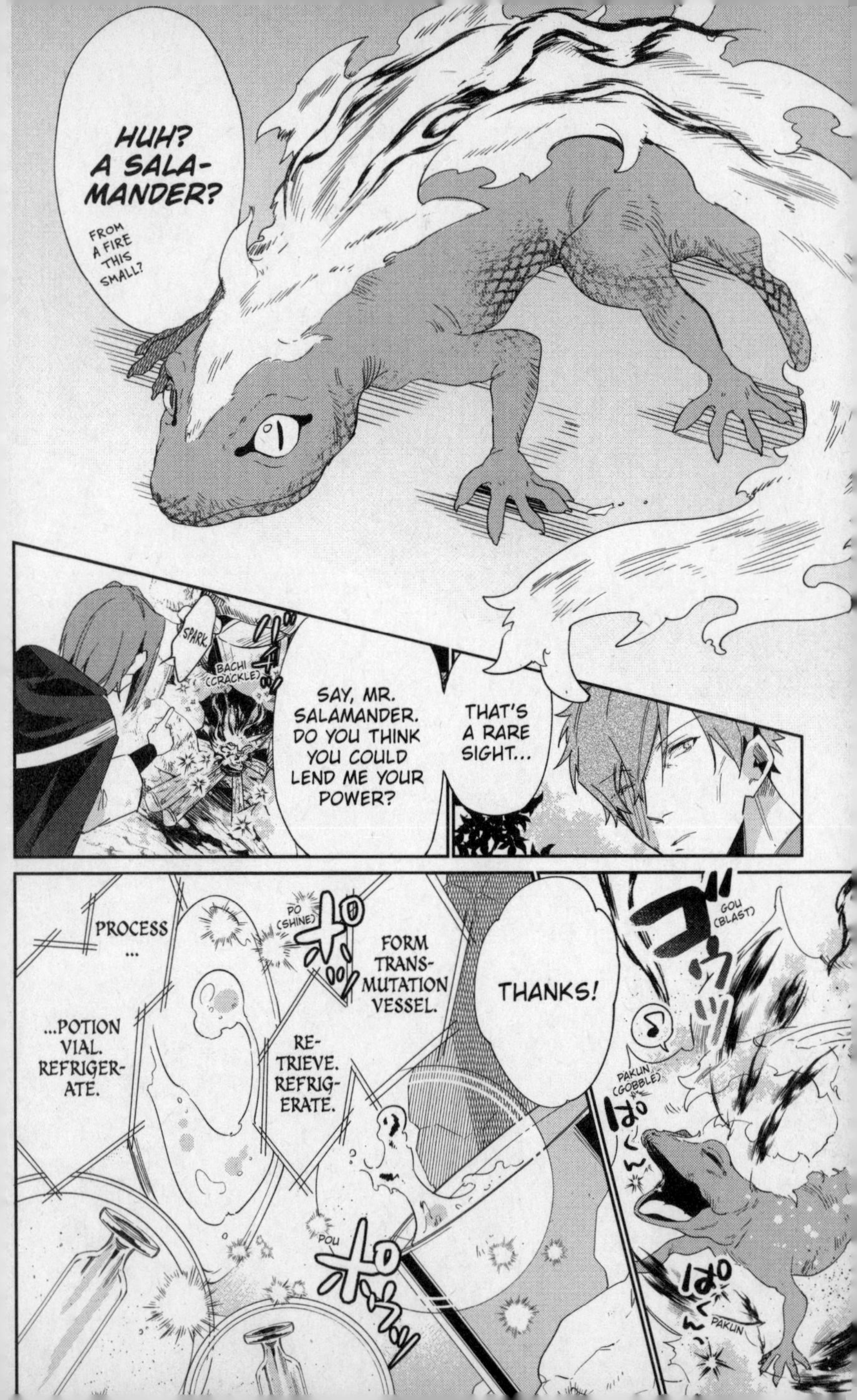
HUH? A SALAMANDER?
FROM A FIRE THIS SMALL?
THAT'S A RARE SIGHT...
SAY, MR. SALAMANDER. DO YOU THINK YOU COULD LEND ME YOUR POWER?
SPARK.
BACHI (CRACKLE)
GOU (BLAST)
THANKS!
PAKUN (GOBBLE)
PAKUN
FORM TRANSMUTATION VESSEL.
PO (SHINE)
PROCESS...
RETRIEVE. REFRIGERATE.
...POTION VIAL. REFRIGERATE.
POU

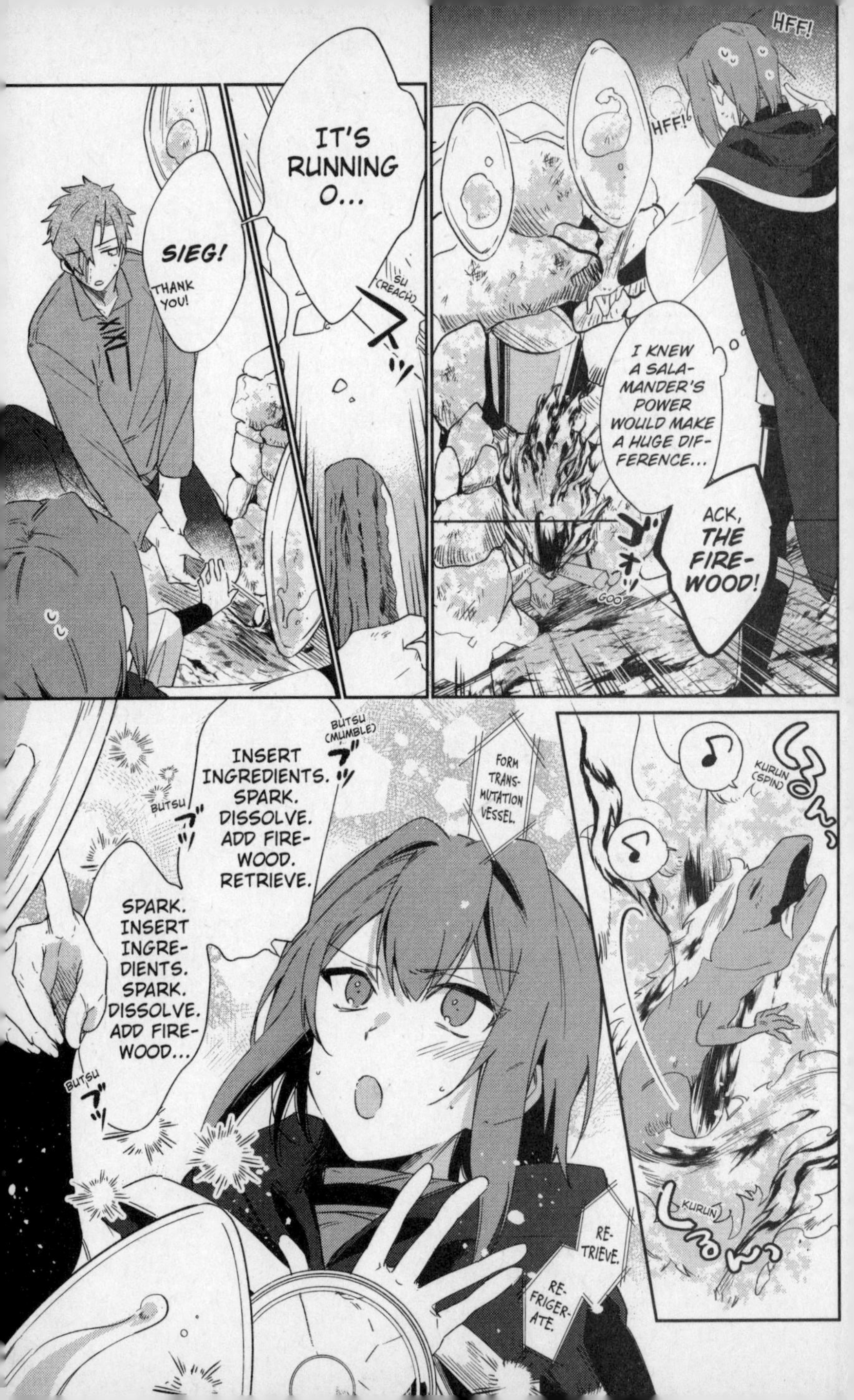
HFF!
HFF!
I KNEW A SALAMANDER'S POWER WOULD MAKE A HUGE DIFFERENCE...
GOO
ACK, THE FIREWOOD!
IT'S RUNNING O...
SU (CREACH)
SIEG!
THANK YOU!
KURUN (SPIN)
KURUN
RE-TRIEVE.
RE-FRIGER-ATE.
FORM TRANS-MUTATION VESSEL.
BUTSU (MUMBLE)
INSERT INGREDIENTS. SPARK. DISSOLVE. ADD FIRE-WOOD. RETRIEVE.
BUTSU
SPARK. INSERT INGRE-DIENTS. SPARK. DISSOLVE. ADD FIRE-WOOD...
BUTSU

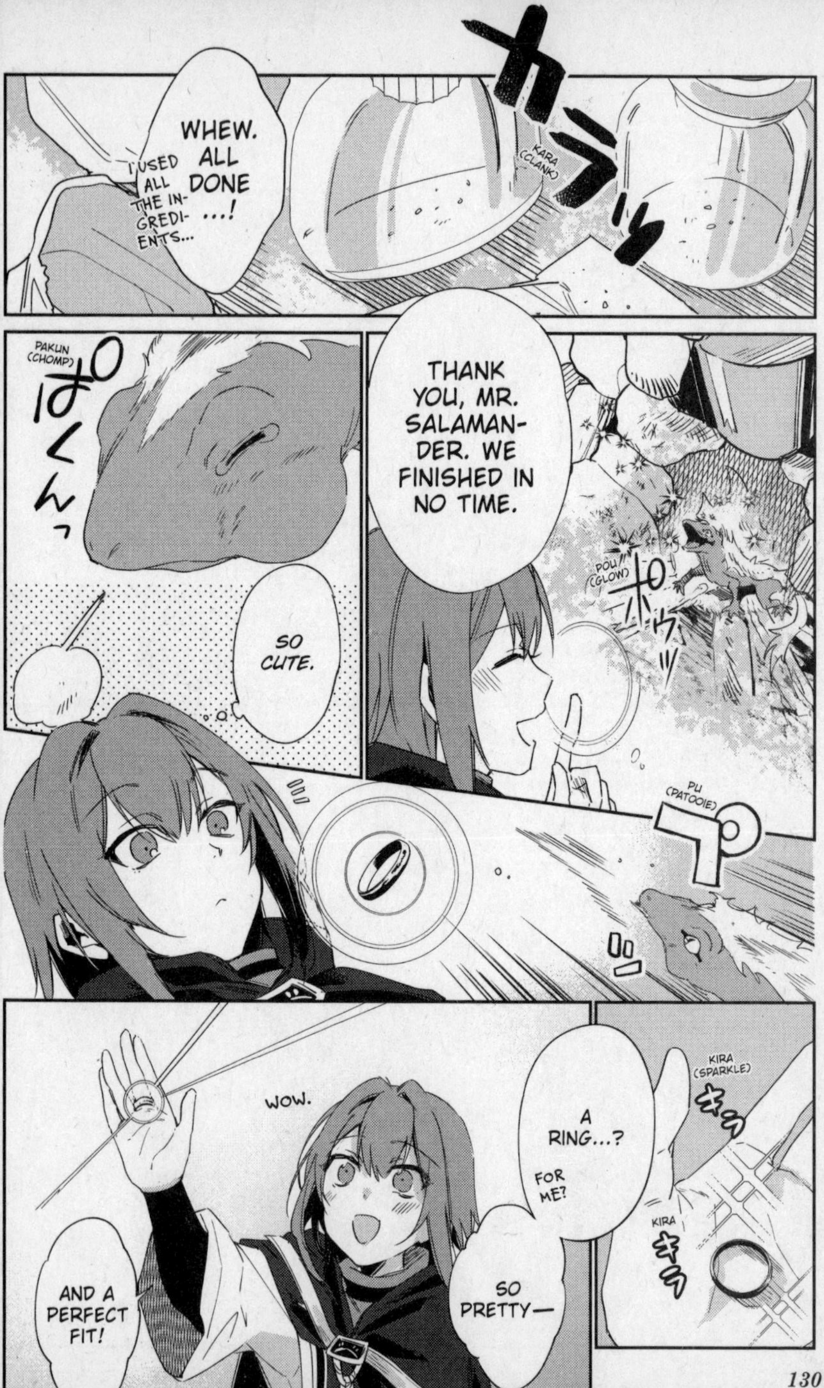
KARA (CLANK)
WHEW. ALL DONE ...!
I USED ALL THE INGREDIENTS...
THANK YOU, MR. SALAMANDER. WE FINISHED IN NO TIME.
POU (GLOW)
PAKUN (CHOMP)
SO CUTE.
PU (PATOOIE)
KIRA (SPARKLE)
KIRA
A RING...?
FOR ME?
WOW.
SO PRETTY—
AND A PERFECT FIT!

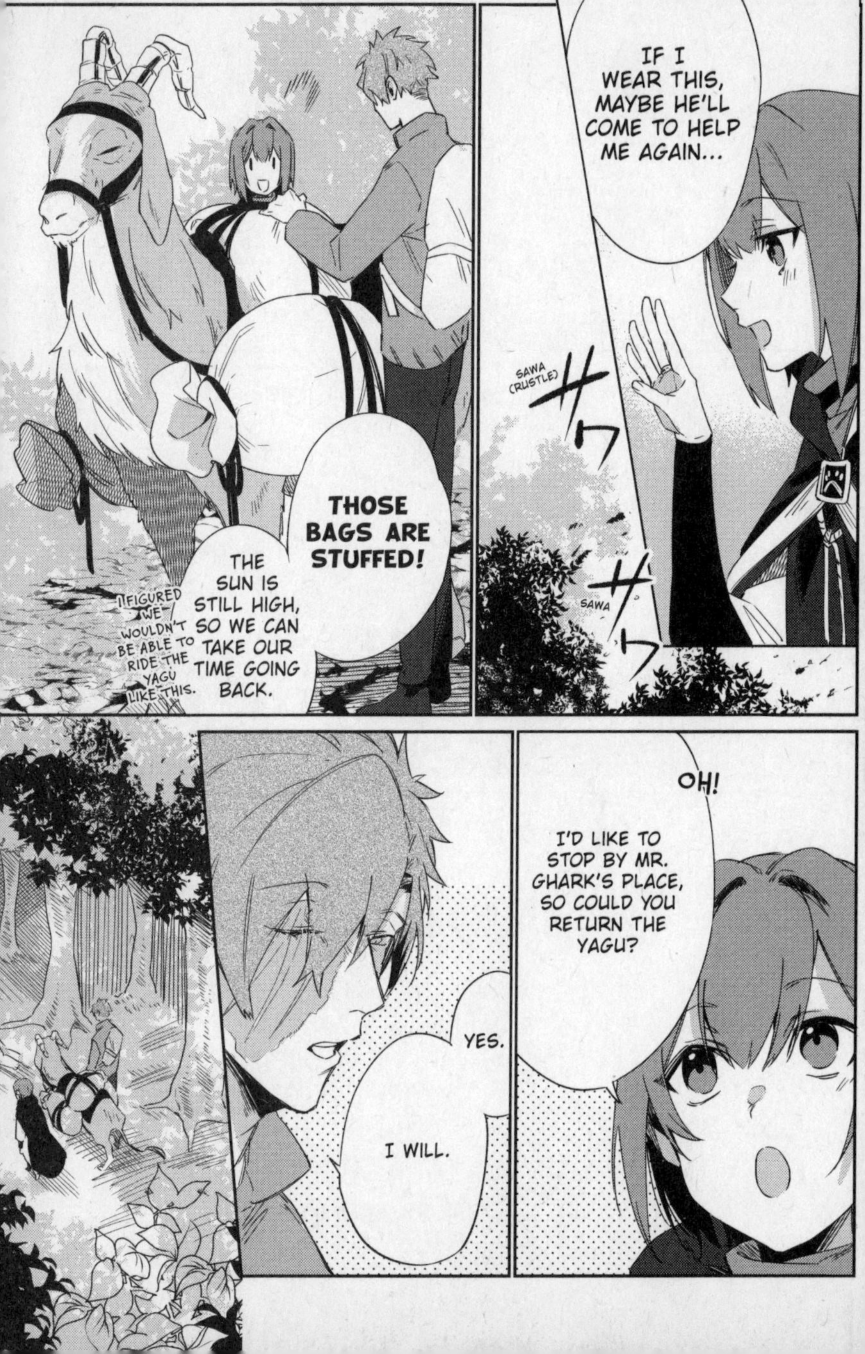
IF I WEAR THIS, MAYBE HE'LL COME TO HELP ME AGAIN...
SAWA (RUSTLE)
SAWA
THOSE BAGS ARE STUFFED!
THE SUN IS STILL HIGH, SO WE CAN TAKE OUR TIME GOING BACK.
I FIGURED WE WOULDN'T BE ABLE TO RIDE THE YAGU LIKE THIS.
OH!
I'D LIKE TO STOP BY MR. GHARK'S PLACE, SO COULD YOU RETURN THE YAGU?
YES.
I WILL.

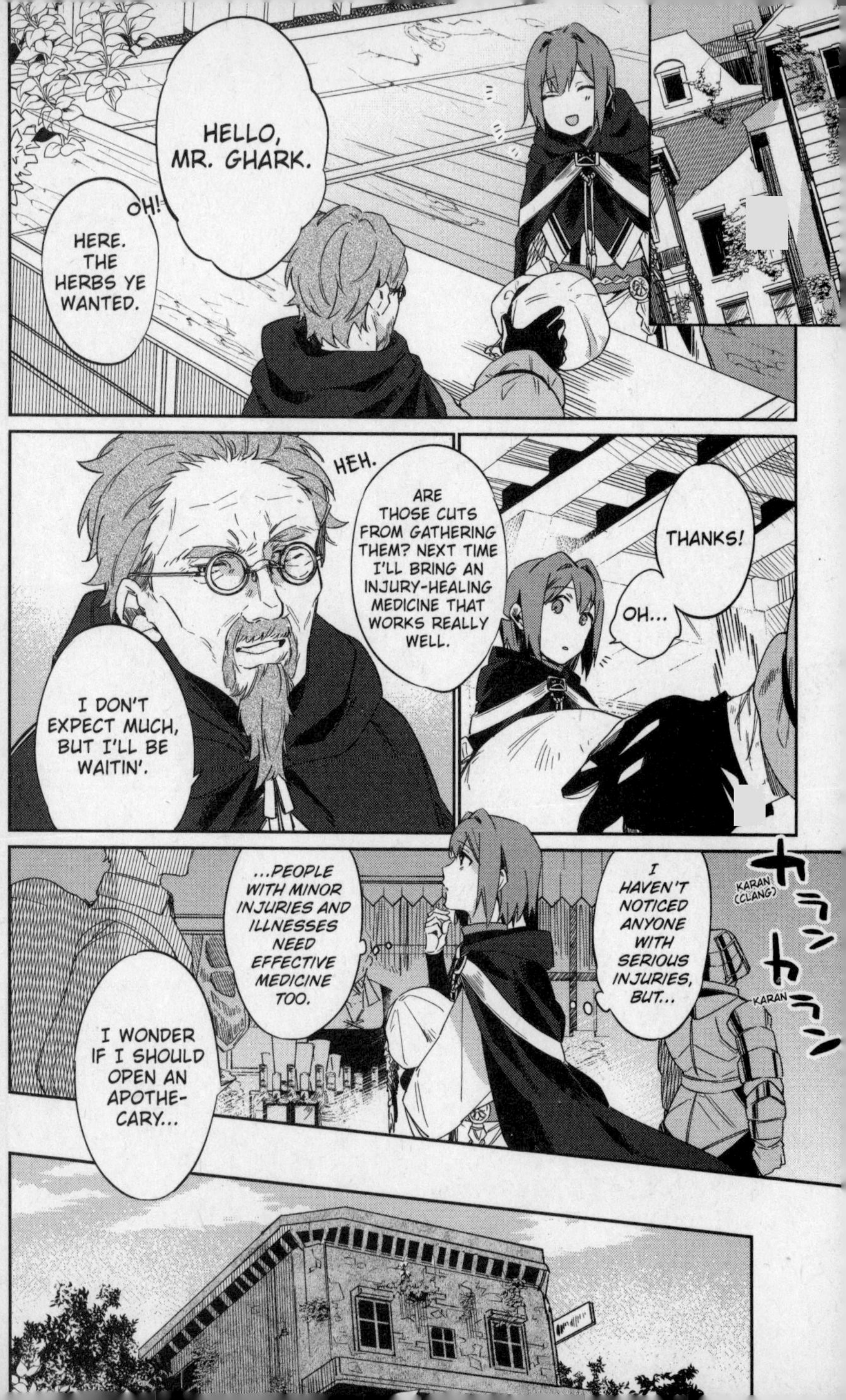
HELLO, MR. GHARK.
OH!
HERE. THE HERBS YE WANTED.
THANKS!
OH...
HEH.
ARE THOSE CUTS FROM GATHERING THEM? NEXT TIME I'LL BRING AN INJURY-HEALING MEDICINE THAT WORKS REALLY WELL.
I DON'T EXPECT MUCH, BUT I'LL BE WAITIN'.
KARAN (CLANG)
KARAN
I HAVEN'T NOTICED ANYONE WITH SERIOUS INJURIES, BUT...
...PEOPLE WITH MINOR INJURIES AND ILLNESSES NEED EFFECTIVE MEDICINE TOO.
I WONDER IF I SHOULD OPEN AN APOTHE-CARY...

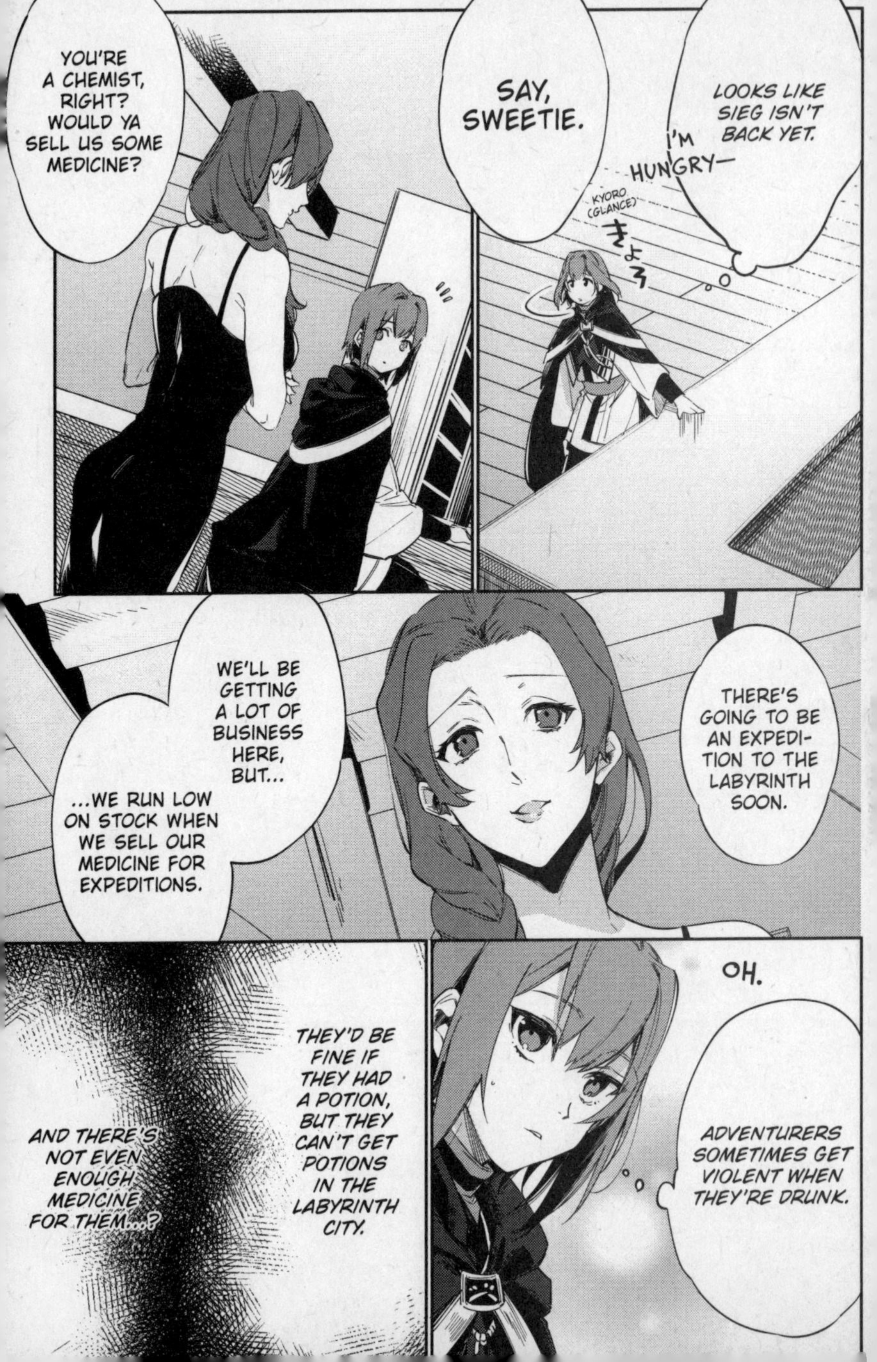
LOOKS LIKE SIEG ISN'T BACK YET.
I'M HUNGRY—
KYORO (GLANCE)
きょろ
SAY, SWEETIE.
YOU'RE A CHEMIST, RIGHT? WOULD YA SELL US SOME MEDICINE?
THERE'S GOING TO BE AN EXPEDITION TO THE LABYRINTH SOON.
WE'LL BE GETTING A LOT OF BUSINESS HERE, BUT...
...WE RUN LOW ON STOCK WHEN WE SELL OUR MEDICINE FOR EXPEDITIONS.
OH.
ADVENTURERS SOMETIMES GET VIOLENT WHEN THEY'RE DRUNK.
THEY'D BE FINE IF THEY HAD A POTION, BUT THEY CAN'T GET POTIONS IN THE LABYRINTH CITY.
AND THERE'S NOT EVEN ENOUGH MEDICINE FOR THEM...?

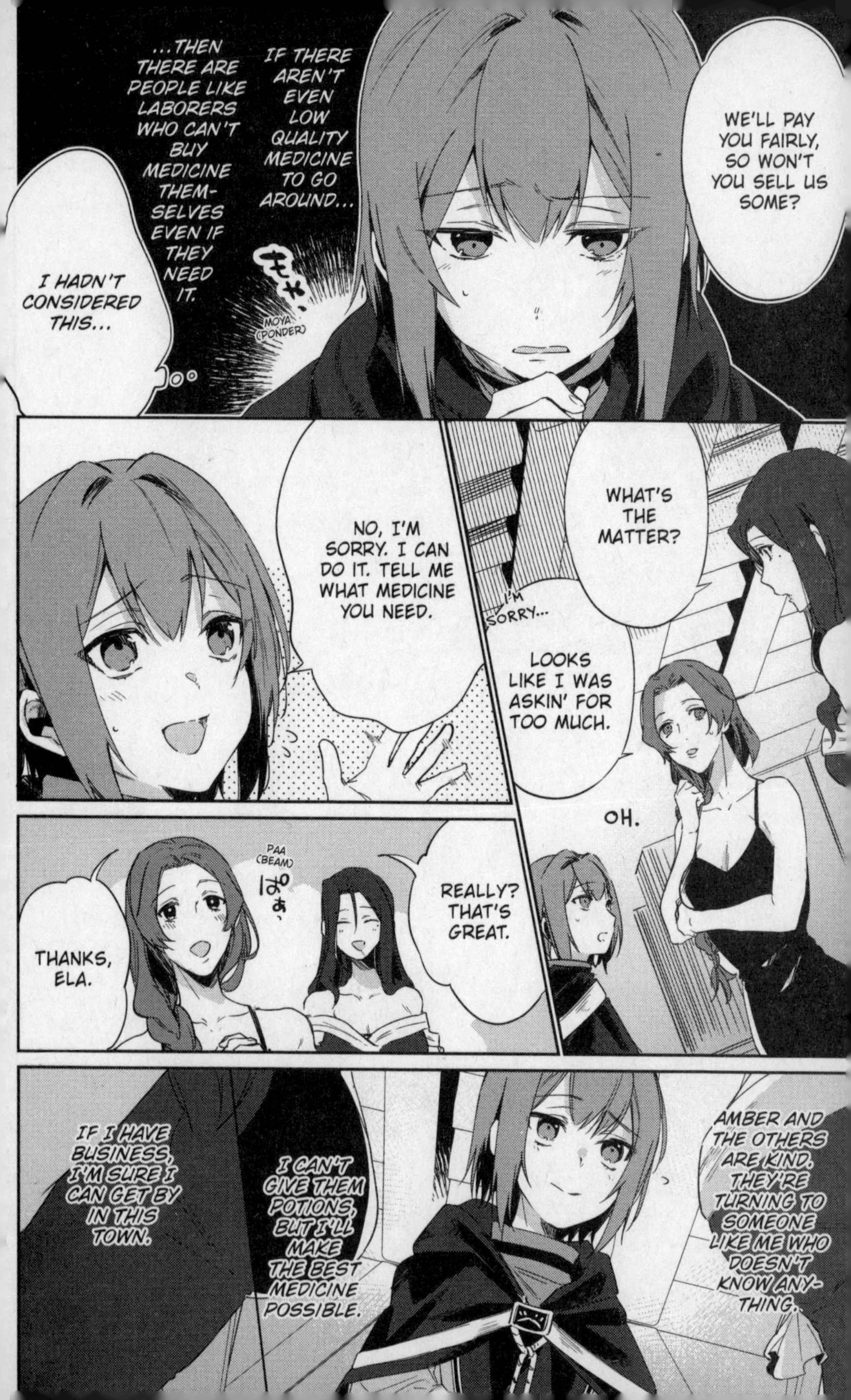
WE'LL PAY YOU FAIRLY, SO WON'T YOU SELL US SOME?
IF THERE AREN'T EVEN LOW QUALITY MEDICINE TO GO AROUND...
...THEN THERE ARE PEOPLE LIKE LABORERS WHO CAN'T BUY MEDICINE THEM-SELVES EVEN IF THEY NEED IT.
もや
MOYA (PONDER)
I HADN'T CONSIDERED THIS...
WHAT'S THE MATTER?
I'M SORRY...
LOOKS LIKE I WAS ASKIN' FOR TOO MUCH.
OH.
NO, I'M SORRY. I CAN DO IT. TELL ME WHAT MEDICINE YOU NEED.
REALLY? THAT'S GREAT.
ぱぁ
PAA (BEAM)
THANKS, ELA.
AMBER AND THE OTHERS ARE KIND. THEY'RE TURNING TO SOMEONE LIKE ME WHO DOESN'T KNOW ANY-THING.
I CAN'T GIVE THEM POTIONS, BUT I'LL MAKE THE BEST MEDICINE POSSIBLE.
IF I HAVE BUSINESS, I'M SURE I CAN GET BY IN THIS TOWN.

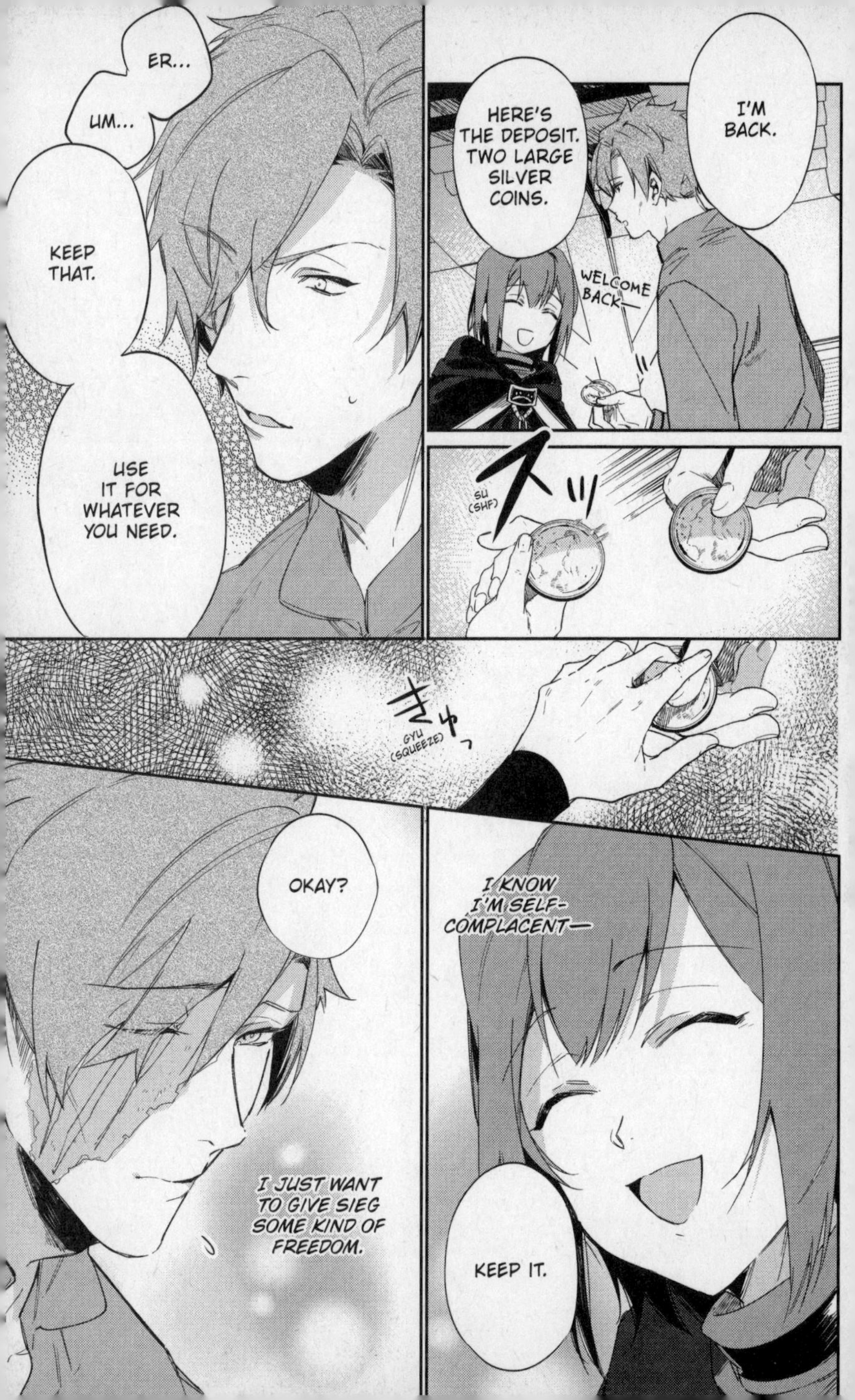
I'M BACK.
HERE'S THE DEPOSIT. TWO LARGE SILVER COINS.
WELCOME BACK—
スッ
SU (SHF)
ER...
UM...
KEEP THAT.
USE IT FOR WHATEVER YOU NEED.
きゅっ
GYU (SQUEEZE)
I KNOW I'M SELF-COMPLACENT—
KEEP IT.
OKAY?
I JUST WANT TO GIVE SIEG SOME KIND OF FREEDOM.

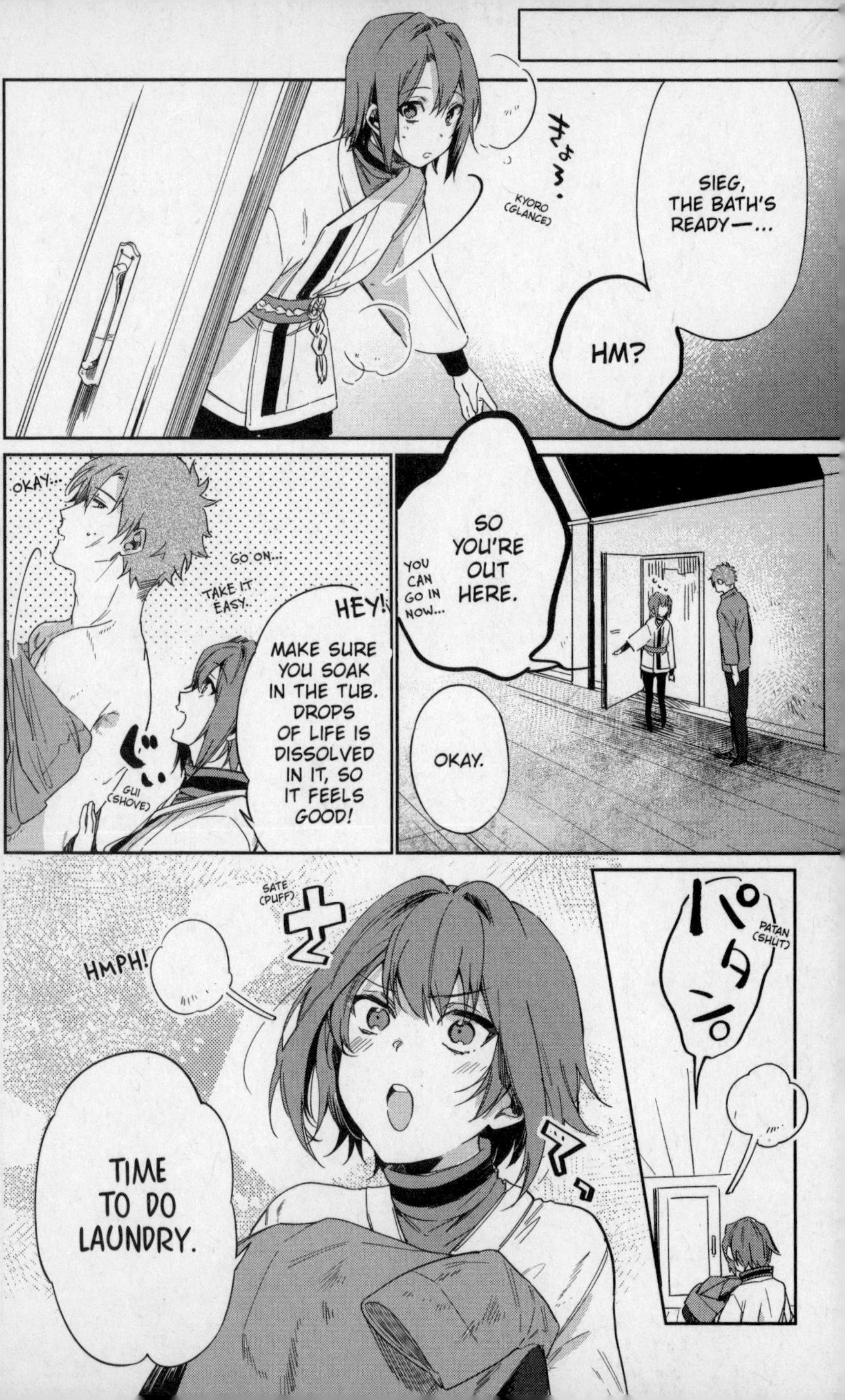
SIEG, THE BATH'S READY—...
HM?
きょろ
KYORO (GLANCE)
SO YOU'RE OUT HERE.
YOU CAN GO IN NOW...
OKAY.
HEY!
MAKE SURE YOU SOAK IN THE TUB. DROPS OF LIFE IS DISSOLVED IN IT, SO IT FEELS GOOD!
GO ON... TAKE IT EASY.
OKAY...
GUI (SHOVE)
パタン
PATAN (SHUT)
SATE (PUFF)
HMPH!
TIME TO DO LAUNDRY.

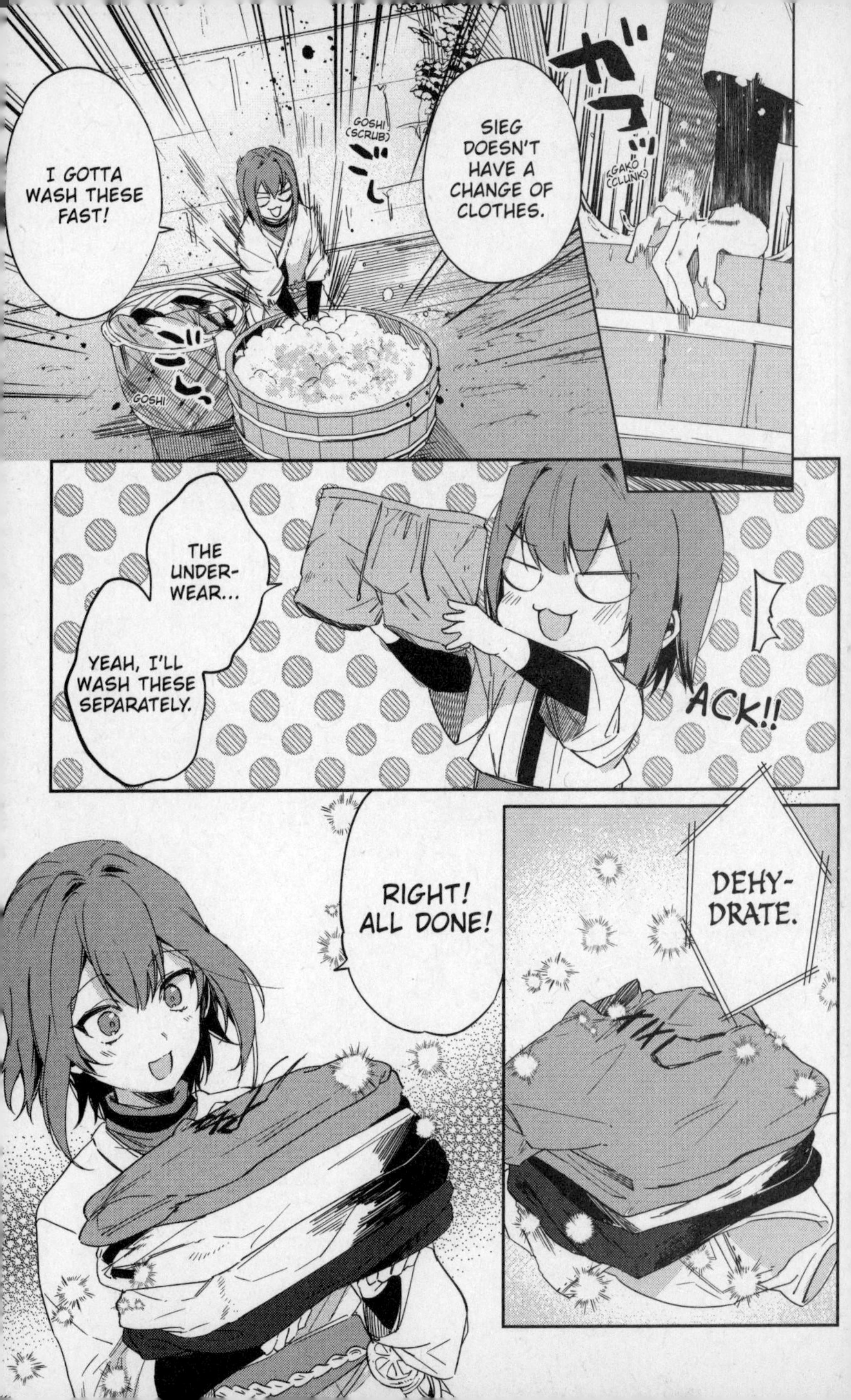
GAKO (CLUNK)
SIEG DOESN'T HAVE A CHANGE OF CLOTHES.
GOSHI (SCRUB)
I GOTTA WASH THESE FAST!
GOSHI
ACK!!
THE UNDERWEAR...
YEAH, I'LL WASH THESE SEPARATELY.
DEHY-DRATE.
RIGHT! ALL DONE!

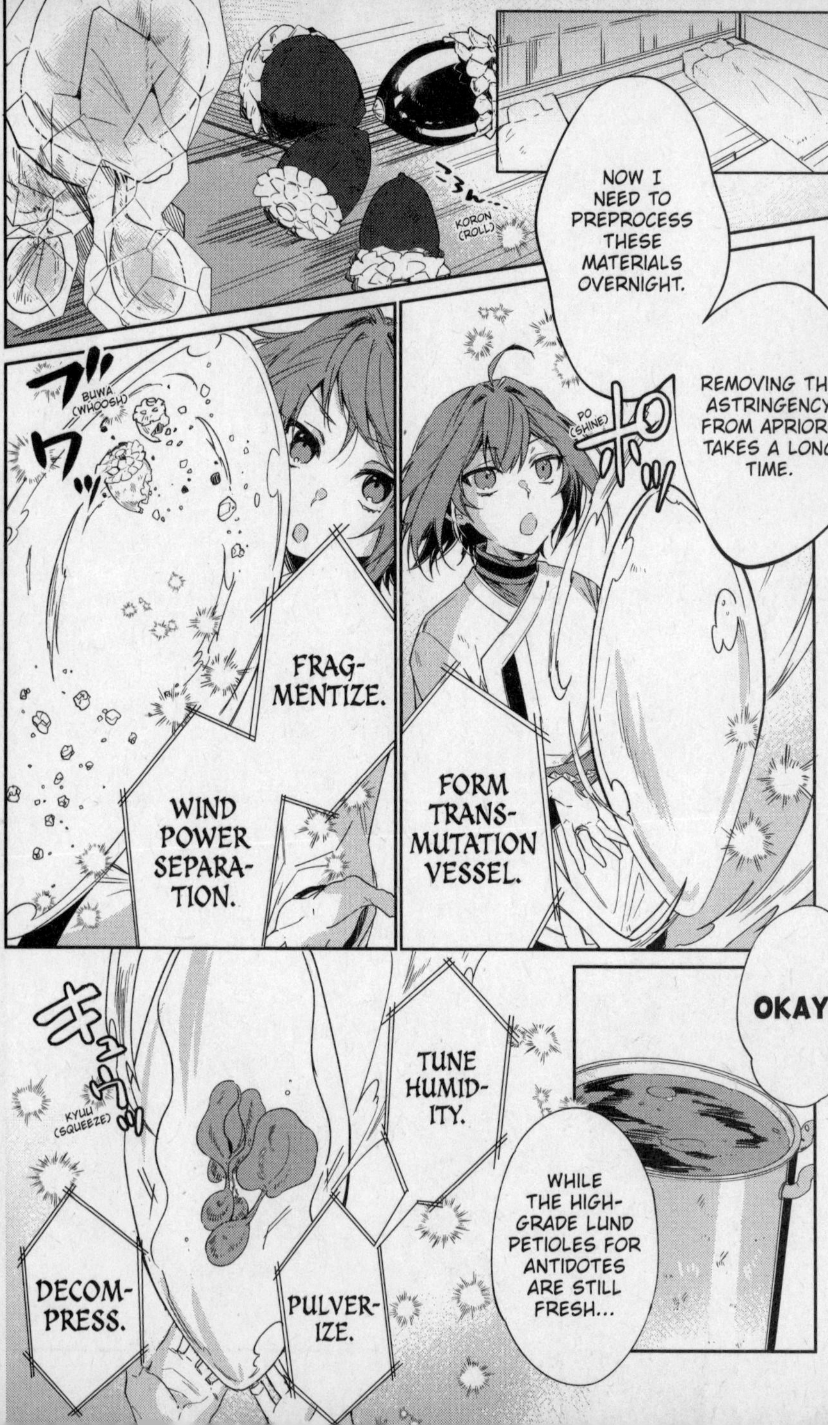
NOW I NEED TO PREPROCESS THESE MATERIALS OVERNIGHT.
KORON (ROLL)
REMOVING THE ASTRINGENCY FROM APRIORE TAKES A LONG TIME.
PO (SHINE)
FORM TRANSMUTATION VESSEL.
BUWA (WHOOSH)
FRAGMENTIZE.
WIND POWER SEPARATION.
OKAY!
WHILE THE HIGH-GRADE LUND PETIOLES FOR ANTIDOTES ARE STILL FRESH...
TUNE HUMIDITY.
KYUU (SQUEEZE)
PULVERIZE.
DECOMPRESS.

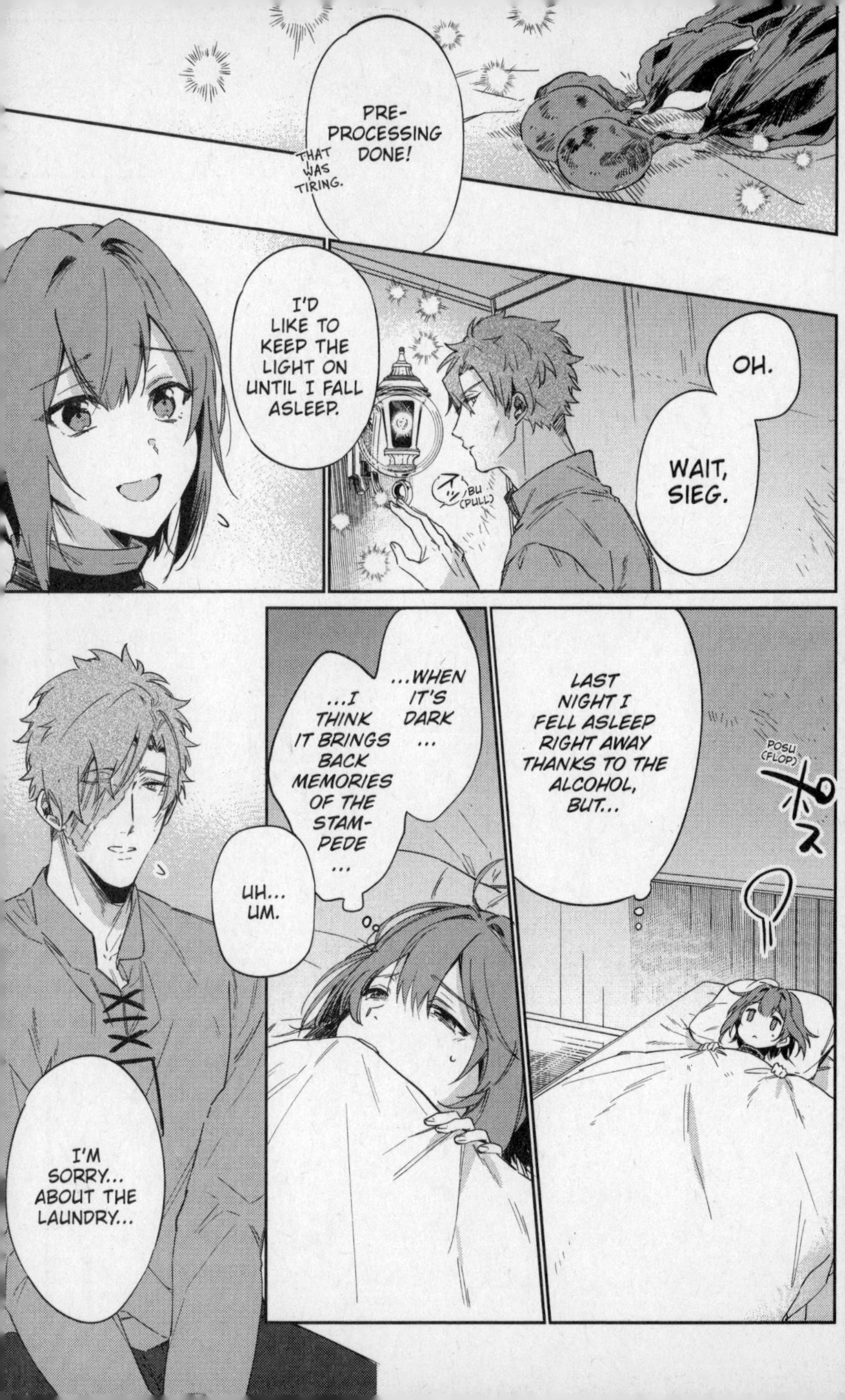
PRE-PROCESSING DONE!
THAT WAS TIRING.
OH.
WAIT, SIEG.
BU (PULL)
I'D LIKE TO KEEP THE LIGHT ON UNTIL I FALL ASLEEP.
POSU (FLOP)
LAST NIGHT I FELL ASLEEP RIGHT AWAY THANKS TO THE ALCOHOL, BUT...
...WHEN IT'S DARK...
...I THINK IT BRINGS BACK MEMORIES OF THE STAMPEDE...
UH... UM.
I'M SORRY... ABOUT THE LAUNDRY...

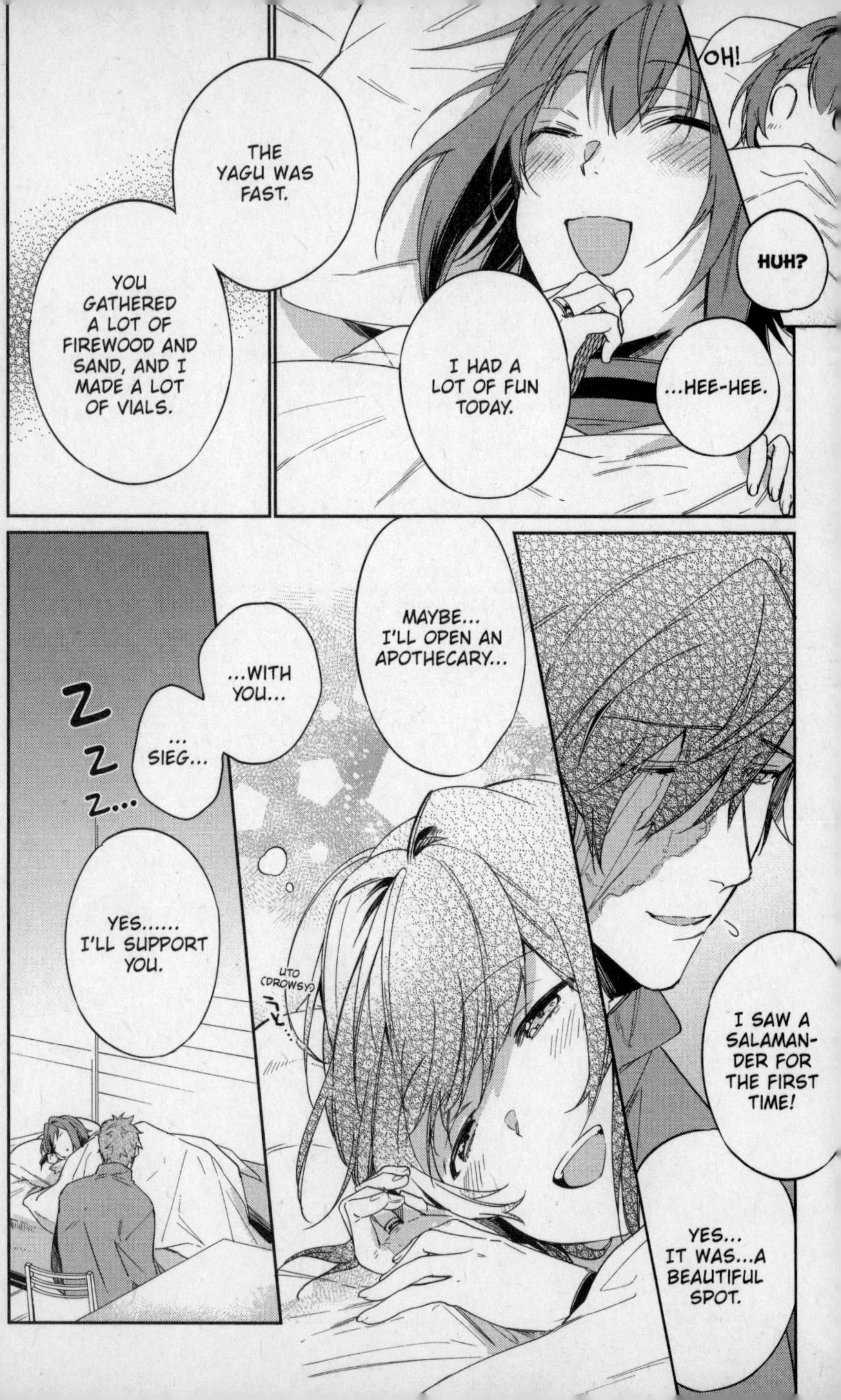
OH!
HUH?
...HEE-HEE.
I HAD A LOT OF FUN TODAY.
THE YAGU WAS FAST.
YOU GATHERED A LOT OF FIREWOOD AND SAND, AND I MADE A LOT OF VIALS.
I SAW A SALAMANDER FOR THE FIRST TIME!
YES... IT WAS...A BEAUTIFUL SPOT.
UTO (DROWSY)
MAYBE... I'LL OPEN AN APOTHECARY...
...WITH YOU...
... SIEG...
Z Z Z...
YES...... I'LL SUPPORT YOU.

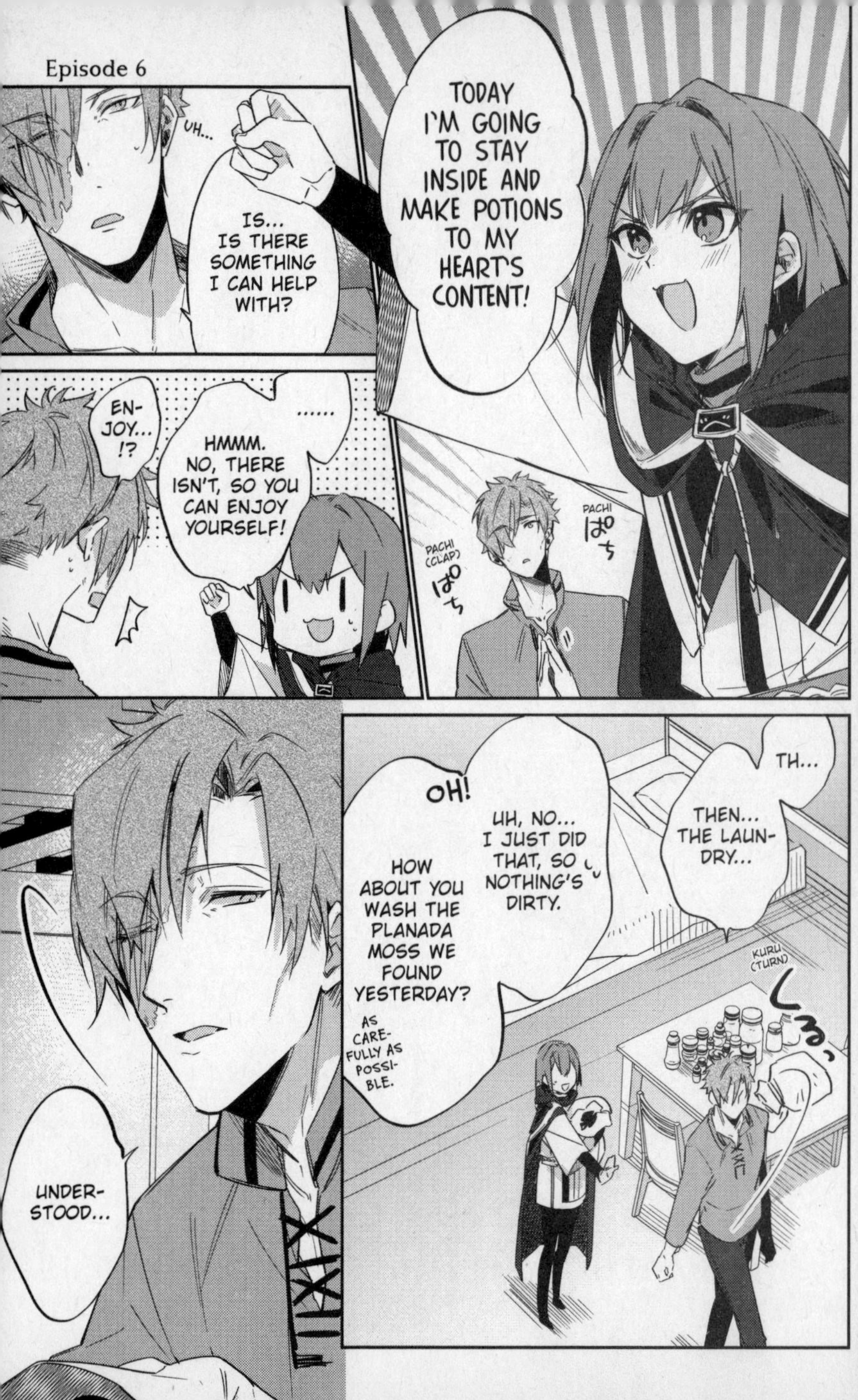
TODAY I'M GOING TO STAY INSIDE AND MAKE POTIONS TO MY HEART'S CONTENT!
PACHI
PACHI (CLAP)
IS... IS THERE SOMETHING I CAN HELP WITH?
UH...
......
HMMM. NO, THERE ISN'T, SO YOU CAN ENJOY YOURSELF!
EN-JOY... !?
TH...
THEN... THE LAUN-DRY...
UH, NO... I JUST DID THAT, SO NOTHING'S DIRTY.
OH!
HOW ABOUT YOU WASH THE PLANADA MOSS WE FOUND YESTERDAY?
AS CARE-FULLY AS POSSI-BLE.
KURU (TURN)
UNDER-STOOD...

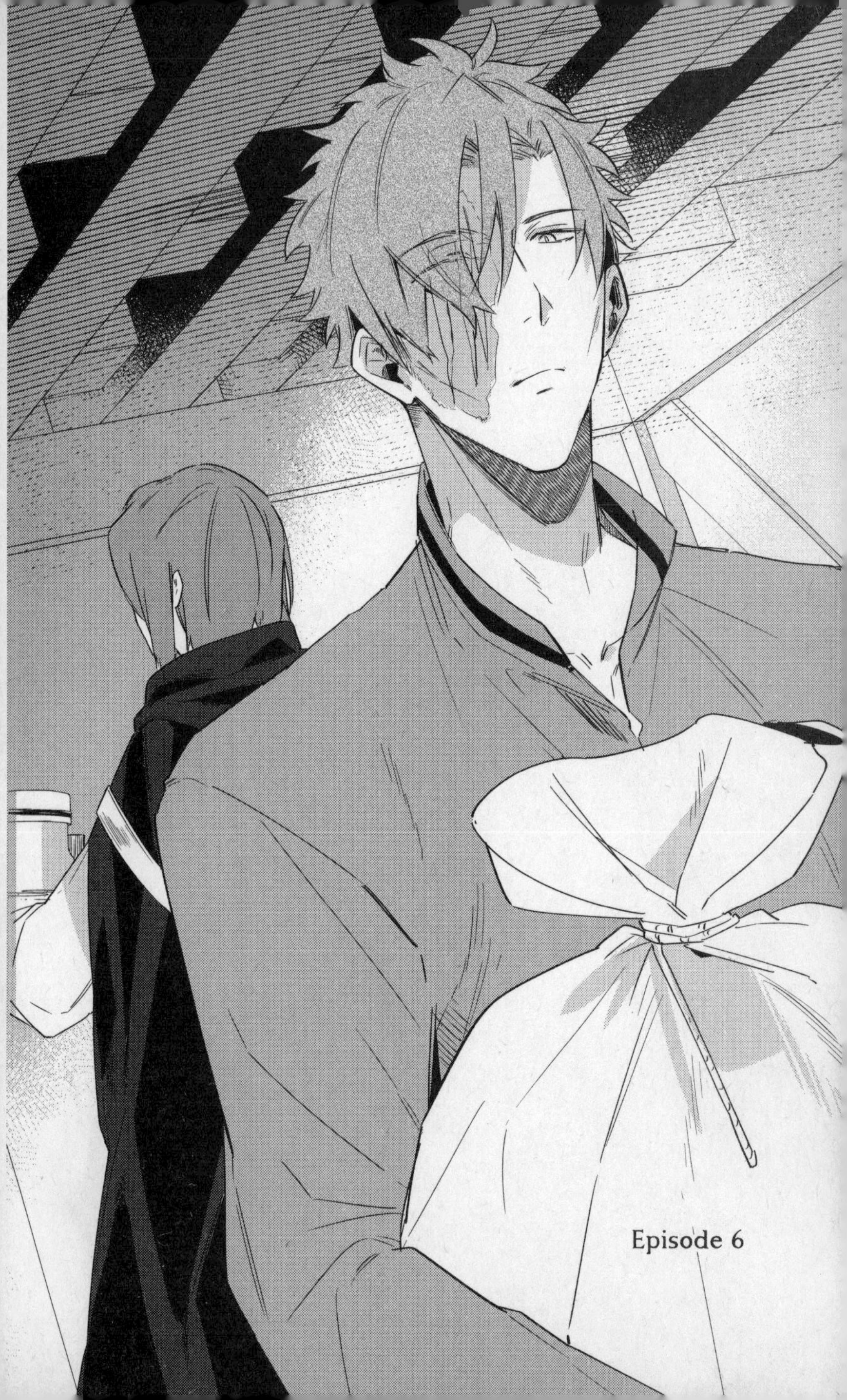

Episode 6

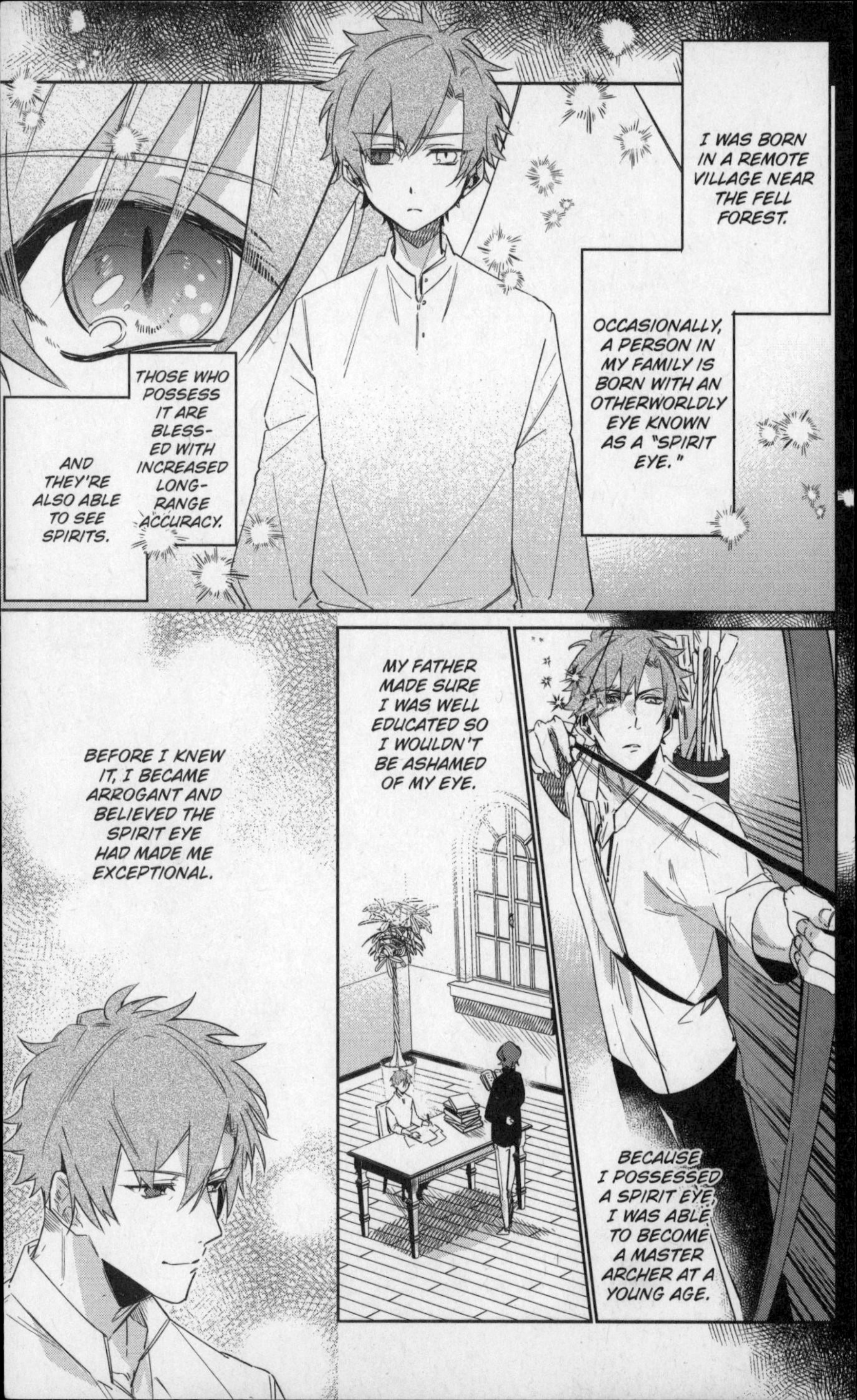
I WAS BORN IN A REMOTE VILLAGE NEAR THE FELL FOREST.
OCCASIONALLY, A PERSON IN MY FAMILY IS BORN WITH AN OTHERWORLDLY EYE KNOWN AS A "SPIRIT EYE."
THOSE WHO POSSESS IT ARE BLESS-ED WITH INCREASED LONG-RANGE ACCURACY.
AND THEY'RE ALSO ABLE TO SEE SPIRITS.
BECAUSE I POSSESSED A SPIRIT EYE, I WAS ABLE TO BECOME A MASTER ARCHER AT A YOUNG AGE.
MY FATHER MADE SURE I WAS WELL EDUCATED SO I WOULDN'T BE ASHAMED OF MY EYE.
BEFORE I KNEW IT, I BECAME ARROGANT AND BELIEVED THE SPIRIT EYE HAD MADE ME EXCEPTIONAL.

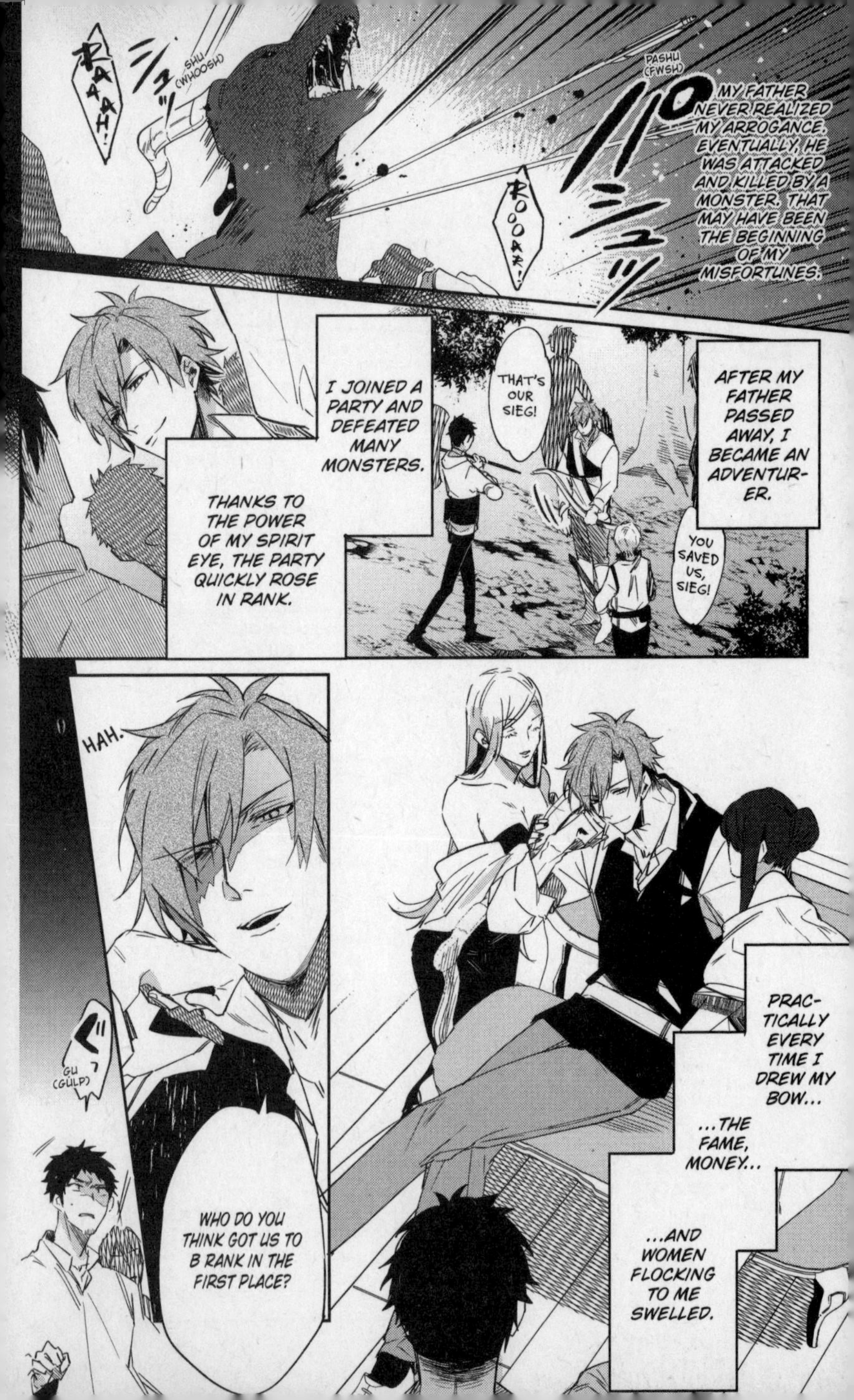
PASHU (FWSH)
MY FATHER NEVER REALIZED MY ARROGANCE. EVENTUALLY, HE WAS ATTACKED AND KILLED BY A MONSTER. THAT MAY HAVE BEEN THE BEGINNING OF MY MISFORTUNES.
ROOOAR!
SHU (WHOOSH)
RAAAH!
AFTER MY FATHER PASSED AWAY, I BECAME AN ADVENTURER.
THAT'S OUR SIEG!
YOU SAVED US, SIEG!
I JOINED A PARTY AND DEFEATED MANY MONSTERS.
THANKS TO THE POWER OF MY SPIRIT EYE, THE PARTY QUICKLY ROSE IN RANK.
PRACTICALLY EVERY TIME I DREW MY BOW...
...THE FAME, MONEY...
...AND WOMEN FLOCKING TO ME SWELLED.
HAH.
GU (GULP)
WHO DO YOU THINK GOT US TO B RANK IN THE FIRST PLACE?

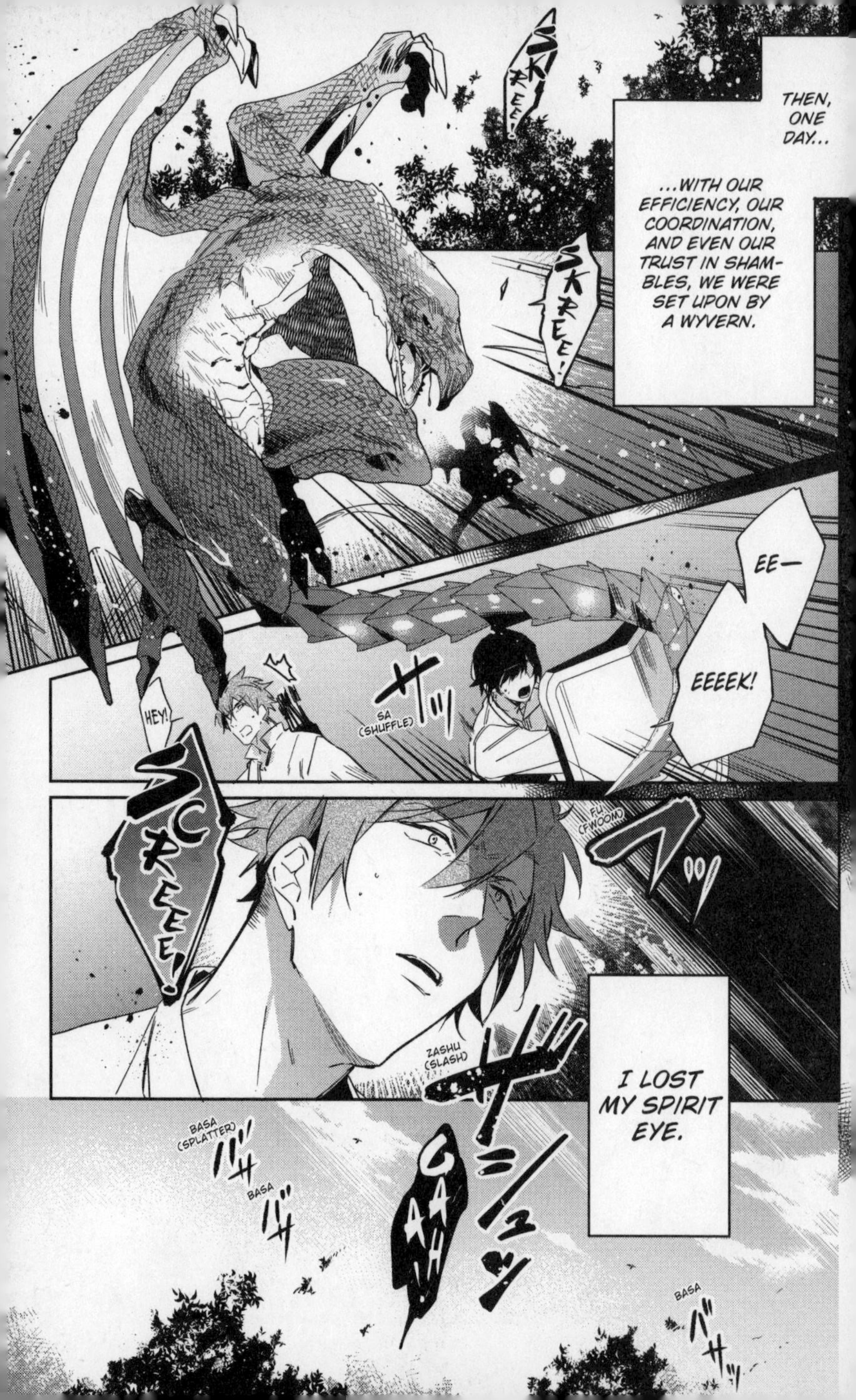
THEN, ONE DAY...
...WITH OUR EFFICIENCY, OUR COORDINATION, AND EVEN OUR TRUST IN SHAMBLES, WE WERE SET UPON BY A WYVERN.
SKREE!
SKREE!
EE—
EEEEK!
SA (SHUFFLE)
HEY!
FU (FWOOM)
SCREEE!
ZASHU (SLASH)
I LOST MY SPIRIT EYE.
GAAHH
BASA
BASA (SPLATTER)
BASA

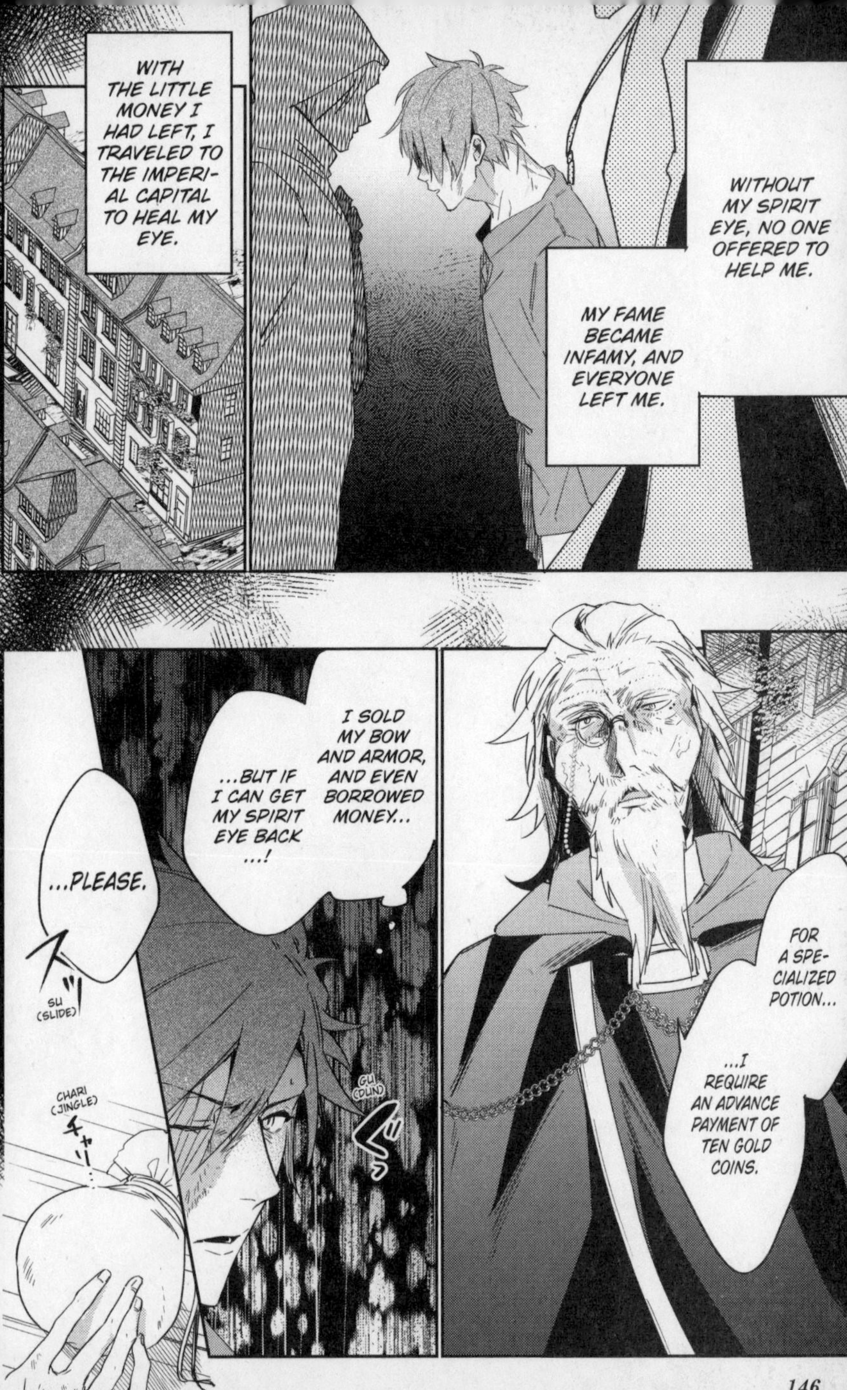
WITHOUT MY SPIRIT EYE, NO ONE OFFERED TO HELP ME.
MY FAME BECAME INFAMY, AND EVERYONE LEFT ME.
WITH THE LITTLE MONEY I HAD LEFT, I TRAVELED TO THE IMPERIAL CAPITAL TO HEAL MY EYE.
FOR A SPECIALIZED POTION...
...I REQUIRE AN ADVANCE PAYMENT OF TEN GOLD COINS.
I SOLD MY BOW AND ARMOR, AND EVEN BORROWED MONEY...
...BUT IF I CAN GET MY SPIRIT EYE BACK ...!
GU (CLUNCH)
...PLEASE.
SU (SLIDE)
CHARI (JINGLE)

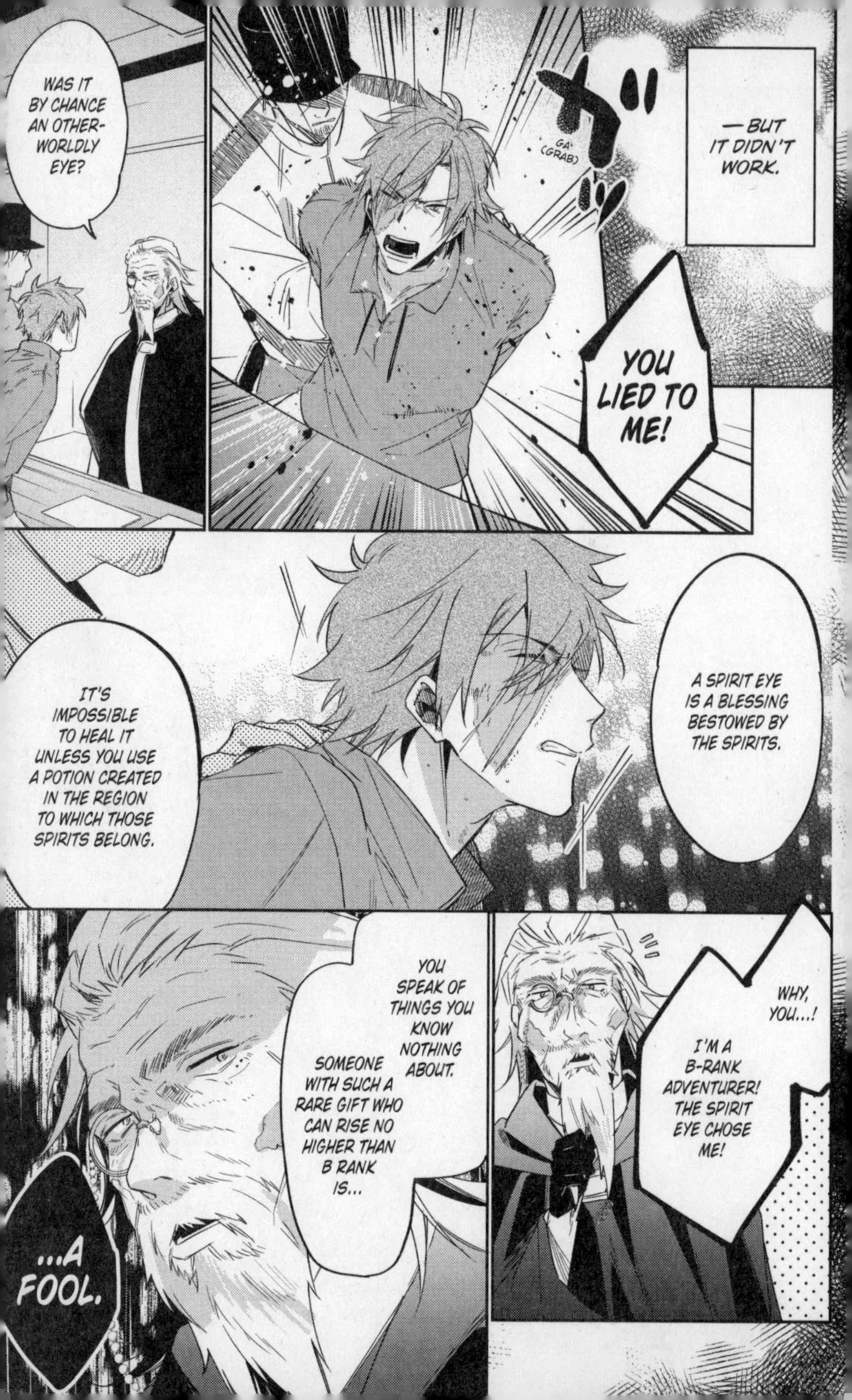
—BUT IT DIDN'T WORK.
GA' (GRAB)
YOU LIED TO ME!
WAS IT BY CHANCE AN OTHER-WORLDLY EYE?
A SPIRIT EYE IS A BLESSING BESTOWED BY THE SPIRITS.
IT'S IMPOSSIBLE TO HEAL IT UNLESS YOU USE A POTION CREATED IN THE REGION TO WHICH THOSE SPIRITS BELONG.
WHY, YOU...!
I'M A B-RANK ADVENTURER! THE SPIRIT EYE CHOSE ME!
YOU SPEAK OF THINGS YOU KNOW NOTHING ABOUT.
SOMEONE WITH SUCH A RARE GIFT WHO CAN RISE NO HIGHER THAN B RANK IS...
...A FOOL.

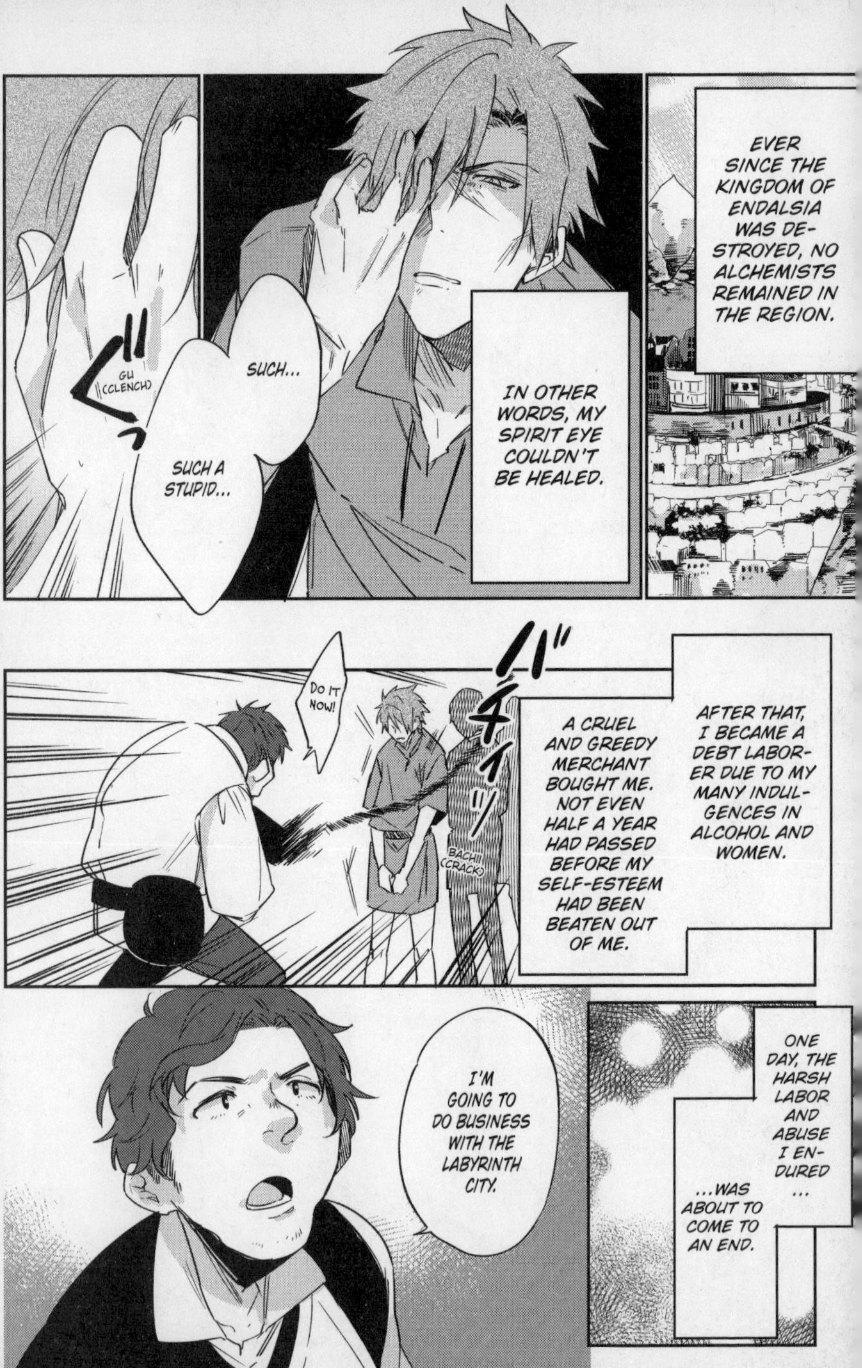
EVER SINCE THE KINGDOM OF ENDALSIA WAS DE-STROYED, NO ALCHEMISTS REMAINED IN THE REGION.
IN OTHER WORDS, MY SPIRIT EYE COULDN'T BE HEALED.
SUCH...
GU (CLENCH)
SUCH A STUPID...
AFTER THAT, I BECAME A DEBT LABOR-ER DUE TO MY MANY INDUL-GENCES IN ALCOHOL AND WOMEN.
A CRUEL AND GREEDY MERCHANT BOUGHT ME. NOT EVEN HALF A YEAR HAD PASSED BEFORE MY SELF-ESTEEM HAD BEEN BEATEN OUT OF ME.
BACHI (CRACK)
DO IT NOW!
ONE DAY, THE HARSH LABOR AND ABUSE I EN-DURED ...
...WAS ABOUT TO COME TO AN END.
I'M GOING TO DO BUSINESS WITH THE LABYRINTH CITY.

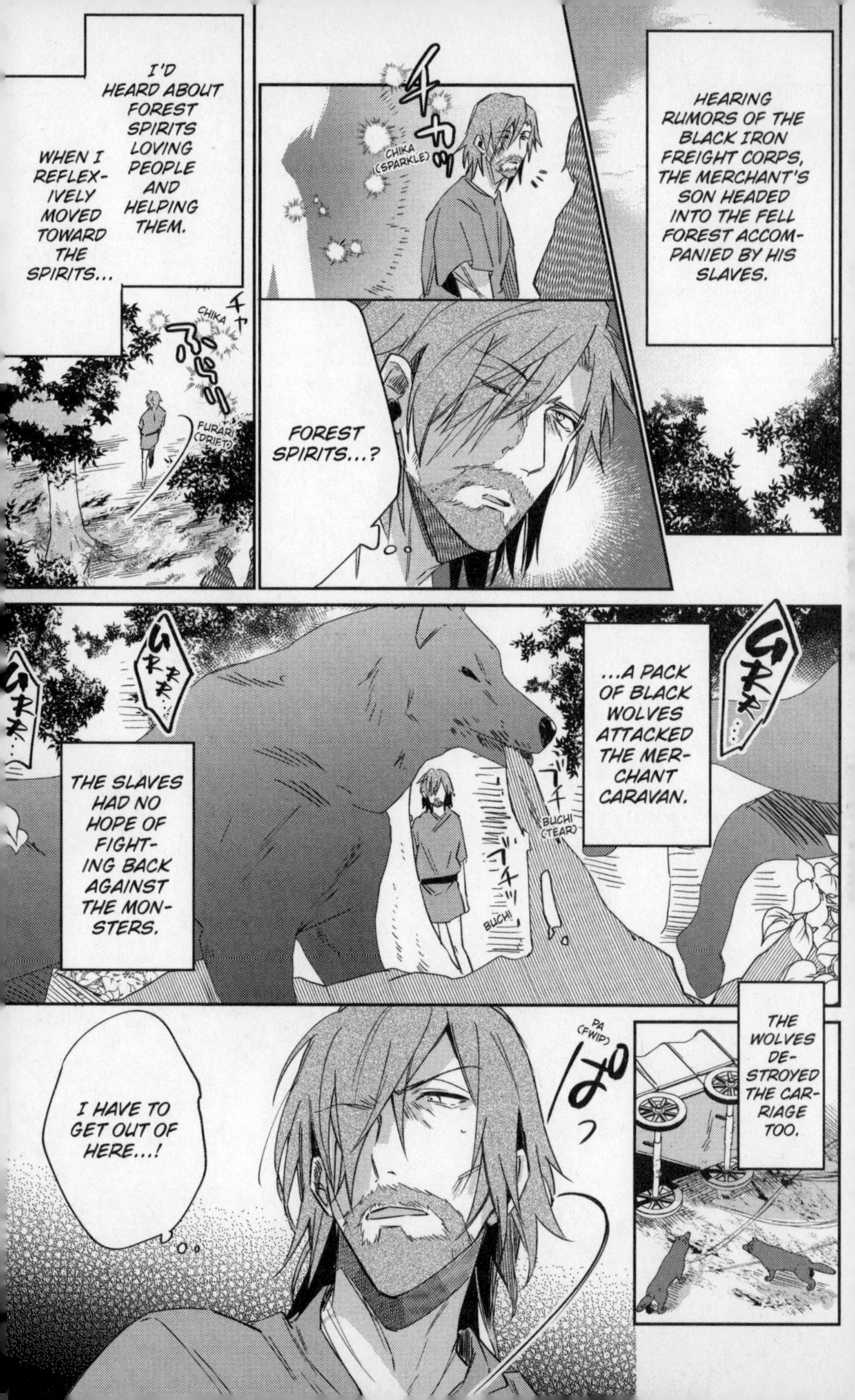
HEARING RUMORS OF THE BLACK IRON FREIGHT CORPS, THE MERCHANT'S SON HEADED INTO THE FELL FOREST ACCOMPANIED BY HIS SLAVES.
CHIKA (SPARKLE)
FOREST SPIRITS...?
I'D HEARD ABOUT FOREST SPIRITS LOVING PEOPLE AND HELPING THEM.
WHEN I REFLEXIVELY MOVED TOWARD THE SPIRITS...
CHIKA
FURARI (DRIFT)
...A PACK OF BLACK WOLVES ATTACKED THE MERCHANT CARAVAN.
BUCHI (TEAR)
BUCHI!
THE SLAVES HAD NO HOPE OF FIGHTING BACK AGAINST THE MONSTERS.
THE WOLVES DESTROYED THE CARRIAGE TOO.
PA (FWIP)
I HAVE TO GET OUT OF HERE...!

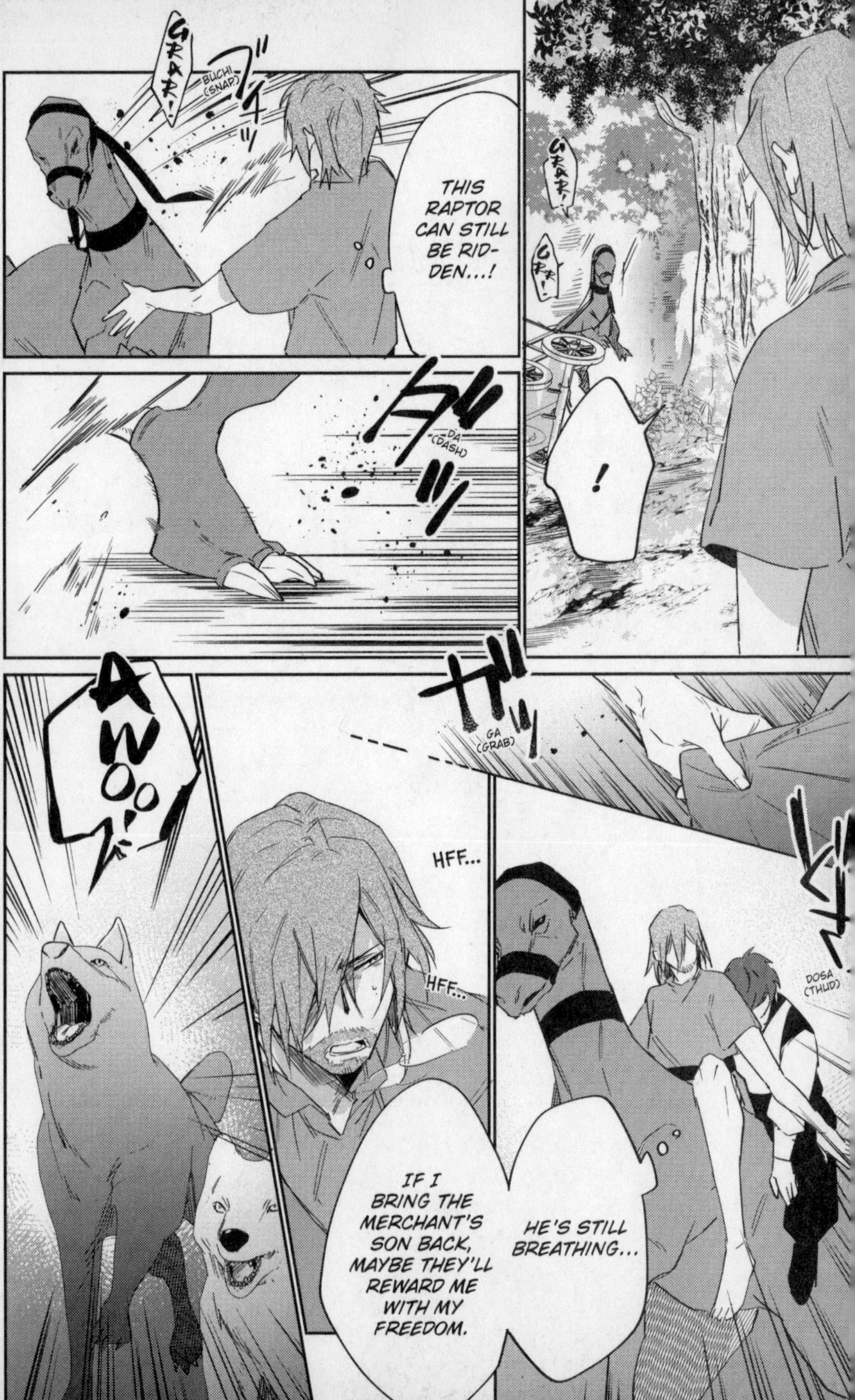
GRAR!
GRR!
!
GRAR!
BUCHI (SNAP)
THIS RAPTOR CAN STILL BE RID-DEN...!
DA (DASH)
GA (GRAB)
DOSA (THUD)
HE'S STILL BREATHING...
HFF...
HFF...
IF I BRING THE MERCHANT'S SON BACK, MAYBE THEY'LL REWARD ME WITH MY FREEDOM.
AWOO

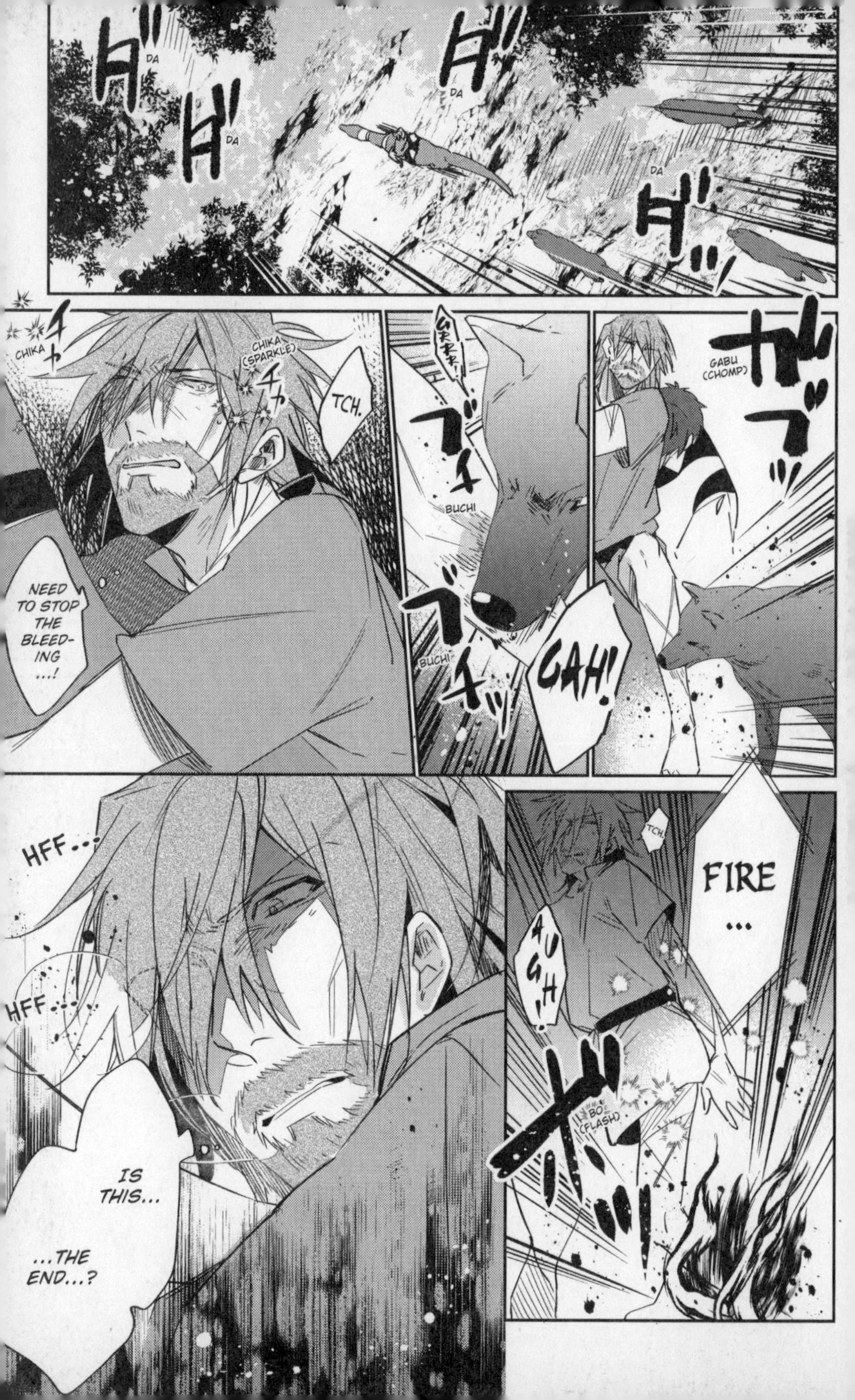
DA
DA
DA
DA
GABU (CHOMP)
GRRR!
BUCHI
BUCHI
GAH!
CHIKA (SPARKLE)
TCH.
CHIKA
NEED TO STOP THE BLEEDING...!
TCH.
FIRE...
AUGH!
BO (FLASH)
HFF...
HFF...
IS THIS...
...THE END...?

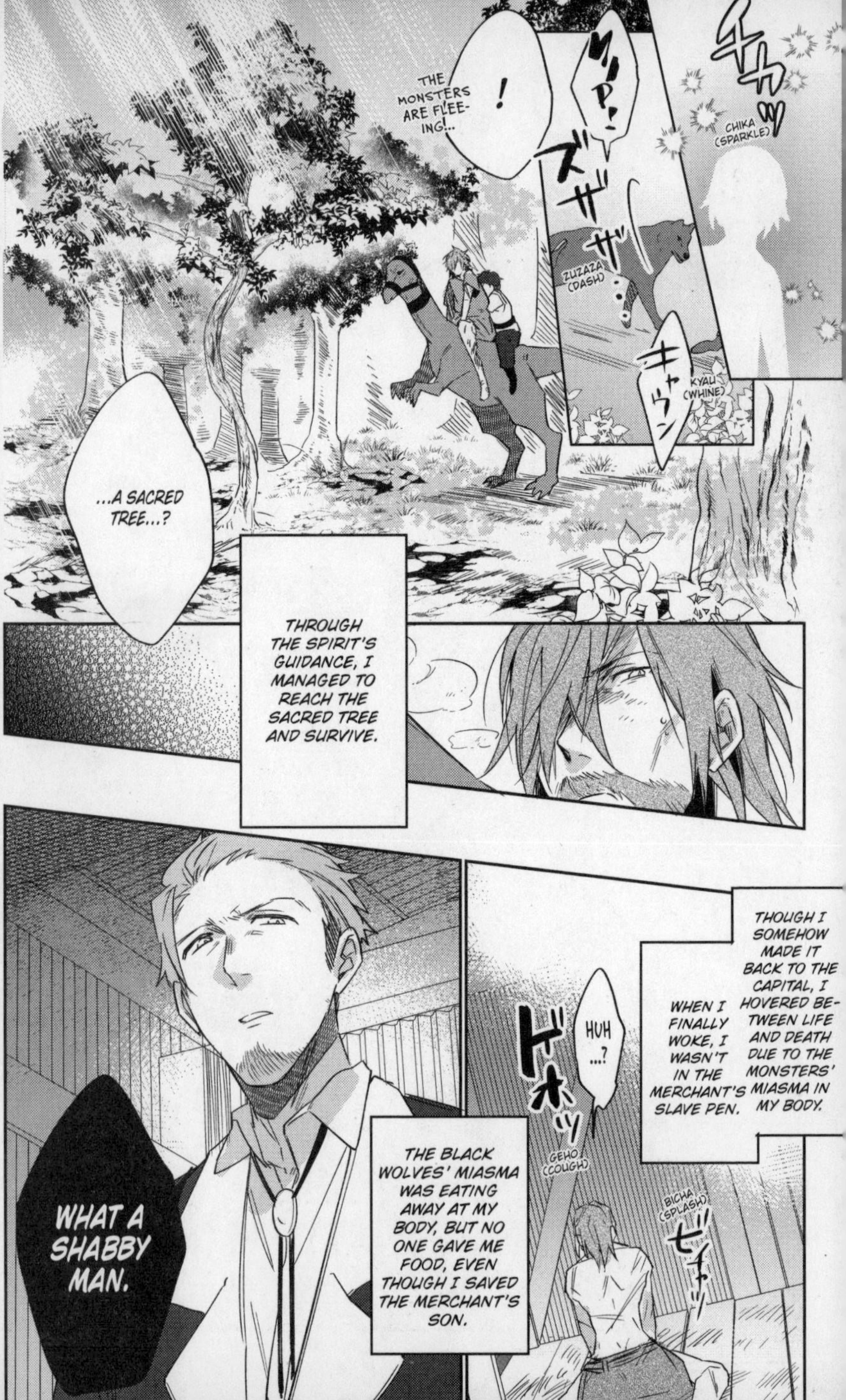

チカッ
CHIKA (SPARKLE)
ズザザ
ZUZAZA (DASH)
キャウン
KYAU (WHINE)
!
THE MONSTERS ARE FLEE-ING!...
...A SACRED TREE...?
THROUGH THE SPIRIT'S GUIDANCE, I MANAGED TO REACH THE SACRED TREE AND SURVIVE.
THOUGH I SOMEHOW MADE IT BACK TO THE CAPITAL, I HOVERED BE-TWEEN LIFE AND DEATH DUE TO THE MONSTERS' MIASMA IN MY BODY.
WHEN I FINALLY WOKE, I WASN'T IN THE MERCHANT'S SLAVE PEN.
ドオッ
GEHO (COUGH)
HUH ...?
ビチャッ
BICHA (SPLASH)
THE BLACK WOLVES' MIASMA WAS EATING AWAY AT MY BODY, BUT NO ONE GAVE ME FOOD, EVEN THOUGH I SAVED THE MERCHANT'S SON.
WHAT A SHABBY MAN.

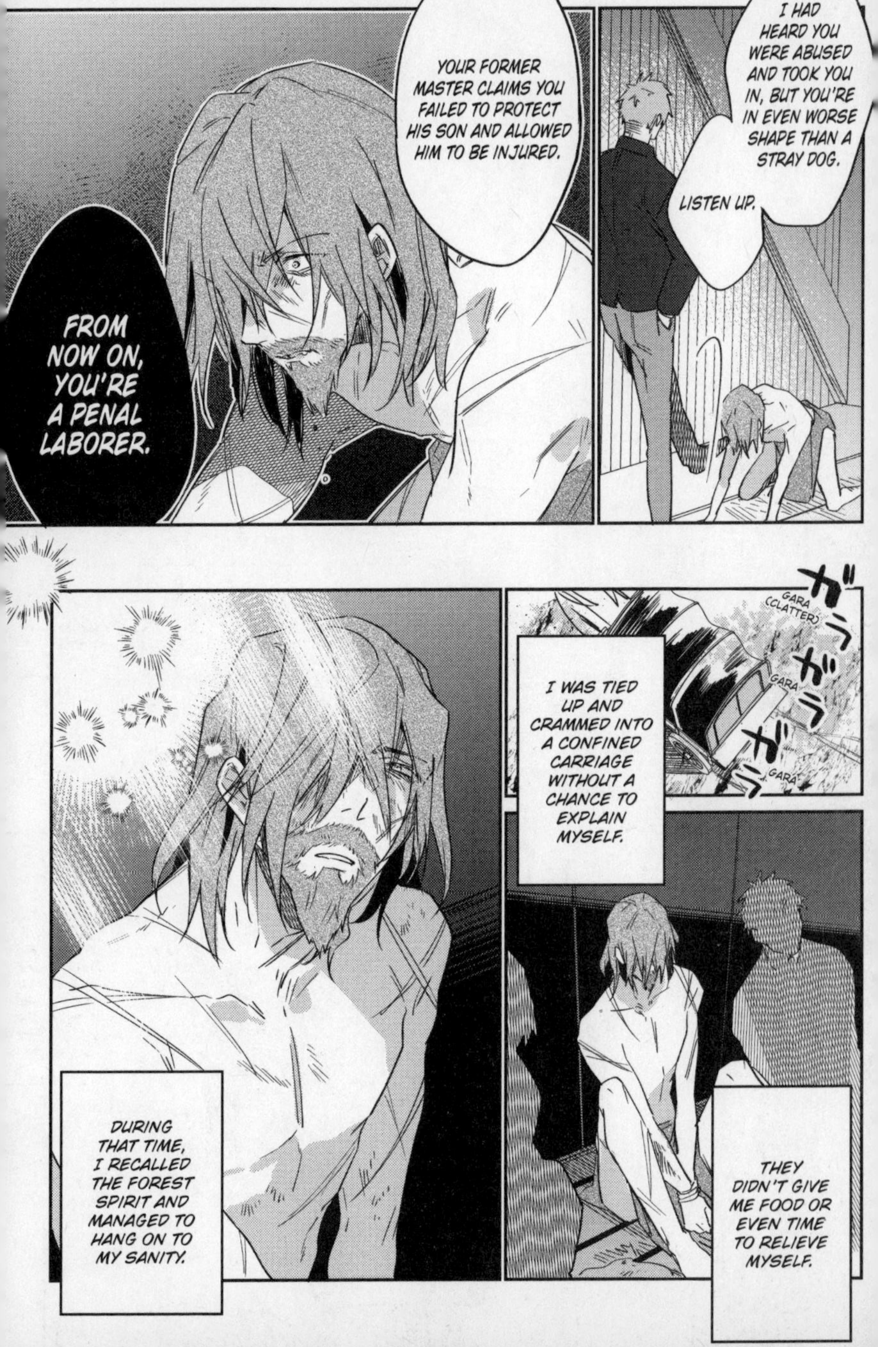
I HAD HEARD YOU WERE ABUSED AND TOOK YOU IN, BUT YOU'RE IN EVEN WORSE SHAPE THAN A STRAY DOG.
LISTEN UP.
YOUR FORMER MASTER CLAIMS YOU FAILED TO PROTECT HIS SON AND ALLOWED HIM TO BE INJURED.
FROM NOW ON, YOU'RE A PENAL LABORER.
GARA (CLATTER)
GARA
GARA
I WAS TIED UP AND CRAMMED INTO A CONFINED CARRIAGE WITHOUT A CHANCE TO EXPLAIN MYSELF.
THEY DIDN'T GIVE ME FOOD OR EVEN TIME TO RELIEVE MYSELF.
DURING THAT TIME, I RECALLED THE FOREST SPIRIT AND MANAGED TO HANG ON TO MY SANITY.

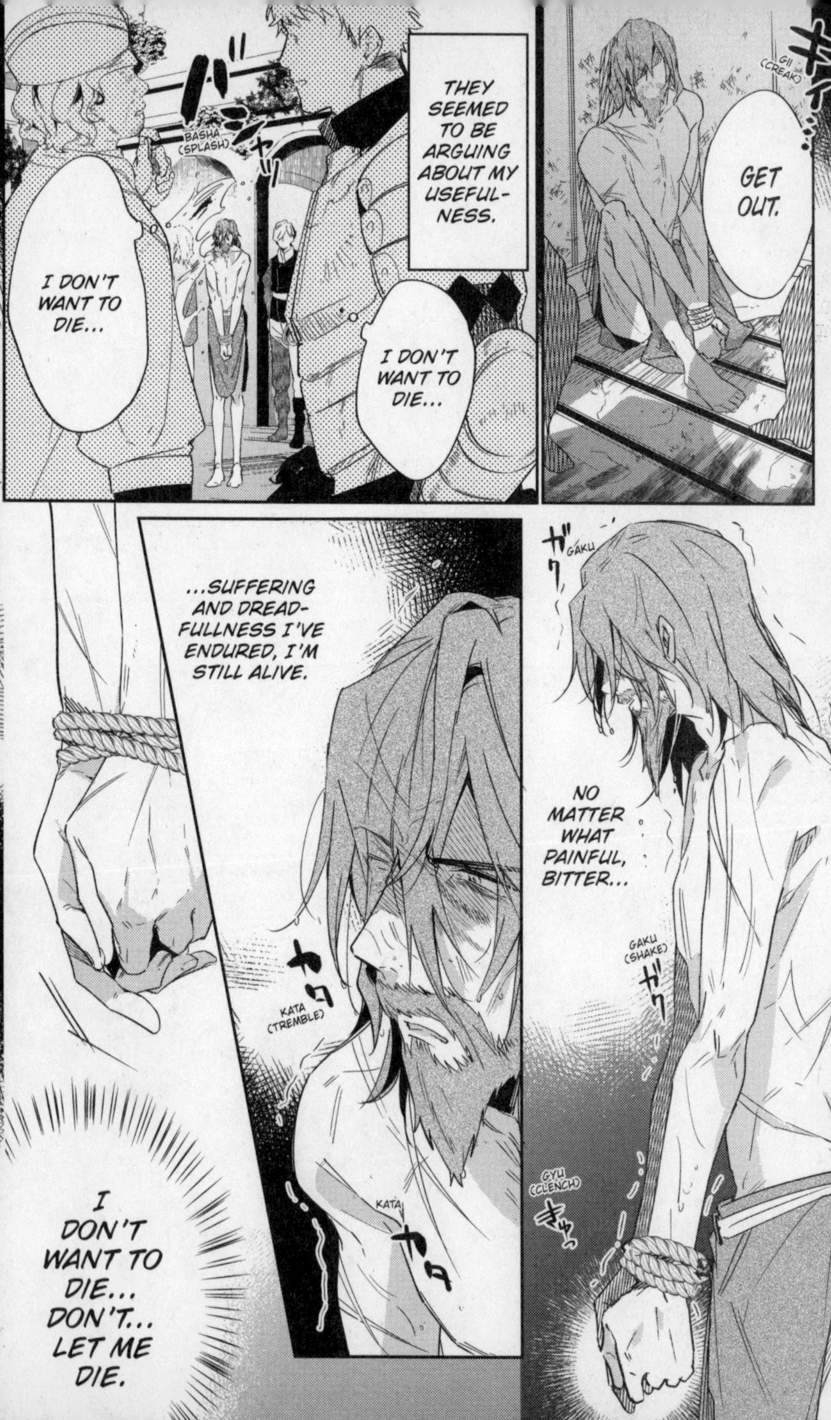
GII (CREAK)
GET OUT.
THEY SEEMED TO BE ARGUING ABOUT MY USEFUL-NESS.
BASHA (SPLASH)
I DON'T WANT TO DIE...
I DON'T WANT TO DIE...
GAKU
NO MATTER WHAT PAINFUL, BITTER...
GAKU (SHAKE)
GYU (CLENCH)
...SUFFERING AND DREAD-FULLNESS I'VE ENDURED, I'M STILL ALIVE.
KATA (TREMBLE)
KATA
I DON'T WANT TO DIE... DON'T... LET ME DIE.

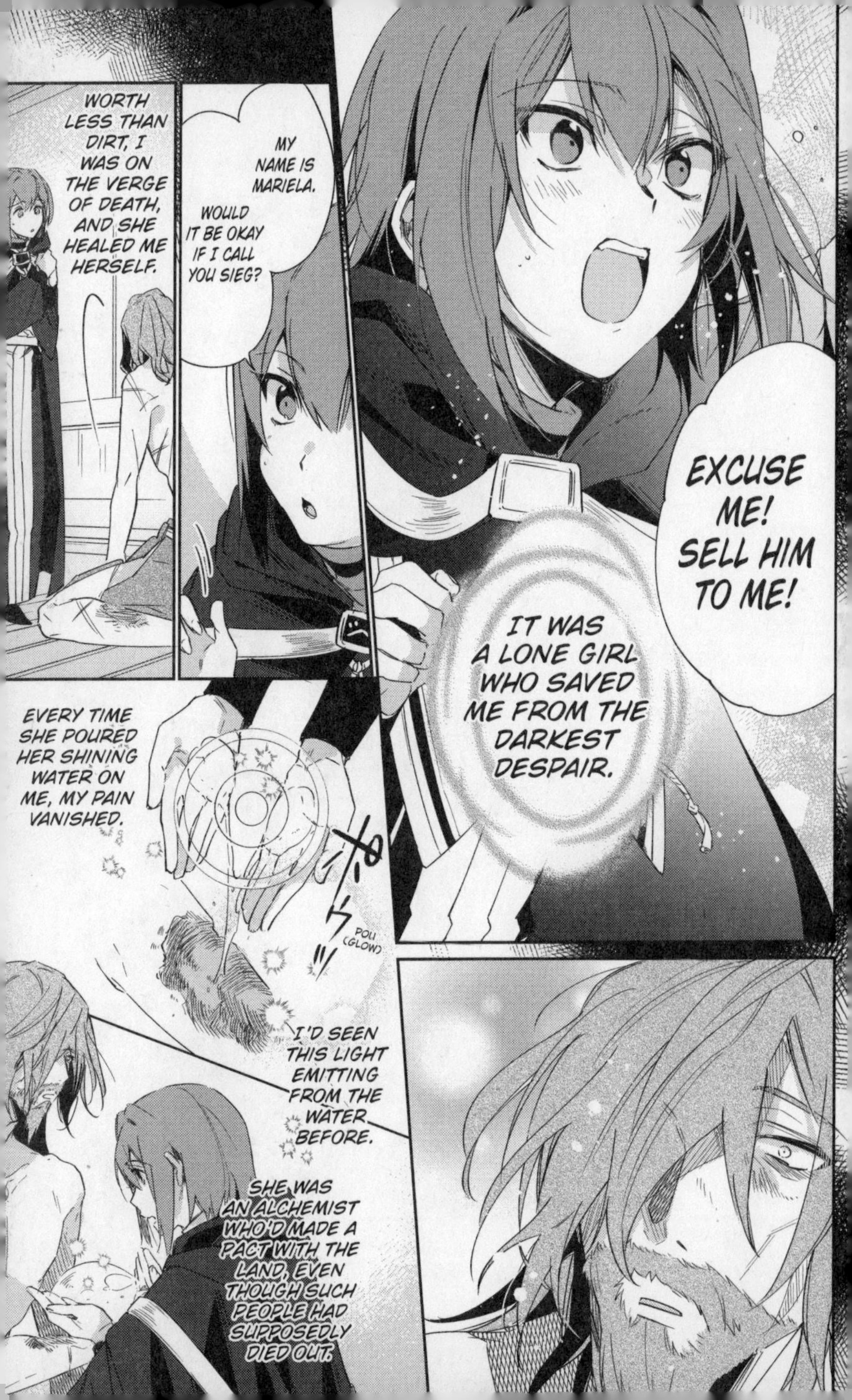
EXCUSE ME! SELL HIM TO ME!
IT WAS A LONE GIRL WHO SAVED ME FROM THE DARKEST DESPAIR.
MY NAME IS MARIELA.
WOULD IT BE OKAY IF I CALL YOU SIEG?
WORTH LESS THAN DIRT, I WAS ON THE VERGE OF DEATH, AND SHE HEALED ME HERSELF.
EVERY TIME SHE POURED HER SHINING WATER ON ME, MY PAIN VANISHED.
POU (GLOW)
I'D SEEN THIS LIGHT EMITTING FROM THE WATER BEFORE.
SHE WAS AN ALCHEMIST WHO'D MADE A PACT WITH THE LAND, EVEN THOUGH SUCH PEOPLE HAD SUPPOSEDLY DIED OUT.

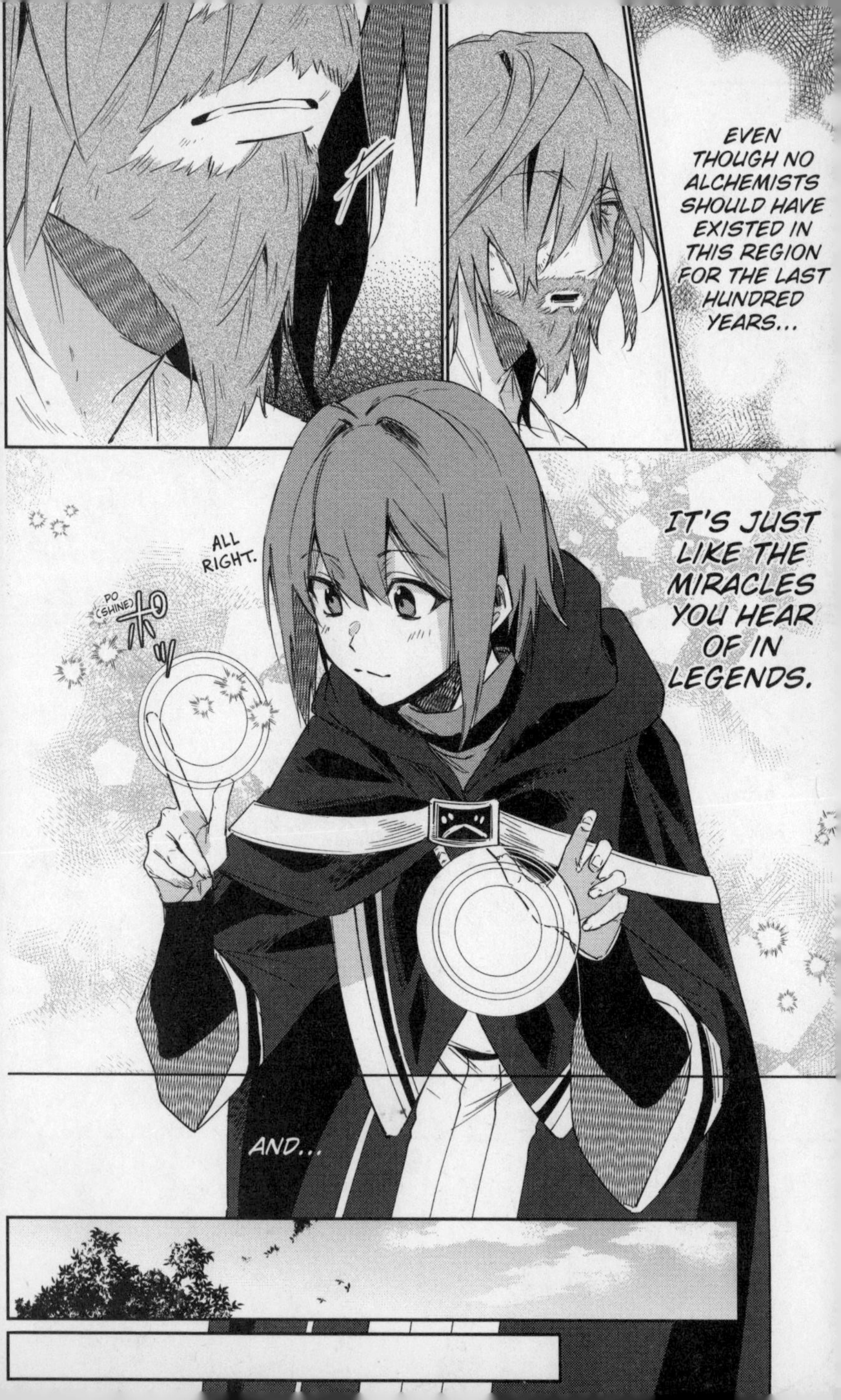
EVEN THOUGH NO ALCHEMISTS SHOULD HAVE EXISTED IN THIS REGION FOR THE LAST HUNDRED YEARS...
IT'S JUST LIKE THE MIRACLES YOU HEAR OF IN LEGENDS.
ALL RIGHT.
PO (SHINE)
AND...

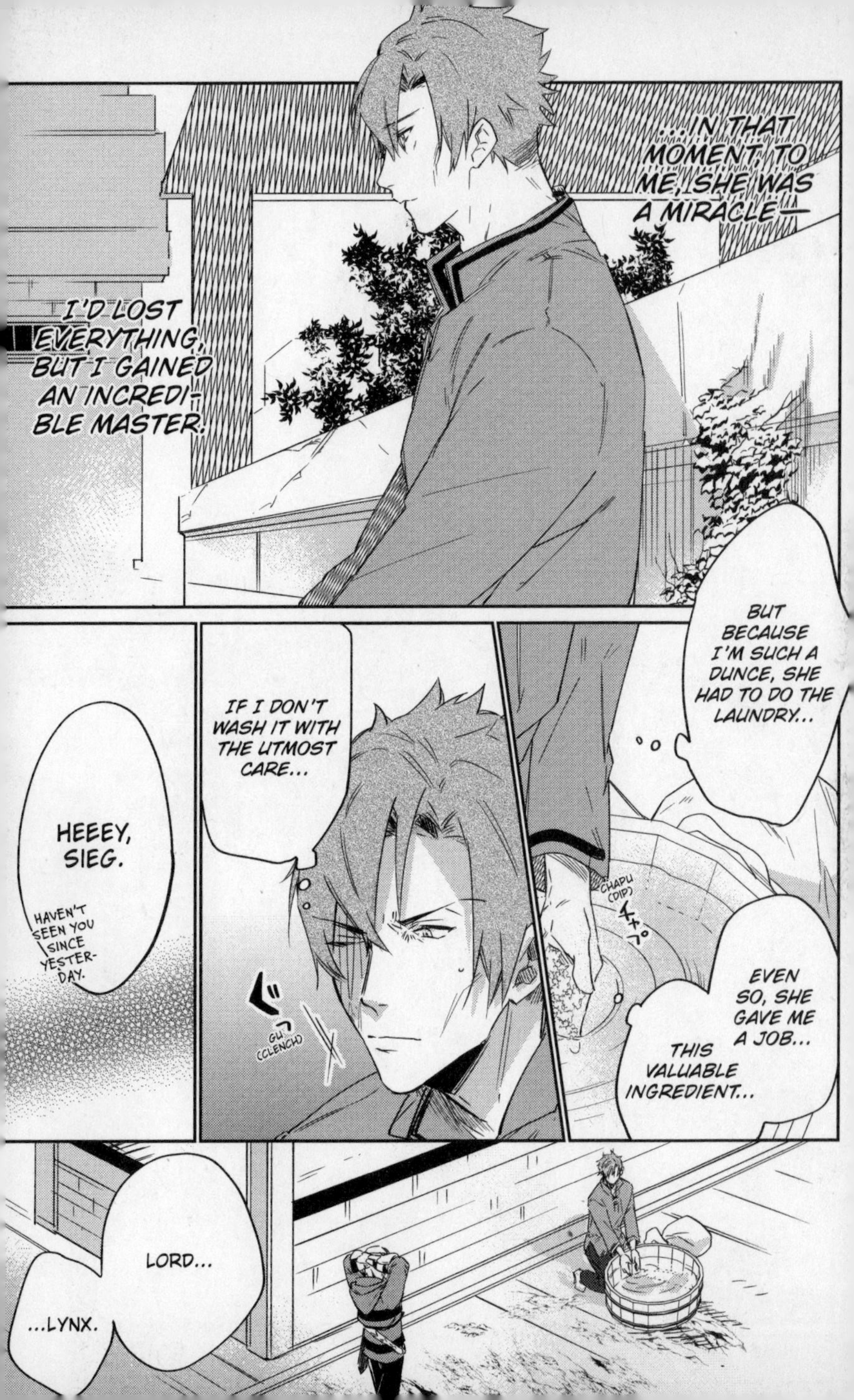
...IN THAT MOMENT, TO ME, SHE WAS A MIRACLE—
I'D LOST EVERYTHING, BUT I GAINED AN INCREDIBLE MASTER.
BUT BECAUSE I'M SUCH A DUNCE, SHE HAD TO DO THE LAUNDRY...
CHAPU (DIP)
EVEN SO, SHE GAVE ME A JOB...
THIS VALUABLE INGREDIENT...
IF I DON'T WASH IT WITH THE UTMOST CARE...
GU (CLENCH)
HEEEY, SIEG.
HAVEN'T SEEN YOU SINCE YESTERDAY.
LORD...
...LYNX.

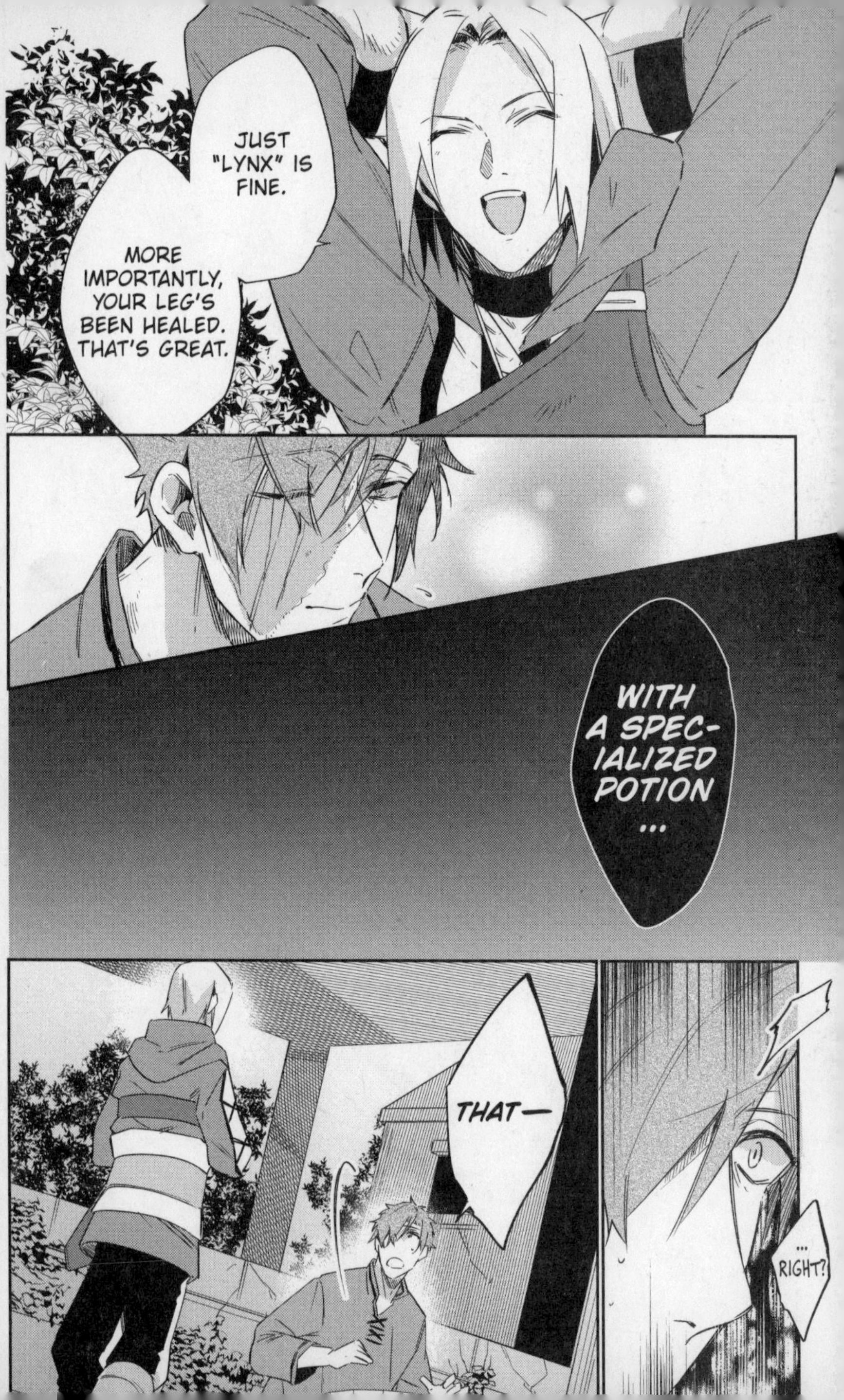
JUST "LYNX" IS FINE.
MORE IMPORTANTLY, YOUR LEG'S BEEN HEALED. THAT'S GREAT.
WITH A SPEC-IALIZED POTION ...
...RIGHT?
THAT—

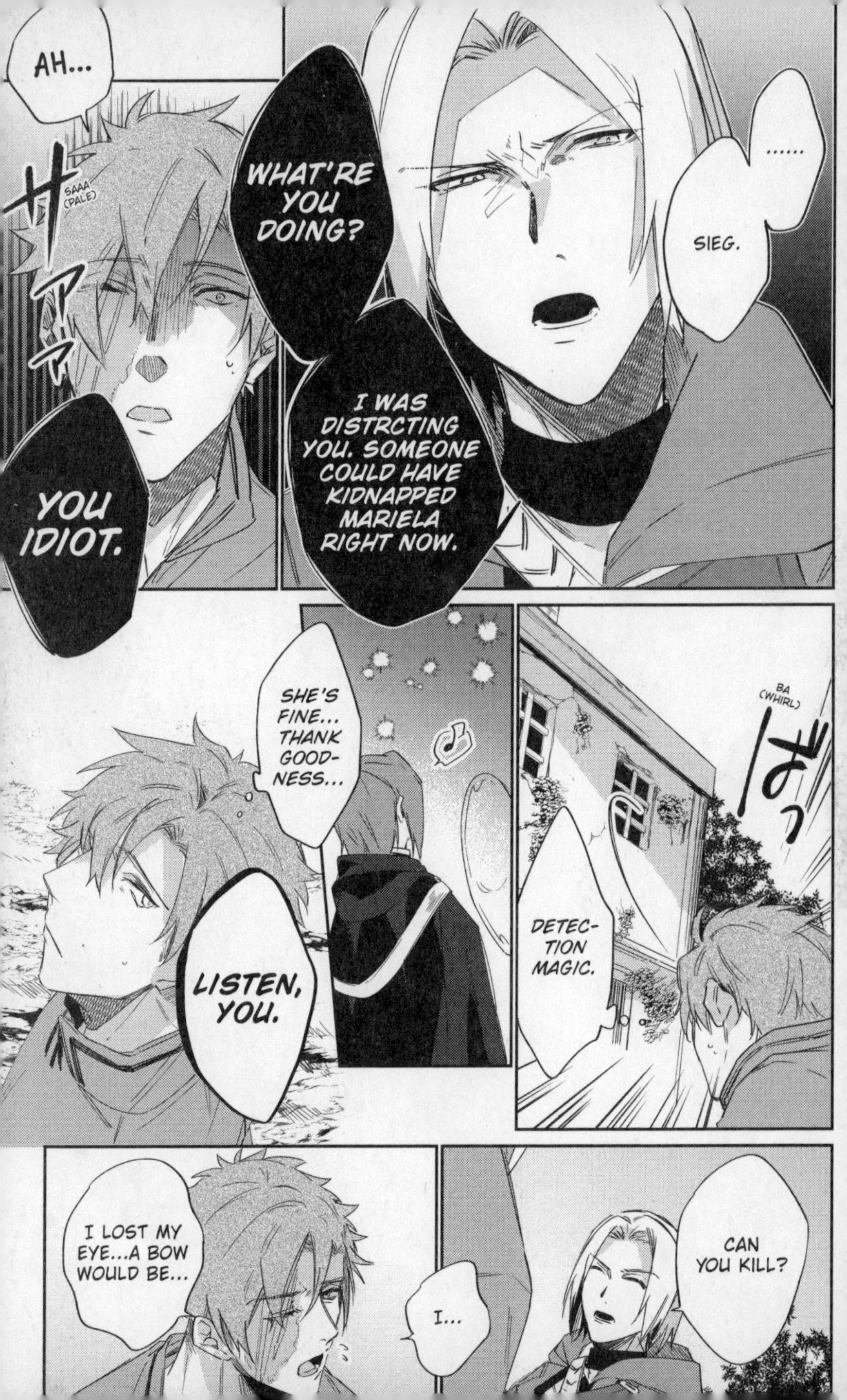
......
SIEG.
WHAT'RE YOU DOING?
I WAS DISTRCTING YOU. SOMEONE COULD HAVE KIDNAPPED MARIELA RIGHT NOW.
AH...
SAAA (PALE)
YOU IDIOT.
BA (WHIRL)
DETECTION MAGIC.
SHE'S FINE... THANK GOODNESS...
LISTEN, YOU.
CAN YOU KILL?
I...
I LOST MY EYE...A BOW WOULD BE...

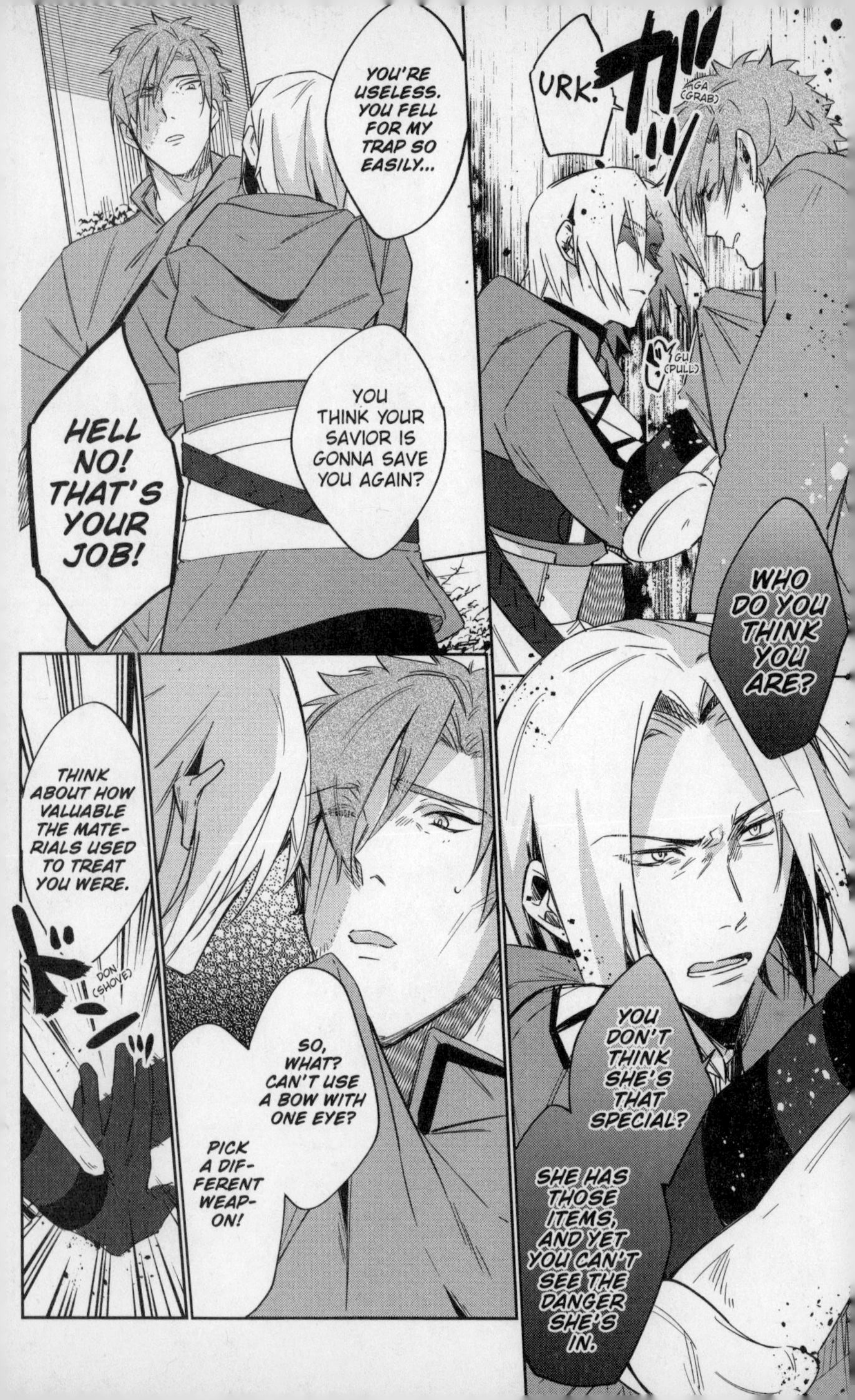
URK.
GA (GRAB)
GU (PULL)
WHO DO YOU THINK YOU ARE?
YOU'RE USELESS. YOU FELL FOR MY TRAP SO EASILY...
YOU THINK YOUR SAVIOR IS GONNA SAVE YOU AGAIN?
HELL NO! THAT'S YOUR JOB!
YOU DON'T THINK SHE'S THAT SPECIAL?
SHE HAS THOSE ITEMS, AND YET YOU CAN'T SEE THE DANGER SHE'S IN.
SO, WHAT? CAN'T USE A BOW WITH ONE EYE?
PICK A DIFFERENT WEAPON!
THINK ABOUT HOW VALUABLE THE MATERIALS USED TO TREAT YOU WERE.
DON (SHOVE)

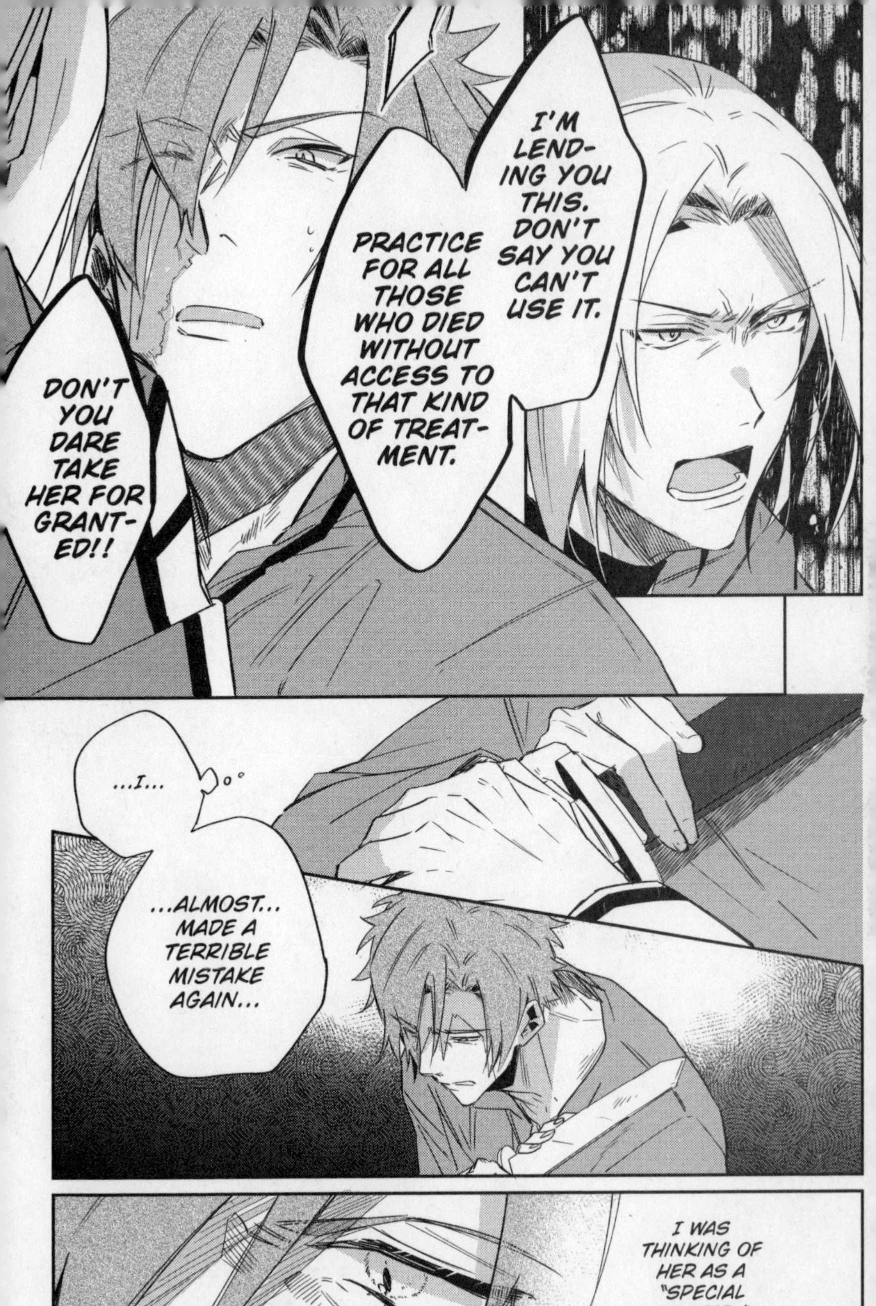
I'M LENDING YOU THIS. DON'T SAY YOU CAN'T USE IT.
PRACTICE FOR ALL THOSE WHO DIED WITHOUT ACCESS TO THAT KIND OF TREATMENT.
DON'T YOU DARE TAKE HER FOR GRANTED!!
...I...
...ALMOST... MADE A TERRIBLE MISTAKE AGAIN...
I WAS THINKING OF HER AS A "SPECIAL MASTER."

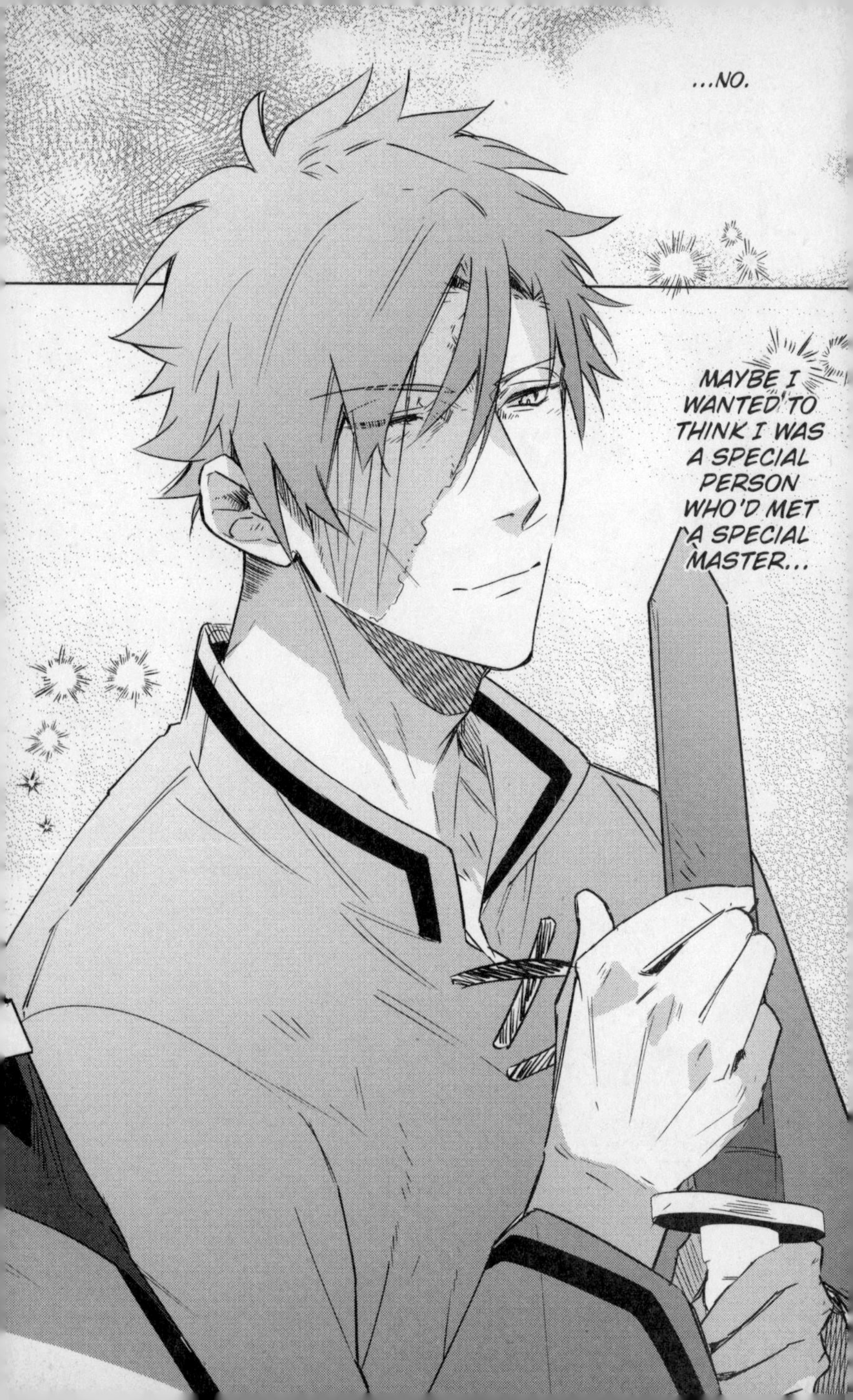
...NO.
MAYBE I WANTED TO THINK I WAS A SPECIAL PERSON WHO'D MET A SPECIAL MASTER...

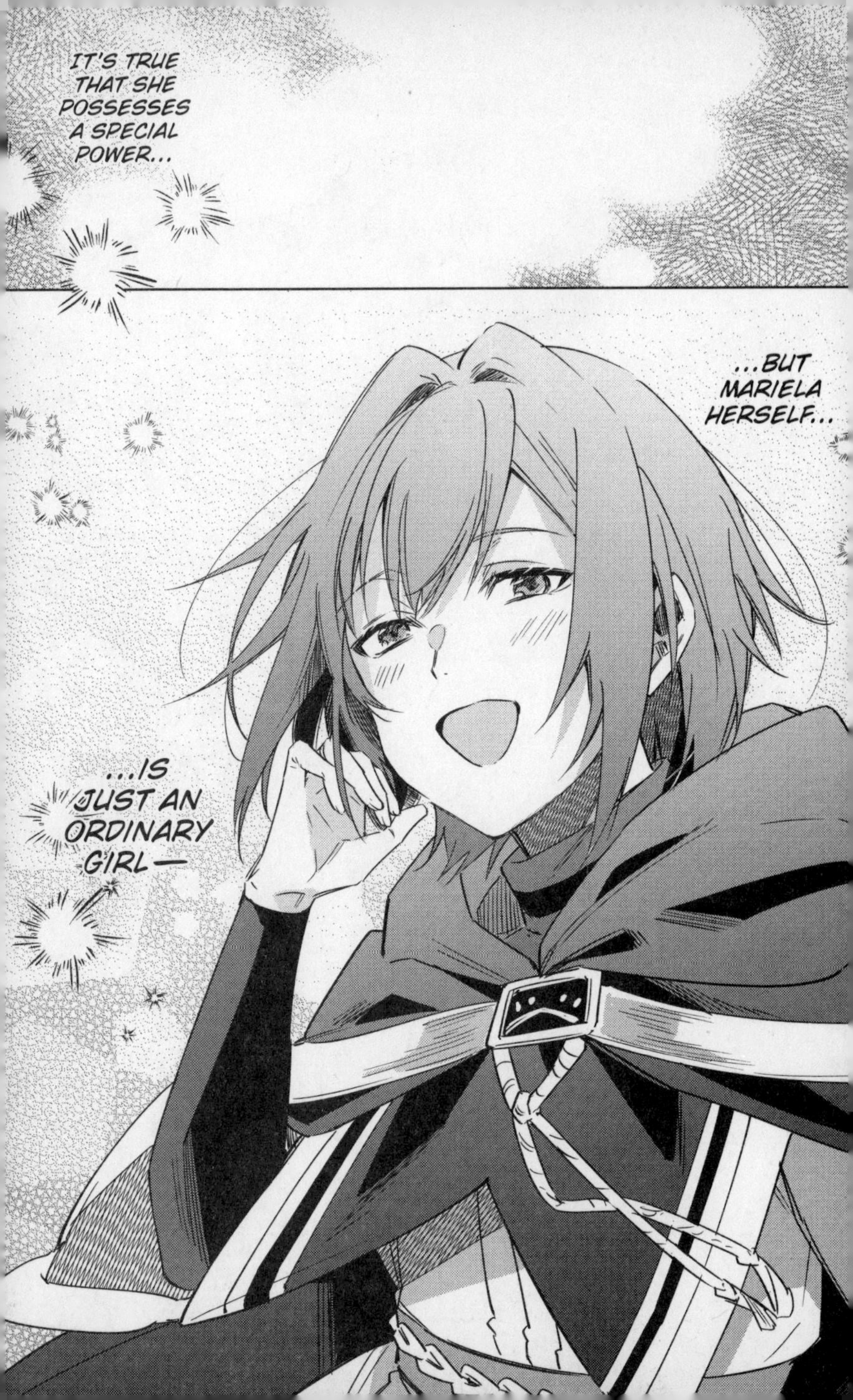
IT'S TRUE THAT SHE POSSESSES A SPECIAL POWER...
...BUT MARIELA HERSELF...
...IS JUST AN ORDINARY GIRL—

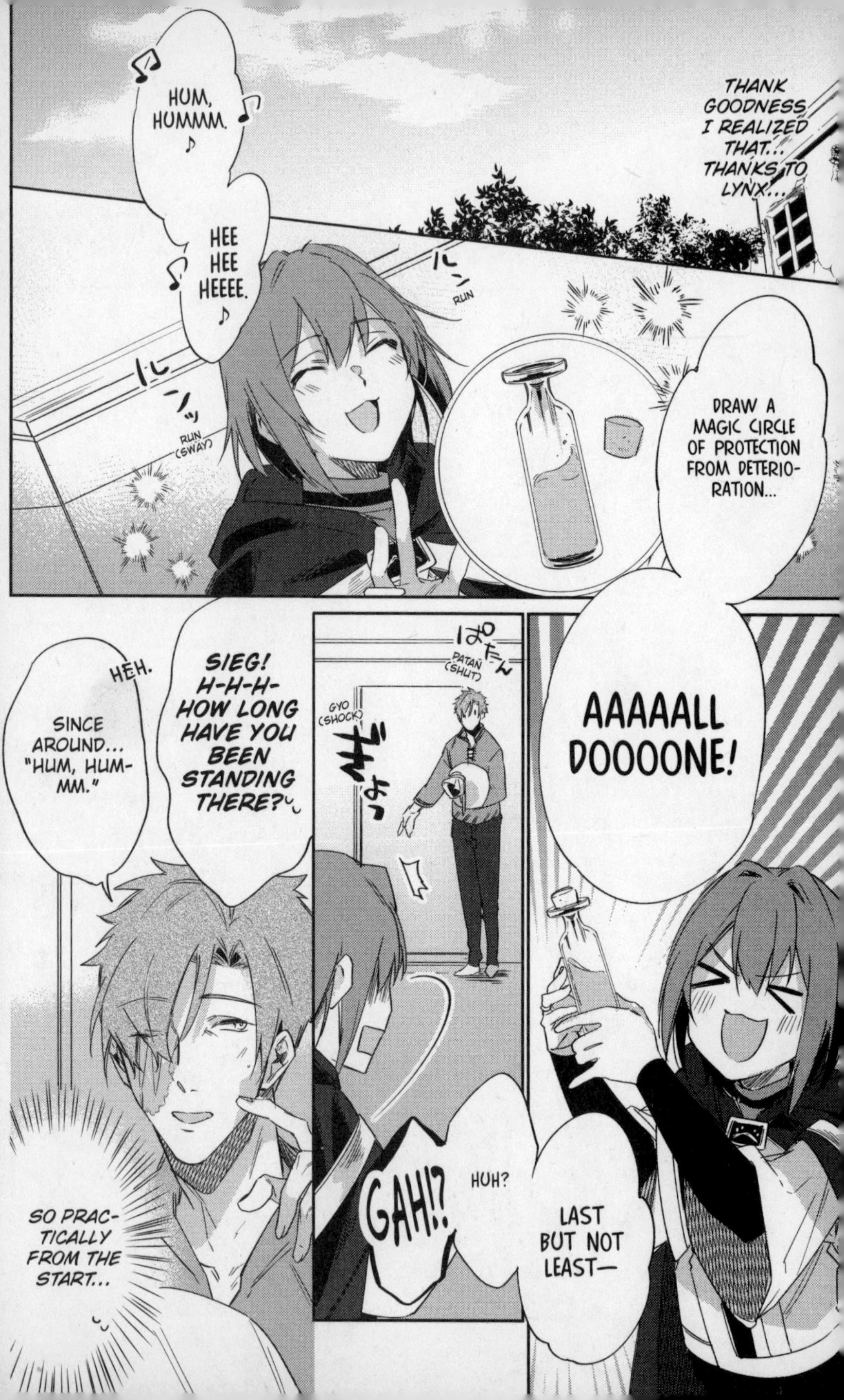

THANK GOODNESS I REALIZED THAT... THANKS TO LYNX...
DRAW A MAGIC CIRCLE OF PROTECTION FROM DETERIO-RATION...
HUM, HUMMM. ♪
HEE HEE HEEEE. ♪
ルン RUN
ルンッ RUN (SWAY)
AAAAALL DOOOONE!
LAST BUT NOT LEAST—
ぱたん PATAN (SHUT)
ぎょっ GYO (SHOCK)
HUH?
GAH!?
SIEG! H-H-H-HOW LONG HAVE YOU BEEN STANDING THERE?
HEH.
SINCE AROUND... "HUM, HUM-MM."
SO PRAC-TICALLY FROM THE START...

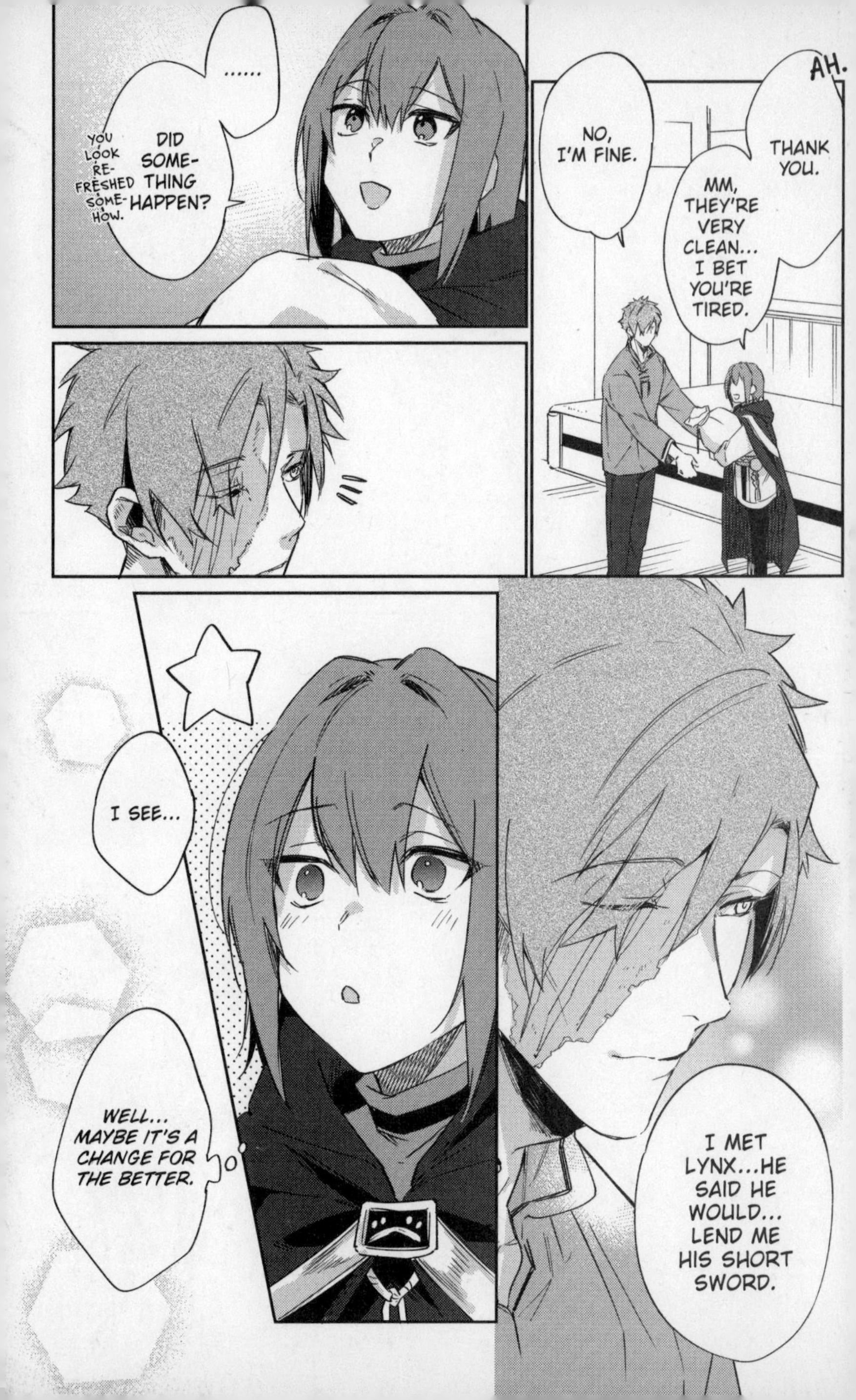
AH.
THANK YOU.
MM, THEY'RE VERY CLEAN... I BET YOU'RE TIRED.
NO, I'M FINE.
......
DID SOMETHING HAPPEN?
YOU LOOK REFRESHED SOMEHOW.
I MET LYNX...HE SAID HE WOULD... LEND ME HIS SHORT SWORD.
I SEE...
WELL... MAYBE IT'S A CHANGE FOR THE BETTER.

The Alchemist Who Survived Now Dreams of a Quiet City Life

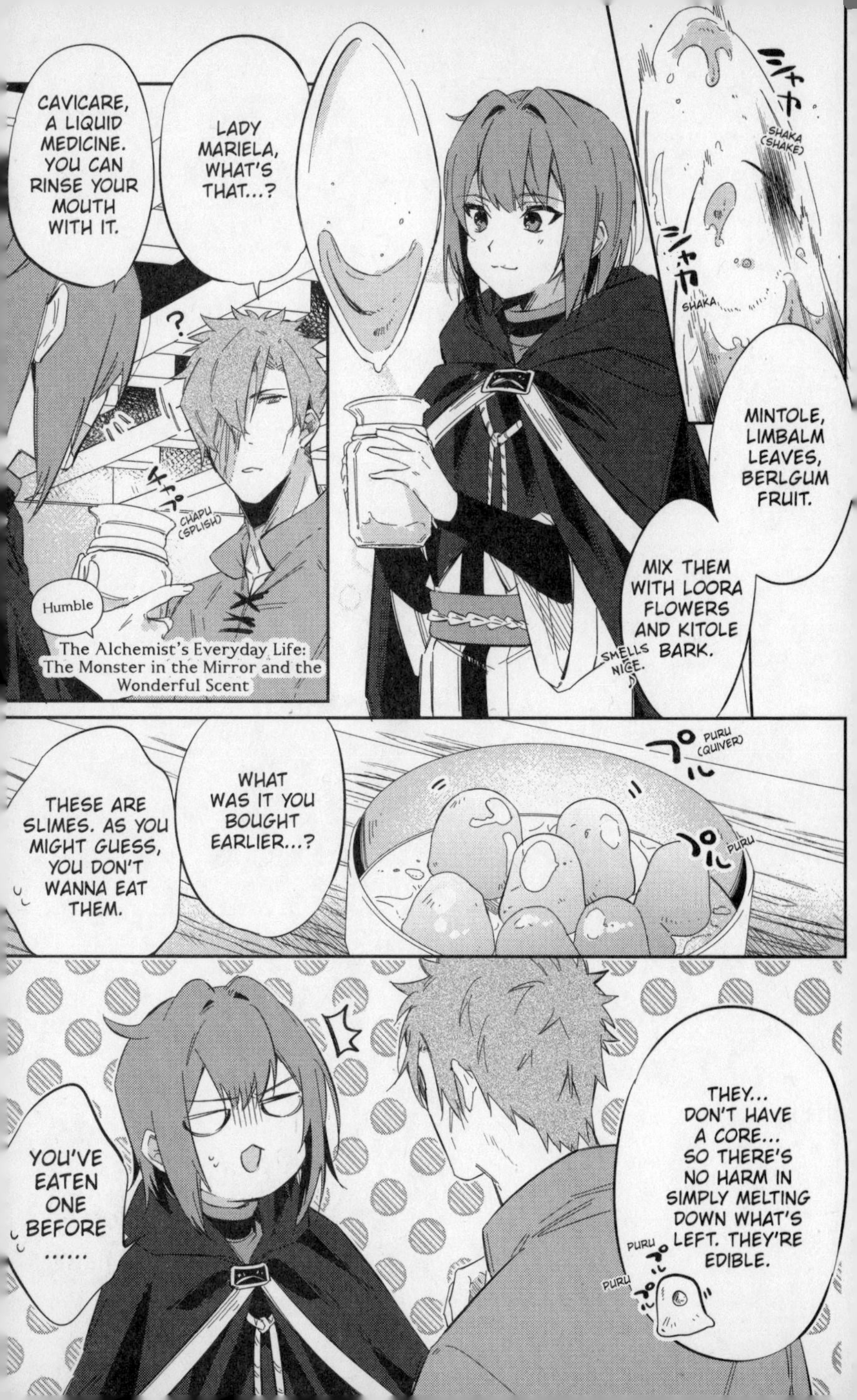
SHAKA (SHAKE)
SHAKA
MINTOLE, LIMBALM LEAVES, BERLGUM FRUIT.
MIX THEM WITH LOORA FLOWERS AND KITOLE BARK.
SMELLS NICE.
LADY MARIELA, WHAT'S THAT...?
CAVICARE, A LIQUID MEDICINE. YOU CAN RINSE YOUR MOUTH WITH IT.
?
CHAPU (SPLISH)
Humble
The Alchemist's Everyday Life: The Monster in the Mirror and the Wonderful Scent
PURU (QUIVER)
PURU
WHAT WAS IT YOU BOUGHT EARLIER...?
THESE ARE SLIMES. AS YOU MIGHT GUESS, YOU DON'T WANNA EAT THEM.
THEY... DON'T HAVE A CORE... SO THERE'S NO HARM IN SIMPLY MELTING DOWN WHAT'S LEFT. THEY'RE EDIBLE.
PURU
PURU
YOU'VE EATEN ONE BEFORE ......

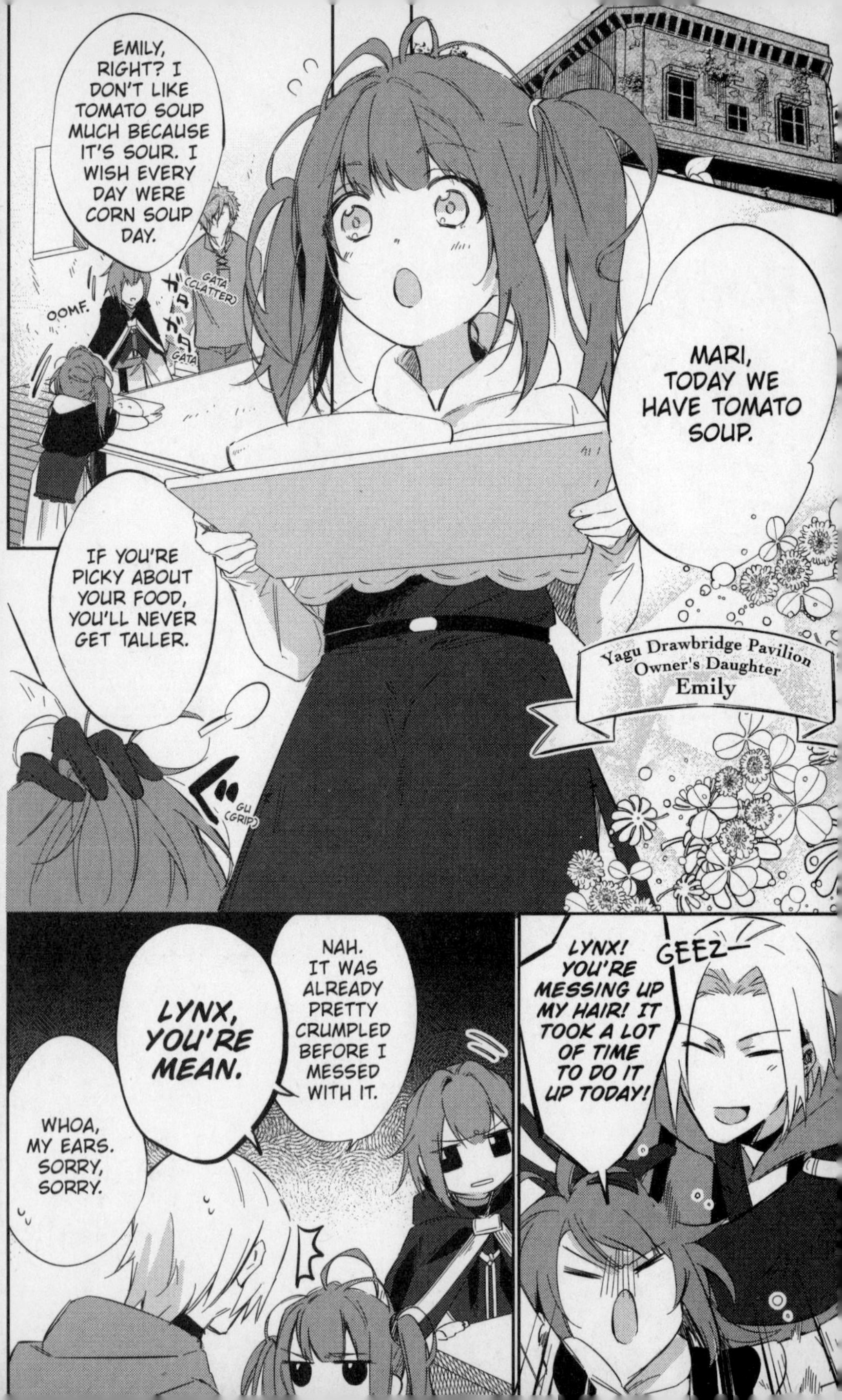
MARI, TODAY WE HAVE TOMATO SOUP.
Yagu Drawbridge Pavilion Owner's Daughter Emily
EMILY, RIGHT? I DON'T LIKE TOMATO SOUP MUCH BECAUSE IT'S SOUR. I WISH EVERY DAY WERE CORN SOUP DAY.
GATA (CLATTER)
GATA
OOMF.
IF YOU'RE PICKY ABOUT YOUR FOOD, YOU'LL NEVER GET TALLER.
GU (GRIP)
GEEZ—
LYNX! YOU'RE MESSING UP MY HAIR! IT TOOK A LOT OF TIME TO DO IT UP TODAY!
NAH. IT WAS ALREADY PRETTY CRUMPLED BEFORE I MESSED WITH IT.
LYNX, YOU'RE MEAN.
WHOA, MY EARS. SORRY, SORRY.

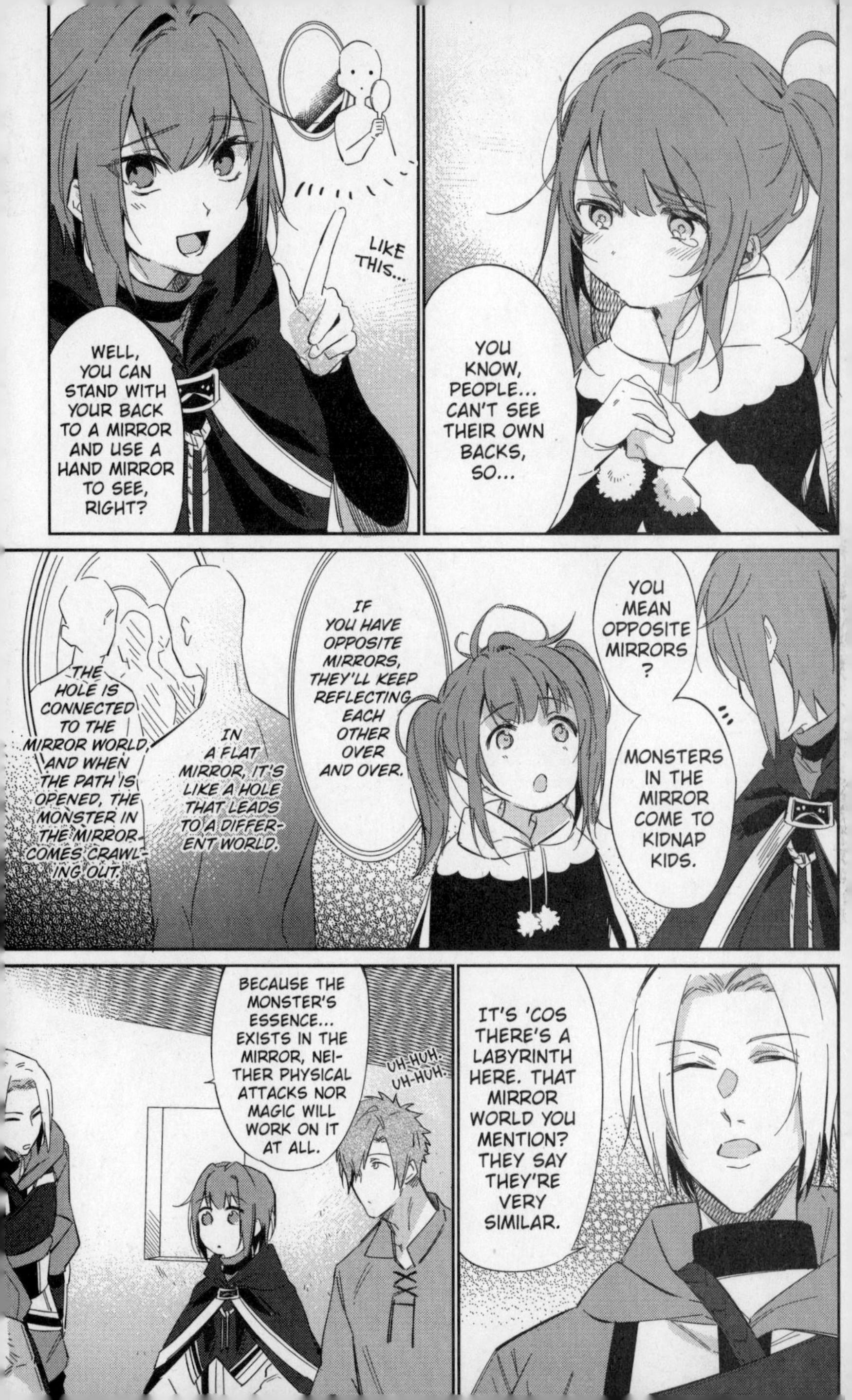
YOU KNOW, PEOPLE... CAN'T SEE THEIR OWN BACKS, SO...
LIKE THIS...
WELL, YOU CAN STAND WITH YOUR BACK TO A MIRROR AND USE A HAND MIRROR TO SEE, RIGHT?
YOU MEAN OPPOSITE MIRRORS?
...
MONSTERS IN THE MIRROR COME TO KIDNAP KIDS.
IF YOU HAVE OPPOSITE MIRRORS, THEY'LL KEEP REFLECTING EACH OTHER OVER AND OVER.
IN A FLAT MIRROR, IT'S LIKE A HOLE THAT LEADS TO A DIFFERENT WORLD.
THE HOLE IS CONNECTED TO THE MIRROR WORLD, AND WHEN THE PATH IS OPENED, THE MONSTER IN THE MIRROR COMES CRAWLING OUT.
IT'S 'COS THERE'S A LABYRINTH HERE. THAT MIRROR WORLD YOU MENTION? THEY SAY THEY'RE VERY SIMILAR.
BECAUSE THE MONSTER'S ESSENCE... EXISTS IN THE MIRROR, NEITHER PHYSICAL ATTACKS NOR MAGIC WILL WORK ON IT AT ALL.
UH-HUH. UH-HUH.

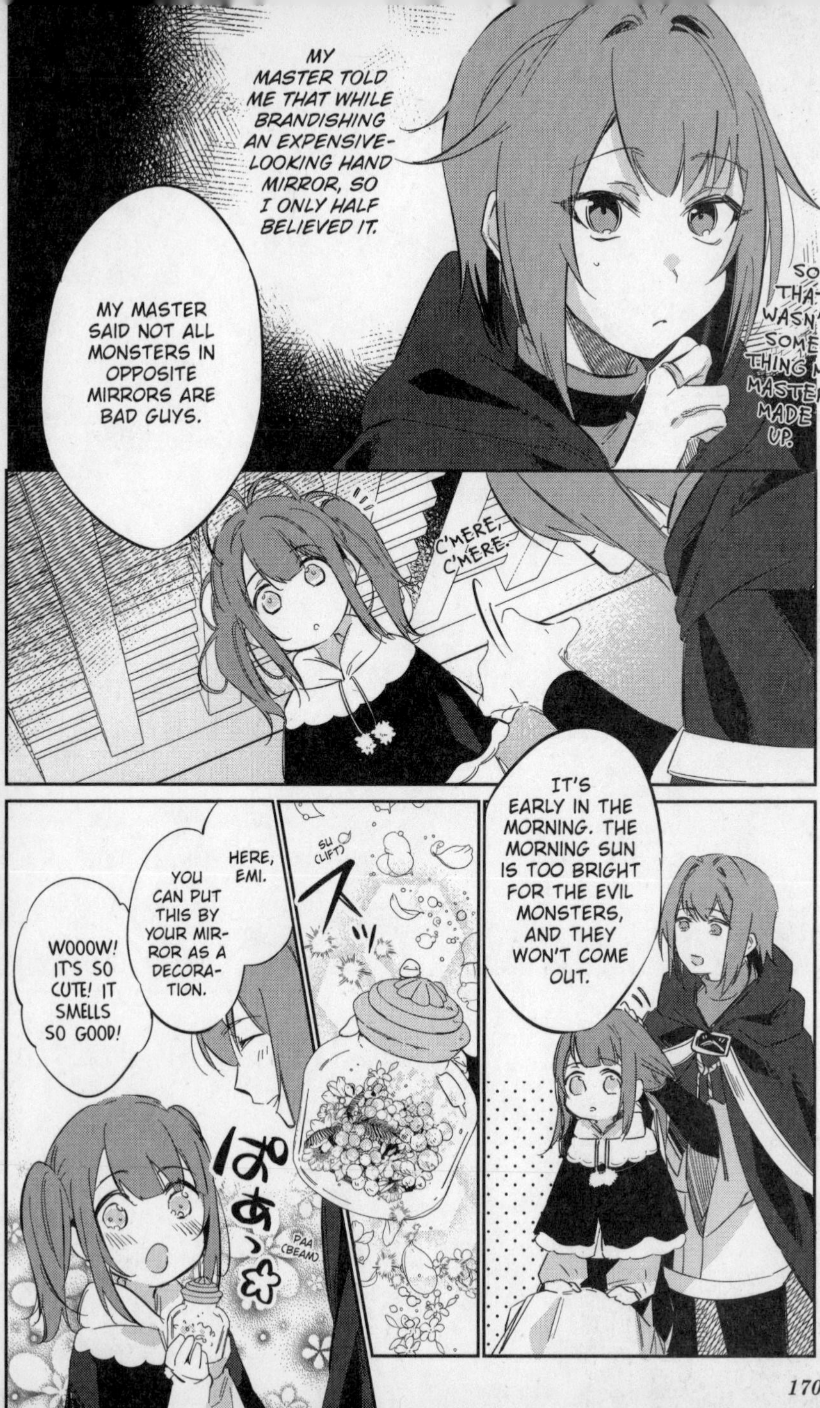
MY MASTER TOLD ME THAT WHILE BRANDISHING AN EXPENSIVE-LOOKING HAND MIRROR, SO I ONLY HALF BELIEVED IT.
SO THAT WASN'T SOME-THING MY MASTER MADE UP.
MY MASTER SAID NOT ALL MONSTERS IN OPPOSITE MIRRORS ARE BAD GUYS.
C'MERE, C'MERE.
IT'S EARLY IN THE MORNING. THE MORNING SUN IS TOO BRIGHT FOR THE EVIL MONSTERS, AND THEY WON'T COME OUT.
SU (LIFT)
HERE, EMI. YOU CAN PUT THIS BY YOUR MIR-ROR AS A DECORA-TION.
WOOOW! IT'S SO CUTE! IT SMELLS SO GOOD!
PAA (BEAM)

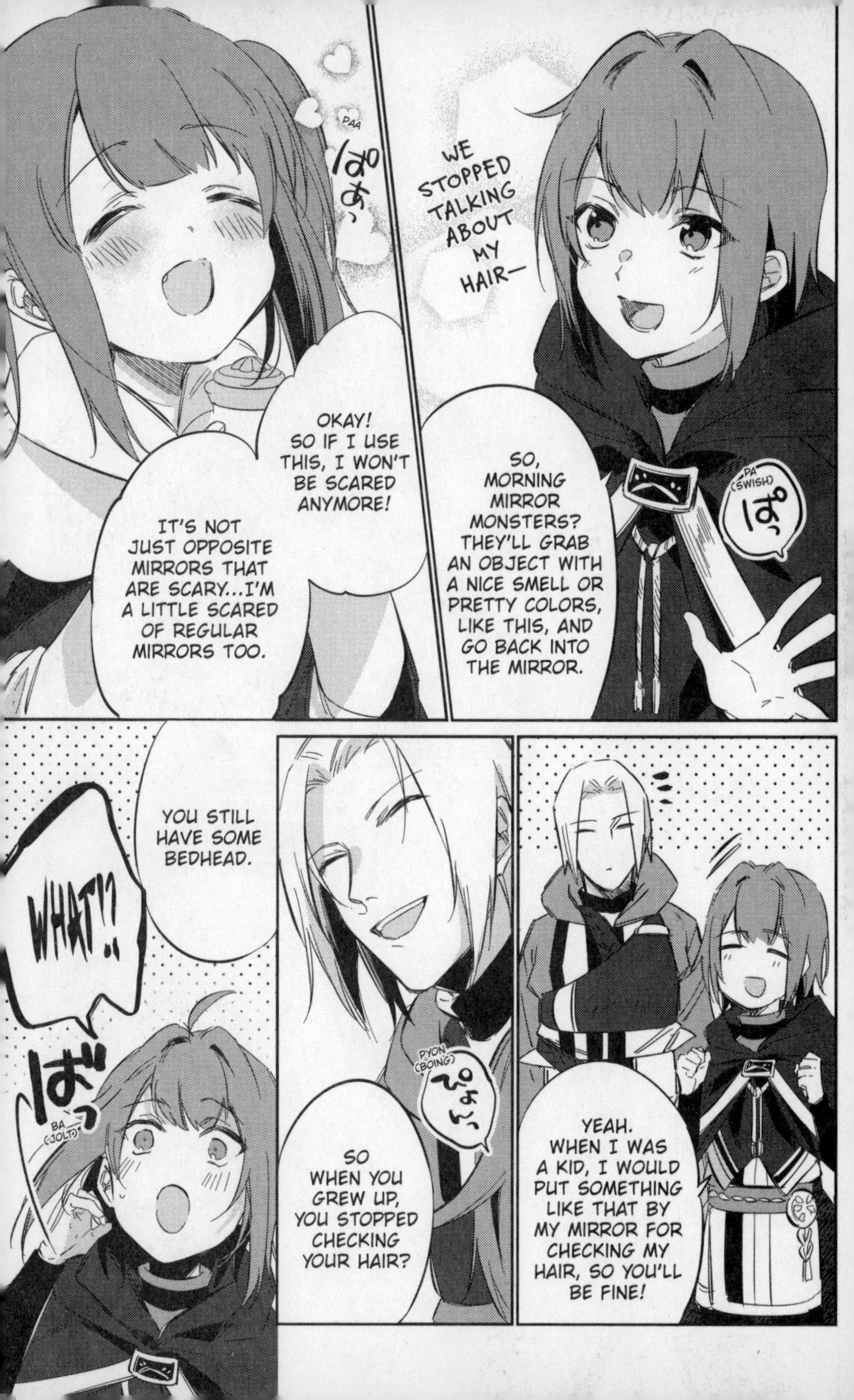
WE STOPPED TALKING ABOUT MY HAIR—
PA (SWISH)
ぱっ
SO, MORNING MIRROR MONSTERS? THEY'LL GRAB AN OBJECT WITH A NICE SMELL OR PRETTY COLORS, LIKE THIS, AND GO BACK INTO THE MIRROR.
PAA
ぱあっ
OKAY! SO IF I USE THIS, I WON'T BE SCARED ANYMORE!
IT'S NOT JUST OPPOSITE MIRRORS THAT ARE SCARY...I'M A LITTLE SCARED OF REGULAR MIRRORS TOO.
YEAH. WHEN I WAS A KID, I WOULD PUT SOMETHING LIKE THAT BY MY MIRROR FOR CHECKING MY HAIR, SO YOU'LL BE FINE!
PYON (BOING)
ぴょん
SO WHEN YOU GREW UP, YOU STOPPED CHECKING YOUR HAIR?
YOU STILL HAVE SOME BEDHEAD.
WHAT!?
ばっ
BA (JOLT)

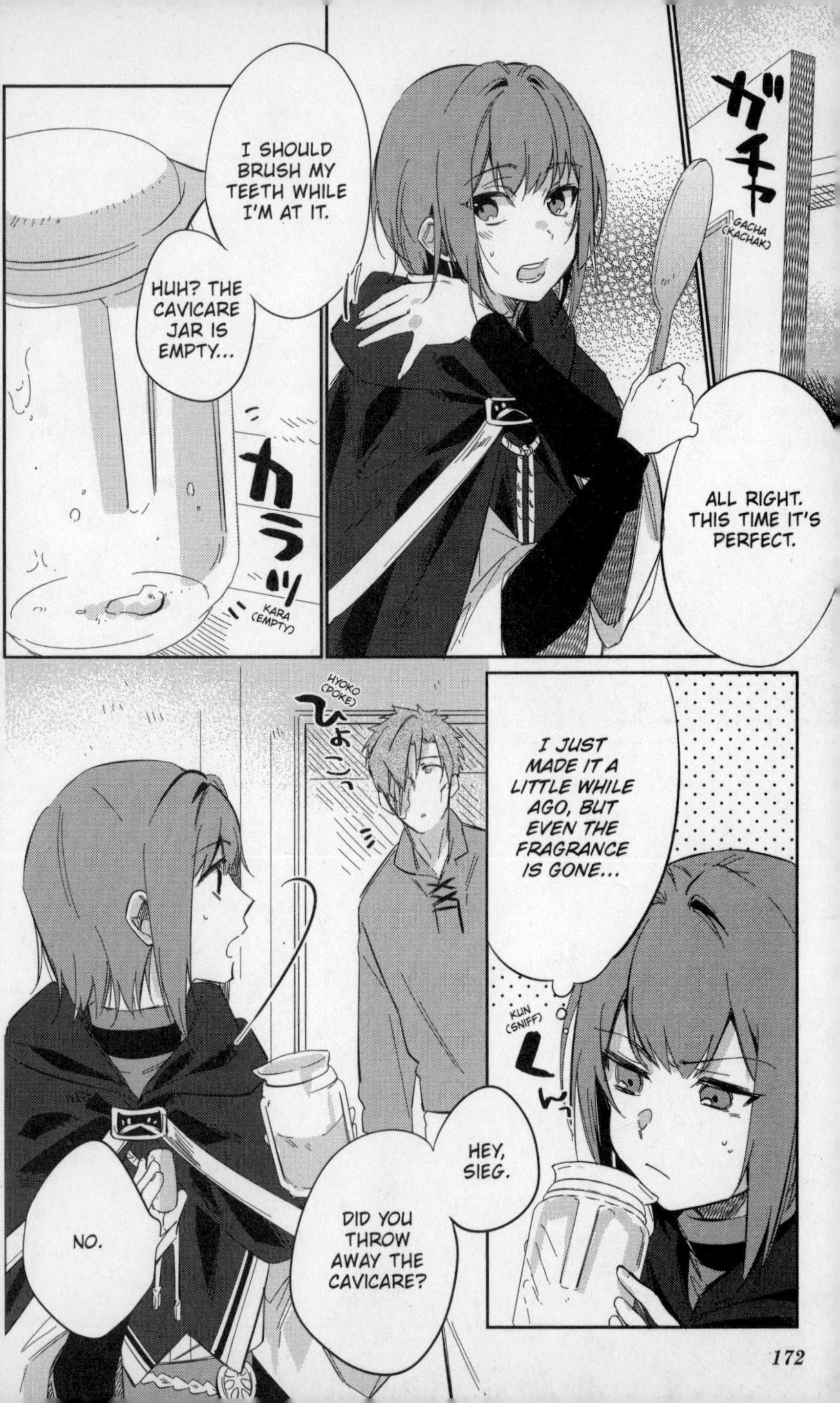
GACHA (KACHAK)
ALL RIGHT. THIS TIME IT'S PERFECT.
I SHOULD BRUSH MY TEETH WHILE I'M AT IT.
HUH? THE CAVICARE JAR IS EMPTY...
KARA (EMPTY)
I JUST MADE IT A LITTLE WHILE AGO, BUT EVEN THE FRAGRANCE IS GONE...
KUN (SNIFF)
HEY, SIEG.
DID YOU THROW AWAY THE CAVICARE?
HYOKO (POKE)
NO.

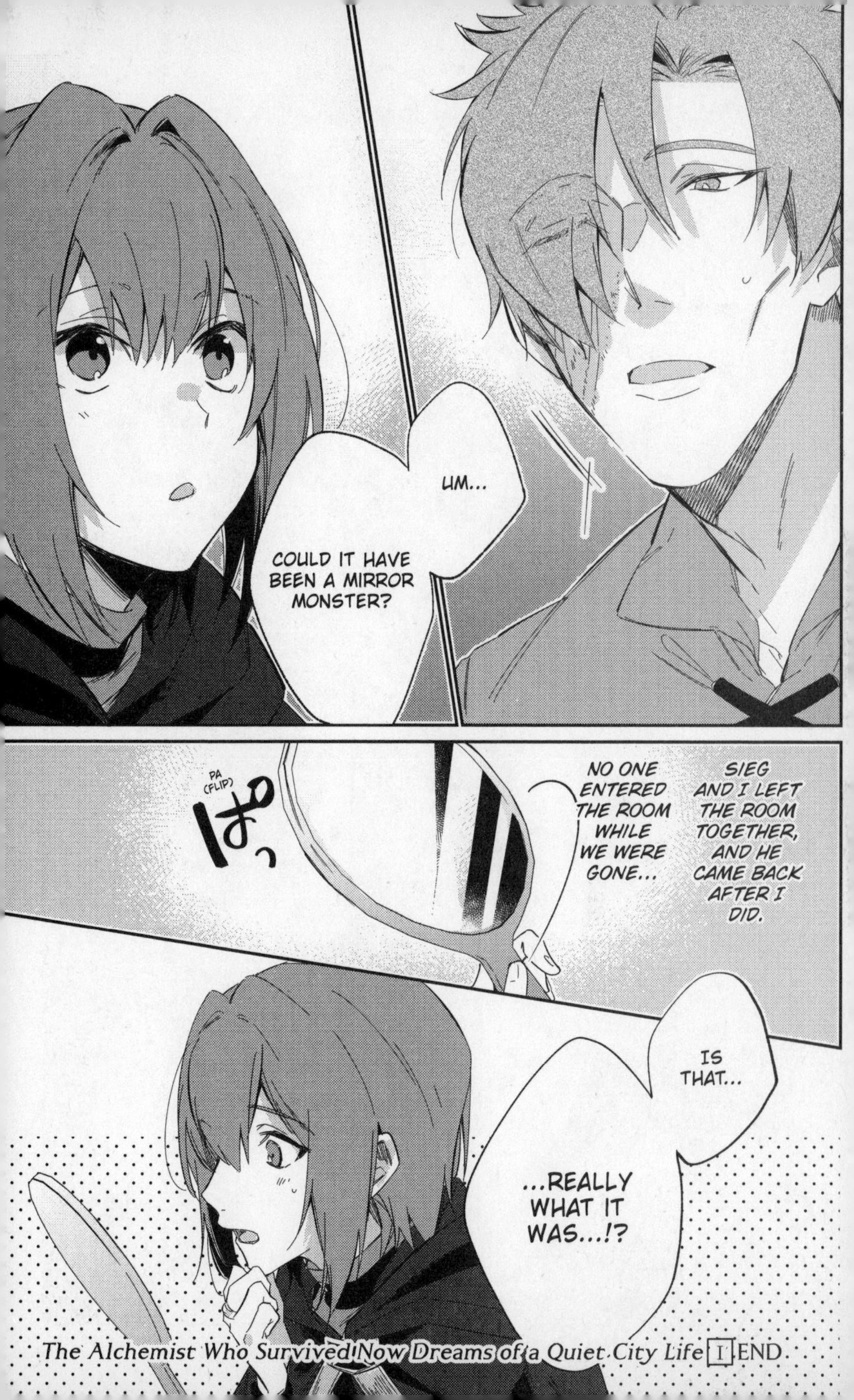
UM...
COULD IT HAVE BEEN A MIRROR MONSTER?
SIEG AND I LEFT THE ROOM TOGETHER, AND HE CAME BACK AFTER I DID.
NO ONE ENTERED THE ROOM WHILE WE WERE GONE...
ぱっ
PA (FLIP)
IS THAT...
...REALLY WHAT IT WAS...!?
The Alchemist Who Survived Now Dreams of a Quiet City Life I END

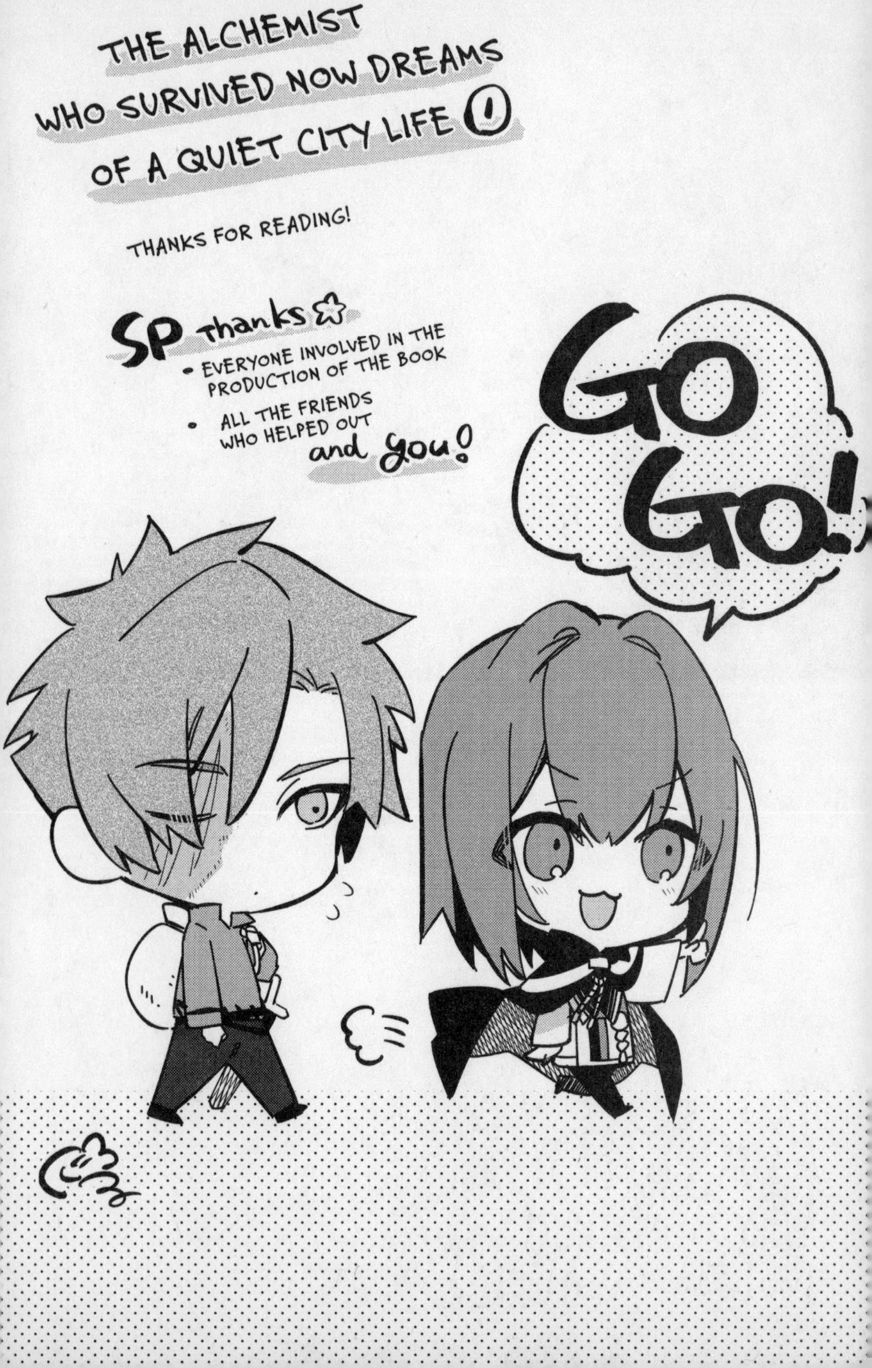
THE ALCHEMIST WHO SURVIVED NOW DREAMS OF A QUIET CITY LIFE 1
THANKS FOR READING!
SP thanks
• EVERYONE INVOLVED IN THE PRODUCTION OF THE BOOK
• ALL THE FRIENDS WHO HELPED OUT
and you!
GO GO!

The Alchemist Who Survived Now Dreams of a Quiet City Life

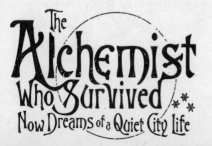

The Alchemist Who Survived Now Dreams of a Quiet City Life

01

Guru Mizoguchi
Original Story

Usata Nonohara
Character Design

OX

Translation: **Erin Husson** ★ Lettering: **Liz Kolkman**

This book is a work of fiction. Names, characters, places, and incidents are the product of the author's imagination or are used fictitiously. Any resemblance to actual events, locales, or persons, living or dead, is coincidental.

IKINOKORI RENKINJUTSUSHI HA MACHI DE SHIZUKANI KURASHITAI, Vol. 1
©Guru Mizoguchi 2018
©Usata Nonohara 2018
©ox 2018
First published in Japan in 2018 by KADOKAWA CORPORATION, Tokyo.
English translation rights arranged with KADOKAWA CORPORATION, Tokyo through TUTTLE-MORI AGENCY, INC., Tokyo.

English translation © 2019 by Yen Press, LLC

Yen Press
150 West 30th Street, 19th Floor
New York, NY 10001

Visit us at yenpress.com ✹ facebook.com/yenpress ✹ twitter.com/yenpress ✹ yenpress.tumblr.com ✹ instagram.com/yenpress

First Yen Press Edition: August 2019

Yen Press is an imprint of Yen Press, LLC.
The Yen Press name and logo are trademarks of Yen Press, LLC.

The publisher is not responsible for websites (or their content) that are not owned by the publisher.

Library of Congress Control Number: 2019938494

ISBNs: 978-1-9753-8427-2 (paperback)
978-1-9753-3130-6 (ebook)

10 9 8 7 6 5 4 3 2

WOR

Printed in the United States of America